Nazis in the New World

Nazis in the New World

German Students in the United States, 1933–1941

AARON GILLETTE

Johns Hopkins University Press
Baltimore

© 2025 Johns Hopkins University Press
All rights reserved. Published 2025
Printed in the United States of America on acid-free paper
2 4 6 8 9 7 5 3 1

Johns Hopkins University Press
2715 North Charles Street
Baltimore, Maryland 21218
www.press.jhu.edu

Library of Congress Cataloging-in-Publication Data

Names: Gillette, Aaron, 1964– author.
Title: Nazis in the New World : German students in the United States,
1933–1941 / Aaron Gillette.
Description: Baltimore, MD : Johns Hopkins University Press, 2025. |
Includes bibliographical references and index.
Identifiers: LCCN 2024033459 | ISBN 9781421450773 (hardcover) | ISBN
9781421450780 (ebook)
Subjects: LCSH: German students—United States—History—20th century. |
Educational exchanges—United States—History—20th century. |
Nazis—United States—History—20th century. | Espionage, German—United
States—History—20th century.
Classification: LCC LB2376.5.G3 G555 2025 | DDC
370.116/208931073—dc23/eng/20250117
LC record available at https://lccn.loc.gov/2024033459

A catalog record for this book is available from the British Library.

Jacket. German exchange student alumni in Berlin listening to the University of
California versus Stanford University football game, November 24, 1934. Rockefeller
Archives Center, RG 4 (FA1288), acc. 2016:070, series 1, box 35, folder 284–86, Early
IIE Photos, 1930s. Courtesy of the Institute of International Education.

*Special discounts are available for bulk purchases of this book. For more information,
please contact Special Sales at specialsales@jh.edu.*

EU GPSR Authorized Representative
LOGOS EUROPE, 9 rue Nicolas Poussin, 17000, La Rochelle, France
E-mail: Contact@logoseurope.eu

In memoriam
Teagle
quem in aeternum amabo

I was . . . subject to deportation at any time. I couldn't go . . . and say, "To hell with Hitler." . . . When you are on a life raft, called a student visa, you don't do that.

—Anton-Hermann Chroust,
German exchange student refugee,
at his deportation hearing

CONTENTS

List of Illustrations *xi*
Author's Note *xiii*
Acknowledgments *xv*

Introduction 1

1 Nazi Infiltration of the Student Exchange 26

2 Recruitment and Training 42

3 Brave New World 78

4 Disillusionment, Resistance, Refuge, and Opposition in Exile 127

5 Propaganda and Espionage Missions 148

6 Consequences of the Nazi-Era German-American Exchange 175

Conclusion 193

Notes *207*
Bibliography *249*
Index *299*

ILLUSTRATIONS

JACKET

German exchange student alumni in Berlin listening to the University of California versus Stanford University football game, 1934.

FIGURES

1.1.	Adolf Morsbach and Ingrid Dybwad at Schloss Köpenick, Berlin, ca. early 1930s	28
1.2.	Ulrich von Gienanth, 1932	35
2.1.	Elisabeth Noelle, 1938	49
2.2.	Herbert Sonthoff	59
2.3.	German-American exchange students at a student assembly, held at Schloss Köpenick, Berlin, 1932	69
2.4.	Anton-Hermann Chroust	72
2.5.	German exchange students en route to the United States on the Hamburg-Amerika Line passenger ship *New York*, September 1938	75
3.1.	International exchange students and staff from the Institute of International Education, Mow Hall, Riverdale Country School, New York City, September 1934 (part 1)	80
3.2.	International exchange students and staff from the Institute of International Education, Mow Hall, Riverdale Country School, New York City, September 1934 (part 2)	82
3.3.	International exchange students and staff from the Institute of International Education, Mow Hall, Riverdale Country School, New York City, September 1935	84–85

xii   *List of Illustrations*

3.4.	American college students mocking Hitler and other dictators, Cornell University, 1939	96
3.5.	Erwin Wickert	117
3.6.	Ruth Hubbard	124
4.1.	Irene Gotthelf	131
4.2.	Ina Gotthelf	132
5.1.	Anneliese von dem Hagen	162
5.2.	Ulrich Pohlenz, dressed as an SS officer for an American film, 1944	171

AUTHOR'S NOTE

To avoid repetition, I have used certain terms interchangeably. *School, educational institution, college,* and *university* refer to American postsecondary academic institutions in general. When differentiation is necessary between teaching colleges and research universities, this is indicated. *Wehrmacht* refers to the German army throughout the Third Reich even though the term *Reichswehr* was used until 1936. Umlauts have been retained, including in the case of names if the person is more commonly referred to in German-language texts. English-language texts from the 1930s rarely used diacritics, so if a German name with diacritics appeared more often in English-language sources, I have used the spelling without them.

Most of the photographs are from microfilm negatives, often the sole extant copies. Digital enhancement was needed to ensure visual clarity. This involved adjustments to brightness and contrast, sharpening, and noise reduction. For the image of Anton-Hermann Chroust, digital darkening of the area to his right removed glare. Shadows on the left side of Elisabeth Noelle's image were mitigated to define her hairline. The background of Annelise von dem Hagen's photograph was lightened for the same reason. These interventions did not alter the essential content or context of the originals, which are available from the author upon request.

ACKNOWLEDGMENTS

I wish to thank my close friend Michael Gelb, who made numerous excellent suggestions on the wording of the text. Over the years, Army Carney and Adam Seipp offered important advice on the project. John R. Thelin provided indispensable advice on the entire manuscript and suggested an essential bibliography for understanding American higher education in the 1930s. The Institute of International Education allowed me unfettered access to its archives and graciously consented to the inclusion of numerous photographs reproduced here.

I began work on the book while a Diesterweg research fellow of the Research Institute for Humanities and Social Science at the University of Siegen, for which I warmly thank Angela Schwarz for assisting me in obtaining the fellowship. My work was also funded by numerous generous grants from the University of Houston–Downtown (UHD), the German Academic Exchange Service (Deutscher Akademischer Austauschdienst, DAAD) and the Center for European Studies of the University of Texas. Two semester sabbaticals from UHD were critical.

During my thirty years of conducting research in archives in the United States and Europe, Sabrina Zinke, assistant archivist at the University of Heidelberg, was the nicest, most accommodating and helpful of any archivist with whom I have worked. Many librarians have been critical to my research endeavors for this book, including the staff at UHD's Interlibrary Loan Office and James Steinbach at the University of Munich Archives. At Johns Hopkins University Press, Greg Britton has been the nicest editor anyone could ever hope for.

Most importantly, I wish to thank my wife, Maria Montserrat Feu-Lopez. If she hadn't taken care of our cat family while I was on research trips, this book would not have been possible.

All mistakes are my own, for which I apologize in advance.

Nazis in the New World

Introduction

> [Regarding the plight of academics against Nazism in Germany,] typical was the lot of those who, sensitive but weak, could not decide the conflict between duty to their families and loyalty to their conscience. Pitiable and unheroic, they demonstrate the fate of scholar, scientist and educator in the modern dictatorial state which, once it is established, inexorably grinds down all human substance . . . [W]hether we must reproach ourselves for insufficient insight and courage to speak, are questions which each must answer before his own conscience.
>
> —*Frederic "Fritz" Lilge, German exchange student,*
> *University of Rochester, 1934–35; professor of education,*
> *University of California, Berkeley, 1958–77*

As usual, students congregated in Florida during their Christmas breaks in the 1930s. They enjoyed their time together by attempting to outdo previous years' students in their antics, exuberantly cruising around in their decrepit autos, surpassing one another in various high jinks, celebrating Christmas Eve with rowdy parties in Miami Beach, and engaging in other mischief. In between such mayhem, they quietly admired the natural beauties of South Florida, discussed their impressions of the United States, and late at night agonized over their future. These are actions one would naturally expect from American college students, but in this case, the students were German Nazis.[1]

Between 1933 and 1939, the German government sent 270 students to the United States for a yearlong period of study. *Nazis in the New World* reveals their fascinating history, framed within current scholarly debates on Germany and the United States during that era. The overarching thesis contends that Nazism, contrary to depictions prevalent today, was not as omnipotent as often portrayed in either country. It did not dictate the ideological beliefs or actions of many German government officials, nor were German university faculty and students universally Nazi zealots or even "Nazis" in the conventional sense. The experiences of German exchange students in America reveals a more intricate dynamic of adoption, adaptation, and opposition to Nazi ideals than commonly expected. Moreover, the political influence of pro-Nazi Americans, with whom some of the exchange students interacted, was not the dire threat to American democracy that some historians have portrayed.

German exchange students who sought to study in the United States were selected to impress the world with the "New Nazi Man."[2] They underwent thorough assessments and submitted the requisite documents to prove leadership in Nazi organizations. Yet, after a year immersed in the United States and its liberal democracy, a quarter of them anxiously sought to remain there. This suggests that German officials sometimes selected exchange students with only a superficial allegiance to the Third Reich. Conversely, by the late 1930s, some German students agreed to engage in covert operations for the National Socialist government, such as subversively distributing Nazi propaganda, intimidating recent German refugees and liberal German exchange students, and engaging in amateurish espionage for the German military. *Nazis in the New World* also illustrates continuity in German society and political culture from the Weimar Republic to the Third Reich as well as how those involved in the German-American student exchange program in the 1930s became pivotal agents in the post–World War II Americanization of Germany.

Background

Interest in pro-Nazi Americans has flourished for more than a decade.[3] Several scholars have asserted that in the 1930s and early 1940s, a significant number of Americans sympathized with Nazi Germany; some even aided covert Nazi agents in gathering military information that posed a substantial threat to the US war effort. These researchers contend that this so-called "fifth column" endangered US democracy. For instance, Charles Gallagher, in *Nazis of Copley Square*, asserts that German agents in Boston significantly influenced public sentiment with their antisemitic propaganda and, by means of their American co-conspirators, played a role in inciting the 1943 attacks on the Jewish community there.[4] Steven Ross, in *Hitler in Los Angeles*, and Laura B. Rosenzweig, in *Hollywood's Spies*, identify Los Angeles, rather than Boston, as the epicenter of Nazi subversion in the United States. *Hitler in Los Angeles*, a Pulitzer Prize finalist, chronicles the efforts of a small group of dedicated Americans who "risked their lives" to thwart "Hitler's minions" from establishing "Germany's New Order in America."[5] Similarly, Bradley Hart, in *Hitler's American Friends*, asserts that if the fifth column had succeeded, "the U.S. would never have entered World War II, Britain would have fallen under Nazi occupation and, ultimately, a version of National Socialism would have taken root in the United States."[6]

Hitler's American Friends and *Hitler in Los Angeles* underscore the relationship between Nazism and the isolationist America First Committee (AFC).[7] *Hitler's American Friends* asserts that the AFC was a product of "years of Nazi disinformation and propaganda, coupled with the extremism of home-grown fascism."[8] It is clear that the German government welcomed the AFC's efforts to keep the United States out of European affairs, warmly appreciating its many pro-German members. With a purported membership of 800,000, it is unsurprising that the group included some Nazi sympathizers. The AFC was, however, united by a single goal: preventing US involvement in a European war. Members included future US presidents John F. Kennedy and Gerald R. Ford; Progressive Wisconsin governor Philip La Follette; anti-fascist novelist Sinclair Lewis; and Socialist Party presidential candidate Norman Thomas. Numerous other accomplished and progressive Americans also joined the organization.[9] As the German Embassy in Washington warned Berlin, America First was "by no means motivated in their attitude by friendship or sympathy for Germany."[10]

The vast radio audience of right-wing populist Charles Coughlin's *Golden Hour of the Shrine of the Little Flower*, reportedly reaching up to 14 million listeners at any one time, is often cited as evidence of a significant pro-Nazi contingent in the United States capable of threatening its democracy.[11] At the peak of Coughlin's popularity, 10 percent of the entire US population tuned into his broadcasts. In contrast, it was only after the Nazi Party (Nationalsozialistische Deutsche Arbeiterpartei, NSDAP) secured 44 percent of the vote in the 1933 Reichstag elections, and then engaged in coercive political maneuvering, that Adolf Hitler was able to establish a de facto dictatorship. Coughlin, though undeniably antisemitic and eventually a Nazi sympathizer, also targeted an impressive roster of opponents, including Communists, Franklin Roosevelt and the New Deal, labor unions, feminists, interventionists, and "the wealthy," as well as perpetrators of anti-Catholic violence in Spain and Mexico and advocates of racial equality. The historians Bill Mullen and Chris Vials have described Coughlin's "fascism" not as a coherent ideology, but as a broad and blanket condemnation of all he opposed.[12] In 1939 an agent likely employed by the anti-Nazi Los Angeles Jewish Community Committee or one of its affiliates, infiltrated American pro-Nazi groups. He reported to the Federal Bureau of Investigation (FBI) that Coughlin's listeners had lost considerable interest in his message following the reduction of anti-Catholic violence in Spain after Francisco Franco's victory in 1939.[13] Without understanding the specific appeals of his rhetoric to various audience segments, one cannot accurately determine which of Coughlin's assertions resonated with his listeners.

Gallagher, Hart, and Ross assert that Nazi-inspired antisemitism was spreading in the United States during the 1930s.[14] Hart shows antisemitism to be the primary conduit for many Americans becoming supporters of Hitler.[15] The Nazi government in Germany actively promoted these sentiments through various means, including German exchange students. *Nazis in the New World* examines anti-Jewish incidents across the country. For example, a national survey conducted a month after Kristallnacht, on November 8–9, 1938, showed that while the majority of US college students expressed sympathy for Jewish German refugees, they still supported barring them from asylum in the United States.[16] This attitude was likely influenced by factors beyond blatant antisemitism, among them financial fears during the Great Depression about job competition from educated Jewish Germans.[17] Furthermore, contemporary reports raised concerns about fifth columnists posing as Jewish refugees, increasing wariness among some Americans.[18]

Logically, while all American Nazis were antisemites, not all American antisemites were Nazis. Antisemitism had deep roots in American history, but it did not necessarily equate to Nazism in the 1930s. For example, the virulently antisemitic Ku Klux Klan viewed Nazism as a foreign ideology and even advocated for the criminalization of the German American Bund, the largest pro-Nazi organization in the country.[19] Many scholars who argue that the United States was rife with Nazis have highlighted the large number of pro-Nazi organizations. Yet Laura Rosenzweig, in *Hollywood's Spies*, has pointed out that a significant portion of these organizations were short-lived "letterhead" rackets, operated by solo propagandists exploiting the era's political anxieties.[20]

Antisemitism was significantly less prevalent in the United States than in Nazi Germany. For instance, in 1936 an anti-Nazi investigator from the Los Angeles Jewish Community Committee told a Nazi sympathizer that the "average American would not lend his support to any religious persecution."[21] Additionally, German diplomats in the United States reported back to Berlin

that the Reich's treatment of Jews and other human rights abuses were fostering an anti-German "psychosis" in America, reviving derogatory references
to Germans as "Huns."[22] In 1937 the German ambassador cabled the Foreign
Ministry to report that the US government's growing antipathy toward Germany reflected widespread American public opinion;[23] the American ambassador to Germany confirmed this assessment in an official dispatch to the
State Department.[24] A Gallup poll that same year reinforced this view. Only
8 percent of Americans favored Germany's policies, a figure that decreased in
subsequent surveys.[25]

By 1938 the Nazis' escalating brutality had further tarnished their already
disreputable image in the United States. Following Kristallnacht, droves of
colleges canceled their participation in student exchange programs with Germany. The dwindling number of institutions still willing to accept German
students often warned the organization responsible for managing international academic exchanges in the United States, the Institute of International
Education (IIE), about the rising anti-German sentiment in their communities and the mounting pressure to terminate the exchange. Meanwhile, antisemitism in the United States failed to gain ground. In 1939 an agent of the
Los Angeles Jewish Community Committee reported on the decline of Coughlin's movement. The widespread revulsion from the American far right in
response to the Nazi-Soviet Pact, he explained, had significantly weakened
pro-Nazi sympathies and antisemitism in New York City. "The Nazi influence has all but disappeared," he wrote. "[The] breach between German Nazis
and American racists has broadened into a chasm which cannot be spanned."[26]

Nazi Espionage and Sabotage in the United States

Some historians assert that American pro-Nazi fifth columnists stealthily
paved the way for agents of the Reich to infiltrate the United States, posing
a dire threat to American democracy. According to *Hitler's American Friends*,
"Throughout the 1930s and early years of the war, Hitler's supporters in the
United States passed a huge number of secrets to their handlers in the Third
Reich."[27] Hart concludes, "An unknown but assuredly substantial number of
Allied sailors went to their graves thanks to the information that slipped from
American ports and ended up with U-boat commanders in the Atlantic."[28]
Hitler in Los Angeles argues that although sabotage by Nazi spies and their
American agents posed a growing danger, the FBI was supposedly almost
oblivious to the menace, as it was "woefully behind in tracking any enemy
other than Communists."[29] Indeed, bureau director J. Edgar Hoover did hesi-

tate to investigate many espionage accusations—because no laws were being broken.[30] According to *The Nazis of Copley Square*, "Before and during World War II, the [German] spy apparatus . . . was vastly more capable than that of the United States."[31] Quite a few German exchange students were involved in these efforts, all but guaranteeing their failure.

Drawing from the work of various historians, Rachel Maddow, in *Prequel: An American Fight against Fascism*, argues that Americans at the time seemingly faced the risk of an "armed takeover of the U.S. government and the installation of something much more like a fascist dictatorship."[32] As she sees it, the "real and violent fascist insurgency" that threatened America before Pearl Harbor was a "close-run affair,"[33] in part due to the FBI and other authorities' delayed recognition of the Nazi threat.[34] *Prequel* also presents the dramatic rise in American antisemitism before World War II period largely as a consequence of Nazi influence. For instance, Maddow cites pro-fascist speaker George Deatherage, who told a pro-Nazi rally in New York that Ulrich von Gienanth, manager of the German exchange students in the United States, had privately told him that American antisemitism had become "ten times more powerful than existed in pre-Hitler Germany."[35]

Furthermore, *Prequel* describes how fascist sympathizers in the American military provided William Gerald Bishop, a Christian Front leader, with a cache of several thousand bullets, a few machine-gun belts, and a limited number of explosives. With this, Bishop and his comrades intended to launch a coordinated terror attack aimed at installing a pro-fascist government in the United States.[36] As Maddow rightly observes, Americans failed to take these fascist terrorists seriously because news reporters dismissed them as "crackpots."[37]

Documents from German archives say much the same thing. Reich officials stationed in the United States perceived the situation much as did the American press. In 1941 Georg Gyssling, the German consul general in Los Angeles, was appalled by several individuals who appeared at the consulate claiming to be Schutzstaffel (SS) intelligence (SD) or Abwehr (military intelligence) espionage agents but who lacked proper identification. Conveying one such incident to a Foreign Ministry colleague, Gyssling recalled an "agent" who lingered around Los Angeles for a year and half, learned almost no English, and was clueless about local German-American relations. The man eventually produced what he claimed were Abwehr identification papers, along with a letter from the Abwehr requesting that he be supplied with "desperately needed funds." Gyssling ordered him back to Germany and provided the money necessary for that purpose. Instead, the agent used the funds to leisurely tour Mexico with a "ladyfriend." Reflecting on this and other incidents, Gyssling speculated that the so-called agent might have actually been an FBI counterespionage operative. Exasperated by such incompetence, he advised his superiors that they could gather more accurate intelligence by simply reading American newspapers or scouting out military installations firsthand.[38]

Nazis of Copley Square portrays Herbert Scholz, Germany's consul general in Boston from late 1938 to 1941, as one of Hitler's premier "spymasters."[39] Scholz was deeply involved in several covert operations and often enlisted German exchange students in the Boston area. In one case, Kurt Ludwig, Scholz's cousin by marriage, initiated Operation Ludwig in March 1941 to gather details about ship movements and military bases.[40] *Hitler's American Friends* notes that one of Ludwig's agents, Lucy Boehmler, was an eighteen-year-old who took part in German in espionage because she thought it would be fun and the promise of a regular salary appealed to her. She worked with her associates to successfully inflict "damage . . . to the [American] war effort [that] will never be fully known."[41] The so-called Ludwig ring, it turns out, operated under FBI surveillance for most of its existence and collected only trivial information. Exposure of the associated Duquesne ring, another Scholz scheme, precipitated Ludwig's panicked attempt to flee the United States. He was so flustered in his rush to escape that he forgot his shortwave radio, which fell into the bureau's hands. The FBI also secured incriminating documents through one of its informants in the German Embassy. After Ludwig's arrest, Boehmler turned state's evidence, angry that Ludwig had criticized her work and refused to continue paying her.[42] The entire debacle not only provided the US government with valuable insights into German espionage activities but also led to a further decline in US-German relations, bolstered Hoover's counterintelligence division, and tarnished the reputation of Wilhelm Canaris, the anti-Nazi chief of the Abwehr (German military intelligence).[43]

In another plot that verged on farce, Scholz persuaded an American engineer, William Curtis Colepaugh, to enroll in a Reich espionage school and return to the United States after graduation to sabotage US industry.[44] Colepaugh attended the school and in late 1944 returned home as part of Operation Elster, a mission aimed at industrial sabotage. Colepaugh quickly lost interest in his mission, however, and instead spent the Reich's funds to maintain a lavish lifestyle in New York City, reconnect with a childhood friend, and attract a new girlfriend.[45] After Christmas, he turned himself in to the FBI, having engaged in neither espionage nor sabotage.[46]

Prequel and *Hitler's American Friends* suggest that German Nazis or their American followers were behind suspicious explosions at munitions plants, especially in New Jersey at the Hercules Powder plant, which operated non-stop, and at three other munitions facilities in New Jersey and Pennsylvania. They imply that the Nazis had advanced knowledge of these catastrophes and might well have been orchestrating them. While *Hitler in Los Angeles* attributes these catastrophes unequivocally to saboteurs, *Prequel* adopts a more nuanced tone, stating, "Whether those explosions were accidents, or strictly a Nazi sabotage operation, or sabotage plotted to help the Nazis but carried out by Americans was never conclusively proven by the government."[47] Two postwar analyses, a 1946 US Navy study and a 2016 FBI report, found no evidence of foreign sabotage in the United States during the war. This is not particularly surprising, given the frantic efforts the German diplomatic corps made to discourage sabotage operations, and the general ineptitude of German saboteurs in the country.[48] Rather, the accidents were very likely due to the rapid pace of rearmament, insufficient training, new supply chain complications, and other mundane causes.[49]

Catastrophes such as munitions plant explosions are almost inevitable during rapid expansions in weapons manufacture, a reality evident in both the United States and Germany before, during, and after World War II.[50] German munitions workers likely faced greater risks and experienced more severe incidents than Americans, driven by the Reich's wartime desperation and working under laxer safety protocols than their American counterparts.[51] Despite the scarcity of detailed records from Germany due to the Reich's secrecy, available evidence indicates frequent and severe accidents.[52] From 1942 to 1945, the years in which US forces fought in the war, 317 workers died in American munitions plant explosions. In contrast, in just two of Germany's larger munitions plants, at Hirschhagen and Ludwigshafen, there were more than 181 deaths from explosions during the same period, with an additional twenty-five explosions for which the number of fatalities remains unrecorded.[53] This suggests that fatalities from munitions plant explosions were much more common in the Reich than in the United States. Notably, both countries experienced such munitions explosions before and after the war, when sabotage would have been particularly unlikely, further underscoring that these tragedies were often due to industrial conditions rather than espionage or sabotage. Despite Germany's frenzied attempts at espionage and covert propaganda operations in the United States, and the self-serving boasts of Nazi supporters and others, not a single case of successful Axis sabotage has been documented.

Introduction   9

Many operatives tasked with espionage were also involved in covert propaganda efforts. Francis P. Moran, a prominent Boston Catholic layman, spent the early 1940s "churning out Nazi propaganda" under the guidance of Scholz and "blazing from his pulpit on behalf of Hitler."[54] Nevertheless, Ernst Bohle, the gauleiter responsible for Nazi organizations outside Germany, admitted to American interrogators after the war that such amateurish efforts significantly undermined the Nazis' attempts to sway American public opinion.[55] The Abwehr's Wilhelm Canaris echoed similar frustrations about the ineffectiveness of these operations.[56]

In the late 1930s, as international tensions escalated, the SS increasingly exploited the German student exchange program for spy operations in the United States, covertly inserting agents under the guise of students. Similarly, the Abwehr sporadically and carelessly employed students for espionage. These interorganizational rivalries, and the escalating stakes as war approached, led to increasingly desperate and risky operations. Many of these plots were so clumsily managed that they culminated in public scandals in the United States, ignited substantial backlash, and contributed to the decline of the exchange program. The absurdity of some of these operations was such that one is tempted to wonder whether Canaris and Hans Oster, his chief of espionage operations, deliberately designed them simply to embarrass Hitler, as they apparently did elsewhere.[57] More plausibly, the failures of Nazi espionage in the United States should be attributed to the sheer incompetence of the agents involved. This was succinctly expressed by a member of a pro-Nazi group in Los Angeles: he admitted that his comrades were "a bunch of numbskulls."[58]

Leo Ribuffo coined the term *brown scare* to describe a trend among some writers of the 1930s and 1940s to sensationalize the threat posed by Nazi propagandists, spies, and saboteurs, often identifying German exchange students in these roles. These writers employed exaggeration and melodrama to convince the American public of an imminent fascist threat poised to subvert the country.[59] One of the earliest examples of brown scare literature is John L. Spivak's *Secret Armies: The New Technique of Nazi Warfare* (1939). Some scholars have been impressed by Spivak's "spectacular exposés" of Nazi machinations in the United States.[60] Spivak accurately deduced that some of the German exchange students were Nazi spies,[61] but also of note, Spivak's more outlandish accusations led to a criminal libel conviction.[62] Presumably, Spivak's readers were unaware that he was a Soviet agent to boot.[63]

John Roy Carlson's *Under Cover: My Four Years in the Nazi Underworld of America* was perhaps the most recognized title of the brown scare genre during the 1940s.[64] Gallagher and Maddow highlight Carlson's assertions that the Nazis' plots posed serious dangers to American democracy.[65] Carlson realized that some German exchange students were dangerous, pro-Nazi "Trojan horses,"[66] but he also had critics. Ribuffo noted Carlson's penchant for presuming guilt based on scant evidence and for transforming casual encounters into close alliances and occasional cooperation into "warm friendships." Rather, official inquiries revealed little beyond the fact that far right propagandists exchanged cordial letters, read each other's magazines, and collaborated to spread prejudice. The well-known Socialist Norman Thomas also did not think much of Carlson, who he described as a "zealot" bent on equating anti-war sentiment with pro-Nazism.[67] Gallagher correctly notes that Carlson had a "flair for drama" and a tendency to make hyperbolic statements.[68] Likewise, Richard Rollins, in *I Find Treason*, also exposed German exchange student involvement in pro-Nazi activities.[69] As Maddow asserts in a related example, such drama certainly contributed to boosting book sales.[70]

Nazism in German Academia, Society, and State Culture

In *The Third Reich in the Ivory Tower: Complicity and Conflict on American Campuses*, Stephen Norwood asserts that American academia was rife with pro-Nazi administrators and faculty.[71] The German scholar Elisabeth Piller notes that during World War I, American Germanist academics were pejoratively labeled "pro-Hun," with many losing their positions. By the mid-1930s, renewed public animosity once again threatened their careers, leading some Germanists to defend Germany perhaps more out of a desire to prevent the closure of their German-language programs, as happened in World War I, than out of genuine ideological adherence.

From a different perspective, Stephen Duggan, director of the American student exchange administration at IIE, and his colleagues, staunch Wilsonian internationalists, believed that student immersion in another country's culture promoted international peace.[72] Duggan also envisioned that students from Germany who studied in the United States could take part in founding a new liberal democratic Germany once the Nazis were thrown out, as would indeed happen.[73] Moreover, Duggan and the German diplomatic corps in the United States were acutely aware that the student exchange program was one of the last remaining German-American cultural connections.[74] At the same time, Duggan and like-minded academics founded organizations to rescue German intellectuals, typically of Jewish descent, by finding them jobs in the United States.[75]

In addition to examining pro-Nazi and other Americans' reactions to the German exchange students, *Nazis in the New World* also considers the German students' relationship to Nazism. In doing so, it devotes attention to opposition to the Third Reich, analyzing the extent to which some students disagreed with Nazi ideology, whether such disagreement motivated them to apply to study abroad, and whether German officials recognized this motivation and were willing to help anyway. Soon after World War II, a flood of books by former Wehrmacht officers, Foreign Office officials, academics, and others sought to distance themselves and their colleagues from the Nazis. For example, the July 20 plot to assassinate Hitler at the Wolf's Lair was often cited as evidence that the Wehrmacht as a whole was anti-Nazi. Regardless of the truth, Cold War imperatives encouraged uncritical acceptance of these claims to facilitate the reintegration of West Germany into the Western alliance. In short, who had been a Nazi, or had opposed the Nazis, became increasingly irrelevant to the superpower struggle. By the 1960s, however, these blanket absolutions came under more critical scrutiny, generally not to the advantage of the suspected.

On the other hand, with the development of social history in the 1970s, interest grew in studying possible signs of anti-Nazi dissent among ordinary Germans. The most notable effort was the Bavaria Project of the 1970s and 1980s, involving the renowned historian Martin Broszat and others. They concluded that the Nazis had, in fact, exaggerated the extent of their popular support. Acts of opposition by various groups, including Catholics, occurred more frequently than previously acknowledged. What constituted genuine resistance, however, became a much-debated topic. Some historians, among them Ian Kershaw, developed a hierarchy of resistance to address this issue, with actions ranging from gestures so mild that they likely escaped notice to lethal acts of defiance (active resistance), demonstrating that not all Germans condoned Nazi actions.[76]

Compared to the clear anti-Nazi imperatives provided by ideologies such as religion, German state culture offered subtler motivators to persuade people to go along with the Nazis. Many scholars have emphasized the traditional proclivity of German officials to obey the legally constituted state, regardless of personal distaste for its policies. Most of these bureaucrats prioritized their own safety, security, and material well-being, even when they had doubts about the ethics of Nazism. Social pressure to conform also played a significant role, with only the bravest daring to face the consequences of openly opposing the National Socialist regime.[77] On the other hand, some officials struggled to maintain their self-identity, personal autonomy, and adherence to religious, political, moral, or professional codes. Thus, many German government employees and academics supported the regime in certain ways, such as emphasizing grievances against the Treaty of Versailles, while resisting other aspects, such as pressure to join Nazi societies, anti-Jewish actions, and the erosion of Christian values.[78]

Voluntary exile served as one form of resistance. As Michael Balfour has noted, choosing exile can be a powerful act of opposition.[79] Research indicates that tendencies toward noncompliance with Nazi policies were most evident among the *Bildungsbürgertum*—the educated, cosmopolitan, upper-middle class, which often included academics, Foreign Ministry officials, international education personnel, and exchange students. Predominantly conservative nationalists rather than National Socialists,[80] many in these groups strove to preserve what they considered the best aspects of German academics and culture, hoping they would outlast Nazism. Although often prioritizing career safety over principle, they still commonly acted on low-risk decisions grounded in personal ethics. In some cases, officials approved students to study abroad even when these exchange candidates' loyalty to the Nazi regime was questionable. The complex interplay of competing organizations and leaders within the German exchange program often facilitated these decisions, allowing decision-makers to justify their actions by aligning them with one or another state authority.[81]

German Foreign Ministry officials had more contact with the exchange program than any others outside the German Academic Exchange Service (Deutscher Akademischer Austauschdienst, DAAD), with the notorious exception of the SS later in the 1930s. Debates about the extent to which Foreign Ministry officials objected to the Nazi regime have been contentious. After World War II, most scholars agreed that the Foreign Ministry was particularly staffed with Hitler opponents and had a widespread aversion to at least some Nazi actions.[82] In 2010, however, Eckart Conze, Norbert Frei, Peter Hayes, and Moshe Zimmermann turned this consensus on its head with the publication of *Das Amt und die Vergangenheit: Deutschen Diplomaten im Dritten Reich und in der Bundesrepublik* (*The Ministry and the Past: German Diplomacy in the Third Reich and the Federal Republic*). These well-respected historians contended that the Foreign Ministry was complicit with the regime, asserting, "The Ministry represented, thought, and acted on behalf of the regime, and documented the integration of Third Reich officials into the post-war West German Foreign Ministry."[83] *Das Amt* unquestionably shows

Introduction 13

that former Nazis were allowed to rejoin the ministry. At the same time, though, recent critics, including Johannes Hürter, Michael Mayer, and Michael Wala, see problems with blanket statements dismissing many Foreign Ministry officials' unease about aspects of Hitler's policies during the Third Reich.[84] Although not "anti-Nazi" as a body, the Foreign Ministry was suspected of harboring non-Nazis or even those seeking the end of the Hitler regime.[85] Consequently, the Nazis generally did not trust the diplomatic corps.

In the early years of Hitler's dictatorship, the Foreign Ministry largely retained its Weimar-era personnel, with only a few Nazis in positions of authority. To foreign observers, this appearance of continuity provided an illusion of diplomatic stability. Several radical Nazi exchange students scorned some of these officials as fossilized remnants of the Weimar era who long before should have been dismissed.[86] Notably, a significant portion of civil servants, particularly at senior levels, never joined the party. Others did so only after intense pressure.[87] Heinz Schneppen has drawn a parallel with Abbé Sieyès, who, when asked what he had done during the French Revolution, responded, "I survived."[88]

Some purported Nazis were not staunch party loyalists, but were motivated by more pragmatic concerns. It is important to recognize that higher-level German government officials, often from the classically educated upper-middle class, joined the Nazi Party for varied reasons, with ideological conviction being only one of them.[89] Many in the German diplomatic corps stationed in the United States despised the Gestapo as well as saboteurs from Germany who showed up from time to time. For example, in 1939 the consulate staff in New York warily eyed Walter Engelberg, a Nazi Party agent imposed on them by Ernst Wilhelm Bohle, gauleiter of Nazi Party Foreign Organization (NSDAP / Auslands-Organisation, AO). In 1940 German consuls in the United States rejoiced that Engelberg had been murdered. They hoped that "this incident will teach the Gestapo and the AO not to pollute the German consular service more than it already is." They also cabled the Foreign Ministry that both sabotage and espionage harmed their primary mission: the promotion of isolationism in the United States.[90]

Several German diplomatic officials in the United States during the Hitler years actively engaged in some sort of "anti-Nazi" activities.[91] Hans Thomsen, chargé d'affaires at the German Embassy in Washington from November 1938 to December 11, 1941, had a highly secret relationship with American intelligence networks. In the summer of 1941, he used his long-time friendship with a Quaker peace advocate, Malcom R. Lovell, Sr., to approach US government officials with secret intelligence. Lovell passed the information on to William Donovan, the US coordinator of information (and a year later, first head of the CIA's precursor, the Office of Strategic Services [OSS]), who then redistributed it, as appropriate, to President Roosevelt; FBI director J. Edgar Hoover; Allen Dulles, an OSS official; and Britain's intelligence representative to the United States, William Stephenson. Thomsen told Lovell that the German diplomatic corps had nothing to do with German Abwehr espionage efforts given that these would only "promote ill will" between the United States and Germany, and, presciently, "gain little information of value." He subtly hinted there might be plans to assassinate Hitler and hoped to play a role thereafter in aligning Germany with American foreign policy. Otherwise, Thomsen hoped to live out his life in the United States. His wife, Annaliese ("Bébé"), was particularly adamant against returning to Germany. The most important information that Thomsen passed on to Donovan, and thus to Roosevelt (reaching him on November 13), was that the Japanese would soon attack the United States, and Germany would immediately join that conflict as well. There is no sign that this information was acted upon, however, presumably due to its indirect nature.[92]

In the early 1940s, both German consuls general serving in California, Georg Gyssling and Fritz Wiedemann, engaged in anti-Nazi activities. Wiedemann, who had once been close to Hitler, fell out with the Führer before his appointment as head of the consulate in San Francisco in January 1939. Despite continuing his consular duties, which included facilitating espionage, he admitted to Gyssling that he hated Hitler.[93] When World War II began months later, one of the German exchange students in Ohio, Gustav Blanke, faced a decision: return to Germany to join the Wehrmacht or remain in the United States. Blanke eventually traveled to San Francisco and sought Wiedemann's advice on the matter. Wiedemann suggested they take a walk in the consulate's garden. Once alone, Wiedemann advised Blanke to remain in the United States.[94] In 1940 Wiedemann began passing critical information, including proposals to assassinate Hitler, to the FBI, OSS, and Britain's MI6.[95]

Gyssling, heading the consulate in Los Angeles from 1933 to 1941, was notorious for pressuring Hollywood producers not to release films critical of Germany or the Nazi regime. At the same time, he also relayed information to a member of the Los Angeles Jewish Community Committee about his conversations with various German consuls in the United States, particularly those who rejected Hitler. This intelligence was then forwarded to General George Marshall and several other military and FBI intelligence officers, although it seemingly did not lead to any significant action.[96] While Gyssling was in contact with several German exchange students, the specifics are unclear. According to his daughter, Gyssling considered making arrangements for her to remain in the United States, but ultimately decided against it, given the potential repercussions.[97] Upon returning to Germany, he was interrogated by the Gestapo for suspicion of disloyalty to the regime.[98]

Gyssling and Wiedemann also engaged in what they regarded as "pro-German" espionage activities and covert propaganda in the United States, but their roles in the diplomatic corps mandates these activities. It seems they perceived themselves as German patriots, rather than Nazis, in a manner reminiscent of German diplomats during World War I. They were aware that any overt objection or apparent reluctance to carry out Nazi directives could result in dismissal from their post at a minimum; if the Gestapo had ever discovered their actions against the Nazis, they would almost certainly have been executed.[99]

Josias von Rantzau, secretary of the German legation at the consulate general in New York during 1936–37, was another active resistor against the Nazis, although he was nominally a member of the Nazi Party, like some of the resistors. For years, von Rantzau had a close friendship with Adam von Trott zu Solz, one of the best-known anti-Nazis in the Foreign Ministry. He also maintained contacts with the Kreisau circle, a leading German opposition group, through Albrecht von Kessel, the diplomatic superior of the former exchange student Sigismund von Baun, also associated with the Kreisau group.[100]

Non-Nazi officials were prevalent in the Foreign Ministry's Cultural Affairs Department (Kulturabteilung), which dealt with exchange programs. Throughout the 1930s, the department struggled to keep Nazi organizations, such as the National Socialist German Students' League, from engaging in their own "cultural-political" activities abroad.[101] Nazi enthusiasts complained that the Cultural Affairs Department "too often forgot the political point of view, and was too deeply immersed in the foreign mentality."[102]

The Nazis' suspicions turned out to be on the mark in some cases. Fritz von Twardowski, head of the Cultural Affairs Department, was loosely associated with the Carl Friedrich Goerdeler circle, arguably the leading resistance group in Nazi Germany.[103] At von Twardowski's postwar denazification interrogation, he never directly mentioned German exchange students sent specifically to the United States, but said that, in general, he only selected individuals for inter-state cultural projects who, in his judgement, "[would be] respected there, regardless of their domestic political stance [in Germany]."

He further asserted that he had opposed any attempt to masquerade Germany's foreign policy goals under the guise of international cultural relations; he also adamantly rejected espionage activities conducted under the cover of inter-state cultural affairs.[104] Von Twardowski thwarted the Nazis in several instances, including one in which he ensured that certain files went missing to protect some Jewish students at the German School in Budapest.[105] Later, the Gestapo suspected him of involvement in the July 1944 assassination attempt against Hitler due to his dubious political sentiments and his acquaintance with some of the plot participants, including Trott. He was eventually cleared, however, perhaps because at the time, he served as the consul general in Istanbul and had not been anywhere near the plotters for an extended period.[106]

Resistance in German Academia

To assess the impact of the German exchange program, it is crucial to consider the extent of Nazification among German professors and university students. Similar to Foreign Ministry officials, academics and students have often been depicted as Nazi sympathizers. Immediately after the war, the historian Max Weinreich asserted, "German scholars from the beginning to the end of the Hitler era worked hand in glove with the murderers of the Jewish people."[107] Robert P. Eriksen echoed this, stating, "Germany's intellectual and spiritual leaders enthusiastically partnered with Hitler's regime, thus becoming active participants in the persecution of Jews and, ultimately, in the Holocaust."[108] Focusing specifically on Heidelberg under Nazism, Steven Remy reached conclusions that reinforced Eriksen's views, though his accusations were not as vehement. For Remy, Heidelberg professors were notably complicit in assisting the Nazis.[109] Wolfgang Benz thought such complicity typical of German academia.[110]

The debate remains ongoing.[111] The historians Hans Rothfels and Gerhard Ritter highlight that many professors were not particularly eager to embrace the Nazis.[112] Most full professors were conservative nationalists who, in 1933, viewed the Nazis as fellow anti-republicans, anti-communists, and ardent German nationalists. They welcomed the National Socialist government's determination to restore Germany to a prominent position among the Great Powers, a move that they believed would include elevating Germany's intellectuals to a preeminent global status. Their initial support for Nazism waned, however, as Nazi radicalism, anti-intellectualism, and academic authoritarianism became increasingly apparent.[113]

The Nazis themselves were suspicious of intellectuals, viewing them as potentially subversive and largely useless.[114] Meanwhile, academics often regarded Nazi functionaries as not very bright.[115] While academics might comply with superficial requirements, like the "German greeting" or the Nazification of university ceremonies, many resisted fully embracing the regime's ideological extremes. Therefore, symbolic gestures of allegiance, such as official university statements, did not necessarily reflect the genuine mindset of the academic community, particularly among senior faculty members.[116]

To placate the regime, scholars sometimes prefaced or concluded their works with obligatory praise for Hitler and the Nazi state, though the core content of these publications often retained its scholarly integrity. This tactic mirrored that of writers during the ancien régime, who would often commence their books with dutiful praise of royal or aristocratic patrons before proceeding to the substantive scholarly content.

Academic rank significantly influenced faculty members' relationship with the Nazi regime. Those striving for tenure were most likely to display allegiance, hoping it would provide them a political advantage. The strategy met with decidedly mixed results.[117] The most influential academic group—the professor ordinarius, or full professors—viewed themselves as the cultural elite and the direct successors to the nineteenth-century German academic and intellectual class. They aimed to preserve their traditions and privileges by retaining control over their universities and promoting faculty on the basis of scholarly merit rather than Nazi Party affiliation. Nazis were forever complaining that academia was only superficially Nazified.[118]

After the war, Gerhard Ritter claimed that he and other professors at the University of Freiburg had formed a tacit pact with Education Ministry officials to resist party interference.[119] Christian-oriented academics seemed particularly willing to risk Nazi attention. Julius Richter, a University of Berlin professor of Christian missionary studies, used his travels to the United States and his contacts with Americans to report on Nazi atrocities against Jews and Christians. Yet his futile efforts left him a "disappointed and broken man." Likewise, several faculty at the University of Freiburg discussed the need for a more Christian-oriented post-Hitler Germany.[120] The Gestapo was aware of such individuals, due to tips from those such as Georg Rettig, a Nazi DAAD official, angered after running into Julius Richter's liberal son Hans, an exchange student at the Princeton Theological Seminary.

Some American students established close relationships with their professors, fellow students, and others during their years of study in the Third

Reich. Aware of Americans' own political proclivities and their "untouchable" status in Germany, quite a few friendly professors and students confided their true opinions of the Nazis to American students. The Americans reported their observations to IIE, which noted that many German academics found the Nazis distasteful.[121]

The Nazis who eventually controlled the German-American exchange lacked the expertise to assess the academic performance of exchange applicants, necessitating reliance on evaluations provided by the students' former and current professors. DAAD could not afford to ignore the academic performance of their exchange candidates without risking complaints about poor performance from the host US institutions, which could jeopardize the entire exchange program. This situation enabled professors to influence the selection process, particularly in supporting students they believed would gain from spending a year in a liberal democracy.[122] In this context, a professor providing a glowing letter of recommendation for a student he knew did not support the Nazis represented a subtle form of resistance. Although writing such a letter may seem rather trivial at first blush, it posed a significant risk under a regime that leveraged fear to ensure compliance. The potential loss of a prestigious academic position during the Great Depression served as a powerful deterrent against open defiance, encouraging only subtle forms of dissent within the academic community during this period.[123]

Many scholars who assert that university faculty wholeheartedly supported the Nazis also argue that university students generally embraced Nazi ideology. Remy, for instance, depicts them as true believers determined to coerce their professors into conforming to Nazi policies or face expulsion from academia.[124] Rolf Uwe Fülbier, among others, details the methods students employed to intimidate professors. These included engaging in verbal confrontations in class, making public accusations of disloyalty to the Reich, planting informants in classrooms to monitor and report on any apparent subversive comments, and even fabricating allegations of political unreliability.[125] Ideologically radicalized students have long used such time-honored tactics for self-empowerment. According to Remy, the most notable instances of Nazi student radicalization occurred from 1932 to 1934.[126] Eriksen draws many of the same observations, focusing particularly on the early 1930s.[127] There is considerably less discussion about student attitudes as the 1930s progressed.

Numerous institutional and social forces hindered the full Nazification of student bodies at German universities. Geoffrey Giles insightfully observes that the vast majority of university students prioritized obtaining their degrees over participating in Nazi activities.[128] Nazi policies challenging social hierarchies alienated many students from the Bildungsbürgertum, who were proud of their class status. Frederic "Fritz" Lilge, a German exchange student who remained in the United States, viewed the Nazification of German universities as a conflict between the traditional elite and the less affluent, culturally unsophisticated newcomers. In his seminal work, *The Abuse of Learning*, Lilge critiqued the decline of German universities as a consequence of modern society's obsession with technological advances derived from science. By the end of the nineteenth century, utilitarian scientific and technological disciplines, growing ever stronger in the eternal battle for academic resources, disdainfully dismissed the contemplative, holistic approach of classical humanism—the foundational ethos of the Bildungsbürgertum elite that Lilge himself represented. The dam broke in the early 1930s, when hordes of young adults, frightened by the Great Depression, sought a university education not for personal enlightenment, its traditional purpose, but as a means to pursue professional careers. Lilge seemed to regard his own class as the potential bulwark against the Nazi incursion, but he also lamented that too many intellectuals failed to uphold the values they professed. Some reluctantly embraced the Nazi state while others remained ambivalent, adopting "inner migration" as a compromise to retain their positions while trying to minimize the affronts to their moral convictions that the Nazi state demanded. Still others, like Lilge, chose exile. He conceded, however, that many émigré academics, possibly including himself, fled more to escape a repressive regime than to maintain moral integrity. Had they possessed true conviction, they would have stayed to resist.

The state that subsequently emerged under the Nazis appeared to try even the university students who eagerly followed the Führer. Soon after the Nazis seized power, German student organizations developed their own Kafkaesque bureaucracies and obligatory, mind-numbing Nazi activities. The bureaucratic inefficiencies and intellectual stultification exhibited by the two competing university student organizations—the German Student Union (Deutsche Studentenschaft, DSt) and the National Socialist German Students' League (Nationalsozialistischer Deutscher Studentenbund, NSDStB)—are exemplary. There was no real ideological difference between the two; both advocated the Nazification of academia and decried the continued role of non-Nazis in the student exchange.[129] The real difference lay in bureaucratic rivalry, as both organizations tended to drown themselves in paperwork and internal bickering, significantly hampering their effectiveness.[130] Giles notes the extent of the pettiness within Nazi student organizations, suggesting that by mid-1936, German students were at risk of getting bored by National Socialism altogether.[131] As he put it, "The real enemy of the NSDStB, and by far its most effective one, was apathy. This was an opponent who could not be thrown into a concentration camp."[132]

Richard Albrecht and Otto Romberg discovered numerous references to university resistance groups within criminal and other student documents. They note that despite the suppression of Catholic, youth, and socialist-communist organizations, these groups remained influential, including among students participating in the exchange program.[133] Students in Germany showed signs of disaffection and engaged in minor displays of opposition at various universities during the Nazi era.[134] Writing to IIE, American exchange students often reported their German classmates' criticism of the Nazis, some of it announced in public.[135] Given these circumstances, it is not surprising that a significant number of German exchange students viewed their time in the United States as a welcome respite from constant hectoring by Nazi leaders, as well as an opportunity to pursue their personal academic interests without ideological oversight.

The German-American Academic Exchange and Postwar Americanization

Selecting students for study abroad involved a variety of assessors, including academics, Foreign Ministry officials, party members, and DAAD management. This range of evaluators, a legacy from the Weimar era, allowed more traditionally minded committee members to retain influence. After mid-1934, however, input from the Nazi Party, often through the SS, began to dominate. The involvement of party zealots in the selection process was almost always inversely proportional to their expertise and managerial acumen. The selection criteria for exchange students focused on four main qualities, only one of which distinctly aligned with Nazi ideology: academic performance; personal attributes such as charisma and physical attractiveness; leadership skills; and devotion to the Führer. The three non-Nazi traits were assessed primarily by professors, university officials, and local leaders of various on- or off-campus organizations, including some indirectly associated with the Nazi state, such as youth community labor directors.

While most of the exchange students focused on advancing their careers during their US sojourn, some pursued highly questionable objectives that aligned with Nazi goals, such as gathering intelligence or fostering pro-German sentiment. This group's "career goals" sometimes involved rising within the ranks of the Sicherheitsdienst (SD, the intelligence agency of the SS) or even engaging in putative medical research using extermination camp inmates.

In contrast, exchange students selected to represent Germany through the program sometimes exhibited un-Nazi attitudes in their applications, displaying only a lukewarm commitment to the regime's ideology. The act of applying for permission and financial support to study temporarily in the United States suggested a desire to experience life in a liberal democracy. Many of those students who adopted American perspectives during their study abroad year often desperately resisted returning to Germany. Inevitably, Nazi officials became aware of their attempts to stay in the United States, and those who failed to secure US residency faced retaliation upon their return to Germany.

A smaller group of exchange students went further in their opposition to Hitler. After two exchange years in the United States, 1934–36, Herbert Sonthoff, who had studied at the University of Georgia, returned to Germany. While back at home, he became friends with members of the Catholic resistance, among them Hermann Siemer and Otto Wirmer.[136] As a German diplomat to the Vatican, Sigismund von Braun, another former exchange student, worked with his superior, Ulrich von Hassell, in planning a post-Hitler Germany.[137] Meanwhile, Von Hassel was acquainted with Wirmer and his brother, Josef Wirmer.[138] Sonthoff and von Braun likely did not know that they were connected through these links to the anti-Hitler resistance. This Siemer-Wirmer opposition group intersected with the more well-known anti-Hitler Goerdeler circle, which included among its associates Adolf Henning Frucht, another former exchange student.[139]

The factors driving German's postwar transformation, including its liberalization, continue to be debated among historians, and this study touches on the role of returned, former exchange students in it. Mary Nolan and other scholars have argued that Germany's apparent "Americanization" was largely due to the significant influence of the United States during and after the Allied occupation.[140] An alternative view, presented by Anselm Doering-Manteuffel, suggests that Germany experienced "Westernization," mainly due to the influence of West German Chancellor Konrad Adenauer as a staunch advocate of membership in the US–Western European alliance.[141] Udi Greenberg believes that revitalized democratic forces from the Weimar era played a crucial role.[142] The analysis in *Nazis in the New World* suggests that "pro-American" German exchange students, who had advanced in their careers by the postwar period, along with other participants from the student exchange program during the Weimar and Nazi eras, significantly contributed to Germany's Americanization.

The issue of continuity in twentieth-century German history is extraordinarily complex and difficult to summarize. Earlier postwar generations of German scholars emphasized a narrative of rupture over continuity, advocating the *Stunde Null* (zero hour) thesis, which posited a complete break with the past after World War II. Today, nearly a century after the war, scholars increasingly incorporate German history within the broader context of European and Western history, shifting the focus from strict continuity to a more integrated historical perspective.[143] This shift is evident in economic and consumerist history studies and has implications for understanding historical continuities.[144] The German-American exchange program, for example, shows considerable continuity between the Weimar era and the Third Reich, particularly in the use of the program to achieve foreign policy goals, such as overturning the Treaty of Versailles.[145] There is markedly less continuity, however, between the Third Reich and the post–World War II years.[146] During the Weimar era, the program had already been structured to support Germany's foreign policy objectives. This structure remained largely unchanged in the Third Reich, during which criteria for selecting exchange students, their socioeconomic backgrounds, preparation for the exchange year, and the propaganda messages they were expected to champion had marked similarities. Nonetheless, during the Nazi dictatorship, ideological selection criteria became crucial, and the students' propaganda messages were modified to serve as apologies for Nazism and the regime's brutal policies.

Book Outline

Examination of the theses in *Nazis in the New World* is organized to reflect, chapter by chapter, a student's typical progression through the German-American exchange program of the 1930s and how it changed over time. Chapter 1 discusses the early days of the German-American exchange program, which was initially based on the national conservative ideology that prevailed at DAAD during the Weimar era. The program was designed not only to enrich the educational experience of German students, but also to serve broader national interests by fostering international goodwill and academic prestige. Besides denying participation by Jewish Germans, with a few notable exceptions, however, little else changed when the Nazis took power. The individual new Nazi government agencies viewed DAAD as a potential conquest in the expansion of their own bureaucratic power. Aside from the SS, most of them generally had little or no success in exerting control over the exchange program. Due to the complex management of student exchange programs in Nazi Germany, the increasingly byzantine bureaucratic rules, and DAAD's relative administrative autonomy, a number of non-Nazi and even some anti-Nazi holdover employees retained considerable influence over the selection of German students for the program. In the late 1930s, Nazi radicals in DAAD's leadership began sending SS spies to the United States in the guise of "normal" students and coerced others into engaging in espionage. The results of these endeavors proved extremely detrimental to the program's integrity. As Nazi brutality and Germany's territorial aggression intensified, American colleges stopped participating in droves, leading to the program's effective end even before the outbreak of war in 1939.

Chapter 2 focuses on the recruitment and training of students for the exchange program, detailing their motivations for studying in the United States, the selection process, propaganda training, and espionage missions. Many German students drawn to modern American culture sought to study in the United States, even during the Third Reich.[147] Applicants for the exchange program were required to demonstrate a range of psychological traits—charisma, charm, extroversion, friendliness, leadership, and in some cases, physical attractiveness—characteristics the German authorities believed would enhance their popularity on American campuses and strengthen their propaganda appeal.

Applicants suspected of excessively admiring American culture or its liberalism were typically disqualified, although some slipped through the selection process. Many students sent to study for a year never returned, while others frantically sought ways to stay or regretted returning home. Some who returned to Germany managed to find their way back to the States before the outbreak of war made it impossible. Chapter 2 also examines the flaws in the Nazis' Kafkaesque exchange program bureaucracy and the continued influence of non-Nazi administrators, which allowed for these apparent ideological anomalies. Before departing Germany, the selected students attended a preparatory course about their host country, which over time evolved into propaganda training aimed at fostering pro-Nazi sentiment among American colleges, a strategy that ultimately failed.

Chapter 3 delves into the transformative experiences of German students upon their arrival in the New World. It describes how they were exposed, often for the first time, to a radically different world, enjoying personal freedoms no longer possible in Germany. The students fully participated in campus life, with some coming to strongly identify with their host universities. Notably, their exchange year allowed them to interact with German refugees who had fled the National Socialist regime, as well as "non-Aryans," challenging their preconceived notions about such people. Most of the exchange students were surprised to find that these individuals were not as they had been portrayed by Nazi propaganda. This exposure generally left them with a positive image of the United States as a progressive, modern country. While there were exceptions, their criticisms of the country were usually grounded in pre-Nazi conservative perspectives associated with the Bildungsbürgertum, rather than a Nazi worldview. Despite Americans' curiosity about the exchange students' views on their homeland, they showed little interest in Nazi propaganda. Until 1938 the students were mostly seen as young, attractive Europeans rather than representatives of Nazi Germany.

Chapter 4 focuses on students who pursued a traditional academic exchange experience. Many of the young Germans were primarily concerned with career preparation, and went to the United States for professional enrichment, often remaining relatively indifferent to the social, cultural, or political life of the country. Nevertheless, most of them came away with predominantly positive impressions of the United States; some even returned to Germany eager to further facilitate German-American friendship. A number of students either opposed the Nazi regime before embarking on the exchange or fell into disfavor with German authorities while in the United States. Quite a few experienced "reverse culture shock"—including anxiety, depression, and fear—upon returning to Germany.[148] Those who dreamed of remaining in States faced daunting impediments due of immigration restrictions or personal attachments in Germany. Those who fought to obtain permanent residency accepted the risk that German authorities would inevitably learn of their efforts. If ultimately forced to repatriate, they could not expect a festive reception for their apparent "resistance" to Nazism.[149] Several of them managed to return to the United States before the war, but often under such odd circumstances that the FBI kept them under observation for some time. The dramatic transformation in the ultimately pro-American students' worldview highlights the Nazis' inability to mold the convictions of young, elite adults as much as has been assumed.

Chapter 5 examines the efforts of German exchange students in the United States who intended to carry out covert propaganda or engage in espionage. Their efforts were almost invariably fruitless. German authorities often misjudged the loyalty of German Americans, overestimated their own espionage skills, and grappled with poorly organized, fractious intelligence organizations.

Chapter 6 explores the postwar careers of former exchange students and others involved in the German-American exchange, such as faculty who served on study abroad assessment committees. Many of them went on to forge prominent careers either in the United States or in Germany. Some actively sought to Americanize postwar West Germany. Still others leveraged their past experiences as exchange students to align with the new political and social realities of postwar Germany.[150]

The conclusion demonstrates how the German-American student exchange program mirrors the Third Reich's administrative bureaucratization, radicalization, and increasing incoherence in many ways. There were numerous opportunities for non-Nazis to exploit the Reich's governance flaws to survive professionally and even exert significant influence on the course of events. Likewise, many students lacking Nazi élan nonetheless managed to study in the United States. The increasingly prominent Nazi radicals who managed the exchange programs were only partially successful in preventing lukewarm "Nazi" students from being selected. The effect of life in the United States on these students was at times profoundly transformative.

While Americans generally liked the exchange students as individuals, they were much less receptive to the propaganda messages they delivered. As Hitler's policies radicalized, German exchange students in the United States suffered the consequences. In line with the Reich's ever-increasing militancy, it used exchange students in its preparations for war through espionage activities and efforts to silence critics. After World War II, former exchange students of all kinds—from refugees to anti-American operatives—sought to use their experience in the United States to benefit themselves or reshape their country.

The theses of this book are validated by documents from FBI and military files and the archives of IIE, the German federal government, and several German universities in addition to information available in college yearbooks, student newspapers, and local and national newspapers. Unfortunately, DAAD's archives were destroyed in World War II. The fascinating history of the exchange students from Nazi Germany and what they experienced has seldom been publicized or has long since been forgotten—until now.

CHAPTER ONE

Nazi Infiltration of the Student Exchange

> It is true that Hitler has assured the world that the Nazi regime will
> last a thousand years. I doubt that it will last many years as it is now
> organized. When the time of change comes we want to be prepared
> through understanding to welcome the revival of the fine old German
> culture.
>
> *—Stephen Duggan, director, Institute of International Education,*
> *September 24, 1937*

The institutional framework of German-American student exchanges in the
1930s functioned as a channel for "academic cultural diplomacy" on behalf of
both Germany and the United States. The distinction between cultural diplomacy and propaganda was frequently unclear. Both countries managed their
academic exchanges at two levels: through their respective exchange administration organizations and the universities taking part in the exchange.

The German government wielded significantly more control over its exchange management organization, the German Academic Exchange Service
(Deutscher Akademischer Austauschdienst, DAAD), than the United States
did over its own, the Institute of International Education (IIE). Regardless,
both institutions sometimes deviated from governmental directives and established their own diplomatic priorities.[1] For example, the IIE often maintained friendlier ties with German authorities than did the US government,
or than the public might think warranted in regard to the Third Reich. DAAD
was inaugurated during the Weimar Republic, on January 1, 1931. In the early
1930s, the German Foreign Ministry dictated its ideology and programs, but
later in the decade, the Nazi Party and the SS (Schutzstaffel) gained increasing
control over both of them.

The German exchange program maintained a consistent structure as well as goals under both the Weimar Republic and the Third Reich, but the Reich's unorthodox governmental structure eventually had traditional government ministries fighting with Nazi agencies in battles for bureaucratic lebensraum. Non-Nazi employees hired during the Weimar era quickly proved themselves adept at exploiting the growing administrative disarray of Hitler's regime, at least temporarily.[2]

Due to Germany's reputation for advanced research, German and American academic ties had been strong long before formal exchange programs were established in 1925.[3] The effects of World War I reversed this relationship. As the United States invested heavily in academia, it became a desirable study destination. German universities, however, continued to attract American students interested in German language, history, and culture.[4]

Stephan Duggan, a professor at the City College of New York and a foreign affairs advisor to Woodrow Wilson, founded the IIE in 1919, with funding from the Carnegie Endowment for International Peace.[5] The organization rapidly became the primary nonprofit student exchange entity in the United States.[6] By 1938 it had sent more than 2,000 American students abroad, and in return had arranged for 1,600 foreign students to study in the United States. At that time, 40 percent of international students in the United States were from Germany.[7] Thus, even as US-German relations deteriorated under the Nazis, and an increasing number of American colleges withdrew from the exchange, the IIE fought fiercely to preserve the American-German exchange program.

Meanwhile, the German government also recognized the potential benefits of international student exchanges. Foreign Minister Gustav Stresemann was particularly interested in using the exchanges to advance cultural diplomacy.[8] In 1931 the German government consolidated its various exchange programs into DAAD. Adolf Morsbach, a well-known Catholic centrist, became DAAD's first director. The organization's overarching philosophy was that international exchange students acted as unofficial representatives of their "people."[9] In 1931 and 1932, the last two years of the Weimar Republic, DAAD exchange students attended a summer preparatory camp that left no doubt about the goals of the exchange program. They attended such lectures as "Germany's World-Political Situation," "Problems of the German East," and one on Arnold Bergsträsser's "The Foundations of German National Self-Consciousness in Today's [Economic] Crisis."[10] They were also expected to promote the German government's view on international issues, especially those condemning the Versailles Treaty (1919).[11]

Figure 1.1. Adolf Morsbach, first director of the German Academic Exchange Service (Deutscher Akademischer Austauschdienst), and Ingrid Dybwad, Morsbach's secretary, at Schloss Köpenick, Berlin, ca. early 1930s. Rockefeller Archives Center, RG 4 (FA1288), acc. 2016:070, series 1, box 35, folder 284–286, Early IIE Photos, 1930s. Courtesy of the Institute of International Education.

Hitler's National Socialist regime, established in 1933, allowed existing governmental organizations, such as DAAD, to continue operating.[12] Given DAAD's generally nationalist, conservative principles, most staff retained their positions. For example, Morsbach, "in no sense and at no time an adherent to National Socialism," continued to direct DAAD.[13] Jewish employees, however, were dismissed by April 1933, and Jewish students, as well as students with only one Jewish parent, were dropped from the exchange programs shortly thereafter.[14] The German government restructured DAAD's governing board in the summer. The Propaganda Ministry, the SA (Sturmabteilung), the Nazi Party Foreign Organization (NSDAP / Auslands-Organisation, AO), and the People's League for Ethnic Germans Abroad (Volksbund für das Deutschtum im Ausland) each gained one representative on board. Of note, the German Student Union (Deutsche Studentenschaft, DSt) was allotted two representatives.[15] In addition, two student union representatives were given seats on the directing committees of each university's Foreign Affairs Office (Akademische Auslandsstelle, AKA).

General Ewald von Massow, a Hitler acquaintance, became head of DAAD's reorganized Presidium, though essentially as a figurehead. Described more as a military general and a Christian than a Nazi,[16] von Massow appeared content with the prospect of enjoying the prestige of being DAAD director while Morsbach and others actually managed the exchange.[17] Indeed, even after the DAAD shuffle, responsibility for sending students to the United States remained to some degree in the hands of a number of non-Nazi officials, including Morsbach; Ingrid Dybwad, Morsbach's highly influential secretary; Georg von Fritsch, in charge of the German-American exchange; and Kurt Goepel, who oversaw the German and American students.[18] This situation did not last long, however.

Beginning in 1934, the DAAD leadership's positions became increasingly precarious. Dybwad was forced out in the spring for her half-Jewish ancestry.[19] Von Fritsch, an aristocratic national conservative and longtime civil servant,[20] was dismissed in 1936 because "he did not sufficiently consider the wishes of the Nazi Party regarding the students."[21] Even some of the exchange students noted his lack of Nazi enthusiasm.[22] During the Weimar era, Goepel had been a prominent adherent of the Volkspartei, a center-right political party. He had also expressed disdain for the Nazis, disapproving of the Nazification of the university student body.[23] After the reorganization, Morsbach suggested to Goepel that it would be a wise career move to experience a pro-Nazi epiphany and officially joined the SA and the Nazi Party.[24] Goepel complied with Morsbach's advice, and even published articles with a Nazi slant, such as his "Kulturpropaganda oder Gastfreundschaft," an April 1934 piece in *Der Deutsche Student*, to demonstrate his newfound faith.[25] Regardless, he was not a practicing Nazi. Instead, he remained devoted to the success of individual students, something in which the Nazis at DAAD showed little interest.[26] One of Goepel's former colleagues noted that he had "remained true to his young nationalist-conservative principles until the bitter end."[27] Goepel ultimately managed to hang on to his position at DAAD,[28] throughout most of the 1930s, overseeing the undergraduates sent to the United States, managing American exchange students in Germany, and directing DAAD's propaganda efforts.[29]

Gerhard Gräfe originally worked for the strongly Nazified Foreign Office (Auslandsamt) of the German Student Union, but in the mid-1930s, was posted to DAAD. There he apparently moderated his views.[30] A *Harvard Educational Review* article published during World War II described Gräfe as a "more scholarly" writer who tried to merge, "in one fashion or another, the National

Socialist gospel with the more humane educational patterns of the past."[31] Ruth Hubbard, de facto administrator of the American-German exchange program for the IIE, praised Gräfe as more open-minded than the Nazis with whom she usually worked. Notably, he approved students to participate in the exchange who stood out as unsympathetic to the National Socialist regime. For example, he appointed Margildis Schlüter to the University of Denver for the 1937–38 academic year. Schlüter hailed from one of the Rhineland's most prominent Catholic intellectual families. Her mother, Maria Hermkes Schlüter, had been president of the Association of German University Women (Akademikerinnenbund) before the Nazis forced it to disband. She was also the leader of the Catholic Women's Organization in Berlin. Her husband, Johannes Schlüter, was a high-level official of the Reich and the Prussian Ministry for Church Affairs (Reichs-und-Preussischen Ministerium für die Kirchlichen Angelegenheiten). He had been denied a promotion because of his close connections with the Vatican. Elizabeth Facht, associated with the University of Denver and a Schlüter family friend, told Duggan that it was "extraordinary that a person of her [Margildis's] type should receive the [exchange] appointment at this time."[32] Schlüter's anti-Nazi beliefs were confirmed by the president of her host school.[33]

In May 1934, Hitler created the Reich Ministry for Science, Education, and Culture, commonly referred to as the Ministry of Education,. The DAAD was administratively placed under this new ministry in late 1934, although it retained considerable independence, due to its connections with numerous other government and party entities. Several quasi-academic organizations were linked to DAAD, such as the Carl Schurz Vereinigung, founded as a German-American friendship association and whose governing ideology always aligned with state policies. During the Third Reich, the association aimed to improve traditional cultural diplomacy and foster German-American friendship among academics, government officials, businessmen, journalists, and politicians, while promoting a positive image of the "new Germany."[34] The association often employed former exchange students to accompany foreign "guests" and ostensibly supported their objectives in Germany. It also managed Carl Schurz Tours, propaganda tours offered to Americans participating in state-affiliated visits.[35] Emil de Haas, the association's executive secretary, was known for his anti-Nazi views and assisted students who shared his ideological inclinations.[36]

As the Nazis grew increasingly assertive, however, Morsbach realized in 1934 that DAAD would benefit from having a connection with a powerful

Nazi patron. Since German law required all men who enrolled in university to join the SA, Morsbach negotiated with the SA's leader, Ernst Röhm, to associate their two organizations.[37] Röhm hoped that DAAD could burnish the SA's image, so the two men met in late June 1934 to discuss the matter.[38] The Führer, however, had other plans. Within days of the Röhm-Morsbach meeting, Hitler began "settling accounts" with almost everyone who had dared cross him since the early 1920s. The Night of the Long Knives began with Röhm's arrest and subsequent execution the next day. Morsbach, due to his recent association with Röhm, landed in a concentration camp, his arrest becoming an international relations disaster.

Throughout the Nazi era, dozens of US college administrators, professors, and students would be invited to a free, two-week tour of Germany, known as the Carl Schurz Tours. In July 1934, when Americans landed in Bremen to start the tour, they expected Morsbach to welcome them. He did not. DAAD representatives, just as bewildered as the Americans, rushed to the scene and had to awkwardly inform them of Morsbach's whereabouts. Apparently, the Gestapo had neglected to check his appointment book for the next day.[39] Morsbach's treatment outraged the international academic community.[40] The Association of Former Exchange Students in Germany organized a petition to demand his release, but von Massow quashed this idea, recognizing the detrimental effect it would have on both the students and DAAD.[41] Given the intense international pressure, the Nazis released Morsbach six weeks later, and he immediately retired. Other student exchange administrators were also caught up in the purge. All the leaders of the University of Munich's AKA, which had been close to Röhm, were dismissed. Friedrich Beck, the most prominent among them, was summarily shot. All of the previously autonomous university foreign offices now fell under DAAD's direct control.[42]

The Röhm purge increased SS influence in DAAD.[43] Wilhelm Burmeister received the appointment as DAAD's new director only a few days later. Ulrich von Gienanth, an officer in both the SD (Sicherheitsdienst),[44] branch of the SS, and the Gestapo, replaced Beck at the Munich AKA immediately after the latter's murder. Both men were raised in the radicalized atmosphere of the 1920s and had joined the SS and the party before 1933.[45] Soon after being promoted, Burmeister ordered all AKAs and DAAD division heads to attend a one-day workshop to receive instruction on DAAD's new party line.[46] Burmeister explained that German exchange students had only one purpose: to serve as international agents of Nazi German "soft power."

Georg Rettig, new deputy director of DAAD, emerged as the primary force behind the radicalization of the German-American exchange program. From the mid-1920s to the mid-1930s, he alternated between pursuing a doctorate in political science and working for industrial concerns in Great Britain, France, and Africa. He joined the Nazi Party and the SS in 1926 and later entered the SD, eventually reaching a rank equivalent to first lieutenant. In 1934 during the Röhm-DAAD purge, Rettig was called in to replace the recently deposed director of the University of Heidelberg's AKA.[47] There, he distinguished himself with his intense efforts to Nazify the exchange program.[48] In 1936 Rettig was transferred to DAAD headquarters in Berlin to "straighten out" the German-American exchange program, which had allowed too many students to permanently leave Germany.[49] Rettig's commitment to hard-line Nazism, his SS-SD status, his overseas experience, and his involvement in university exchanges made him well qualified him to carry out his mission.[50] Burmeister and Rettig got along splendidly.

To stop the student exchange serving as a source of German refugees, Rettig instituted a more rigorous selection procedure; henceforth, ideological commitment was to be the sine qua non for successful candidates.[51] He also thoroughly Nazified the preparatory training program. Once in the United States, the students' indoctrination would continue, along with more stringent monitoring.[52] German students were no longer permitted to study in the United States for more than a year, to decrease the likelihood of their "Americanization."[53] Burmeister seems to have been perfectly prepared to shut down the German-American exchange if it failed to change along the intended lines.[54]

With DAAD's new management in place, some of the exchange students began to receive covert operation assignments in the United States. While recruiting, the German Student Union sought candidates most committed to the Nazi cause who would agree to engage in covert activities while in the United States, for instance, reporting on the refugees at their host school.[55] The students' reports were sent to Rettig or to von Gienanth, soon to be restationed Stateside as the students' mentor, who added notes regarding the student's demonstrated aptitude for "political work." The end product went to both the German Student Union and the National Socialist German Students' League (Nationalsozialistischer Deutscher Studentenbund, NSDStB). If it contained "important political or cultural-political observations or suggestions," the Ministry of Education, the Foreign Ministry, and the AO also obtained copies.[56] All of the exchange students, were also supposed to continue submitting the Weimar era–type reports about conditions in the United States, but now in a more comprehensive manner. Revealing how little he actually knew about college students, Rettig was surprised that only 10 to 20 percent of the exchange students who went to the United States ever submitted such reports.[57]

To Rettig, the exchange students were essentially an abstraction, a common equation in the dehumanization typical of Nazis. He had no interest in them as individuals, nor in the benefits they might gain from a year abroad.[58] He kept his distance, and apparently only spoke to them regarding official matters, and then, usually in an intimidating posture. Almost everyone who met him seemed to dislike him. The 1935 exchange students, the last cohort from the relatively "liberal" post-Weimar DAAD, considered Rettig a "laughing stock."[59] The IIE was not particularly fond of either Burmeister or Rettig, to put it mildly.[60]

Furthermore, IIE director Duggan infuriated Burmeister and Rettig with his efforts on behalf of German refugee academics. In 1933 Duggan and several colleagues founded the Emergency Committee in Aid to Displaced Foreign Scholars, an organization dedicated to funding academic positions at American institutions for German academics fleeing National Socialism. The committee successfully relocated hundreds of prominent Jewish German intellectuals to American universities.[61] From 1934 to 1937, Duggan made it a point to denounce totalitarian dictatorships—Germany's being the foremost example—in IIE annual reports. After returning from a trip to Germany in 1934, Duggan observed, "The average decent German, horrified by the repressive measures introduced [by the Nazis], is in a condition of great mental distress. He will admit that he has been accustomed to regimentation, bodily regimentation, but not intellectual. His has been the land of Lern- und Lehrfreiheit and he is anxious to return to a state of intellectual freedom now non-existent in the German university."[62]

Although the IIE generally maintained a cordial relationship with the German Embassy, Duggan's involvement in the emergency committee was a potential powder keg, poised to explode if the wrong people became aware of his role. In 1935 the German Embassy in Washington complained to the Foreign Ministry that Duggan's "leftist political views" and "the growing influence of anti-German academic institutions on the IIE" were negatively impacting the exchange.[63] Aware of such sentiments, Duggan attempted to quell the growing tension. He advised the embassy to resist the influence of Burmeister and Rettig, cautioning that yielding to them would only lead to the eventual collapse of the entire German-American exchange program, "one of the last remnants of German-American cultural exchange still remaining," as Duggan put it.[64] Hans Luther, the German ambassador and no friend of the Burmeister-Rettig faction, strongly agreed. Duggan also had friends in Germany—possibly including covert anti-Nazis, to whom he occasionally alluded—who worked to reduce tensions. Karl Bertling, director of the Amerika-Institut of the University of Berlin and a Duggan ally, wrote to Hans Dieckhoff, a Foreign Ministry expert on the United States, arguing that Duggan was simply trying to secure more top academics for the United States. Even more importantly, Bertling noted, Germany was far better off having Duggan exerting influence on the fate of refugees than leaving the task to "Messrs. Dickstein and Comrades."[65]

Burmeister and Rettig then began maneuvering in an attempt to circumvent the IIE.[66] Rettig, with good reasons, suspected that the IIE was encouraging the Americanization of the German exchange students. From 1935 onward, he made annual visits to the United States. As his schedule allowed, he made a point of speaking with as many German exchange students as possible, trying to discern if any of them seemed a bit too enraptured with the United States. This effort also served as a warning to the students that they were being watched. Rettig's primary goal, however, was to assess the host American colleges to determine which of them were sufficiently friendly to the "New Germany." He planned to test this by offering the prospect of direct "university to university linkages," bypassing the IIE. During his annual visits to the IIE in New York, Rettig persistently lobbied for the establishment of a DAAD branch office in the city, a concept initially floated almost a decade earlier, during the Weimar era. As he envisioned the office, however, it would control all German university affairs in the United States and closely monitor German exchange students; Rettig himself would serve as its director.[67] Von Fritsch, still at DAAD, warned the Cultural Affairs Office at the German Foreign Ministry about Rettig's grandiose schemes and the need to thwart him; von Fritsch savvily anticipated that Americans would view such a German-run center in Manhattan as a Nazi propaganda outlet, which would be "disastrous" for German-American cultural relations.[68]

As the SS gained power within DAAD in the mid-1930s, Joseph Goebbels, Reich minister of public enlightenment and propaganda, suddenly took a renewed interest in the student exchange programs. Helen Appleton-Read, *Vogue* associate editor and art critic, caught Goebbels' attention in 1935 while collaborating with him on an exhibition of German art in the United States. Appleton-Read suggested that Germany could significantly improve cultural relations with the United States through its student exchange programs, but, she noted, the current setup was repeatedly running into obstacles.[69] Seizing the opportunity, Goebbels began arguing that in addition to the logic of having student exchanges housed within the Propaganda Ministry, the lack of coordination between the welter of Reich offices was severely hindering the development of cultural-political ties between Germany and other nations. Naturally, the Ministry of Education and the Foreign Ministry opposed these attempts to poach their territory.[70] While Goebbels could not fully absorb DAAD into his ministry, he did secure a consolation prize: the authority to send Propaganda Ministry—officially designated as cultural and educational attachés—to key German embassies. These attachés would oversee Germany's student exchange programs in their assigned countries. The attaché at the German Embassy in Washington now also served as the official overseer of the German-American exchange. This arrangement echoed the earlier idea of a DAAD New York branch office. Whereas, in previous years, an exchange student had been indirectly appointed as the "leader" of German students in the United States, this role would now be filled by a government attaché.[71] Richard Sallet, the first propaganda attaché to the United States, had limited involvement with the exchange program, likely due to his short tenure. His successor, however, von Gienanth, would become a key figure in it.

Von Gienanth, scion of a wealthy, baronial industrialist family in the Ruhr,[72] joined the Nazi Party and the NSDStB in 1930, followed by the SS in 1931, a pattern not uncommon for young nobles who now found themselves disoriented in a republic.[73] He soon left for the United States for graduate studies at Johns Hopkins University. By the time he returned to Germany, Hitler had assumed power. With his US master's degree in hand, von Gienanth applied to join the diplomatic corps but was rejected. Determined to enter the international affairs field, he convinced NSDStB officials, who now sat on DAAD's governing board, to find him a suitable post there. Thus, in 1934 he was appointed director (*leiter*) of the University of Munich's Foreign Office, with the special assignment of reviving the Junior Year in Munich program, a victim of the Röhm purge.[74]

Von Gienanth had numerous ties to the Propaganda Ministry. Soon after reconstituting the Munich program, Goebbels sent von Gienanth to the United States to set up the German Library of Information in New York City, attached to the German consul's office. Once Sallet left the attaché position, von Gienanth assumed the role. It was perhaps at this time that von Gienanth was also made a Gestapo and SD officer. In this capacity, he served the SS-Ausland

Figure 1.2. Ulrich von Gienanth, 1932. US-based "manager" of German exchange students and covert operative for the Sicherheitsdienst (SD). Early IIE Photos, 1930s. Courtesy of the Institute of International Education.

Abteilung III, foreign intelligence, and after the creation of the Reich Security Main Office (Reichssicherheitshauptamt), he was assigned to Amt VI D, which dealt with SD intelligence operations in the United States.[75] Given that the Nazis considered Foreign Ministry officials a bit too independent-minded, von Gienanth had the added duty of watching over those stationed in Washington.[76] It was also widely believed that von Gienanth had the right to order any recalcitrant German citizen in the United States to return home and, if required, arrange for their suitable punishment.[77] In addition, the exchange students were obligated to follow his orders.[78]

Thus, with this roster of duties, von Gienanth found himself simultaneously beholden to DAAD (theoretically in the Ministry of Education); the Propaganda Ministry; ; the SS (specifically its SD and Gestapo branches); and the Foreign Ministry (since he worked out of the German Embassy).[79] Given the combination of these roles, von Gienanth was often referred to as the "head of German espionage operations" in the United States, although numerous other such operations were being run simultaneously by the departments he worked under and by other German entities.[80] Von Gienanth was certainly energetic, juggling perhaps a dozen projects at the same time while also maintaining a remarkably active social life.

Von Gienanth and Rettig had a fractious relationship, perhaps because von Gienanth was, in a sense, usurping powers that should have rightfully gone to a DAAD employee—presumably Rettig himself. They worked together on certain projects, however, including Rettig's plan to set up student exchanges managed solely by DAAD.[81] In 1936, Rettig took another step in this direction with the institution of the new Carl Schurz Exchange, arranged with the National Exchange of Foreign Students of Fraternities in the United States. The national exchange engaged with German universities directly, outside of the IIE's control, although the two organizations were on good terms. Günther Hans Grueninger, a former German exchange student who had secured a tenure-track position at DePauw University, directed the national exchange.[82] The Carl Schurz Exchange program appears to have been chaotic and not entirely legitimate.[83] As evidence of this, in 1937, dozens of American students from various fraternities and sororities, seemingly chosen at random, were offered the chance to study in Germany for an academic year, with all costs paid by the German government; there were no German-language requirements. German authorities paid little attention to the students after they arrived. In fact, they did not even need to be enrolled at a German university. Rather, the actual purpose of the Carl Schurz Exchange was apparently to secure reciprocal slots at American universities for ideologically passionate Nazi students to undertake intensive propaganda and espionage work in the United States.[84] Several of the most active students in this regard, such as Elisabeth Noelle, who engaged in propaganda, attended American colleges through the exchange.

Rettig's attempts to divert the student exchange to his control naturally worsened relations between DAAD and IIE, which were already strained after Morsbach and von Fritsch's ouster. In 1938 the ripple effects of growing American hostility to German aggression in Central Europe reached the student exchange. In several instances, antagonism toward Germany manifested itself as antagonism toward German exchange students. Furious over such treatment, Burmeister threatened to shut down the program with a number of American colleges unless they apologized for various insults hurled at the students or at the New Germany.[85] Burmeister also used the anti-German incidents as evidence of the IIE's inability to impartially manage the exchanges; thus, he relentlessly asserted, a DAAD branch office in New York City was essential, regardless of IIE's stance. Duggan, clearly losing patience with Burmeister's constant hostility toward the IIE, told him that he expected to be treated with more respect, since he was already under attack in the United States for maintaining the German-American exchange amid Americans' hostility toward the Nazis.[86] Duggan insisted that such an office would be viewed as a propaganda agency and would cause severe harm to the student exchange program.[87]

Oblivious to such warnings, in October 1938, Rettig inaugurated the New York DAAD branch office, christened the German University Service. A month later, he sent a letter to three hundred college presidents across the United States, announcing the office's opening and offering its services. The timing of the letter—dated November 10, the day after Kristallnacht—attracted notice. Rettig then embarked on a tour of East Coast universities to encourage them to establish exchanges directly through DAAD's New York branch. Whenever his approach failed to yield the desired result, Rettig rather ghoulishly approached students directly on campus, dangling offers of generous scholarships to German universities—and thus bypassing not only the IIE but university administrators as well. The IIE was inundated with letters from university presidents outraged by his aggressive tactics.

An article in the December 3, 1938 edition of the *New York Times*, *criticizing* the German University Service, marked a new phase in the decline of the German-American exchange. Rettig boasted to the IIE's Hubbard that such

Nazi Infiltration of the Student Exchange 39

an article was actually free publicity for his new exchange service. However, she did not find the whole episode quite as amusing. Reproachfully, she asked Rettig why he had sent a letter announcing his exchange service to the City College of New York, "a college which is 99 percent Jewish." Rettig, in an astonishingly tone-deaf reply, stated that even CUNY students might wish to study in Germany. Hubbard fired back that he should understand that "no Jewish student would care to study in Germany or have anything to do with a Nazi office like his."[88] As a consequence of the article, Rettig received threatening phone calls from across the United States.[89]

Were that not bad enough, the following month Rettig issued Circular Letter no. 1 to the German exchange students, ordering them not only to submit their usual reports but also a new, "secret report," which was to include details such as the "political and financial influences" on the host schools and how these influences shaped the schools' "attitudes." He also insisted that the students report information they could obtain on any "conventions" held near the schools as well as articles from school publications concerning academic and political relations between the United States, Germany, and various other countries.[90] While the secret reports had long been standard practice for the "special" exchange students engaged in undercover work, this was a new task for the rest of the students. Several sought to distance themselves from it by showing the letters to their professors or school administrators. One student, Gertrude Achenbach, even sent a defiant letter to Rettig, informing him that his circular had made life even more difficult for the exchange students in the United States.[91] Host school administrators, the IIE, the US government, and even the German Embassy recognized Rettig's demands as a thinly veiled solicitation for espionage. Rettig ludicrously attempted to explain that he was only interested in gathering facts about a school's suitability for students and to satisfy his "own curiosity."

The circular debacle gave Duggan the perfect opportunity to rid himself of Rettig once and for all. He approached Sumner Welles, a close advisor to President Franklin Roosevelt, and asked him to inform the German Embassy of Rettig's disastrous actions and their potential diplomatic consequences. Welles sent an emissary to Hans Thomsen, the German chargé d'affaires to the United States, warning him that the secret reports clearly constituted solicitations of espionage and would trigger American laws to that effect. As expected, Thomsen expressed genuine outrage over the situation; fully aware of American antipathy toward Germany at that time, he had been struggling to keep his country out of the American spotlight. He confided in Welles that the embassy had never supported the establishment of Rettig's office, and had voiced its opposition, but obviously to no avail.[92]

From a broader perspective, the Rettig crisis arose in the context of the ongoing power struggle between the "moderates" at the German Embassy in Washington and the more radical Nazi agencies operating in the United States. Thomsen bluntly informed Rettig that his German University Service had caused enough trouble during its brief existence, was viewed by the US government as an illegal propaganda and espionage center, and was to be immediately shut down. Rettig began closing shop in late January 1939, as news reports of his espionage activities continued to spread.[93] He left the United States in March 1939, never to return.[94] Thomsen then ordered the German academics and students in the United States to avoid any "underground activities," warning that such actions would inevitably lead to "violent repercussions." While Thomsen's first demand was fulfilled, the second, due to von Gienanth's efforts, was not.

By the spring of 1939, the German-American exchange had become nonviable. Countless American colleges were abruptly dropping out of the program, now widely regarded as a cover for propaganda and espionage operations. American universities faced imminent public backlash if they continued participating in the exchange. Moreover, the program threatened the legitimacy of the IIE through its ongoing association with the German government. Nazi atrocities and the deteriorating international situation further rendered the German-American exchange untenable. Hubbard found herself spending most of her time dealing with German students in the United States as refugees.[95] For various reasons, nearly fifty exchange students from the United States and Germany remained in their host countries as late as the beginning of the war between their two nations.[96] The German students still in the United States were often either attempting to avoid returning to Germany or were involved in espionage activities.

Duggan wisely recognized that the IIE could not continue relying on the increasingly precarious German and broader European exchanges if it wished to survive. Thus, in 1935 the institute inaugurated exchanges with Latin America, followed by China the next year.[97] In 1941 the IIE began administering US government–sponsored academic exchange grants, which quickly grew to become its core function. After the war, the IIE would essentially become a bureaucratized quasi-governmental organization, largely funded by the US government, with a vastly expanded mandate. Germany would never again be a particularly significant exchange partner with the IIE.

The history of the German-American student exchange in its institutional context reveals that non-Nazis existed throughout DAAD, German universities, and the Foreign Ministry, many of whom maintained essential aspects of the late Weimar exchange program. By keeping their heads down and outwardly showing approval of Hitler's dictatorship, they retained their positions, as few Nazis were qualified to replace them. Consequently, many exchange students were more focused on presenting a charismatic view of Germany rather than justifying Nazism. While nearly everyone acknowledged that improving US-Nazi German relations was impossible, non-Nazis at least sought to preserve a modicum of friendly relations in the academic sphere. They also recognized the importance of the exchange in shaping the careers and characters of highly gifted students. These perspectives stood in stark contrast to Nazi plans to turn the exchange into an espionage apparatus.

If the Nazis had developed a sophisticated understanding of American society, they would have realized that their activities through the exchange would only serve to undermine it, while yielding no useful espionage or covert information. Even on the verge of World War II, it is evident that numerous German Foreign Ministry officials and diplomats were not Nazi fanatics. Many non-Nazi and even anti-Nazi students managed to slip through the web set intended to ensnare them, thanks to the tacit cooperation of German university professors, DAAD officials, and others, who followed their consciences and helped deserving students the opportunity secure opportunities to study abroad.

CHAPTER TWO

Recruitment and Training

The exchange students sent to America each year . . . represent one of
our most important and effective cultural propaganda assets.
—*Richard Sallet, propaganda attaché, German Embassy, Washington,*
to Propaganda Minister Joseph Goebbels, June 4, 1936

Numerous students who sought refuge in the United States or defied the
Nazis in other ways continued to be selected for the German-US exchange
program despite the Nazification of the German Academic Exchange Service's (DAAD) recruitment and training processes. In many cases, certain
questions went overlooked, while in others, obvious nonconformists, students
with close connections to Jewish Germans, and potential refugees were either
undetected or permitted to advance in the selection process. Analyzing the
selection process to identify the "weak points" that permitted such students
to escape the Third Reich sheds light on the German institutional and ideological forces that resisted the Nazis in the 1930s.

As the Americans and Germans annually negotiated each new round of
exchanges—usually in the summer or fall preceding the selection of the new
cohort—the US schools with available slots outlined the desired characteristics of students to be selected by German officials. Gender was often indicated,
and religion (Catholic or Protestant), essential for denominational colleges,
identified. Schools might also specify other details, such as educational level
(e.g., undergraduate, PhD, postdoctoral, medical residency), age range (typically linked to educational stage), and field of study. Frequently, however,
schools provided vague preferences, such as asking for students "just like" or
"not like" previous exchange students. One institution even insisted that its
German exchange student be a "Nazi."[1] Decisions occasionally came very late

in the process, without the student having much time to learn about their host college. Herbert Sonthoff, for instance, informed just before he had to leave that his host school would be the University of Georgia, asked, "Where the devil is Georgia?"[2] German officials tended to assign the most intellectually gifted candidates to large US research universities, while often sending students with a particularly engaging personality to smaller, more isolated colleges. The German Embassy in Washington reported that German students had a more significant impact on Americans in these environments than at major universities.[3]

The Application Process

After reaching agreement with US administrators on the number and location of exchange slots, DAAD authorized the Foreign Affairs Office (AKA) at German universities to post notices specifying the basic requirements for each slot and to encourage students to apply.[4] The offices also guided potential candidates through the application process, which required them to obtain numerous documents to complete their application portfolio (*Bewerbung*).

All applicants had to secure recommendation letters from two or three professors, who were required to complete two forms: one assessing the student's academic ability, the other evaluating his or her political reliability. This second form was marked with a printed red band along the margins and labeled "Confidential! For Office Use Only!"[5] The confidential form delved deeply into the applicant's character, requesting comments on the student's sense of duty, reliability, responsibility, leadership skills, and other traits. It also asked whether the applicant would likely feel comfortable working outside his or her academic field. Potentially disqualifying factors had to be indicated, as did the student's political affiliations, commitment to the regime, and so on.[6]

As one exchange student who chose to remain in the States later noted, a surprising number of recommendation letter writers ran afoul of the regime.[7] Others were not Nazis. One of Gerhard Wolfgang Lüdtke's references, Georg Kartzke,[8] headed the German Institute for Foreigners at the University of Berlin and was described by his friend H. L. Mencken as a "lifelong liberal" who once denounced the Nazi regime in his company while strolling along the Unter den Linden. Kartzke had spoken in English, but Mencken nonetheless warned him to quiet down.[9] Herbert Sonthoff and Elisabeth Noelle received letters of recommendation from their University of Berlin journalism professor, Emil Dovifat, who had been a member of the Catholic Center Party before the Nazi *Machtergreifung* (seizure of power), and apparently remained a "moderate" afterward.[10] According to Noelle, Dovifat was "incredibly brave to openly criticize the Nazis" in and outside the classroom.[11] One of his biographers wrote, "Dovifat knew how to express himself . . . so that students knew what he meant."[12] Noelle claimed that his students "felt like resistance fighters," relishing the freedom of thought and expression they experienced in his classes.

Ursula Schäfer obtained a reference letter from Max Dessoir, her philosophy professor at the University of Berlin, who had suggested that she apply for an exchange scholarship to the United States, apparently hinting that it could be a way out of Germany. Having a Jewish grandparent and considered suspect by the regime, Dessoir was fired in 1935, forbidden to publish in 1940, and apparently marked for execution by the Gestapo later during the war, but the chaos from constant bombardment made it impossible to locate him.[13] Another Schäfer reference, Gerhard Masur, was a fiercely nationalist professor who also had some Jewish ancestry. He eventually left Germany for a teaching position at Sweet Briar College in Virginia.[14]

The applications also had to include recommendations from two Nazi authorities.[15] Again, the status of the letter writer could influence outcomes. For example, Jenni Karding secured a letter from Hans Luther, the German ambassador to the United States and an acquaintance of her father.[16] Anneliese von dem Hagen included a letter of recommendation from Hans-Wilhelm Scheidt, a division chief of the Nazi Party's Foreign Organization.[17] In such cases, acceptance to the program was likely a formality. A letter of recommendation from the head of the Foreign Affairs Office at the student's university might prove less decisive. Applicants were at a distinct disadvantage if they lacked familial connections or if they proved unable to secure letters of recommendation from influential officials or professors.[18]

The questionnaire that applicants had to fill out required them to outline their educational and personal record in a résumé (*Lebenslauf*) and also to highlight involvement in both Nazi and non-Nazi organizations as well as any associated awards. Early during the Nazi regime, from 1933 through 1935, selection committees advanced candidates who had demonstrated desirable qualities in non-Nazi organizations, such as the Bund Deutsche Freischar, which was somewhat similar to the Boy Scouts.[19] Male applicants often emphasized their Hitler Youth or SA activities, while females might highlight their work in the League of German Girls.[20] An administrative order from the Ministry of Education required all college students to complete a six-month stint in the Labor Service, which also presented opportunities to distinguish oneself. The service mixed community service—such as helping farm families with their heavy summer workload—and ideological, paramilitary, and gender indoctrination. All candidates had to demonstrate at least "provisional" membership in the German Student Union (DSt), which was subsumed by the National Socialist German Students' League (NSDStB) in 1934. Given the corruption that permeated Nazi organizations, it is unsurprising that many exchange students were also leaders in the union. Since the union participated in the selection of both local and national exchange candidates, its leaders were in a position to essentially secure themselves an exchange slot.[21]

Exchange candidates who were members of the SS or the Nazi Party had the greatest advantage of all. While enormously beneficial, membership in the Nazi Party was not a requirement, primarily because the party had stopped accepting most membership applications after May 1933 due to the overly "enthusiastic" rush of Germans to join after it took control of the state earlier in the year.[22] Before 1933, many students were too young to join. Membership in the SS, however, was not similarly restricted. Although the number of exchange students in the SS grew over time, it always remained a minority.

Finally, the students had to write a short personal statement (*Anschreiben*). Here, an applicant explained why she or he wanted to study in the United States, with emphasis on "cultural-political" motivations.[23] Quite a few mentioned promotion of the "New Germany" as an important, if not principal, reason for their interest in studying abroad. Some emphasized a desire to strengthen their Nazi convictions.[24] In 1936 Ilse Giesing explained in her statement, "A year abroad should help me see Germany not from the standpoint of the self-satisfied citizen, but from that of a German living abroad; such a critical vantage point would allow me to become a better champion of Germany."[25] More students gave what might be called "conventional" reasons for wanting to study in the United States, often relating to professional goals or prior contact with Americans. Several candidates had lived in the same accommodation as an American exchange student who had piqued their curiosity about their country.[26] While working for the Carl Schurz Vereinigung, Eugen Lahr encountered American professors who encouraged him to apply for an exchange fellowship.[27] One common reason was acquaintance with German students who had studied in the United States, and who, upon returning home, regaled their peers with tales of America.[28] In other cases, applicants might have had relatives in the United States, sometimes academics themselves.

Selection and Criteria

In the Nazi era, the process for reviewing exchange student applications consisted of three tiers. First, the applications and letters of recommendation were judged by a local committee that included the university rector or his representative; the heads of the university's Foreign Affairs Office, the Teachers' Union (Dozentenschaft), and the German Student Union; a former exchange student; and one or two academics who were "especially trustworthy" on foreign relations. Prior to the 1934 Röhm purge, a representative of the SA University Office (SA-Hochschulamt) also sat on the committee.[29] Eventually, representatives of the German Student Union's Foreign Office and of the Hitler Youth (Gebietsführung der Hitlerjugend) were appointed as well.[30]

For the local selection process, essentially a university function, the committees conducted rigorous, quantifiable assessments of the applicants' characters and achievements to tally numerical scores. After the summer of 1933, the German Student Union's Foreign Office at each university did much of this work, which was then passed on to the national DSt Foreign Office for evaluation and subsequently submitted to DAAD. Its representatives discerned applicants' leadership capabilities, social skills, and observable commitment to "National Socialist principles," including nationalist enthusiasm.[31] The applicant had to convince them that they would "stimulate interest in and understanding for the New Germany" through personal relations with students at the host school as well as through their "total disposition" while abroad. Successful applicants had to be "energetic," reliable, sociable, likable, and able to "gain from life experiences."[32]

The exchange candidates and those recommending them had to be careful not to provoke suspicions about their ideological views, as occurred in several cases of German exchange students applying to study in liberal democracies. In one instance, a student from the University of Marburg, Gerda Trojandt, applied to study at the Sorbonne. Her interview with the student union representatives was disastrous because she made the unforgivable error of praising democratic, liberal government. Furthermore, her letters of recommendation were oddly generic. One reference avowed her political reliability on the grounds that her father was a senior civil servant and Nazi Party member who had fought in World War I, and her brother was currently serving in the military. "The family enjoys the best reputation in my hometown," he noted.[33] Furious at being rejected, Trojandt raised a fuss—threatening to expose the corrupt selection practices to the media, informing her powerful friends, and so on. The student union evaluators retaliated by writing letters to Trojandt's Nazi character references, detailing her liberal attitudes and aggressive behavior and asking whether they still wanted to support her (obviously anticipating their responses). One of Trojandt's references apparently did not know her all that well and was so indignant to learn of her transgressions that he informed the evaluators of his intention to report her to the Gestapo.[34] Much like the case with professors who recommended students for the exchange, he no doubt did not enjoy contemplating the possible consequences of helping a "liberal" student go abroad to study in a democracy.

At the same time, the German Student Union's Foreign Office at each university did not always take their duties terribly seriously as guarantors of exchange student ideological purity, as evidenced in several cases.[35] In the case of Werner von Rosenstiel, the union's Foreign Affairs Office at his university approved his application at the end of 1934. They noted that von Rosenstiel seemed satisfactory both academically and socially, but added, "Unfortunately, we personally don't know him enough to render a final verdict, although his overall impression is sufficient for us to not oppose his application."[36] Another successful candidate, Peter Wecker, made it through after a year of trying, despite some rather lukewarm evaluations. He received a weak recommendation from the University of Munich's National Socialist German Students' League, which noted that he had never been a leader within the organization, but seemed sufficiently politically reliable enough to study in the United States.[37] The university's Foreign Affairs Office felt Wecker made an excellent impression in terms of personality and athletics, but showed little understanding of German foreign policy, likely due to his limited time at the university. The assessor believed Wecker otherwise deserved to be at the top of the list of potential exchange students to the United States, encouraging him to work at the Foreign Affairs Office for a year, after which the assessor felt confident Wecker could be recommended.[38] One reference, however, declined to endorse Wecker's political reliability, and the local committee suggested he seek a different endorsement.[39]

An administrative scandal involving the application of a University of Kiel student to study in Denmark reverberated through the labyrinthine bureaucracy of the exchange student apparatus. The University of Kiel's Foreign Office rejected the student's application, deeming the student unqualified, possibly due to concerns about the student's political reliability. Nevertheless, the application was sent on to DAAD headquarters in Berlin, possibly with the endorsement of a powerful official in Hamburg, perhaps the student's home city. Upon the application's arrival in Berlin, DAAD approved it. This infuriated the University of Kiel administration, as the application had not only been forwarded, but was then also approved despite its earlier rejection. Accusations of incompetence, bureaucratic confusion, personal animosities, and mysterious backdoor maneuverings ensued involving the University of Kiel's rector and its Foreign Affairs Office, the German Student Union's Foreign Office at the university, the Student Union's Foreign Affairs Headquarters in Berlin, DAAD's director, DAAD's vice director, and the Ministry of Education. Eventually, tempers got so heated that the Gestapo was called in to try to make sense of it all.[40]

In addition to political reliability, exchange student assessors looked for charm, charisma, and attractive physical appearance in an applicant. They recognized that charisma could be converted into "social capital," potentially bolstering a student's effectiveness as an unofficial propagandist for the Reich.[41] Judges were therefore instructed to ensure that the candidates appeared friendly, "fresh" and exhibited "physical grace."[42] The physical attractiveness of exchange students—both male and female—did not go unnoticed by German and American observers alike.[43] Anneliese von dem Hagen, one of the exchange students, remarked that DAAD favored candidates who were good-looking.[44] Similarly, Elisabeth Noelle recounted overhearing members of the national selection committee noting her beauty while reviewing photos of the candidates. Her striking appearance apparently drew the attention of the Führer himself, who invited her to tea, a relationship that proved instrumental in securing her opportunity to study abroad.[45]

In 1942 an Alien Enemy Hearing Board decided to intern one post-exchange student still in the United States, Irene Gotthelf, deciding that she would make an excellent German spy, given that the "subject is an unusually attractive character, physically of striking beauty, great intellectual ability and charm of personality."[46] In another context, Gotthelf was described as "tall, blonde, a real Valkyrian figure."[47]

If one removed the references to political ideology and the prohibition of "non-Aryans," the qualifications important for selecting German students were not very different from those used to select American students for study abroad. The IIE did not consider the selection of charming students as unusual.[48] Indeed, Ruth Hubbard, the de facto administrator of the German-American exchange program at IIE, believed that potential host schools were influenced by German applicant's looks.[49] Additionally, IIE preferred to send

Figure 2.1. Elisabeth Noelle, June 1938. A Nazi propagandist who studied journalism at the University of Missouri and later became a prominent West German pollster. "Miss Elizabeth [*sic*] Noelle," *Joplin Globe*, June 12, 1938, 13. Courtesy of the *Joplin Globe*.

Americans of northwestern European descent to Germany. In a letter, Hubbard told Ingrid Dybwad, secretary of DAAD managing director Adolf Morsbach, that IIE sought to send to Germany "only those Americans who seem really representative." The "wrong" type of people, Hubbard continued, included students at the New Jersey State Teachers' College at Montclair, which, she noted, drew its students from Newark, Paterson, and similar cities, populated by "anything but a class of people from whom good American representatives can be drawn!"⁵⁰

Since the résumé required information about the applicant's parents, potential host universities knew something about each candidate's familial background. Some American host schools, particularly small private colleges, expressed a preference for students from elite families.[51] Research universities that hosted German exchange students, however, viewed the matter from the opposite perspective. An administrator at Johns Hopkins University complained that students were seemingly chosen for their wealth and social background rather than their intellectual accomplishments.[52]

Nazi Intervention

Once in power as DAAD deputy director, Rettig micromanaged the selection process. Previously, much of the exchange program had been controlled at the local level by university Foreign Affairs Offices, but Rettig sought to bring them under greater centralized control.[53] In 1935 diktats were sent to all the Foreign Affairs Offices, stressing that exchange applicants had to prove that they were "bearers of National Socialist thought . . . not on the basis of an objective academic interest in National Socialism, but on the basis of an inner experience that shapes their further training."[54] To achieve this, Rettig decreed that students had to wait until their second year of college before applying for an exchange slot, lest they prove too naïvely open to foreign influences. The delay in going abroad also allowed an additional year to assess the prospective applicant's devotion to the Führer.[55] Likewise, exchange students were not to remain in the United States for more than a year. Rettig claimed that this would allow more German students to participate in the exchange, but the Americans involved in the program's management saw through his reasoning.[56]

Rettig also ordered the local selection committees to conduct more thorough background checks on the students.[57] Perhaps Rettig had two goals in mind: in addition to selecting students who were loyal Nazis, he might have been concerned with his own self-preservation. If a student highly ranked by the local committee then failed to return to Germany, he could absolve DAAD headquarters, and thus himself, of responsibility for missing any signs of disloyalty. The local selection committees ceded power to Rettig, as they were only allowed to rank students according to an established rubric and then passing that along to DAAD. They would no longer select the candidates for final evaluation at the national level.

Rettig would further narrow the selection committees' list of qualified candidates through personally interviewing each of them.[58] It was at this point in the selection process that almost all the exchange candidates met Rettig.

Some of the German exchange student refugees, who remained in the United States, had pegged him as an unpleasant, zealous Nazi.[59]

Although it is hazardous to draw conclusions based on a few incidents, the possibility exists that some non-Nazi applicants surreptitiously escaped Rettig's ideological net because of him. His decision to abrogate much of the German Student Union's power in selecting exchange candidates, along with the additional work required to investigate their ideological backgrounds, may have led to a loss of interest in the selection process.[60] If this was indeed the case, it suggests that the SS-aligned centralization of Germany, as represented by Rettig, was negatively affecting even Nazified civil organizations.

The new measures caught quite a few "moderate" student applicants who might have otherwise more easily passed the ideological assessments in the selection process. In one case, the student union representatives on the exchange selection committee offered a nuanced evaluation of a candidate for a US slot, emphasizing his unsuitability for the position. While he was a diligent, ambitious, and capable academic, he did not meet the "charm" standard: he was too introverted and too focused on academic pursuits, whereas the union sought leaders who could be influential on an American campus. Additionally, he was judged to be overly enthusiastic about American institutions. Instead, the evaluators recommended a female student known for her enthusiastic support of Nazi ideals. She was eventually chosen to fill the exchange slot.[61]

A national-level committee (Auswahlausschuss für Austauschstudenten) convened at the University of Berlin each January for the final stage of the selection process. Before the Nazi era, the committee consisted of representatives from DAAD, the Prussian Ministry of Education, the Foreign Ministry, and the Reichstag Committee on Cultural Relations.[62] Since a few communists number among the exchange students selected during the late Weimar-era, it can be presumed that representatives of leftist parties were also members of the selection committee at that time.

Within only several months of Hitler's accession to power, DAAD officials were required to assess the applicants' dedication to National Socialism. Morsbach also pointedly reminded the judges that such dedication alone was not sufficient for approving an applicant; personality and academic ability remained paramount.[63] Furthermore, the national selection committee could grant exemptions from certain requirements if an exchange position required special skills, thus limiting the number of applicants who excelled in all categories. Though understated, this provision essentially allowed the committee to select whomever they wished for the exchange.[64] Because of this, candidates during the Morsbach era who struggled to prove their dedication to National Socialism were occasionally "given another chance" to demonstrate their loyalty to the Führer.[65]

Horst Janson, destined to study at Harvard and never return home, fit into this category. Officials interviewed him about his lukewarm service to the Nazi cause two months after he filed his application. Janson responded to their questions in an impressively gruff, militaristic manner. Although the investigators likely remained unconvinced of his trustworthiness, Janson suspected that officials deemed him worth the risk, given the pressure to find a suitable candidate for the Harvard exchange slot. Janson also believed that he may have been the only qualified candidate, as Nazi organizations drained so much of the students' time and energy from their academic studies.[66]

In the summer of 1933, the Nazis expanded the national selection committee to include various party entities and others, each ostensibly with equal influence in DAAD's management:

- *Amerika-Institut*—Karl Bertling, director
- *Cultural Affairs Division, German Foreign Ministry*—Friedrich Stieve, head of the division, or Fritz von Twardowski, deputy division head
- *Cultural Affairs Division, Nazi Party Foreign Organization* (Kulturabteilung der Auslands-Organisation der NSDAP)—Emil Ehrich, also designated to judge applicants' political reliability based on reports by the Gestapo and the SD,[67] with the latter's influence increasingly felt after 1937 according to one exchange student[68]
- *DAAD*—Ewald von Massow, DAAD president; often delegated to Morsbach, DAAD's managing director, and after 1934 to Burmeister or Rettig; Burmeister, Rettig, and von Massow belonged to the SS; von Massow had connections to the Abwehr
- *Foreign Affairs Department, Ministry of Education*—Herbert Scurla, a senior administrative officer in the Education Ministry, (also with SD ties), or DAAD managing director Wilhelm Burmeister (also an Education Ministry senior administrative officer)
- *German Research Council* (Notgemeinschaft der Deutschen Wissenschaft)—August Wilhelm Fehling
- *German Student Union*—two representatives, one of them being the current chairman of the Association of Former Exchange Students (Vereinigung Ehemaliger Austauschstudenten)
- *University of Berlin*—the rector or a faculty member delegated by him

The selection committee also included several members of the professoriate: Alfred Baeumler, Arnold Bergsträsser, Ludwig von Dienes, Constantin von Dietze, Conrad Matschoss, and Hans Rothfels.[69] Fritz Beindorf represented the business elite.

In the first few years of the Nazi regime, the national committee was dominated by "moderate" Nazis, non-Nazis, and even anti-Nazis, representing various academic offices or the Foreign Ministry. Many of the committee members, such as Morsbach, would eventually run afoul of the regime. Stieve and von Twardowski, officials from the late Weimar era who had retained their posts, had not "sympathized with the Nazis," and both complained about the Nazis' attempts to mix cultural policy with propaganda.[70]

Fehling had spent several years as a student in the United States, after which he became an adviser to the Rockefeller Foundation's fellowship program in Germany.[71] He informed the foundation's representative that he was opposed to the Nazis.[72] In 1934 he appealed to the foundation to retain its fellowship program in Germany, despite the Nazis' poisoning the country's academic atmosphere, to give young scholars the chance of "escaping for a year" from the intellectual isolation that had descended upon his country. Fehling also attempted to persuade the foundation to directly support the research of Jewish German scholars in Germany, in hopeful anticipation of the Hitler regime's eventual downfall.[73]

Constantin von Dietze was one of the most active academics in the anti-Nazi opposition, leading the Freiburger circle, a group of like-minded professors and students at the University of Freiburg. The circle focused on planning intersections of Christian ethics, politics, and economics in a post-Nazi Germany, an outlook that also formed the basis of their connection to another opposition group, the Goerdeler circle.[74] The SS eventually uncovered von Dietze's activities, and he narrowly avoided execution in 1945.[75]

Gerhard Ritter, a conservative historian during the Third Reich and a member of the Freiburg circle, noted the continued existence of non-Nazis in various government offices, especially the Education Ministry and the Foreign Ministry, both of which controlled DAAD to some extent.[76] Arnold Bergsträsser, who helped establish the University of Heidelberg exchange program, moved through the school's academic hierarchy to become a professor of economics and business in 1933. However, in the mid-1930s, Bergsträsser's Jewish ancestry was revealed. Several high-level acquaintances attempted to obtain an Aryanization certificate for him, but failed, so Bergsträsser left for the United States in 1937.

Hans Rothfels was Jewish German and apparently also a Nazi sympathizer. He taught at the University of Königsberg until his dismissal in 1934. Rothfels also campaigned for an Aryanization certificate; although a number of leading Nazis supported his pleas, the request was eventually denied. Minister of Education Bernhard Rust found Rothfels work in the Prussian State Library in Berlin, but he was finally forced out of Germany in 1938, emigrating to the United States and eventually landing a position at the University of Chicago.[77]

Fritz Beindorf was a wealthy manufacturer from Hannover and unquestionably a Nazi sympathizer. He was also, however, somewhat broad-minded, serving as a patron of modern art, a Freemason, and governor (president) of the German Rotary Clubs in 1934. The Nazis closed down the few remaining Freemasonry Lodges in 1935 and the Rotary Clubs in 1937.[78]

Years later, Scurla described Bergsträsser, Rothfels, and Biendorf as "very clear-thinking men" who preserved their integrity in their work on the selection committee.[79] With these exceptions, there is no reason to doubt that the other members of the national selection committee were dedicated and active Nazis who most likely placed a much higher emphasis on candidates' dedication to "the cause" than the members discussed above. Even so, given their known political predisposition, and possible numerical advantage at times, it is conceivable that the non-Nazis on the selection committee could have outvoted the Nazis.

The Students

Both DAAD and IIE were fully cognizant that the Germans chosen for the exchange program with the United States came from the old German elite along with a sizeable number from the new Nazi elite.[80] The former were from the governing class, often with foreign, sometimes American, connections. This class included diplomats and Foreign Ministry officials, scientists and academics, prominent Germans with close American ties, industrialists, financiers, and general officers of the Wehrmacht. Among the students from this class was one related to the Reich minister of food and agriculture; Heinrich Sahm, son of a Berlin mayor; and Hans Schemm, son of the Bavarian minister of culture. Exchange students with parents in the government bureaucracy included four sons of government councilors (*Oberregierungeräte*) and three children of Reichsbahn (government railroad) executives.[81]

German diplomats with American ties used the exchange program to send their children to study in the United States. From this group, two students were related to the German consuls in New York and Boston; Friedrich-Heinrich von Boetticher was the son of the German military attaché in the United States, Lieutenant-General Friedrich von Boetticher.[82] One student, Gunther Bischoff, did not have known connections to the United States, but his father was the German consul general in Japan.[83]

Other students with notable ties to the United States included Hans Erich Schurer, a nephew of Paul Haertl, a member of the Georgia Warm Springs Foundation, who helped design its spa and consequently became acquainted with President Franklin Roosevelt.[84] Eva Strasmann was the niece of Ferdinand Thun, president of the Philadelphia-based Carl Schurz Memorial Foundation (unrelated to the Carl Schurz Vereinigung in Germany), which provided a significant portion of IIE's funding. Her brother-in-law was editor of the *Reading (PA) Eagle* and a prolific historian. Were that not enough, she also had a letter of recommendation from the president of the Dusseldorf Senate.[85]

Among the students with parents in industry and finance were Gerhard Wolfgang Lüdtke, son of Gerhard Lüdtke, owner of Walter de Gruyter, a major publishing firm.[86] Another exchange student was the nephew of an I.G. Farben executive.[87] Hermann Wetzer's father owned a factory,[88] and two or three were children of bank directors.[89]

Among family members of the military leadership who went to the United States to study was Egloff von Tippelskirch, nephew of Major General Kurt von Tippelskirch, chief of German army intelligence (distinct from the Abwehr). Baron Hans von Preuschen was related to Reich President Paul von Hindenburg, and his father was a lieutenant general.[90] Heinz Mass-Protzen was also the son of a high-ranking Wehrmacht officer.[91]

The children of Nazi officials included Erika Hanfstaengl, niece of Ernst Hanfstaengl, who had played a critical role in helping Hitler establish himself in the early 1920s. She also had close connections to the traditional elites, as her father served as director of the German National Gallery of Art (Deutsche Nationalgalerie). Elisabeth Hühnlein's father, Adolf Hühnlein, had participated in the Beer Hall Putsch, and, like Hitler, was subsequently incarcerated in Landsberg prison. After being released, Hühnlein rose rapidly in the Nazi ranks to become corps leader (*Korpsführer*) of the prestigious National Socialist Motor Corps (Nationalsozialistisches Kraftfahrkorps), one of the party formations (*Parteigliederungen*).[92] SS and German Labor Front (Deutsche Arbeitsfront) officials also had children in the German-American exchange program as well.

Conversely, it appears that relatively few exchange students came from lower-middle- class families. There were a number of children whose parents were teachers and ministers, several had fathers who worked as lower-level railroad employees. The parents of two exchange students were farmers. The working class was even less represented. Friedrich "Fritz" Lilge's father worked as a cashier in an insurance company, while Herbert Sonthoff's father was a traveling salesman. Other students had fathers who worked as a postman, butcher, baker, tailor, and fireman. It is not known if any of these parents held higher-level Nazi Party positions. In short, the selection of exchange students did not reflect the putative class blindness of the Third Reich. The national selection committee also skewed the process in favor of the German elite by considering parents' ability to repay state loans for the students' travel expenses and other costs not covered by the host institution.[93] The most notable exceptions were students who received scholarships reserved for those whose fathers had died in World War I.[94]

Of course, the most dramatic change among exchange students in the Nazi era compared to their predecessors was the nearly total prohibition on Jewish Germans. Most of the Weimar-era program's Jewish students, who apparently made up a significant number, had their scholarships revoked in the summer of 1933.[95] Stunningly, Helene Mayer, an Olympic gold medalist then studying in the United States, lost her DAAD scholarship that summer because her father was Jewish. Immediately after the Nazis took power, the few remaining exchange students with some Jewish ancestry joined their Gentile peers in rushing to pledge allegiance to the Nazi regime.[96]

In another case, a Jewish German exchange participant attended a meeting of foreign exchange students in Germany and was singled out by DAAD official Herbert Scurla as an example of the government's supposed non-discrimination against Jews. She courageously refuted his claim.[97] Not surprisingly, many Jewish German students, like Mayer and Ewald Schnitzer, remained in the United States or returned there if the opportunity arose.[98]

There is considerable evidence that the most active anti-Nazi exchange students were heavily involved in the Protestant or Catholic Churches. This is not surprising given the Confessing Church's distrust of the Nazi influence on Christianity and the well-known reluctance of many Catholics to fully embrace Hitler's program for Germany.[99] Albert Ickler, on his exchange application form, listed his membership in the German Confessional Church, where he had been illegally ordained. He explained that he thought it a good idea to participate in an international exchange to "enlarge [his] perspectives by learning about the non-German world."[100] Later, in a letter to Hubbard, he lamented that it would be impossible for him to ever obtain a position in the German government.[101]

In late October 1938, Rettig visited Princeton University on one of his college tours. His encounter with Hans Richter, a theology exchange student, left him appalled. Rettig denounced Richter for his preference for speaking English and his "absurd" views on Nazi Germany, which Rettig claimed were as hostile to the Fatherland as one would expect from an émigré. As evidence, Rettig noted that Richter had praised Albert Einstein, whom Richter knew quite well, and deplored Einstein's emigration as a "great loss for Germany." Richter added that there was "of course" no place for National Socialists at Princeton and advised Rettig to be "restrained" when dealing with the faculty and administration.

Consequently, Rettig advised DAAD that the German Student Union, and apparently the Ministry of Education as well, be apprised of Richter's heretical view given that he intended to return to Germany the next year for his theological state examination.[102] The incident took on greater importance because, in a telegram, Rettig emphasized that Richter was the son of Julius Richter, a theology professor specializing in missionary studies at the University of Berlin. Rettig also noted that Julius Richter had established the German-American theology exchange with DAAD, and remained involved in it, and that Hans's selection for the exchange had stemmed from his father's influence.[103]

At the time the telegram was written, the Gestapo had already deemed Julius Richter a "person of interest." He had been a visiting theology professor in New York shortly before his son began his degree at the Princeton Theological Seminary. Julius was also a friend of Dietrich Bonhoeffer, the theologian known for his involvement in circles seeking to assassinate Hitler. By the late 1930s, Julius had become a notable advocate for Christians of Jewish descent and, according to one of his American colleagues, "a stout fighter against Hitlerism."[104]

In the summer of 1937, Julius Richter hosted the patently liberal "American Seminar." He was involved in an "official" presentation to the seminar participants and another, "unofficial" presentation at his home. Bonhoeffer attended the latter, during which they conferred on the true state of affairs in Germany.[105] One of the seminar participants believed that the Gestapo was aware of the unofficial and frank discussions.[106] Nevertheless, Hans Richter was still permitted to leave to study in the United States several months later. Richter was at the seminary alongside Hans-Werner Gensichen, another German exchange student. The two associated with Germans on the Princeton faculty who had maintained ties with the Confessing Church in Germany and also with German émigré faculty.[107]

Gensichen later described their exchange year as a "temporary escape from Nazi Germany." Like Julius Richter, Gensichen's father, Johannes Gensichen, had also defied the Nazis. In the spring of 1935, Johannes, an Evangelical Lutheran pastor in Leipzig, read a proclamation to his congregation protesting the arrest of a group of ministers. Hans-Werner later claimed that his father was "literally carried from his Leipzig church pulpit to the Gestapo prison."[108] As with Richter, it is startling that this episode seemingly did not obstruct his son's application to study in the United States under DAAD auspices in 1937.

Catholics were also well represented among the anti-Nazi exchange participants. As previously noted, Margildis Schlüter, from a prominent Catholic family in the Rhineland, was accepted. Herbert Günther Sonthoff, born into a staunchly Catholic family, was apparently of Polish descent. He went by the last name Samozinski until he was fifteen, when his father changed it to something that did not sound Polish; Günther was an assumed name.[109] In the final years of the Weimar Republic, Sonthoff was a member of the Catholic Center Party and he worked for the leading Catholic newspaper *Germania* until late 1934.[110] He joined the SS in November 1933, allegedly to satisfy enrollment requirements for the University of Berlin.[111]

The SS was apparently unaware of his continued association with *Germania*, despite his habit of staunchly defending Catholicism against criticism within his SS unit.[112] They also somehow failed to note his Polish ancestry, even though all prospective members of the SS had to present rigorous evidence of Aryan descent.[113]

According to Sonthoff, in the summer of 1934, while working for *Germania*, he was ordered to prepare for the Röhm purge and await instructions. Instead, he immediately disappeared on a "sailing trip." This, plus his "violent political Catholicism" and "lukewarm" Nazism, led to his expulsion from the SS in July 1934. He was forced to endure a humiliating ceremony in front of his unit, during which his insignia was ripped from his uniform.[114] He had just been accepted as an exchange student by the University of Georgia, and consequently left Germany only weeks later. When asked by the FBI years later why his disgrace had gone unnoticed by the Gestapo and DAAD, Sonthoff replied, "The SS did not keep good records at that time."[115]

Figure 2.2. Herbert Sonthoff, ca. 1937. Expelled from the Schutzstaffel (SS) for his Catholicism and therefore unable to pursue an academic career in Germany after studying in the United States; after a brief repatriation, returned to America, but continued to be haunted by his Nazi past. Humboldt University of Berlin Archives, Z-D 1/977. Ka. 031, application for graduate studies at the University of Berlin. Courtesy of the Humboldt University of Berlin Archives.

Horst Janson, born in Russia, only became a German citizen in 1929. At the University of Hamburg, he studied under the Jewish German art historian Erwin Panofsky, who fled Germany for the United States in 1933. Panofsky encouraged Janson to apply for an exchange fellowship as a means of emigrating.[116] Amazingly, the German authorities who investigated Janson for the exchange program overlooked his prior association with Panofsky.

Many other successful exchange candidates expressed decidedly unorthodox ideas in their personal statements. One of Luzie Kossack's references, Karl Viëtor, was married to a Jewish German and had already fled to the United States as a refugee before Kossack's exchange program application was filed.[117] In addition, Kossack expressed her love of Thomas Wolfe's books, which had already been banned in Germany.[118] Ulrich Pohlenz's brother-in-law was Jewish; Kurt Neumann, in his personal statement, praised "rabbinic literature" and the piety of pre-Christian Jews. All of these students were awarded exchange slots, even in the final years of the 1930s. Many of them never returned.[119]

A number of personal statements sounded "progressive," even by today's standards. Several exchange students studying journalism expressed a desire to see the world from a different perspective. Ilse Maria Wössner hoped to be inspired by living among a different people in an "impressive" foreign country, such as the United States. She wrote that not only would her professional horizons "infinitely expand," but "my experience would deepen, my empathy increase . . . My horizons would broaden under the influence of a different worldview; borders would fall, and be rebuilt anew."[120] Maria Wiemers believed that learning foreign perspectives on issues would make her a better journalist.[121] Another journalism student, Herbert Hörhager, agreed, and added, "After all, it is not the task of the editor to give an opinion that was preconceived by others, but to form an independent judgment of the matter."[122]

Some students in other fields echoed similar sentiments. In late 1937, Hannalene Kipper explained in her application that by learning about American perceptions of Germany, she hoped to expand her perspective beyond "European narrowness." This, she believed, would allow her to form "a distinct and impartial judgment of our situation" in Germany.[123] Ilse Giesing was confident that viewing Germany from the outside would help her break away from the mindset of a "self-satisfied citizen."[124]

Some students continued to express these ideas once in the United States. In June 1934, Carl Ringer, a German exchange student at Dickinson College, told the local Kiwanis Club, "Here I had a valuable opportunity to see my own Germany through the eyes of the Americans about me and in this manner I was able to learn much of our strengths and weaknesses."[125] Even in 1935, Ingeborg Oesterlin explained to the local community newspaper in Lincoln, Nebraska, that one of the reasons for the German-American exchange was to give "young students a broader point of view. In this way, they were able to see another country from the inside as well as their own from the outside."[126]

Some theological students wrote that studying in the United States would facilitate their understanding of other types of people. Wolf Weber trusted that such an experience would help him overcome "the misconceptions that made it almost impossible to understand other people or ideas." As a future pastor, he anticipated that a better understanding of people elsewhere and their mentalities would help him minister to individuals from all walks of life.[127] Albert Ickler wrote much the same thing.[128]

The continued prevalence of pro-American sentiment in 1930s Germany, along with increased teaching of American studies and the English language, fueled Germans' interest in the United States and boosted the number of students wanting to study there.[129] Inge Lindenmeyer applied for the exchange because of her "sympathy" for and ever-increasing desire to get to understand American economics, politics, and cultural relations, which, she added, had a powerful influence on Europe.[130] Guenther Bischoff was excited about the opportunity to exchange views in American debating clubs, "which are unknown to us" in Germany.[131] Some successful candidates favorably compared the United States to Germany.[132]

Given the apparent incongruity between the statements in these personal applications and DAAD's criteria for selecting exchange students, one might suspect that the students were being disingenuous, writing only to impress the American academics who ultimately chose which of them would attend their universities. The IIE and host universities received an even greater number of applications from German students who expressed a desire to present the Nazi viewpoint to Americans, that is, represent the New Germany, and included statements redolent of Nazi propaganda. If DAAD was willing to send those personal statements to IIE, along with résumés listing Nazi affiliations and "achievements," then perhaps there was no need for DAAD to insist that others lie about their motivations for wanting to go to the United States. Ruth Hubbard, who would know better than anyone, considered the effusive résumés genuine.[133] One of the longest-living exchange students, Ursula Dibbern, wrote only one application, rather than both a "pro-Nazi" application and another that downplayed any Nazi affiliations.[134]

Final Preparations and Problems

Those selected by the national committee could generally expect to secure an exchange slot, but additional hurdles remained before they could finally depart for the United States. First, IIE had to locate American host institutions willing to accept each of the German students recommended by DAAD. Additionally, the students were required to complete a six-month "training" program, which brought together former exchange students, those preparing for their exchange year, students interested in foreign affairs careers, and others curious about other countries.[135] The program essentially combined lectures on German foreign policy and relevant "country" studies with discussion workshops.

In the late Weimar years, the training program had an informal structure. The lectures, often held in private homes, focused on preparing the students for the various "problems" they would likely encounter in their host countries. Once abroad, the students were expected not only to concentrate on their academic work but also to spend time associating with their American classmates and giving talks about Germany.[136] They had to keep in mind that they represented Germany, rather than a particular political party or some other sectarian group. They were to convey their government's position on such issues as their country's innocence in World War I, the sorrowful mistreatment of German Americans during the war, the iniquity of the Versailles Treaty, the burdens of reparations, and so on.[137]

The lecture format drastically changed over time. In the first year of the Third Reich, various organizations haphazardly ran the training seminars, among them the German Student Union, the National Socialist Students' League, humanities faculties at universities, and the Association of Former Exchange Students.[138] The atmosphere of the seminars remained very informal: notetaking was not required; no exams were given.[139] The exchange students were told to accept every speaking opportunity offered, but not to seek them out or engage in overt propaganda. Given American sensitivities, lecturers also told them to avoid obnoxious pro-Nazism.[140] Despite this, they received few specific talking points. Although the Weimer-era complaints about the Versailles "travesty" remained in vogue, the training program's propagandistic-political goals were quite different from those of the Weimar era. The students reviewed "racial theory," for instance.[141] They also received instructions to play up the "achievements" of the Third Reich—such as national unity, social equality, volunteerism, economic prosperity—and, of course, the people's love of the Führer.[142] The students were also encouraged to foster German Americans' pride in the New Germany;[143] they should refute the "atrocity stories" and "lies" prevalent in the (supposedly Jewish-controlled and refugee-influenced) US press, such as the mistreatment of Jewish Germans, the Nazi regime's stifling of civil liberties and personal expression, and so on.

When Burmeister and Rettig took control of DAAD, in the fall of 1934, they became aware of the seriousness of the exchange student refugee problem. From their perspective, Western democracies, especially those with large Jewish populations and significant numbers of German refugees, were filling the heads of naïve young German students with heretical liberal notions.[144] Even worse, anti-Nazi German students were using the exchange to flee abroad.[145] Given the large number of German students going to the United States, that country stood out as the worst offender. At the national training conference for Foreign Affairs Office personnel that fall, Burmeister made DAAD's new management philosophy perfectly clear. Attendees received notice that returning exchange students, "particularly from the Anglo-Saxon countries," would require "re-education" to rid their minds of "foreign perspectives." This became one of the duties of the Association of Former Exchange Students,[146] whose measures were partially effective.

The German Student Union was relieved to learn that Burmeister and Rettig were just as focused as it was on the danger of the liberal West and on stanching the student refugee flow.[147] They agreed that the students selected for study abroad had to be better inoculated against ideological confusion through more intensive training to understand the host country's "mentality."[148] As a consequence, the student union took on many training seminars, which it subsequently regimented and radicalized.[149] In 1935 in the Berlin suburb of Dahlem, the Nazi Party established the Foreign Policy School (Aussenpolitisches Schulungshaus), a training center for those intending to go abroad for long periods or work in a Nazi agency focused on foreign relations. Documents also identify exchange students as one of the groups suitable for training at the school. Lectures not only focused on the Nazi Party's version of foreign affairs, but guest speakers from other countries gave lectures as well. There is no known record of an exchange student having studied at the Foreign Policy School.[150]

Regardless of who sponsored the training, it became highly politicized after about 1935. The exchange students going to the United States received instruction on the usual array of anti-American stereotypes: American democracy was a sham, and corrupt, mafia-like political "machines" ran its cities and states, with Huey Long's Louisiana exemplifying this state of affairs. American capitalists, unlike their German counterparts, had no sense of social responsibility; meanwhile, self-interested, venal bosses controlled US labor unions. The much-vaunted American freedom of the press was an illusion; the American press did not report the news, it "made" the news, based on the wishes of Jewish media barons. The US government suspended freedom of speech whenever it feared dissent, as during World War I. Thus, the so-called freedoms of the press, speech, and thought, and the entire panoply of democratic virtues, simply constituted the veiled "superstructure" of the ruling classes.[151]

The trainers also emphasized police brutality in the United States; additionally, they pointed out police allowed dangerous subversives and illegal businesses to flourish. The US government was said to be indifferent to the economic destitution of its people, and trainers highlighted the irony of self-satisfied American claims of egalitarianism while government manifestly denied Black Americans their civil rights. Other courses were more reminiscent of their Weimar-era predecessors, covering the US Constitution, US foreign affairs, various aspects of American culture (such as literature and music), social etiquette, and college life. In 1938 the students were instructed to advocate isolationism in US foreign policy. The lecturers dared not praise the United States, and sometimes even ridiculed it.[152]

Lectures also reiterated the correct responses to questions the exchange students would likely be asked in the United States, to create a positive image of the New Germany. The students were taught to emphasize Germany economic recovery from the Great Depression, the brilliance of German academic life and culture, the country's pacifist international politics, and the voluntaristic egalitarianism of the Reich Labor Service; they should downplay the supposedly exaggerated "Jewish question," emphasize the inherent qualities associated with race, and defend Germany's right to "peaceful" expansion. After the promulgation of the Nuremberg Laws in 1935, it became impossible to deny that Jewish Germans were being discriminated against, so the students were told to bring up the treatment of African Americans in the South as a counterargument.[153] The lecturers encouraged them to attend social events, especially those hosted by German American organizations, and join group tours, outdoor activities, and "games." These were considered excellent venues for intermingling with American students and influencing their attitudes.[154]

The discussion workshops retained the open format of previous years. Anneliese von dem Hagen, a student at the University of Berlin, attended a number of such workshops at the university's Humboldt Club in early 1938. According to von dem Hagen, American exchange students studying at the university made up about 50 percent of the attendees, with German students making up the other 50 percent. Some of the German attendees wore the uniforms of the SA or SS. Topics included "issues of the day," such as press freedom, the relationship between church and state, and cultural matters. She asserted that attendees were allowed to speak freely and that debates could at times get "extremely heated."[155] Although there were reportedly instances of America-bound students making statements that irritated the Nazis involved at this stage of the selection process, no evidence suggests a student being expelled from the program at this point. After the training course ended, the students received the required certificate of completion by their local student union.

Before the students left for the United States, the Foreign Affairs Offices provided them with propaganda materials designed for Anglophone or specifically American audiences.[156] The students had to promise to join the Association of Former Exchange Students upon their return. Those going to the United States then had to submit themselves to yet another oversight organization, the Association of Former German Students in America, founded earlier in the Nazi period by Heinrich Rocholl, a former exchange student. Also a dedicated Nazi and espionage agent employed by the US Consulate in Berlin, Rocholl attempted to steal secrets obtained from the consulate and was summarily dismissed. The implication was rather obvious: the students who had studied in the United States should understand that they would be watched after their return, so arriving in Germany with openly "liberal" attitudes would be unwise.

Burmeister and Rettig also instituted measures to better monitor the ideological proclivities of German students while abroad.[157] Apparently through Burmeister's prodding, the Ministry of Education repeatedly issued warnings to the exchange students to report to their local German consulate, particularly in countries with large Jewish or German émigré populations. The repeated demands suggest a persistent noncompliance issue throughout the history of the German-American exchange program.[158] To better suppress dissent, the students were supposed to keep an eye on one another, and meet in regional groupings more frequently.[159]

Working with DAAD caused IIE frequent headaches. Principal problems included the perennial lack of qualified German students capable of performing reasonably well at American colleges. The situation worsened over the course of the 1930s.[160] As previously noted, after June 1933, the Foreign Affairs Offices were instructed to only advance those applicants who demonstrated loyalty to the New Germany. To do so, students had to devote a great many hours to "the cause," time that could otherwise have been spent studying. As schools and universities Nazified, the academic rigor in most fields declined precipitously. The preference given to students with Nazi connections only exacerbated the problem.

By the second half of the 1930s, American host schools frequently complained about the German students' academic incompetence.[161] The percentage of poorly performing students increased with each academic year from 1935–36 onward. By the final year of the program, 1938–39, such students had become the majority.

The IIE frequently expressed irritation about the Germans' failure to fill all the exchange slots available to them. By mid-decade, the situation had become so troubling that Duggan personally discussed the matter several times with Hans Luther, the German ambassador. Luther was livid to find IIE more eager to secure German students than DAAD was in providing them. In a May 14, 1935, letter to the Foreign Ministry, Luther expressed his disbelief that a populous nation like Germany could not produce enough qualified students to fill fifty or sixty exchange posts.[162] Richard Sallet, propaganda attaché in the United States, informed Goebbels that such a problem was "incomprehensible."[163] Other German officials in the United States echoed the same concerns.

The next year, Luther and Sallet frantically informed their bosses that the situation had deteriorated even further. Luther reminded DAAD that the exchange program was the conduit for "enormous" German influence on American colleges. He emphasized that simply filling the slots with any available students was not a solution, as American colleges had academic requirements that they would not waive.[164] German officials frequently trotted out a line about the French pouring money and soft power into chiseling away at Germany's influence in American academia.[165] Luther amplified their complaints, informing the Foreign Ministry that Duggan had threatened to offer unfilled German slots to the French if Germany could not find a sufficient number of qualified students.[166] The implication of these missives was clear: "moderates" like him felt that exchange officials needed to relax the ideological requirements for selecting students, if only for the practical reason of filling otherwise empty slots. Even less ideologically excited students would nevertheless prove a credit to the German nation.

The pressure from US-based German authorities and American host schools might explain the continued presence of some high-achieving students in the German-American exchange program. Helga Boursé, an exchange student for 1938–39, explained in an interview with a local US newspaper that students with the highest grades at her German university, Stuttgart, were encouraged to apply for an American exchange slot.[167] The radicals at DAAD and the student unions, however, were determined to push back against such ideological laxity. To them, the exchange program lost its raison d'être if they did not place hard-core Nazis abroad to impress the world with the New Nazi

Man, as well as carry out covert propaganda and espionage. Conveniently, many officials involved in the exchange blamed the student union for this sorry situation, since the union was responsible for finding the exchange candidates in the first place. The student union's Foreign Office in Berlin pressured its university affiliates to do whatever was necessary to drum up good exchange candidates, even though their demands for ideological purity made this task all but impossible.[168] A 1936 conflict involving German exchange students in another democracy, Switzerland, which the US government was monitoring, illustrates this dynamic, closely paralleling the conflict involving the United States.

Attempts by German exchange students at the University of Lausanne to encourage their friends back home to apply for study in Switzerland proved unsuccessful due to the endless paperwork, the required and extensive proof of dedication to Nazism, and the time-consuming preparatory training demanded by the German Student Union. The rigid rules were choking the flow of qualified German students who were, in fact, staunch supporters of Germany and National Socialism but simply could not meet the excessive bureaucratic requirements. The exchange students warned that if the situation continued the German exchange student presence at Lausanne would end. Otto Riese, a German faculty member who taught law there, fully supported the students' complaints. The students further buttressed their arguments with the clever threat that if the situation persisted, only German refugee students would remain at the university, dealing a propaganda blow to the New Germany that, ironically, the ideologically stringent selection requirements back in Germany were meant to counter in the first place. On top of that, previous experience had shown that most German students who had lived abroad became even more attached to Germany and to National Socialism, not less.[169]

The headquarters of the German Student Union Foreign Office hit back, arguing that its role was to ensure that only the most dedicated followers of National Socialism be selected for study abroad. Furthermore, the office asserted that other Reich administrative bodies, not the union, held responsibility for the extensive paperwork and bureaucratic hurdles involved.[170] Several months later, the Education Ministry took up the issue, siding with the German students in Lausanne. The student union's Foreign Office responded that none of the student complaints were the real cause for the declining number of exchange students. Rather, the decline had been ongoing since World War I. The Reich Economic Ministry's extraordinary currency restrictions had made study abroad almost financially impossible. With this practical consideration in mind, it only made sense to reserve the few well-funded exchange slots at Lausanne for "politically immaculate . . . proven National Socialists." Indeed, the student union insisted that it was actually quite tolerant of students who lacked some of the political requirements.[171] This episode demonstrates, once again, the tendency in Nazi Germany to thwart the Reich's larger goals due to bureaucratic tussles, mutual recriminations, and exhausting demonstrations of political purity.

The German students selected for the exchange program had to attend a final multiday preparatory meeting before leaving for the United States. In 1933 the four-day assembly held in early September remained similar to its Weimar-era predecessors. The central focus was a "reunion" of post-exchange students, who participated in discussion groups with the new exchange students, organized by host country. The former exchange students familiarized the new students with the innumerable practical details they would encounter in the host country, such as health insurance requirements and employment opportunities. Whenever possible, students who had just returned from their exchange year met those who were about to leave for the same host college.

The students also attended lectures by various "experts," typically former exchange students or professors.[172] In the 1933 keynote address, Morsbach gave what could be considered rather un-Nazi like instructions: he asked the students to display "reticence and modesty" in their host countries. This, he asserted, would best serve Germany.[173] He recommended that the students demonstrate the virtues of the New Germany through their personal example and conduct, rather than speeches and propaganda. Perhaps not coincidentally, this would be his last address at such an assembly.

The contingent of Nazi officials at the 1933 assembly was determined to impress upon the students the necessity of conforming to the new ideological orthodoxy, obliging them to participate in a "handshake ceremony" as a pledge to willingly represent the New Germany.[174] Various participants reported a palpable tension between the Nazi and non-Nazi officials in attendance.[175]

The subsequent predeparture assemblies followed a different pattern: they were longer (eventually, ten days), more regimented, and increasingly focused on teaching propaganda techniques. In 1935 Burmeister's presentation primarily consisted of threatening the exchange students with "disciplinary action" if they misbehaved, which did not go over well with his audience. He also made it clear that "going native" was intolerable. The students were to remain steadfast Nazis; they should observe their host cultures, not absorb them or return to Germany with "silly democratic ideas, customs, etc." Even

Figure 2.3. German-American exchange students at an assembly, Schloss Köpenick, Berlin, 1932. Courtesy of the Deutscher Akademischer Austauschdienst.

Burmeister, however, warned them against bragging about the Reich or belittling the host country. On another occasion, he stressed that the nineteenth-century liberal academic world that had strived for international peace, harmony, and self-enrichment had been a mirage. Rather, the real world was a struggle of peoples. Since the New Germany was being increasingly isolated by its enemies, the students had to view themselves not as individuals, but as soldiers of the Reich in a hostile world.[176]

By 1937 Burmeister had instructed the students to regard themselves as full-fledged "political soldiers" fighting for the Reich in a global ideological war, played out on foreign college campuses.[177] In this, he proved himself oblivious to the potential international consequences of his rhetoric, exhibiting the limited horizons typical of many Nazis. On August 27, the *New York Times*, having learned of his speech, ran the article "Nazi Students Drill on Converting World: Those Who Go Soon to Foreign Colleges Are Trained for Propaganda Abroad." The fallout in the American academic community was predictable: a large number of colleges canceled their exchange programs with Germany, with some citing Burmeister's speech as the reason.

Soon thereafter, Walter Wilcox, a professor of economics at Cornell University, informed Duggan that he and Alvin Johnson, director of the New School for Social Research, were considering organizing a committee to protest the continuation of the German-American exchange. They had lost patience after the *New York Times* article. Duggan awkwardly advised them not to take Burmeister's comments literally, claiming that they were simply meant to impress the regime.[178] The 1938 cohort of exchange students received instructions to "completely submerge themselves in the American mode of life," even to the point of losing their German accent, which may have been intended to facilitate espionage. They were also told to "keep their ears open at all times."[179]

Germany's invasion of Poland preempted the assembly scheduled for September 1939, and the country's exchange programs now relied on exchanges with allied and neutral countries on the European continent.

Aside from Nazi officials' pep talks, a considerable amount of time at the assembly was spent on hiking and various sports activities, in line with the Nazis' emphasis on physical fitness. A 1935 handball match held one afternoon between the US-bound students and those headed to other countries seemed an odd decision, considering that the differentiation led the students to identify with the United States as a cohort. Additionally, the numerical division between those going to the United States versus "everyone else" revealed the predominance of the German-American exchange. One of the less-cheery social evenings featured Rettig reading aloud the letters of German students killed in World War I.

As far back as 1926, the student assemblies provided German authorities a venue for selecting an "exchange student leader" for the most important host countries.[180] These assemblies were the first occasion when all of the German students destined to study abroad were gathered together. DAAD officials clearly wanted to assess the students' interactions before making such a significant leadership decision. As became evident during the Nazi era, waiting until practically the last minute to make such an important determination could be fraught with problems.

The student leader position, originally conceived to facilitate the students' exchange year, became increasingly political and propagandistic in the last year of the Weimar Republic. The selection and responsibilities of the student leader seem to have been extremely haphazard, especially for the one going to the United States. From 1933 to 1936, it appears that the German Student Union selected the US exchange student leader, with DAAD officially confirming the candidate. The partial Nazification of the exchange program in June 1933 opened new vistas for party control over the exchange students. In the case of the German-American exchange, however, such efforts only led to disastrous embarrassments.

Around that time, Ernst Wilhelm Bohle, a protégé of Rudolf Hess, deputy Führer of the Nazi Party, was appointed gauleiter of the Nazi Party Foreign Organization, with Hess as his superior.[181] Bohle attempted to burrow into the student exchange program by declaring that his remit over Nazi Party members abroad gave him the right to supervise German exchange students. To Bohle, Anton-Hermann Chroust, about to begin his exchange year at Harvard, must have seemed an excellent choice to represent the Nazi Party for German students in the United States. Both Bohle and Hess knew Chroust personally.[182] Chroust, a somewhat older student, was working toward his PhD at the most prestigious university in the United States, in its most populous region. In short, he appeared mature, intelligent, and potentially influential, and, in addition, he was an SS member.[183]

Chroust received his "appointment" as the Nazi Party's exchange student leader in the United States at the 1934 predeparture assembly.[184] It was entirely unclear what this meant, as Bohle made the appointment outside the normal administration of the exchange program. It is uncertain what role, if any, DAAD had in confirming Chroust's appointment, perhaps because the assem-

Figure 2.4. Anton-Hermann Chroust. A Harvard law student in the early 1930s who became a fervent Nazi; later clashed with German diplomats in the United States; refused to return to Germany and eventually joined the faculty at Notre Dame University. Early IIE Photos, 1930s. Courtesy University of the Institute of International Education.

bly took place just a few weeks after Burmeister replaced Morsbach as DAAD's managing director. Oddly, no one thought to provide Chroust with a list of the exchange students he was supposed to oversee. As a result, he turned to the IEE, informing it that he was the new exchange student leader and, as such, wanted the names of the other exchange students. He also asked pointed questions about the whereabouts of Ernst Lampe, a Jewish refugee student.[185] Startled by this odd request, IIE asked DAAD for clarification.[186] DAAD confirmed that Chroust was indeed the German exchange student leader in the United States. Several months later, however, DAAD contacted Hubbard to admit that, as it turned out, Chroust was not the exchange student leader after all.[187]

In the midst of such confusion, Chroust essentially appropriated whatever powers he thought befitted his position. This quickly came to encompass monitoring the exchange students to ensure ideological conformity, rooting out deviants, spying on refugees, and ultimately exercising unchecked control over the exchange students.[188] His efforts did not go over well. To assert his authority, he began annual "inspection trips" around the United States, checking up on students.[189] During the 1934–35 Christmas holidays, he accompanied several dozen exchange students on their vacation to Florida. While they were enjoying themselves on Miami Beach, Chroust insisted that they conduct themselves in a manner befitting the Nazi elite and ordered them to sing the Nazi Party anthem, the "Horst Wessel Lied." Chroust's exhortations were "very badly received" by the students, who were not his fans in any event.[190]

Chroust displayed a sort of megalomania. At various times, he claimed to "speak with the authority of the German government" and thought he had "absolute power over the exchange students," including the right to have them imprisoned if he determined their behavior warranted it.[191] Incredibly, at one point, Chroust even declared himself to be Hitler' personal representative in the United States.[192] His delusions of grandeur were so extreme that even Kurt von Tippelskirch, the German consul general in Boston, concluded that Chroust was, quite literally, insane.[193]

As the Nazi Party student leader, Chroust apparently viewed himself as invulnerable. At one point, he refused to speak to von Tippelskirch, following an earlier encounter. Whereas Chroust was a radical Nazi, von Tippelskirch was not even a party member, which might have played a role in their mutual animosity.[194] In the fall of 1935, von Tippelskirch filed a formal complaint to his superior, Ambassador Luther, regarding Chroust's outrageous behavior. No doubt, Luther saw it as an opportunity to assert the authority of the Foreign Ministry in relation to the Nazi Party Foreign Organization. In December 1935, Luther summoned Chroust to Washington and demanded that he explain himself. During the meeting, Chroust seems to have fallen into the trap of asserting that the party's writ superseded that of the Foreign Ministry's and that, in fact, Nazi authorities had granted him all the powers he claimed. Any other validation, he suggested, was merely paperwork not worth the effort. Chroust even told Luther that if he had a problem with this arrangement, he could take it up with his friend, Hess.[195] Luther did just that. He pointed out to Hess that most of the exchange students were not party members and thus did not answer to the party's Foreign Organization or its representatives.[196] The Foreign Organization quickly backpedaled, asserting that it had never granted Chroust authority over anyone. This allowed von Tippelskirch and Luther to declare that Chroust had lied. The German diplomatic service in the United States publicly declared that it considered Chroust an "incorrigible renegade" who was "messing up" the student exchange.[197] As a result, at the end of 1935, Hess personally informed Chroust that he was being removed from his party-assigned post—a rather odd move given that Chroust ostensibly had never been appointed to it.[198] The Education Ministry also warned Chroust that his leadership claims lacked any official basis.[199] Both the Foreign Ministry and the Education Ministry agitated for Chroust to be repatriated.[200] Thereafter, one of the surest ways to irritate diplomats at the Boston consulate was to mention Chroust's name.[201]

Neither the German Student Union nor the Nazi Party Foreign Organization ever again appointed a student leader for the United States. Instead, Ulrich von Gienanth, the new propaganda attaché at the German Embassy in Washington, as well as the chief SD representative, was granted full authority by DAAD over the exchange students. Although von Gienanth claimed no less power than Chroust had, he was taken at his word; it was also an open secret that von Gienanth held a high-ranking position in both the Gestapo and the SD. Furthermore, he was fairly popular with the exchange students and exercised his authority with a lighter hand than Chroust.

Conclusion

The confusion and tension surrounding the Chroust affair represents yet another example of the organized chaos that characterized the Third Reich. It also highlights, in microcosm, the constant struggle between the Nazi Party and the state bureaucracy. In 1935 the state, in the form of the Foreign Ministry, won a battle against the party in the Chroust matter. The victory turned out to be hollow, however, given that Chroust's replacement, von Gienanth, represented the party rather than the state.

It is easy to see that the selection of German students for the exchange program was fundamentally flawed from the Nazis' perspective. Discerning the reasons for this, however, is far from simple. The structure of the selection process seemed to align well with the generally accepted modus operandi of

Figure 2.5. German exchange students en route to the United States on the Hamburg-Amerika Line passenger ship *New York*, September 1938. Gustav Blanke, *Vom Nazismus zur Demokratisierung Deutschlands* (Hamburg: Dr. Kovač Press, 1999), 26. Courtesy of Dr. Kovač Press.

the Third Reich. Much like their approach to the Foreign Ministry, the Nazis retained Weimar-era state institutions and processes while gradually Nazifying them. Even as late as 1935, the structure and function of selecting exchange students would have been recognizable to a Weimar-era official.

Some aspects of DAAD's core philosophy did not radically change in the Nazi era. The exchange students were expected to present an appealing image of Germany in their presentations, personal appearance, and behavior. They were instructed to propagandize carefully, ensuring they avoided backlash from IIE, host universities, or their audiences. Despite these guidelines, students frequently breached the established parameters.

The selection and training processes for the exchange program were most radically transformed when under Burmeister and Rettig, when an original goal of the program—maximizing the students' benefits—was largely replaced by a determination to maximize the students' usefulness for the Reich. Concern over German students' Americanization or pursuit of permanent residency became an incentive for DAAD's new Nazi leadership to scrutinize exchange candidates with suitable National Socialist vigor and to radicalize the preparatory training programs. These "reforms" curtailed the number of exchange students who refused to return home, but by no means stopped the flow entirely.

It is unclear why, even after the Burmeister-Rettig safeguards, some students still ended their exchange year markedly less amenable to the regime. Some non-Nazi and other officials, whose worldview still reflected certain pre-National Socialist notions of academic excellence and international cooperation, remained in the exchange bureaucracy and ancillary government offices for the duration of the German-American exchange, until 1939. Clearly, they were responsible for advancing non-Nazi students through the selection process. Also, the Gestapo appears to have done a poor job of weeding out students who, from a Nazi perspective, should not have been sent abroad. The Gestapo administration, like so many other Nazi organizations, was inundated with paperwork, understaffed, and disorganized, making such an unexpected outcome easy to occur. Any investigative work it actually managed to conduct was likely superficial, if tips were even followed up at all. Racial crimes topped the list of the various categories of crimes the Gestapo most zealously investigated.[202]

The overburdened German Student Union also proved incapable of adequately filtering out non-conformists. Indifference or, to put it bluntly, laziness, might also have contributed to the loopholes evident in the student selection process. Growing pressure to find academically suitable exchange candidates undoubtedly led to haphazard investigations into applicants' political commitment, even during the Burmeister-Rettig era. The Foreign Ministry periodically expressed frustration over the lack of qualified candidates for American exchange slots, while the Propaganda Ministry voiced its dissatisfaction with the situation as well. In some cases, a student's family or references carried enough weight to make approval a mere formality. Sometimes the required recommendations by Nazis were based on the flimsiest connections or had little to do with a student's Nazi credentials, instead relying on such traditional criteria as family reputation.

The majority of students applied for the exchange program due to a purported interest in presenting Germany in a favorable light, a desire to enhance their career prospects, or a fascination with American culture. Nevertheless, a new type of exchange student emerged in the Burmeister-Rettig era. With the Nazi's dramatic reorientation of DAAD, the SS—particularly the SD—began to infiltrate the exchange program. As was their habit, they planted espionage agents among the exchange student cohort. Von Gienanth, with his SS-SD and Abwehr credentials, intensified the covert propaganda aspects of the exchange while also facilitating espionage efforts. In the end, the Nazis' espionage and propaganda efforts did little to benefit the state, but did a great deal to worsen US-German relations.

CHAPTER THREE

Brave New World

The U.S.A. is such a beautiful country—no, more like a continent—
filled of richness, of good people, full of problems, and full of great
possibilities! I love this country.
—*Heinz Rudolph, German exchange student, 1937*

For the vast majority of Germans in the German-American student exchange program, their stint studying abroad in the United States represented their first time living in a liberal democracy since the end of the Weimar Republic. That the students' "liberalization" so infuriated radical Nazi officials was evident. This unexpected outcome among the students demonstrates the need for a less mimetic and reductive examination than is typical of most studies on Nazification. Further, the interactions of Americans with the German students, while often friendly, reveal no significant tendency toward the spread of Nazi sympathies in the United Sates. The numerous comments, observations, and efforts to encourage the exchange students' liberalization, as apparent in this study, demonstrate that the majority of American university professors and administrators actively opposed Nazism. In short, when Germans from the Third Reich encountered citizens of a liberal democracy, the ideology that prevailed was certainly not Nazism.

While in the United States, many of the students relished being free from the constant control they experienced in Germany. This translated into a general disregard for the rules established by DAAD, a lackadaisical attitude toward required contacts with German authorities in the United States, and an insouciance toward Nazi attempts at behavioral enforcement.[1] In most cases, however, such behavior did not reflect anti-Nazi sentiments. Rather, it provided a respite from the "pressure cooker" environment that had permeated their lives in Germany.

Each year, at the conclusion of the national exchange program assembly, the students destined for the United States immediately departed together. They sailed together on a German ship, spending the week-long voyage practicing their English language skills by conversing with American passengers. Oftentimes, an official involved in the exchange accompanied them, such as Ulrich von Gienanth, the Nazi Party official and DAAD manager of the German-American student exchange who also watched over the students abroad. For those destined for espionage or covert propaganda missions, von Gienanth haphazardly continued their training during the voyage.[2]

Upon arrival in the United States, the exchange students attended an IIE conference at the Riverdale Country School, in the (then) tranquil Riverdale neighborhood of New York City. There, they joined hundreds of other students from around the world. Beside covering practical matters related to the US collegiate system, the Riverdale conference program included proselytizing American ideals of freedom, democracy, and "universal brotherhood." The conference also provided IIE officials the opportunity to observe the students, identify potential troublemakers, and individually warn them about the unpleasant consequences that would follow any attempts at aggressive propagandizing.

After departing Riverdale, the students traveled to their host schools, where those attending larger universities found themselves forming into small groups, and those at smaller colleges suddenly became the only German student on campus. They maintained contact through the *Rundbrief deutscher Austauschstudenten in den U.S.A.* (*Newsletter of the German Exchange Students in the U.S.A.*), which first appeared in 1931. The students' articles in the *Rundbrief* covered eclectic topics, ranging from tongue-in-cheek reports on their social activities to humorous or noteworthy encounters with Americans, to playfully written accounts of their traditional annual trip to Florida. The newsletter also carried what the students considered erudite observations on American culture. The student leaders, Anton-Hermann Chroust and later von Gienanth, also contributed articles to keep the students up to date about events in Germany and the perspectives they were expected to convey.

The students' private assertions and the semi-private statements in the *Rundbrief* offer insight into what they actually believed, especially when comparing Germany and the United States. National stereotypes often focused on

Figure 3.1. International exchange students and staff from the Institute of International Education, Riverdale Country School, New York City, September 1934 (part 1). Rockefeller Archives Center, RG 4 (FA1288), acc. 2016:070, series 1, box 35, folder 284–286, Early IIE Photos, 1930s. Courtesy Institute of International Education.

Edna Duge, secretary to IIE director Stephen Duggan (1st row, 2nd from right)

Ruth Hubbard, IIE German-American exchange secretary (1st row, far right)

Ruth Laué (2nd row, far left [light collar, plaid dress])

Ina Gotthelf (2nd row, 2nd from left [curly hair, dress with jacket])

Herta Warnholtz (2nd row, 3rd from left [beaded necklace])

Jenni Karding (3rd row from back row, 5th from left) [short braided hair, light outfit, relatively short stature])

Eva Gennes (2nd row, 6th from left [short hair parted on left, white belt])

Janna Hanser (2nd row, 4th from right [dark hair parted in middle])

Maria Hörmann (2nd row, 3rd from right [short hair, parted on right, white horizontal blouse seam and cardigan])

Hildegard Kerkhof (2nd row, 2nd from right [dark jacket, light dress])

Richard Abel-Musgrave (3rd row, 5th from left [glasses, suit, coat draped over shoulders])

Annemarie Weber (2nd row from back row, 6th from left [dark hair parted in middle, white collar, darker dress])

Fritz Lilge (2nd row from back row, 7th from left; 14th from right) [short hair]

Liselotte Roennecke (2nd row from back row, 8th from left) [Pearls, belt, white blouse, dark suit, buttons on lower center of dress downwards, hair somewhat curly, relatively short, dark])

Karl August Maelzer (back row, 3rd from left [hair parted on left, large tie, open suit coat])

Guenther Plathner (back row, 4th from left [only head visible, glasses, white shirt])

Ulrich Lebsanft (back row, 5th from left [hair parted on left, glasses])

Ingrid Förster (back row, 6th from left, center [V-neck floral dress, bow, hair parted in middle and pulled back])

Elisabeth Borgwardt (back row, 7th from left [head and right side only visible, mid-tone woman's suit])

Friedrich Wilhelm Böge (back row, center [hair parted left side])

Margildis Schlüter (back row, 9th from left [hair parted on left, somewhat curly, white blouse])

Friedrich Keppler (back row, 4th from right [full hair, parted on left])

Hans Werner Kübitz (back row, far right)

Figure 3.2. International exchange students and staff from the Institute of International Education, Riverdale Country School, New York City, September 1934 (part 2). Rockefeller Archives Center, RG 4 (FA1288), acc. 2016:070, series 1, box 35, folder 284–286, Early IIE Photos, 1930s. Courtesy Institute of International Education.

Edward R. Murrow, IIE assistant director (1st row, far left)

Jessie Douglass, IIE secretary of the Student Bureau (1st row, 2nd from left)

Gertrud Hermes (1st row, 4th from left [legs crossed, hands on knee)

Marianne Lautsch (1st row, 3rd from right [white shirt under mid-tone dress])

Günther Kiersch (1st row, 2nd from right)

Kurt Naumann (1st row, 1st from right)

Bruno Wehner (2nd row, 3rd from right [mid-tone jacket, dark sweater, white shirt, tie, hair parted on left])

Elisabeth Huehnlein (2nd row, 2nd from right [thick hair pulled back, white blouse, open dark jacket])

Theordor Georg Clausen (3rd row from back, last on the right [dark receding hair, black handkerchief, looking to the right, checkered tie])

Hermann Wetzer (2nd row from back row, 4th from right [blond hair parted on left, only head and left shoulder visible])

Herbert Müller (3rd row, 3rd from right [receding hairline, looking to his right])

Erika Hanfstaengl (3rd row, 2nd from right [darkish hair, white shirt, only face and left shoulder visible])

Ingeborg Oesterlin (3rd row, far right [curly blonde hair, white blouse, light jacket])

Ferdinand von Weymarn (back row, almost center, 17th from left [white shirt, dark tie, square white handkerchief])

Hans Gatzke (4th row, 7th from left [blond hair, tall stature])

Fritz Vöhringer (back row, 11th from right, center of photo, [head and chest visible, tall])

Wilhelm Blank (back row, 6th from right [only head visible, dark hair])

Herbert Sonthoff (back row, 5th from right [short blond hair, dark tie, mid-tone suit])

Gerold von Minden (back row, 4th from right [dark hair parted on left, dark sweater and tie])

Friedrike Waltz (back row, 3rd from right [white blouse, jacket draped on shoulders])

Paul Schenk (back row, 2nd from right [hair parted on left, checkered tie])

Georg von Lilienfeld (back row far right [dark tie, mid-tone jacket, left hand in pocket])

Figure 3.3. International exchange students and staff from the Institute of International Education, Riverdale Country School, New York City, September 1935. Rockefeller Archives Center, RG 4 (FA1288), acc. 2016:070, series 1, box 35, folder 284–286, Early IIE Photos, 1930s. Courtesy of the Institute of International Education.

Karl Wolf
(1st row, far left)

Maria Wiemers
(1st row, 2nd from left)

Horst Griehl
(1st row, 3rd from left)

Ursula Kaufman
(1st row, 4th from left)

Werner Ruch
(1st row, 5th from left)

Edward R. Murrow
(1st row, 9th from left)

Jessie Douglass
(1st row, 10th from left)

Magdalene Schepp
(2nd row, 2nd from left)

Norbert Beyer
(2nd row, 4th from left)

Werner Von Rosenstiel
(2nd row, 6th from left)

Heinz Loefke
(2nd row, 7th from left)

Dora Pfeiffer
(second row, 9th from left)

Eike Dornbach
(2nd row, 11th from left)

Gerhard Lenschow
(2nd row, 9th from right)

Ernst Mahr
(2nd row, 8th from right)

Walter Knoepp
(2nd row, 7th from right)

Philipp Kaffenberger
(2nd row, 4th from right)

Ilse Woessner
(2nd row, 3rd from right)

Horst Voigt
(2nd row, 2nd from right)

Georg Theil
(2nd row, far right)

Ernst Foerster
(3rd row, 10th from left)

Kurt Weege
(3rd row, 11th from left)

Hermann Ruehl
(3rd row, 12th from left)

Gerutha Kempe
(3rd row, 13th from left)

Hans Rupp
(3rd row, 14th from left)

Fritz Bartz
(3rd row, 7th from right)

Hanns von Steagel
(3rd row, 6th from right)

Hermann Schelp
(3rd row, 5th from right)

Erwin Wickert
(3rd row, 4th from right)

Gertrude Achenbach
(4th row, 10th from left)

Ursula Schäfer
(4th row, 7th from right)

Gottfried Rosenthal
(4th row, 6th from right)

Dietrich Zwicker
(5th row, 6th from right)

Irene Boner
(5th row, 5th from right)

Bruno Weber
(5th row, 4th from right)

Eugen Lahr
(5th row, 3rd from right)

Horst Jansen
(5th row, 2nd from right)

Herbert Voigt
(5th row, far right)

Hans von Dobeneck
(6th row, 5th from right)

Gerald von Minden
(6th row, 4th from right)

Ulrich von Gienanth
(6th row, 3rd from right)

Hermann Reissinger
(6th row, 2nd from right)

contrasts between the "normality" of their homeland and the peculiarities of the host society. Whatever they found particularly exciting about the United States implied a lack of that characteristic in Germany. At times, *Rundbrief* articles praised the openness and liberalism of American society to an extent that must have made their Nazi overseers nervous. After the Nazis took power in Germany, perhaps one-third of *Rundbrief* articles overtly criticized the United States, one-third were neutral, and one-third expressed generally positive attitudes about the country. With the onset of the Georg Rettig era at DAAD in late 1935, the *Rundbrief* took on a decidedly more Nazified tone.

Missionaries for "New Germany"

The German exchange students generally kept busy after arriving at their host schools, speaking to campus clubs, local civic groups, and churches. In the early years of the Nazi regime, Americans' interest in hearing from the students mostly stemmed from curiosity about the German people and culture, of which most Americans had at least some vague awareness, though few had in-depth knowledge. Some exchange students felt overwhelmed by the onslaught of American curiosity. Writing to IIE's Ruth Hubbard, Annelise von dem Hagen described the inquisitiveness as nearly oppressive at the small, provincial Texas Women's College: "The whole day long is six or ten girls sitting in my room asking questions: how do you like Hitler and what about our 'hot dogs' all this in the same breathing [*sic*]. Reporters are coming and going and interviews are published. 'How glad to meet you, come over to see us . . .' I hear it [a] hundred times during the day."[3] Others apparently tired of having to repeat the same formulaic answers to the same old questions. At Muskingum College in Ohio, Helga Boursé grew frustrated after being asked the same questions for the "steenth" time: "Do you think Hitler's crazy?" and "What do you think of America?"[4] Eva Schröder, at the University of Vermont, constantly delivered lectures to various clubs and church groups.

As public speakers, the exchange students inevitably indulged their hosts with expected commentaries on typical aspects of German life, sometimes interweaving these with musical presentations or other elements of traditional German culture. DAAD had anticipated this and readily encouraged it. The purpose as that exchange organization saw it, however, was to warm up the crowd to better absorb the propaganda messages at the core of the German student exchange program. These messages evolved starkly from the late Weimar period to the end of the 1930s. In public remarks before 1933, the students inevitably complained about the iniquities of the Versailles Treaty, but with Adolf Hitler and the rise of the National Socialists, the focus shifted. In the summer of 1932, Rudolph von Wistinghausen, recently returned home from the University of Illinois, wrote to his host school's student newspaper, describing his newfound hero, Adolf Hitler, as "simple, modest, able and idealistic, with almost a superhuman love for his people, a person of absolute integrity."[5] At the same time, other exchange students detested Hitler with equal passion. A German exchange student at Stanford confidently reassured his classmates, "There is no danger that Hitler's followers will become a menace to world peace."[6]

The students who arrived in the United States in the fall of 1933 represented the first trained "missionaries" of the "New Germany." Several themes illustrate the general tenor of Nazi propaganda in the United States, which has been well documented.[7] Their public remarks shifted from foreign affairs issues to the beneficent changes in domestic conditions under the new regime. The New Germany was depicted as a prosperous, peace-loving, and happy land of a confident, proud, and dedicated *volk* (people), finally united under the wise leadership of the Führer. All the exchange students claimed that Hitler had saved Germany from chaos and Bolshevism. A "modest man of the people," Hitler was portrayed as virtually preordained to save his country. Elisabeth Noelle, studying at the University of Missouri and one of the most ardent and best-drilled Nazi propagandists among the exchange students, explained, "Hitler came neither from a military caste nor from the social elite, but he had worked his way up from a poor mason [*sic*] to the highest political position."[8]

The exchange students lauded the Nazis' version of "democracy." Ilse Wiegand, hosted by Barnard College, displayed an astonishingly self-contradictory naivety in an interview with the college newspaper when explaining the results of the March 5, 1933, election, which became a cornerstone of Hitler's dictatorship: "One half [of German voters] were for the communists, one half for Hitler. And then—we all decided for Hitler. There was so much enthusiasm that no education of the lower classes was necessary. We all trust in him because he does what is best for the whole nation." German refugees, Wiegand confidently explained, simply had ideas "different from ours and so they left."[9]

Regarding freedom of speech, Elisabeth Noelle explained that Germans also enjoyed this liberty, within reason. For instance, Germans were not allowed to hold "regular meetings" to listen to hateful, propagandistic radio broadcasts, if the purpose was "obviously to spread communist propaganda."[10]

Liselott Traun-Strecker, studying at Vassar College, explained that when it came to press freedom in Germany, anyone could buy the major foreign newspapers from public newsstands and read letters from foreign friends abroad, provided they were "sincere letters."[11] The exchange students also occasionally pointed out that foreign visitors were always allowed to tour their country, as long as they behaved correctly. In a letter to IIE, Erwin Wickert, hosted by Dickinson College, in Pennsylvania, admitted that there might be a certain "supervision" of foreign professors in Germany—though he preferred the term "hospitality." In any case, Wickert believed this was justified, as foreign professors eager to write about the Third Reich only sought out "scandals, little failures of governmental institutions and so on."[12]

When pressed to elaborate on German "freedom," some exchange students eventually admitted that real freedom did not exist, but then enumerated reasons why the people were better off without it. Ilse Dunst, who probably caused ulcers among German officials in the United States,[13] admitted to a reporter from the *Barnard Bulletin* that Germans had knowingly exchanged liberty for national concord. Since younger Germans were unaware of personal liberty in the American sense, she explained, they did not miss it. Exacerbating the impact of her earlier comments, Dunst wrote a letter to the paper's editor a month later, claiming that Germans did have the right to criticize their government, as long as it was "constructive" criticism.[14] In the spring of 1939, Peter Brix, studying at the University of Rochester, similarly admitted that Germans lacked some of the liberties enjoyed by Americans. Brix's peculiar rationale was that greater restrictions on individual freedom were necessitated by "the crowded conditions of her peoples."[15]

American audiences frequently asked about the German state's treatment of Jews. Typically, the students responded by claiming that the few instances of Jewish mistreatment in Germany had been dramatically exaggerated by Jewish Americans and German refugees.[16] Elisabeth Noelle asserted that the Jewish-owned media in the United States was so biased and distorted that the American claim of "freedom of the press" had no real meaning.[17] It was widely known, she claimed, that no Jews worked in Germany's media organizations, which she argued was justified because, during the Weimar period, Jews had so dominated the German media that they "endangered German cultural life and national unity."[18]

The German exchange students sometimes produced their own "media scandals" when discussing Jews in their lectures. Dietrich Zwicker reportedly said in a lecture, "If the Jewish question continues to be raised in American newspapers, there will be real barbarism toward the race in Germany." He later claimed that his remark was picked up by a "Jewish reporter" from the local *St. Joseph Gazette*, who interviewed him and then distorted his responses to create a scandal. The incident attracted enough attention that Stephan Duggan, IIE director, investigated the matter. Zwicker explained that he had been discussing Jewish Germans, not Jewish Americans. Given this, he complained, he could not see how the interviewer, "Mr. Jacobs, as a Jew, could find anything offensive in these statements, or, could even pretend that I attacked the Jews in this country!"[19] Zwicker faced few consequences for his overt antisemitism; the chancellor of the University of Kansas merely requested that he stop giving speeches.[20]

It appears that some of the exchange students realized sooner or later that the official party line did not impress Americans. Thus, a number of them sought to adapt their responses to questions more creatively. In one example, Henning von Dobeneck, at the University of Massachusetts, Amherst, claimed that Hitler actually sought to eliminate antisemitism, not inflame it. By excluding Jews from the German nation, the Führer had eliminated the racial tensions that gave rise to antisemitism in the first place and "rendered invaluable service to the Jewish race as a nation."[21] Portraying himself as an objective observer willing to call out Nazi falsehoods when he recognized them, von Dobeneck ridiculed those in Germany who claimed that the United States was ruled by Jews.[22]

In a fall 1933 interview, Gerhardt Paul, studying at the University of Georgia, implicitly admitted that there had been some atrocities in Germany. Paul then asked, however, why Americans weren't equally concerned about the persecution of the Catholic Church in the Spanish Republic or, for that matter, the "murders of Nazis" in Germany before 1933.[23] Other students cited the relatively small percentage of Jews among the German population in inane attempts to argue that their fate therefore did not matter within the broader context of the German people. At Columbia University, Detlef Sahm articulated this in particularly absurd terms: since Jews made up only 1 percent of the German population, they deserved only 1 percent of his time for discussion.[24] In June 1936, Dietrich Zwicker used the same excuse when addressing a German-American singing society. Finally, a few students made an argument that must have hit home: Jews were also mistreated throughout the United States, and in the South, African Americans were treated even worse.[25]

Other students sought to preempt uncomfortable topics by emphasizing what they regarded as the more positive aspects of life under the Nazis, such as the Nazi version of community "socialism." Paul Freiling, at Bethany College, was proud that German university students were expected to work in the mines or factories alongside their working-class comrades.[26] Ernst Wilhelm Foerster, studying at Williams College, had worked on a farm and in a factory, where he learned what "socialism" truly meant: Everyone in the national community was equal. If this equality didn't appear obvious, it was due to the harsh working conditions, as he had personally witnessed. With wages barely sufficient for survival, he understood wage laborers' bitterness.[27] Marianne Lautsch, studying at Oberlin College, found her volunteer social work in Germany to be a liberating experience.[28] Helga Prym-von Becherer, a Middlebury student, asserted that the German labor service was "intended to remove social barriers" allowing "telephone girls" to work in the fields or farmers' kitchens alongside peasants and college students. In so doing, she imagined, "They lost all class prejudice."[29] At Vassar, Liselott Traun-Strecker waxed lyrical about the community service required by German colleges, such as making clothes for the poor or lecturing impoverished families on the importance of self-improvement. In this way, she explained, the college elite remedied their "alienation" from the masses; they abjured "study for study's sake" in favor of applying their newfound knowledge to community betterment, as "an inseparable part of all studies."[30]

It is possible that the German students' interpretation of this *Volksgemeinschaft* (national community), more pronounced than in most descriptions of Nazism, reflected a certain idealism on their part. These students largely came from upper-middle-classes families and were interested in interacting with people from different backgrounds and perspectives, as evidenced by their participation in an international exchange program. It was convenient for them to assign meaning to Nazism according to their own predilections, suggesting that "Nazis" could have differing, preexisting value systems that, at least theoretically, were separable from Nazi ideology.

Propaganda, Cultural Misunderstandings, and Shifting Perspectives

Given Americans' increasing antipathy towards Nazism, complaints about the German students' propaganda efforts inexorably intensified. One college administrator complained that the German students at his school had "either openly or furtively spread antisemitic and pro-Nazi propaganda. It is as if the exchange were being used to send Nazi agitators to this country."[31] Another wrote, "We have been subjected for the past several years to a good deal of embarrassment by the apparent inability of these young Germans to avoid public expression of pro-Nazi opinions of one kind and [sic] another." Similar examples abound.[32] The increasing numbers of complaints about propaganda led Duggan to send a letter to all the German exchange students in mid-February 1938 warning them that any propagandizing would be dealt with harshly.

As the chorus of complaints became ever louder, Duggan launched an ostensibly comprehensive investigation of the problem. He sent a circular letter to all the host colleges and universities, requesting that a responsible administrator inform him whether propagandizing by German students was an issue on their campus. After receiving sixty responses, he publicly declared that only five administrators perceived such a problem, while six others were unsure.[33] The vast majority allegedly did not regard the German students' statements as constituting "propaganda" per se. An FBI agent reviewing the replies in 1944, however, disagreed. He judged that at least half the schools had reported to what he called "quite marked" propaganda. Furthermore, many other schools had already dropped out of the exchange program due to disapproval of their Nazi-era German students, severely skewing Duggan's sample. In addition, for fear of adverse publicity, many colleges had been "anxious to dismiss or hush up" news of propaganda activities. Thus, the agent concluded, "It is clear that the German exchange students did carry on a substantial amount of propaganda in this country despite denials by IIE."[34]

With Berlin's dangerous foreign and domestic radicalism becoming increasingly apparent in US newspapers, requests for speaking appearances by German students multiplied. These engagements were dominated more by criticism of Germany's current government than any interest in traditional German culture. In 1938 Iowa State College informed IIE that the German exchange student there was "besieged to talk to various groups about conditions in Germany."[35] In January 1939 at the California Institute of Technology, a postdoctoral exchange student, Otto Schmauss, was shocked when more than 200 people attended his lecture, "The Nazi Party in Germany." He noted the "strong interest, even excitement, to learn what the Nazi at Caltech would say." In a letter written days before the outbreak of World War II, he complained that he had accepted so many invitations to speak that he hardly had time to sleep.[36] By then, some less cautious school administrators encouraged these public events, recognizing the deepening concern in the United States over Germany's actions. As one college president reported back to IIE, audiences wanted to hear "the Nazi side of the story."[37]

Surely, the German exchange students did not themselves believe all the claims they blithely offered to American audiences. Apparently they justified their obvious mendacity to themselves as the price they had to pay to participate in the exchange.[38] Some Germans realized that, if nothing else, life in Nazi Germany had taught them that dishonesty was the price for survival. Occasionally, an exchange student would send a letter to the United States containing sentiments out of line with Nazi dogma, yet include a sentence loudly endorsing the regime. For example, in Fritz Brandi's letter to the *Furman Hornet* emphasizing how much he missed the United States, he concluded it with "We are confident and loyal to our Fuehrer forever."[39] Americans relaying these letters to their college newspapers sometimes recognized such remarks as politically expedient means to avoid attracting suspicion as having been "Americanized," an increasingly dangerous crime in Nazi Germany.[40]

For some German students, the jarring contrast between what they knew and what they were compelled to say likely contributed to their reluctance to discuss German politics. Others remained silent on the subject, fully aware that the attention their propaganda brought them was anything but greater esteem.[41] Margrit Martin, at Carleton College, explained her reluctance to answer political questions: "I know no more about Hitler, what he thinks and what he does, than you people do about your president."[42] Another student told the *Mount Holyoke News* that she "didn't know or care a great deal" about either American or German politics, enigmatically adding, "Perhaps it is because I've seen too much and been asked far too many questions."[43] An article in the Bates College student newspaper about their 1938–39 German exchange student recommended that readers not "stop him on campus and start firing political questions at him. He won't be interested."[44] A significant number of students also displayed similar reserve.[45] By the late 1930s, some anxious host college administrators were often relieved by this behavior. The chairman of Harvard's Committee on Graduate Studies, T. R. Powell, commented that the German exchange student Karl Arndt was "quiet and unassuming" and had "made a very favorable personal impression on all of us."[46] The president of Wesleyan University described Gerhard Hess as "admirable . . . quiet and retiring and very well-liked by our student body."[47] Anneliese von dem Hagen pleaded with her classmates not to ask her opinion of Hitler, as she had already answered this question many times, and it was difficult for her to respond.[48] It did not go unnoticed that a refusal to discuss German politics might signal disagreement with their country's policies, but in such cases, silence might be the better part of wisdom.[49]

Given the hundreds of German exchange students on American campuses during the Nazi era, a few documented cases show that they occasionally had an impact that DAAD had hoped for. Yet, rather than suggesting an attraction to National Socialism, such instances appeared to have had more to do with the students' personal charisma and American academics' general appreciation of traditional German and European culture than with any attraction to Nazism. For example, one faculty member at Duchesne College in Omaha considered Annemarie Closterhalfen "a very stimulating student to have in class, because, having had a broader cultural background than so many of our American girls, her comments and questions bring out points of view that would otherwise not be forthcoming." As a result, she "meant a great deal in the lives of our students to have these contacts with the greater world."[50] Herbert Beyer's efforts were described as "spreading much good will" toward Germany.[51] At Furman University, Fritz Brandi and Hella von Schwerin "increased student interest in the German language, literature and customs."[52] Most notably, at a December 1937 YMCA Hi-Y club presentation in Springfield, Ohio, Wittenberg College student Günter Müller appeared to interject what may have been disparaging remarks about Jews into an accordion recital. An attorney relaying the incident to Duggan wrote, "Quite a few boys in the audience were so impressed by [Müller's] personality and his address, that they all sought his autograph."[53] The most notable report, from Wheaton College in May 1938, complained to IIE that their last few German exchange students were

> adroit in fastening on susceptible members of the student body or of the staff of the college and persuading them that the American newspapers are all in the hands of Jews and do not give a truthful account of any of the affairs going on in Germany. Undoubtedly these influences has spread among a limited number of students and outside the college into its locality, but we do not look upon this influences as serious because the reaction of the average student to the propaganda of the German student is rather salutary [by rejecting such overtures].[54]

Some of the German students mistakenly got the impression that their American audiences were absorbing the "right" lessons from their propaganda.[55] These fantasies of success stemmed from their misunderstanding American culture, as well as to wishful thinking. In the spring of 1934, an American exchange student Homer Richey learned from various sources that the German students' efforts as "cultural ambassadors" to the United States had made little impact.[56] Among the dozens of accounts of public lectures and conversations involving German exchange students and Americans examined for this study, the only instances of possible propaganda successes are those just mentioned.

The Germans often mistook Americans' politeness for approval. Especially when interacting with a foreign visitor, Americans considered it good manners to show a certain deference toward visitors' views about their own country. It would have been natural for college students or audiences in the United States to tolerate an exchange student's beliefs, even if they thoroughly disagreed with the views expressed.[57] When it came to Germans, several other factors reinforced this tendency. Like other Americans, college students tended to be more critical of the German government than of the German people. An IIE-supported French academic touring colleges in the United States in 1936 noted, the college students' hostility towards a foreign power was nearly always aimed at the government or its leaders. The students felt that if "the masses" were led toward a catastrophe, it was the leaders alone who were responsible.[58] Similarly, a few months after the beginning of World War II in Europe, a poll found that 66 percent of Americans regarded the German people as "essentially peace-loving and kind," although prone to following aggressive leaders.[59] An American correspondent in Europe recalled an illustrative example of reactions to a German exchange student during the war. The former exchange student and friend,

> ["Heinrich"] lived in a fraternity house and the boys were crazy about him . . . Girls like Heinrich because of his manners. "Isn't he cute?" they say. . . .
>
> When a person thinks of the Reich in terms of a mustached, neurotic monster with no respect for men or God, it's easy to hate the Reich, it's easy to think—"Kill the dirty Germans." But when a person thinks of the German army in terms of thousands of bewildered Heinrichs, muddled by past teaching and present loyalties, hate becomes impossible.[60]

In short, American attitudes toward "old" Germany and its people remained relatively positive until 1945, when American soldiers discovered the concentration camps.

One German exchange student was struck by the willingness of his classmates to discuss diverse views in a relaxed and respectful manner.[61] This intellectual open-mindedness led many German exchange students to question the dogmatic orthodoxy they encountered at German universities. Likewise, Americans were eager to demonstrate the value of free speech, which is why one college president tolerated Eva Schröder's pro-German lectures despite their controversial content.[62]

During the Great Depression, many college students had more on their minds than the latest pronouncements of a foreign government as relayed by its exchange student representatives. Rather, American students knew that the closer they got to graduation, the sooner they would have to confront the disconcerting lack of professional jobs for which they were supposed to be preparing.[63] Facing the prospect of poverty did wonders for improving students' focus on their academic work, as opposed to catching up on the latest international news. In this context, Walter Lippman's advice to the American college student—to not let himself "be absorbed by distractions about which as a scholar he can do almost nothing"—must have seemed like wise advice indeed.[64] The educated public also expressed such concern. In a July 1931 *Harper's Magazine* article, "Why Don't Your Young Men Care?," Harold Laski lamented that American college students were just not concerned with politics.[65] Annoyed educators noted this phenomenon. One of Hubbard's correspondents at Brown University remarked that her students simply were not that interested in foreign affairs.[66] Even after the Anschluss, Germany's annexation of Austria, W. H. Freeman at the New Jersey State Teachers' College wrote to Duggan that the "current German [exchange student] girl seemed quite distressed that no one appeared very much interested in the German situation."[67] The growing visibility of isolationists by the end of the decade reinforced the notion that what went on in Germany was not America's problem.

On the other hand, the nearly obligatory social networking and image-making that accompanied college life did not avail itself to foreign political ideologies. Quite simply, fascism in any guise had nothing to do with American college student culture or aspirations. Bruno Wehner, an exchange student at Harvard, complained to Gerhard Gräfe, an employee of the Foreign Office of the German Student Union, that American college students showed little interest in his preachings on the glories of Nazism. Rather, their response was essentially, "Let's go get some ice cream and have a good time."[68] Helga Boursé, arriving at Muskingum College in 1938, encountered a similar environment. "Americans are just little children—always looking for a good time and seldom getting serious," she wrote. As evidence, she noted that her American "co-ed" peers were, overall, "so silly." She added, "They sit around and gab about their dates, who kissed who, and what ever became of Sadie.

Figure 3.4. American college students mocking Hitler and other dictators, Cornell University. *Cornellian* (yearbook), May 1939, n.p. Courtesy of Cornell University Archives.

Why don't they ever wise-up to themselves and think about something more worthwhile."[69]

Not everyone appreciated these observations by privileged young Germans in late adolescence. The editors of a local newspaper in Zanesville, Ohio, responded, "Germans should understand that Americans are not only dedicated to having a good time. If they [Germans] believe that Americans do not take their heritage of democracy and liberty and justice seriously, they should then sit down and carefully read a bit of authentic history."[70]

At that time, Hitler did not necessarily stand out among the world's dictators as being any more threatening than Mussolini, Stalin, Hirohito, or their other less newsworthy peers. As a result, it was not unusual for American college students to treat the Führer's histrionic speeches, self-importance, and Nazi pomposity as more amusing than dangerous.[71]

In 1939 at West Virginia University, the Phi Sigma Kappa fraternity held a "Hitler party," where fraternity brothers wore Hitler-themed costumes. German authorities learned of the event, and a German newspaper described it as "insolent, shameless and silly." Continuing the joke, the fraternity chapter sent a cable to Hitler, declaring, "West Virginia University students hereby sever relations with Germany, *prosit.*" The incident, reported by the Associated Collegiate Press, noted that "the humor that seems to make U.S. citizens less susceptible to hysteria and mass-ignorance" was apparently missing in Nazi Germany.[72] Not everyone's sense of humor regarding Nazism was in particularly good taste. The president of Springfield College in Ohio greeted the newly arrived German exchange student by clicking his heels, raising his arm in a Nazi salute, and barking, "Heil Hitler!"[73] At Middlebury College, while the American students may have liked the German exchange students as individuals, they laughed at the pro-Nazi views the German students espoused.[74]

Americans' Growing Disgust

As other scholars have emphasized, it would be a mistake to conclude that Nazism had no impact on American academics or the public. Yet disgust, not admiration, was their most frequent response, which intensified in the late 1930s.[75] The Nazi regime's internal radicalization and external aggression provoked ever sharper reactions from most Americans. Whatever admiration American students might have felt for their "cosmopolitan, savvy" German guests deteriorated into pity for their obtuseness or anger at their mendacity.[76] In late 1933, Otto H. F. Vollbehr, a German espionage agent and propagandist residing in the United States, wrote to his superior in Hamburg that Americans were increasingly hostile to Germany.[77] The historian Susan Pentlin has also stressed that the American public, including teachers of German, were generally negative toward Nazi Germany. In 1934 Friedrich Schönemann, a well-known German professor and propagandist frequently sent to the United States on various academic propaganda assignments, confirmed this, noting, "Americans are no longer friendly towards Germany. Since the National Socialist Revolution, we in America have had to reckon with a very bad, even openly hateful, and in any case always unfavorable opinion from the entire public opinion, from official America right through to the masses of the people."[78] In 1935 Ben Cherrington, a nationally known educator at the University of Denver, reported to IIE about his university's German exchange student, Hans Werner Kubitz, who, Cherrington noted, "has been quite successful and self-controlled in an environment extremely hostile to many of the convictions he holds sacred."[79]

Colleges dropped out of the German-American exchange in increasing numbers as the National Socialists transformed Germany and demonstrated increasing intolerance at home and belligerence abroad. In 1936 Tyler Dennett, president of Williams College, received national attention when he explained to the *New York Times* that he had withdrawn his college from the German-American exchange program because it was pointless to have German students come to Williams if they did not arrive with "an open mind." Dennett also snidely remarked that if his college needed anyone to give lessons about Nazism, there were numerous refugee German professors who would be happy to do so.[80] Ernst Wilhelm Foerster, the German exchange student at Williams at the time, described as a "dyed-in-the-wool Nazi," displayed an astonishing arrogance regarding Dennett's decision. He wrote letters to various college officials across the United States, urging them "not to pay attention to the statement of the president of a small provincial college." He also helped organize an informal student poll at Williams on the issue of continuing the German exchange program. Of those who responded, 71 percent wanted to keep the exchange going. Farnsworth Fowle, an editor at the Williams College student newspaper, told IIE that it likely was not the students' interest in the exchange program with Germany that they favored; rather, it was most likely "the reaction of an easy-going campus to Dr. Dennett's holier-then-thou attitude."

As if that were not enough, Foerster wrote a witheringly sarcastic article for *Sketch*, the student literary magazine at Williams. In "Youth in Danger," he claimed that the German students were taken aback to learn that their minds had been ruined by "seductive" Nazi propaganda, which had destroyed their critical faculties. As Nazi "propaganda machines," they wandered through the United States, blind and deaf, unable to appreciate real civilization, which was no longer possible in Germany.[81] Unsurprisingly, Fowle believed that Foerster's impertinent article and obnoxious letter-writing campaign had increased the number of students supporting Dennett's position.[82] One Williams professor told IIE, "Our student this year [Ernst-Wilhelm Foerster] has taken upon himself the role of a missionary and propagandist, and as a result has succeeded in isolating himself pretty completely."[83]

A growing number of Americans were becoming increasingly sensitive to disparagement of Jews, in both the United States and Germany. Responses to German exchange students' crude remarks about Jews occasionally reached a wider audience than the students may have wished. In the 1937 YMCA youth group incident, Günter Müller, an exchange student at Wittenberg College, informed his young audience that the Jews were doing quite well in Germany. As evidence, he offered, "Many of the delicatessen stores in Germany are still in the hands of Jews." As Rees Edgar Tulloss, Wittenberg College president, would later note, Müller admitted to a personal aversion to Jews, though he apparently attempted to avoid discussing his own antisemitic feelings and was generally uncomfortable with discussing the "Jewish question" insofar as possible. Müller's humiliating comments brought two fourteen-year-old Jewish boys in the audience to tears. When Henry Arnold, a Wittenberg College faculty member, learned of the incident, he asked an attorney, Benjamin Goldman, to bring the matter forcefully to the attention of IIE director Duggan. Goldman demanded Müller's expulsion from Wittenberg and his deportation to Germany. Indeed, given the antipathetic propaganda activities of the German exchange students, Goldman questioned the wisdom of maintaining the German-American exchange program at all.

The Anti-Defamation League was also notified of the incident. Richard Gutstadt, the league's director, appealed to a non-Jewish friend, the prominent educator Alvin Johnson, to intervene. Gutstadt argued that Duggan might note that Gentiles as well as Jews were growing tired of the German exchange students' propaganda. In his ensuing letter, Johnson acknowledged that while antisemitic propaganda from a few exchange students might not seem like a direct threat to American tolerance, their antisemitic rhetoric was harmful to American institutions. Duggan promised "drastic action" to resolve the situation involving Müller and pledged to investigate the broader problem of German exchange student propaganda. Duggan stressed that the exchange students would be taught once and for all that Jews were not "second class citizens" in the United States and that "all citizens are alike."

The Müller episode began to die down after Wittenberg president Tulloss determined that the root of the problem stemmed from Müller's poor ability to speak English. According to Tullos, Müller had not meant to say he "wouldn't touch a Jew," but "he did not wish to touch upon the Jewish problem." Despite this clarification, Tulloss recognized that Müller was deeply antisemitic. In a letter to Duggan, Tulloss claimed the incident had been exaggerated due to Jewish families' "oversensitivity" to racial insults.[84]

Ilse Wiegand's 1937 interview in the *Barnard Bulletin* exemplified the sharpening, fierce backlash at American colleges against the German exchange students' apologies for Nazism. One of Wiegand's classmates responded to her interview with withering criticism:

> Miss Wiegand is here in America as the guest of Barnard College and is therefore in a sense the guest of the Barnard student body, which to our pride, is made up of students of many nations, faiths and races, living and working to-

gether in the spirit of mutual toleration and respect. It seems to me that the duty of a guest in such an environment is to adjust herself to its spirit as fully as she can. Ideally she should avoid expressing herself in such a way as to offend personally any member of the group which is her collective host. It seems to me that it is quite possible to accept this concession to courtesy without in any way limiting one's freedom to express political opinions.[85]

Likewise, in early 1936, Henning von Dobeneck delivered the lecture "Germany Today" at his host school, the University of Massachusetts. As one would expect, his presentation was an apology for Hitler's regime. Von Dobeneck's remarks sparked an eruption of anti-Nazi sentiment, with critics writing to the *Massachusetts Collegian* to express their outrage. One student, Nicholas Jacobson, believed the dictator was using Jewish Germans as scapegoats for the country's problems when the real culprit was militarism. Jewish Germans were fully assimilated into German society, Jacobson asserted, and considered themselves German above all else. Such a population could not possibly have committed the crimes the Nazis attributed to them. Furthermore, Hitler's dictatorship employed all the techniques of repressive governments to crush opposition. Jacobson believed he had recognized the root issue: "The greatest of peoples can be duped, misled and horribly victimized by unscrupulous leaders who are able to . . . profit when catastrophe and hopelessness overtake the nation." This even extended to the "intellectual classes," who prostrated themselves before "the hysterical and unreasonable claims of a ruling clique" controlling the nation's destiny.[86] Another student was equally adamant, calling the exchange students' propaganda "exceedingly absurd." Like Jacobson, he blamed the Nazis for transforming "a great nation of otherwise reasonable people into a nation temporarily insane with fear, hatred, and suspicion."[87]

Germany's increasing bellicosity during the second half of the 1930s worsened the reception of its exchange students in the United States. By 1937 a Gallup poll reported that 58 percent of Americans were convinced that Nazism posed a threat to the United States. Three-fourths of those surveyed thought Hitler was prepared to risk another European war to achieve his expansionist goals.[88] After the German occupation of Austria in March 1938, the tolerance for German exchange students in the American academic world dwindled. Fritz Brandi, in a letter to the *Furman Hornet*, extolled the unification of Germany and Austria, praising, the "legally and constitutionally held plebiscite" as evidence of the "the free and unanimous will of the Austrian as well as the German people."[89] A former classmate, Bernie Fischer, fired back, condemning Brandi's claim. Fischer said the principles Brandi cited had nothing to do with what had happened to Austria. He described the invasion as "a ruthless repudiation of human rights," pointing out that civil liberties were being rapidly extinguished in Austria just as they had been in Germany five years earlier.[90]

Students at the University of Vermont viewed Eva Schröder as a surrogate for the German government. That same month, following Germany's annexation of Austria, a student sent her a dead mouse along with a note that read, "'Deutschland über Alles.' The Austrian problem is solved. Austria is dead. Let this be a lesson to all who oppose international Nazism. Let this be a lesson to anyone who dared to think for himself. What nation will be next to have people's intelligence crucified on a swastika? Poland? Czechoslovakia?" The incident quickly reached a furious Wilhelm Burmeister.[91] Jane Daddow, a doctoral student at Brown University, informed Hubbard that anti-Nazi feelings had sharply risen among the student body since the Anschluss, whereas earlier, students had been quite passive toward Germany. Daddow warned that if the college were to accept another German exchange student, they would surely "have a difficult time" and could expect to be "forced into a good many unpleasant situations." Despite this, Daddow sympathized with the German exchange students: "It is rather hard on the person who wants to come here to study and learn about America to have to spend so much energy in defending and explaining in a hostile atmosphere."[92]

In some instances, college professors and administrators stopped trying to shield their German exchange students from the embarrassment of representing Nazi Germany. Marie Luise Habermann, the German exchange student at Wheaton College, in Massachusetts, was appalled when, during a chapel service, the college president condemned the "murderers who rule Germany." She immediately reported the remarks to DAAD.[93] In another case, Hans-Georg Baare-Schmidt, a German student at Colgate University, took a course on dictatorships and became incensed when the professor criticized the Nazis for abolishing civil liberties in Germany. The instructor denounced the actions of the Nazi government, calling them "the height of dishonesty and shamelessness." He went further, referring to Germany's leaders as "gangsters.[94] Details of this episode reached Berlin, further fueling Bürmeister's fury at both American academia and IIE.

In March 1939, Hans Grueninger, studying at De Pauw University, informed IIE, "There is a great amount of antagonism toward German exchanges at various universities. Even if [fraternity] chapters want to continue the exchange with German universities they have to overcome opposition on the part of faculty members, alumni, and university administration."[95] Shortly after that, the president of Oberlin College wrote to Duggan to explain that the school was dropping the exchange program, partly because "any German student sitting in our chapel, our lecture halls, in our classrooms will inevitably hear severe attacks on Nazism."[96]

American college students increasingly adopted a critical perspective towards Nazi brutality. The Auburn University school newspaper reported an incident involving an American exchange student studying at the University of Freiburg. He had watched a military parade but did not give the requisite Nazi salute. Having spotted this apparent disrespect, an SA squad severely beat him. In an editorial, the newspaper's editors contrasted this episode with one likely experienced by the German exchange student at Auburn. They quipped, "Amusing, isn't it? We can't imagine patriotic Americans jumping Rau some fine morning while he watched an ROTC parade. It's quite a contrast between American and German methods of treating visiting aliens."[97] At around the same time, in May 1938, one college president reported to IIE that American students were ever more convinced that debating Nazism with German exchange students was a waste of time.[98]

The rising anti-Nazism in the communities near colleges hosting German exchange students mirrored the growing tension felt by many on the campuses. In June 1938, Helene Wurlitzer, a wealthy contributor to the German-American exchange in Cincinnati, wrote to Duggan expressing concern about the environment that incoming German students might face in the fall. She hoped they would be "entering less hostile atmosphere than the outgoing ones have experienced."[99] Here hopes were futile. Cornelius W. Prettyman, head of the Department of German at Dickinson College, informed IIE that it was impossible to continue the student exchange program with Germany, not because of any misconduct by the German exchange students, but due to "the hostile criticism which prevails against Germany at this time."[100] German students reciting their public presentations in their college communities could not avoid discussing the rising anti-Nazism among Americans.[101]

Charm Offensive, Attachment, and Fascination

The German exchange students failed in their goal of seducing Americans with the "charms" of Nazi Germany. In fact, if these encounters changed any minds, it was clearly those of the German students themselves. By the 1920s,

US college life was primed to captivate students from such bleak dictatorships as the Third Reich.[102] American undergraduates had created their own insulated world.[103] It centered on cultivating social networks, becoming campus leaders, exuding attractive personalities, gaining athletic renown, and achieving self-realization through clubs and organizations.[104] Fraternity parties, dances, pranks, romance, pseudo-intellectual conversations, and the broader "college experience" were integral to university life.[105] One perhaps slightly exaggerated estimate from the time suggested that college students devoted the vast majority of their time on such activities.[106] The lively atmosphere on US campuses, vastly more engaging and entertaining than any found in Germany, exposed the German students to American school loyalty, especially during sporting events, which played a key role in attracting alumni donations.[107] Altogether, the culture of American colleges encouraged German students to develop a sense of attachment to their host institutions, offering them an alternative, American anchor for their identity.

Unsurprisingly, the more German students exhibited the characteristics that tended to guarantee success in this environment, the more successful they became. American college officials overwhelmingly reported that their German students were popular, suggesting that DAAD had indeed selected charismatic and sociable students for the program. In particular, the students had an exceptional aptitude for making friends.[108] Kurt Naumann, for example, was reportedly "one of the best-known and best liked students in the group" at an intercollegiate conference. A Yale professor commented on Naumann, "As an exchange student, sent here both for purposes of study and to represent Germany, I do not see how a much finer choice could be made."[109]

In some cases, particularly at the small, less prestigious, and more isolated schools, the German students were met with almost incredible adulation. Annemarie Closterhalfen, studying at Duchesne College in Omaha, "has caused such a furor of interest among the girls that I sometimes wonder if we'll ever get them calmed down again . . . We can't say too much of the excellent impression this young lady is making here."[110] Another student was a hit at the Randolph-Macon College for Women, where she quickly adjusted, becoming helpful to both faculty and students. Her "charming personality" ensured that upon arrival, she was almost immediately elected to join a sorority. As a German instructor at the college remarked "We shall hardly know what to do without her."[111] At Colgate University, a German student "took the college by storm," enjoying "unprecedented popularity and adulation," yet remaining humble and "fine, frank and appreciative."[112] Georg von Lilienfeld, according to a dean at his school, was a "social lion."[113] Another exchange student "endeared himself" to everyone at Iowa State College," while elsewhere a male student was simply described as an "ace."[114]

Among the "charismatic" exchange students, the least dogmatic ones gained the most popularity. Ursula Dibbern exemplified "the best cultural German type, not at all politically aggressive."[115] Irmgard Rein was described as "a sweet child and the girls love her, everybody loves her." Although "an enthusiastic Nazi," Rein's refraining from proselytization seemed crucial to her appeal, a trait shared by all the most popular German students.[116] Albert Ickler, studying at Princeton Theological Seminary, was considered a "moderate Nazi," yet his social grace "in the end succeeded in persuading his American friends, who could not share his political views, that one can be a responsible and socially attractive human being, in spite of a National Socialistic outlook upon political and social life."[117] Other responses highlighted the German students' good manners, particularly their sense of humor, gentility, refinement, courtesy, and astuteness.[118] Overall, from the 1935–36 to the 1938–39 academic year, colleges reported generally positive assessments in about 90 percent of their replies to IIE.

As DAAD authorities had hoped, a student's physical attractiveness often played a significant role in their social success.[119] At IIE, Hubbard occasionally commented on the general attractiveness of the German students.[120] At times, a commentator might even highlight a student's sex appeal. Carl Scheve, a University of Denver student, told Hubbard that Hans Werner Kubitz "is so good looking that all the girls are anxious to meet him and at D. U. that means he will get along splendidly."[121] Similarly, the president of Clark University mentioned to Duggan that he had gotten to know "two attractive" female German exchange students.[122] Such remarks, regarding both male and female exchange students, were common.[123]

The intimate environment of American dormitory life captivated many of the German exchange students.[124] In the spring of 1938, one student reported to Hubbard that participating in American campus life had been his most rewarding experience in the United States. Interaction with dormmates often proved critical for early assimilation into American culture. For instance, one German student popular in his dormitory was praised for being particularly "open minded."[125] Many decades later, Werner von Rosenstiel recalled that "dorm life" was one of the key moments in his Americanization. His first experience with freedom of speech—during a heated debate at the University of Cincinnati over the New Deal—left a lasting impression. In a so-called bull session with his dormmates, one of the American students referred to Roosevelt as a "son of a bitch." Taken aback, von Rosenstiel remarked that in Germany, such a comment about Hitler would lead straight to a concentration camp. His dormmate replied, "You're in America now."[126]

Erika Mann, an ethnically half-Jewish refugee visiting her father, Thomas Mann, in Princeton, New Jersey, was present at a bull session at Princeton University when the German exchange student there remarked, "Hitler would be no good in America." The entire group, including the exchange student himself, found the idea of Hitler in America ludicrous.[127] Fritz Brandi spoke about how dorm life helped him acculturate to his host school.[128] The informal conviviality between students and professors delighted some of the German students.[129] For Edeltraut Proske, the liberating feeling of intimacy and close interactions she experienced at Mt. Holyoke—something she had never encountered in Germany—was why she raved about the sense of belonging she felt at her host school.[130]

Dances and parties frequently provided opportunities for the German students to immerse themselves in American social life and overcame national barriers, much as IIE had hoped. Theo Claussen recalled to friends back home that even during his passage to the United States, the male German students whiled away their time dancing and flirting with American girls.[131] Eike Dornbach wrote a humorous article for the *Rundbrief*, describing how he and his friends fought through a northern Illinois blizzard to attend a party, succeeding against all odds. They downed several whiskeys and danced the night away with apparent aplomb. "As far as how the rest of the night went, it's best not to report," Dornbach teased.[132] Gerhard Lenschow quipped in the *Rundbrief* that his host institution, Carlisle College, was a terrific place to meet girls (*Mädchenhändlerzentrale*).[133] Gustav Blanke made an impression at Miami University of Ohio when he paid particular attention to a female French exchange student at a school dance.[134] These romantic and social behaviors demonstrated not only a desire to bond with non-Germans, but also resulted in a notably large number of marriages to Americans.

German exchange students generally developed excellent relationships with other exchange students from adversarial countries. While this may have been intended to impress Americans with Germany's "peaceful, amicable intentions" toward its neighbors, in some cases the students' remarks suggest a genuinely cosmopolitan outlook. In a letter to Hubbard, Godber Godberson, studying at Cornell University, wrote, "I am awful [*sic*] proud because there are living in the [international] House [where he resided] people of all nations, races and minds." He eagerly added that he would soon participate in an internationally diverse racing rally held by Cornell fraternities; his team included a Chinese student, an English student, and a Jewish American student.[135] Similarly, reports highlighted the strong rapport between German and French exchange students.[136] For instance, the University of Rochester's student newspaper featured an article on the close friendship between the school's German and French exchange students. The French student, having developed a friendship with his German peer, remarked, "I certainly could not take an antagonistic attitude toward Germany."[137] In 1937 Duggan was impressed to find that a group of German, Italian, and French exchange students had become "the best of friends" and spent their holidays traveling together in the United States.[138]

Demonstrations of school loyalty, especially during sporting events, could sometimes be intense. One morning in 1936 at Dickinson College, Herbert Hörhager was disgusted to find "Beat Dickinson" scrawled in ugly green oil throughout his dormitory hallway. "Damned Gettysburgers!," he cursed, certain that students from neighboring Gettysburg College had snuck in overnight to spread such "infamous words" across the campus. This moment, he later reflected, made him realize that he had become a true "Dickinsonian."[139] At the subsequent football match, Hörhager felt the same pride in Dickinson's Red Devils as his American classmates did, enthusiastically joining them in singing the school anthem. When the Red Devils scored a touchdown, he screamed himself hoarse. His account, originally published in the *Rundbrief,* was later imprudently reprinted by the Association of Former German Students in America in its newsletter during the war years.[140]

Fritz Brandi also became aware of his intensifying attachment to his American host school during a football game. As a member of the Furman College band, Brandi regularly attended sporting events. During a November 1937 game, Furman finally took the lead, raising hopes that a long line of defeats at the hands of its rival might come to an end. Brandi remembered, "For the first time I was up there cheering and crying and going crazy."[141] His loyalty to Furman persisted even after his return to Germany. In one of many letters he wrote to the *Furman Hornet,* he enthused, "I greet you, Alma Mater, from far away Germany, with all my heart"[142] Several other German students hosted by fraternities, such as Gustav Blanke, found that the "Greek" organizations, much like sports, were vital bridges for their acculturation.

Some students took pride in their host institutions for various other reasons, ranging from aesthetic appreciation to general emotional attachment.

One student, for instance, proudly told her German peers that her host school, Connecticut College, "was the most beautiful women's college in the United States."[143] In December 1935, Irmgard Erhorn and her fellow exchange students traveled through the South en route to Florida, stopping at various colleges along the way to pick up other students. Later, when comparing the host schools they had seen, Erhorn expressed her attachment to Mount Holyoke, remarking, "I have the feeling that it is my college."[144]

With the common desire to "see America," a large contingent of the exchange students traveled throughout the United States and neighboring countries whenever possible, sometimes skipping classes for weeks at a time to do so. Students from Eastern schools often went west to California; some even ventured down to Mexico.[145] All the students of course encountered physical environments in the United States that did not exist in Germany. Their fascination with the landscape reflected their aesthetic and cultural values.[146] Wide open spaces, palm trees, and modernist architecture—signifiers of "exotic" spaces and places—proved as intoxicating as any of America's other charms. The exchange students of the Third Reich sang the praises of the American landscape, connecting it to the cultural values they believed it embodied. Ulrich Jetter, for example, was filled with an almost religious awe during a visit to the "magical" Carlsbad Caverns in New Mexico.[147] In other *Rundbrief* article, one writer extolled the Midwest:

[W]hy is the feeling of freedom here so pronounced that it can't be denied? . . . And isn't it wonderful when you feel so free that it pervades your imagination? Have you ever seen someone here who felt inferior? Doesn't everyone think that he's capable and could eventually "become someone"? Why is that? I'd almost say that a main reason is the nature of the country. If you walk along the railroad tracks here in the Midwest and see how straight, how relentlessly they lead into the distance, endlessly, until they lose themselves on the horizon, don't you rejoice inwardly over such vastness, such limitlessness. If you stand on the edge of a highway and see hundreds of cars rush by, don't you want to join them, follow the wild urge to go West, up and down hills, but always looking straight ahead, restless, unstoppable? It's the spirit of the savage, mighty steppe. It breaks through again and again, it grows between trees and gardens, blooms and withers. Isn't it liberating when you leave our [German] home, where everything is so jammed together, where not even a handful of soil remains unturned, to find a wilderness right next to a metropolis? And the cities themselves: in one place they build enormous, multimillion-dollar mansions, only to tear them down later; next to a sumptuous hotel lies an empty lot. Everything is an expression of haste, unrest, nomadism, detachment, and freedom.[148]

German exchange students began spending Christmas vacations in Florida during the final years of the Weimar Republic, and it became a tradition for many East Coast students. Each year, they tended to follow similar itineraries, spending Christmas on Miami Beach and then vacationing at a house rental or other accommodation in Naples, on the Gulf Coast.[149] In Florida, the German students tended to "run wild," acting more like American college students reveling in the freedom of a school break and less like steely representatives of Nazi Germany. The annual Florida pilgrimage provides a snapshot of the evolution of German students' attitudes toward their host countries after residing there for several months or more. The impressions they developed were not what the German authorities had in mind.

The exchange students most often hitchhiked to Florida, took buses or, for the most fortunate, caught rides with fellow German students or classmates.[150] It was not uncommon for several American students or others from other countries to tag along. Once reaching Florida, the students worked their way down the peninsula, visiting tourist sites where they could and inevitably finding themselves in humorous situations, especially given their bare-bones budgets.[151] Elisabeth Hühnlein recounted her Florida adventure in a sort of extended haiku: "Christmas Eve on Miami beach and dancing in Miami, swimming and motorboat rides in the Gulf of Mexico, eating grapefruits and oranges until one feels sick, Indians, coconuts, palm trees, rattlesnakes, tarantulas, jungle, cactuses, motorboat rides on the Gulf of Mexico."[152] No wonder Helga Boursé, who initially ridiculed American, ultimately admitted that she was having "heaps of fun."[153]

Early attempts by DAAD to get the Florida vacations under control and infuse the students with proper Nazi enthusiasm led to rare instances of direct confrontation and rebelliousness against German authorities. This rebellion was driven by the clash between the exuberant experiences of freedom in America and the rigid Nazi conformity expected of them. As discussed in the previous chapter, the vacationing German students opposed Anton-Hermann Chroust, their putative "leader," in his efforts to press them into appropriate Nazi-like behaviors during a 1934 Christmas vacation in Florida. This stands as a striking example of Nazi authorities' frequently unsuccessful attempts to enforce their expectations on the students.

During Rettig's oversight of the German-American exchange, from late

1934 to spring 1939, German officials became more determined than ever to Nazify the Florida vacation. Henceforth, the focus of the trip was to be an estate in Naples owned by a Nazi sympathizer where they expected to force certain activities on the students, including propaganda refresher sessions led by von Gienanth.[154] Despite these efforts, the attempts failed to break some students' newfound nonconformity as they continued to "have a hell of a good time," as one of them put it.[155] Ursula Schäfer was so critical of the Nazi regime during the trip that Rettig canceled her stipend.[156] Furthermore, the students continued to use the holiday as an opportunity to candidly "compare notes." In the last year of the exchange, 1938–39, Gustav Blanke reported that at the Naples gathering, the students lamented DAAD's poor understanding of American public opinion and, more ominously, discussed their plans for when they returned to Germany. They imagined dedicating themselves to presenting a "truer" image of their host country to their compatriots. Some of the students apparently also considered their "options" if war in Europe broke out. Whatever possibilities they might have considered, after returning to school, Blanke, for one, launched frantic efforts to obtain asylum in the United States.[157]

In many instances, American school officials suspected that their exchange students might be having a bit too much "heaps of fun." In one typical example, IIE assistant director Edgar Fisher dryly remarked that Marie Luise Habermann, at Wheaton College, was "rather popular with the students, so perhaps she is making up in her social activities what she has failed to contribute in her academic work."[158] Lilian Stroebe, a professor at Vassar, irritably noted that the German exchange students had been more interested in having a good time than in explaining the political acts of their government back home.[159]

Some of the German students found themselves attracted to other aspects of American college life. Margrit Martin gloried in the freedom she experienced at Carleton College in 1937: "Freedom from duty, it is wonderful! At home everything is duty, all your life, and here, why you have fun while you are in school, it's the first time I've ever heard that." She especially appreciated the American educational concept of elective subjects, "of everything being up to you, and your own business." If this were not sufficiently alarming, she crossed into rank heresy by asserting that "although we admire Hitler himself very much, there are a lot of things done by the government that we do not like." This attitude, she added, was particularly the case among the older generation.[160] Another German student extolled the sense of liberty she felt in the United States, where "everything is an expression of oneself."[161]

The *Heimatrundbrief deutscher Austauschstudenten in den U.S.A.*, edited by Erwin Wickert, Herbert Hörhager, and Werner Seydlitz, was composed during the war and circulated to former exchange students who had studied in the United States from 1935 to 1938. It featured a mix of new and reprinted articles from the *Rundbriefs* from those years. The *Heimatrundbrief* exuded a distinctly melancholy tone. One of the reprinted articles, by Heiner Häring, described an American friends' disenchantment with his own government. The subtext was quite obvious—Americans cherished exercising free speech, unlike in the Third Reich, where the concept did not exist.[162] In a similar use of rhetorical subtlety, Kurt Weege, who studied the American penal system during his exchange year, reported in a *Rundbrief* article that criminal justice in the United States employed education to reduce recidivism, unlike in Germany, which focused on punishment. Viewed in a broader context, Weege deduced that criminal justice reflected differences in national character and ideology.[163] These were bold observations for German exchange students to publicly articulate in the Burmeister-Rettig era.

Years later, several of the exchange student refugees pointed to their college libraries as the places that ultimately challenged their worldview. Exposure to American newspapers as well as books banned in Germany revealed a reality that the German media and government cynically denied. Gustav Blanke developed a special relationship with the German refugee librarian at Miami University of Ohio, who introduced Blanke to new works published by German exiles, including Paul Tillich. Blanke was especially impressed by Tillich's denunciation of Kristallnacht and "German Christians" as well as his support of Confessional Church leaders Dietrich Bonhoeffer and Martin Niemöller.[164] One of Blanke's professors also sought to enlighten him, referring him to numerous articles in the *New Republic* about the terrible experiences refugees from Nazi Germany had suffered.[165] These works profoundly shook Blanke's worldview. He confided in Hubbard that the longer the German students were allowed to stay in the United States, the better. In his view, the German student in America was "turned in upon himself and his nationality," and more time in the United States meant he had "longer to face the outside world objectively and sympathetically."[166] Repeating the sentiments he had expressed in Florida, Blanke reaffirmed to one of his professors his determination to "explain the real America" to the German people.[167] Werner von Rosenstiel reported a somewhat similar experience. He was astonished by the differences between American and German media accounts of events in his homeland. The more humane American perspectives made him more aware than ever that the United States was "very, very different" from Germany.[168] These students experienced a perceptual reversal—from that of a German Nazi looking at American society to a German in the United States looking at Nazi society—and what they saw was not pleasant.

Ethnic and Material Wealth

For some of the German students, interactions with various demographic groups in the United States began to erode their Nazi perspectives. The ethnic, religious, and ideological diversity of the country fascinated them.[169] The concept of ethnic tolerance, nonexistent in Nazi Germany, influenced some of the German students' attitudes toward the Jews with whom they encountered. In general, the students condemned Jews in the abstract far more often than they did individual Jews with whom they had personal contact. Many of the German students combined ideologically driven antisemitic remarks with polite behavior toward Jewish Americans or Jewish German exiles. A German exchange student from Leipzig studying at Princeton casually socialized with Erika Mann, for instance, despite it being widely known that she was ethnically half-Jewish and a refugee. On one occasion, Mann mentioned Erwin Panofsky, the renowned Jewish German art historian who mentored Horst Janson while both lived in Germany and later in the United States. At the time, Panofsky was teaching at the nearby Princeton Institute for Advanced Study. The Leipzig exchange student "quite quietly and mechanically" stated, "'Panovsky is a Jew,' with a complacent little bow like a schoolboy who knows he's given the right answer."[170] When the discussion became a bit heated, the Leipzig student made clear that the misfortunes of Jewish Germans were not his concern.

On another occasion, when Mann met the exchange student for a "date," they chatted about her father, Thomas Mann, the Nobel Prize–winning author also at Princeton University at this time. She felt compelled to compare her father's brilliance with Hitler's intellectual poverty. The Leipziger conceded that Thomas Mann was indeed a brilliant writer but found Erika's comparison to Hitler amusing. He then sarcastically added that her father had been a well-known liberal in Germany and that his political orientation had led to his exile after the Nazis took power. The student called Thomas Mann a "poor devil, to back the wrong horse like that." Mann shot back, "The race isn't over yet." Suddenly fearing the possible repercussions for her family in Germany due to this indiscretion, she added, "God grant it turns out well for Germany."[171]

In a more typical encounter, Elizabeth Noelle had begun a friendship with a University of Missouri classmate, Esther Priwer, until she learned that Priwer was Jewish. Thereafter, Noelle "was neither unfriendly nor friendly," restricting their conversations to pleasantries.[172] In 1938, The famous psychologist Carl Rogers commended the "almost friendly" behavior that his two German exchange student interns showed toward their Jewish colleagues. Rogers speculated that this behavior stemmed from their enthusiastic admiration for "American institutions." One of the two exchange students married an American woman during his internship.[173] Gerhard Goy, studying at Penn State, experienced a profound transformation while at a Quaker work camp dedicated to community projects and communal living. Goy roomed with a Jewish participant at the camp, but did not display the antisemitism camp authorities feared. His time with the Quakers gave Goy a new perspective on international friendship "which has little in common with Nazism," his advisor noted. The experience also instilled in him the desire to remain in the United States.[174]

While serving as an intern at a San Francisco hospital in 1938, Gerhard Brecher developed a friendly relationship with a Jewish German refugee. Brecher purportedly told him that Hitler was "dangerously obsessed with the idea that only he and nobody else is right."[175] In 1939 Gustav Blanke caught a ride while hitchhiking and during the ensuing conversation explained that he was a German exchange student. The driver wished him success in his American experience. As he was leaving, the driver revealed that he was Jewish.[176] This display of astounding tolerance, Blanke claimed, was the moment he realized that liberal American culture outshone that of his homeland. Godber Godberson reported to Hubbard that the Jewish students in his dormitory "are all my friends here in America."[177] Willi Soyez told the University of Rochester student newspaper that, regardless of the realities in Germany, he regarded all races as equal while in America.[178]

In several cases, such as with Janson and Panofsky, German students developed special relationships with Jewish mentors, while in others they had romantic relationships with Jewish students. Werner Boehr, studying at Bates College, dated a Jewish student while still representing Nazi Germany. In a conversation replete with irony, Bates College president Clifton Gray complained to Edgar Fisher of IIE that Boehr, while "brilliant," had "morals not at all to be desired." The reason: Boehr had dated the daughter of the local Jewish rabbi, a "negress," and (the presumably more suitable) president of the Bates Christian Association. Indeed, Gray kept a close eye on Boehr, watching for any overtly sexual behavior, with the implication that if such was found, he would be sent packing to Germany.[179] In an example of a familial relationship, Ulrich Pohlenz, studying at the University of Kansas, worked to save his Jewish brother-in-law by helping him escape Germany. These incidents occurred just months before the outbreak of World War II, at a time when the Nazification of the exchange program was at its most extreme.

While Hitler and his followers did not display the same violent hatred of blacks as they did toward Jews, the Nazis nevertheless denigrated people of African descent as the most "barbarous" race. The Nazis portrayed Jews as an existential threat due to their supposedly cunning plans to supplant Aryans as the dominant human race. Blacks were considered a threat because of what the Nazis saw as the decedent Western tendency to embrace the so-called primitive sensuality of African and African American cultures. According to Hitler, miscegenation was even worse, producing racially "bastard" children.[180]

Most of the German students who mentioned African Americans reported respectful, even admiring encounters. After World War II, Erwin Wickert wrote that while an exchange student at Dickinson College, he had developed a close friendship with Candler Lazenby, a black Quaker from Alabama who worked as a German teaching assistant. Wickert was ostensibly impressed by Lazenby's clear-eyed, peaceful yet determined ideas on fighting racism in the United States.[181] While Wickert may have made up some of his stories about his experiences in the United States, he did publish an essay supposedly written by Candler, "Some Contributions of the Negro to American Culture," in the *Rundbrief*.[182] Regardless of the actual details, such an article in a semi-official Reich newsletter was not exactly in line with the Third Reich's ideological precepts. Gustav Blanke had an encounter with blatant racism when he took a seat in the front row of one of his classes in Ohio. A student in the row behind Blanke told him that he had to move, because only African Americans were supposed to sit up front. Blanke pointed out that the student next to him was also white. The objecting student responded that the man was mixed race and thus considered African American. When Blanke next ran into the university president and was asked about his experiences thus far, he complained about the incident. At the next class session, the biracial student was sitting in a back row and smiled appreciatively at Blanke.[183]

Some of the exchange students showed a special interest in African American religion, with several attending church services. On a lark, Eugen Lahr gave a speech at an African American Church in Harlem one midnight during a New York City gathering of students, around Thanksgiving.[184] Ilse Woessner wrote an article in the *Rundbrief,* "Black Memories," about her visit to an African American church in Cincinnati. The minister who welcomed her, she wrote, had, "black, wise eyes in an ivory face, surround by snow white hair. A curious, warm cordiality suffused his whole being." She found the parishioners friendly, curious about her, and respectful, though she also mentioned the stereotypical "childlike naiveté" of the congregation.[185]

The exchange students sometimes made appreciative references to African American music. At Springfield College, in Ohio, Theo Claussen sought to join a black choir.[186] In 1939 Helga Prym-von Becherer extolled "the great pleasure" of meeting Roland Hayes, an African American classical singer who years before had experienced both racism and admiration during a tour in Germany.[187] Erwin Wicket praised African American slave ballads, stating, "Even a European can be moved by their simple, pretty melodies and ornate words."[188] On the whole, these and other statements of encounters with African Americans showed a greater degree of respect than one might expect from many white Americans at the time.[189]

The egalitarianism that some German exchange students observed in the United States surprised them.[190] Fritz Hubertus Scheibe marveled at the Americans' ability to forge a common culture from the great variety of racial, religious, and regional differences that characterize the country.[191] Another student reported to his university's Foreign Affairs Office the heretical notion that although Americans remained separate in ethnicity, they had built a collectively beneficial life together based on mutual respect and the recognition of the value of different cultural traditions.[192]

Naturally, the German exchange students wrote extensively about their perceptions of American society and culture. They were particularly struck by the natural wealth of the United States, the consumerist ethos of the culture, the fast-paced modernity of its cities, and the overall friendliness, warmth, and hospitality of Americans. Although the students were, of course, aware of the possible unpleasant consequences of openly praising the wonders of US democracy, admiration of American open-mindedness and personal freedoms was nonetheless a fairly frequent occurrence. For a minority of the students, the revelations they experienced about the United States permanently eroded their allegiance to Nazism, leading them to question their very identity.

Perhaps nothing struck the German students as much as the wealth of the United States. Either in admiration or with sarcastic irony, a number of the exchange students referred to the United States as "the land of limitless possibilities" (*das Land der unbegrenzten Möglichkeiten*), The phrase originates from the 1903 book by Ludwig Max Goldberger, a Jewish German economist. For the students, the ubiquity of car ownership was a common symbol of American material wealth.[193] To many of the them, the American automobile also represented freedom to travel and thus explore the seemingly endless expanse of the North American continent. For some, this translated, perhaps subconsciously, into an intoxicating sense of personal freedom that stood in direct contrast to the Nazi worldview.[194]

The German students usually attributed American wealth to the vast natural abundance of the continent-sized country. Because of the United States' geography and peaceful borders, it did not, unlike Germany, have to contend with threats from belligerent neighboring countries. In a report to the University of Jena's Foreign Affairs Office, one exchange student concluded that Americans must be the luckiest people on earth, given their geographical location, with friendly countries north and south, and two vast oceans to the east and west. This freed them from the geopolitical threats that Germany constantly faced. It was because of this "splendid isolation" that American students seemed so unconcerned about their country's geopolitical future.[195] Oskar Bezold, in a *Rundbrief* article, came away astonished by the plenteous country he had encountered: "Wow—America! A good God has poured into this country all the riches he had to give away . . . They do not know how rich they are or how rich they might become."[196] Among the students rather less favorably impressed, Bruno Wehner, at Harvard, sarcastically remarked that Americans could afford to pursue their insipid, carefree lives, given the natural abundance of their country and their luck, as he put it, "to sit atop the massive oil well that lay beneath American soil." He complained that being of such wealth, these people had blithely interpreted the Aryan race's supposedly desperate struggle for existence against the Jews as "cultural barbarism."[197]

Fritz Hubertus Scheibe believed that the wealth he observed in the United States derived from the nation's strong work ethic and persistent "frontier spirit." He was impressed by Americans' willingness to take on any job that offered itself, work long hours, but always remain cheerful. He also found Americans to be quite generous. Like Scheibe, many German students who developed a positive view of the United States noted Americans' friendly and upbeat character, even clearly hinting that Germans were much less so.[198] They remarked on Americans' readiness to help them in whatever way possible.[199] In sum, Scheibe wrote in the *Rundbrief*, "They are the best companions."

It would be misleading to claim that all German students integrated well into American collegiate life. Various German exchange students in the 1930s expressed some of the same critical reactions that exchange students today might feel toward a foreign country after living there for a while. The German students' negative stereotypes of Americans were often infused with the elitism typical of Germany's educated, cosmopolitan upper-middle class, the Bildungsbürgertum, as well as perhaps envy of American prosperity and the United States' natural resource wealth. The "anti-American contingent" of the German students viewed their American classmates as too provincial, lacking sufficient awareness of the world's serious problems (i.e., those that concerned Germany) and ignoring important "philosophical questions." Americans ostensibly spent their time in college not in pursuit of academic enrichment, but focused on having fun, socializing, climbing the popularity ladder, and perhaps meeting a future spouse. Erwin Wickert dredged up the usual stereotypes in his account of American college life, " 'American Way of Life' oder: Eine denkwürdige Teestunde" ("American Way of Life" or, a Memorable Teatime). He complained that "manly" subjects—such as world politics, science, history, and high culture—held no interest for American students. Rather, a college degree was seen as a sign of belonging to the economically privileged, and these "young scholars" swallowed the expensive education their parents paid for as if it were a distasteful medicine necessary to transform them into the next generation of the elite.[200] Several German students also claimed that many American women seemed to be in college solely to find a husband.[201]

Some of the German students pointed to the materialism of US culture as the cause of a variety of distasteful consequences.[202] Ursula Schäfer's comments on these matters were infused with "land-of-limitless-possibilities" jealousy. In her Rundbrief article, "Kleiner Triumph im grossen Amerika" (A Small Triumph in Big America), Schäfer scoffed at the other women attending her expensive, private host school, Smith College. They dressed in their winter finery, with hats perched daintily on the sides of their heads, and their clothes, much like Christmas trees, were decorated with accessories. They sat in class playing with the expensive trinkets overflowing from their purses. Only their exposed, unadorned arms and legs were "democratically equal." Such extravagant American vulgarly contrasted with the elegant simplicity of a German student such as Schäfer, who with her small pocketbook, unnoticed and unenvied, efficiently carried all that was needed for class.[203] She ridiculed the intersection of the "American dream" with American modernism. The

Figure 3.5. Erwin Wickert: A Dickinson College student and prolific writer who viewed the United States skeptically; later served as West German ambassador to Romania and China. *Microcosm* (yearbook), 1935–36, 161. Courtesy of Dickinson College Archives.

United States, to her, was a shallow, uniform consumer paradise lacking any sense of aesthetics: "American Frigidaires, houses stuffed with furnishings, and other marvels ordered from Sears and Roebuck, with free, incredibly speedy delivery." But where, she implied, was the beauty of European life? "How does it stand with the much-praised, time-honored elegance in other things? You'll be amazed when you look around."[204] Apparently she was unaware that Hitler was promising Germans similar material abundance—someday.[205] Given the disdain for American academic culture Schäfer expressed, it is ironic that she eventually became an American citizen herself. Some German students felt that material life in the United States was not always up to German standards. At Clark University, Angelika Sievers was upset that as a German girl, she did not find her dorm room "proper, clean, or friendly-looking."[206]

Wickert, in describing his adventures in the United States, adopted the persona of a Nazi anthropologist studying a benighted people. He proffered almost textbook imagery of Americans according to the Nazi ideology, presented through often lurid vignettes.[207] After visiting Chicago, perhaps second only to New York City in its popularity as the symbol of "crass American materialism," Wickert oddly described the city's beauty as only "skin deep, like that of so many American girls." While the "Gold Coast" shined along the lakeside, extreme poverty lie in full view just a few streets away.[208] He reportedly saw homeless Americans sleeping on cold pavement, covered only in newspapers for warmth. The sewage from an adjacent prison poured out nearby. He observed that the men behind their barred windows resembled animals; they slept, turned away, or looked fixedly at him as he walked by. During his Chicago odyssey, Wickert discovered one of the dangers inherent in US democracy—insidious, subversive, and revolutionary-minded elements allowed to propagate their ideas. He found "a swaggering ideological blowhard" haranguing a "ragtag crowd" of "grim, disillusioned men, chaff from all the lands of the Earth" with promises of a communist paradise. He observed that other "perversions," such as homosexuality, flourished in the conditions fostered by American freedom.[209]

Wickert and Martin Mohrdiek were aghast at Americans' attitude that time equals money.[210] While briefly working in New York, apparently after his exchange year, Wickert moved through his day at a civilized pace compared to the frenetic Americans who surrounded him. Each morning, as he sauntered from the subway station up to the street, New Yorkers, in a rush to get to work, hurried around him, cursing his slow pace. Walking the streets, he found every telephone booth occupied by men who, he speculated, were making business deals. The frantic tempo was contagious. Eventually, Wickert found himself imitating New Yorkers by rushing through lunch, although he had no reason to hurry. "No, slowly working or slowly doing anything—that's impossible in New York," he concluded.[211]

In what may have been a response to Wickert's portrayal of the United States, another exchange student, Ulrich Jetter, wrote that Europeans tended to view Americans as "always on the hunt for the dollar" because they had limited their visits to New York or Chicago. "This verdict," Jetter wrote, "owes its origin to those critics who attribute the undeniable productivity of this people to a moral defect." While American materialism could indeed degenerate into a naked greed for wealth, he saw more to it than that. American success, he argued, rested upon the people's practicality and freedom from the inhibitions of authority, tradition, and prejudice.[212]

One German student introduced a novel complaint: US culture was stiflingly uniform. He complained about the "standardization" of American schools, colleges, newspapers, magazines, radio, books, and advertising.[213] Astonishingly, he asserted that such bland cultural uniformity and standardization had no place in the German "national community."[214]

"Anti-Americans" emphasized that Europeans had developed a long, refined, and sophisticated culture over millennia, whereas Americans were seen as a raw, unsophisticated, and primordial amalgamation of peoples. For Georg von Lilienfeld, the sense of community prevalent in European culture was superior to American individualism. Nazis, in particular, viewed the Aryan German nation much like a family of blood relations (which, of course, the United States could never achieve, given the country's heterogeneous ethnic composition). Thus, von Lilienfeld explained, Germany was much more advanced in social welfare than the United States.[215]

Herbert Sonthoff offered his summation of the German students' views on American greatness: "Our American hosts seem to expect unconditional praise, so self-satisfied are they with their own political and social system. However, there isn't much in this country that deserves our total admiration and esteem. Too much confronts us that we could criticize, with, perhaps, an ironic smile."[216] The reader might not be surprised to learn that Sonthoff made desperate, and ultimately successful, efforts to obtain asylum in the United States a few years later.

Poor language skills represented another type of barrier to German students understanding or appreciating American culture. Exchange students lacking good English inevitably felt disoriented, although many became more adjusted as their grasp of the language improved.[217] Similarly, students alienated from their host culture were more likely to spend time with other Germans in their local community.[218] As their college mentors sometimes realized, these reactions may have stemmed from loneliness, homesickness, and insecurity. Because of this, exchange students who projected a disgruntled and antagonistic manner might not have been anti-American, per se, but instead suffered from culture shock.

Such seeming anti-Americanism might apply to the case of Eva Schröder. In 1938, with the radicalization of the German exchange program, the increasingly bitter reactions of some Americans toward the German students exacerbated the already palpable tensions between IIE and DAAD. Mary Jean Simpson, dean of women at the University of Vermont, complained to IIE that Schröder seemed to be more interested in propagandizing than in learning. She remained an outsider, Simpson continued, unable to acculturate to campus life or see the world from an American viewpoint. Schröder irritated her dormmates with her general intolerance and dismissive attitude toward the US news media, which she claimed was so biased and distorted in matters related to Germany and Japan—presumably because of Jewish influence—that the American claim of freedom of the press had no real meaning. She came across as arrogant and defensive, "even belligerent," when questioned about her views on Nazi Germany, and she "considered the faculty very stupid and uncooperative" because they didn't support her opinions. Overall, Schröder gave the impression of "having a chip on her shoulder" and thinking that she was "in a class all by herself." Simpson acknowledged, however, that such disagreeable behavior might actually have been a defense against loneliness or insecurity.[219] Duggan attempted to defuse this antagonistic episode by asking Simpson to consider the matter from the German students' perspective. He explained that "their position is an extremely difficult one," given "the strong anti-Nazi feeling almost everywhere" in the United States. The students were bombarded with criticism of their country and therefore tended to "be a little bit too aggressive," coming across as missionaries for Nazism.[220]

In contrast, the Americanophile German students praised the United States' exciting potential to forge a new future. In a 1938 article published in the DAAD journal *Geist der Zeit*, Heinz-Horst Schrey wrote, "Finding that the American type is different from the European does not give us permission to disparage the former." Rather, he insisted, American culture should be judged on its own merits, not as some poor reflection of a more refined Europe.[221]

Another student found Americans' "strong originality and naturalness" appealingly refreshing.[222] America was boundless and fluid, capable of being guided by the country's own propensities. Given its youthful culture, its tremendous resources, and its buoyant optimism, the United States was indeed "the land of the future, with unlimited possibilities." The American dream bound the people together and undergirded their national mentality. The power of this idea, with its leveling influence, made the common man in the United States the truest representative of this new form of democracy. With the right tools and a willingness to work hard, the United States had the glorious prospects that its people anticipated.[223]

Oskar Bezold regarded the typical American as a kind of noble savage, once again invoking a traditional European stereotype of Americans.[224] He saw the American male as "so boyishly strong, so impertinent and uneducated . . . sentimental, . . . so easy to excite, full of romantic longing, so simple and straightforward in his thinking," while also being naïve, carefree, remarkably hopeful for the future, and strikingly honest, kind, and generous. Yet not all was to be admired. Like so many other students, Bezold also found life in the United States too materialistic, blinkered, and superficial.[225]

Fritz Hubertus Scheibe in a *Rundbrief* article, predicted that American culture would lead the world to a more exciting modern age, free from the worn out, increasingly irrelevant, and destructive forces permeating Europe. For example, he strikingly denigrated the German academics who traveled through the United States, pompously disparaging American skyscrapers for lacking the harmonious proportions of classical buildings or disdaining the nation's intellectual heritage because it could not boast of producing great minds over the course of millennia, which lent such gravitas to the European intelligentsia.[226] Again using modernist architecture as a symbol of American culture, another German student lamented that young architects in the United States were forced to design poor imitations of Gothic or classical structures, all the while eagerly awaiting professional independence so that they could throw away these stale designs and plunge into modernism, their natural element.[227]

Overall, the German exchange students made a number of interesting points in contrasting American and German culture. In many cases, they viewed the United States from a European perspective, rather than a specifically German one; they regarded themselves as representatives of a Western European civilization stretching back to antiquity, rather than the more narrowly defined German kultur.[228] While in no way contradicting Nazi orthodoxy regarding northwestern European culture, it remains curious that a specifically German identity was not asserted in the passages above, nor in many others scattered throughout the sources. This may reflect a vestige of the broader perspectives of exchange program pedagogy, as well as remnants of an open-minded liberalism that had been temporarily suppressed in Germany's modern history.

The difference in personal freedom between the United States and Nazi Germany would have been glaringly obvious to anyone. Many of the exchange students appreciated the freedoms in the United States that Germany lacked. The contrived rationalizations taught to the exchange students before they left for the United States may have exacerbated this contrast and could have engendered resentment toward their own mendacious government. For many, there seems to have been a discomforting cognitive dissonance between what they expected (or were told to expect) and what they found. This dissonance often led those with any degree of open-mindedness to quietly begin questioning Nazi dogma.

For the majority of exchange students, it appears that their previous views of the United States changed substantially, if not profoundly. Gerald von Minden probably spoke for many in an interview with the *Dickinsonian*. When asked if he still held the same impression of the United States that he had back in Germany, von Minden replied, "decidedly no." He had imagined the United States as a combination of Sinclair Lewis's novels and Wild West movies. Now, he explained, "Practically all former impressions are gone because they were untrue."[229] Hella von Schwerin exulted in her exchange-year experience and promised Hubbard that when she returned home, she would tell her compatriots "what wonderful people I have met over here and that the Americans are not all gangsters, as so many Europeans believe!"[230] This general attitude was common in the students' letters to IIE.

Duggan knew that such self-questioning was occurring for many German exchange students, and this helped justify continuing the American-German exchange program even in the radicalized Rettig era. In trying to head off a nascent anti-German exchange committee at Cornell, Duggan explained that by the end of their exchange year, the students uniformly "speak with enthusiasm of their year in a college in the United States as one of the most happy and memorable of their lives." He thought there was no question that the exchange programs were like "lighthouses of information in a surrounding sea of ignorance and prejudice. And this is true also of Germany which I visited at length since the inauguration of the Nazi regime."[231] Many American faculty members and administrators agreed. They often noticed the German students' appreciation of freedom of speech and, in particular, Americans' ability to criticize their own government.[232] In a typical example, a February 1937 report by a Bryn Mawr administrator noted that their German exchange student, Erika Simon, had an "open quality of mind," which informed her study of "controversial issues."[233] The president of Wheaton College told IIE, "We comfort ourselves with the thought that the student [Marie Luise Habermann,] narrowly indoctrinated as she is, cannot go back to her homeland quite as one-sided in her views as she was when she came."[234] Another college president wrote to Duggan, "I have reason to believe, as a matter of fact, that the sojourn of these German students . . . considerably modifies their opinions and attitudes."[235] In another case, a dean at Wittenberg College reported that the German exchange student there was "giving evidence of catching something of our spirit."[236] A. B. Faust, in Cornell's German Department, told IIE, "I am sure the freedom that the German exchange students experience in the United States reacts at home on their return in a liberal direction."[237]

Their classmates also made conscious efforts to liberalize the German students in their midst. A dean at the University of Kansas, interviewed by the FBI regarding the credibility of Ulrich Pohlenz's pro-American sentiments, explained that Pohlenz was at the university courtesy of Delta Upsilon, and "the boys in the fraternity house worked on the German exchange students with that thought [changing the German students' Nazi beliefs] in mind."[238] Indeed, it was widely regarded that at least some of the German exchange students would become "Americanized" and thus might act as a force for the better.[239] Hans Borchers, the German Consul in New York, wrote to Berlin that one of Duggan's primary aims in the German-American exchange was to seduce the German students with Western liberalism. By extension, Duggan hoped that American exchange students in Germany would have a similar effect on the Germans there.[240]

Hubbard served somewhat as a mother figure to the German exchange students. It was not unusual for them to express their innermost feelings to her. She received many letters similar to Hella von Schwerin's: "In a way, I am glad and on the other hand I am terrible [sic] sorry to leave America! I love this beautiful, strange and big country and I like its people! I really spend till now, the most wonderful year in all my life over here! . . . And at home I am going to tell my friends what wonderful people I have met over here.[241] In a 1936 letter to Hubbard, another student said her stay in the United States had made he "open-eyed." She added that it seemed "good for all times to look with critical eyes at things, especially today in Germany!"[242] Ruth Dieffen-

Figure 3.6. Ruth Hubbard. Oversaw the US side of the German-American exchange; served as a mother figure to many German students. Rockefeller Archives Center, RG 4 (FA1288), acc. 2016:070, series 1, box 35, folder 284–286, Early IIE Photos, 1930s. Courtesy of the Institute of International Education.

bacher described her "love" and admiration of the United States, and fascination with its democratic institutions.[243] Another student wrote that year that he had become "deeply . . . attached" to these same institutions.[244] Godber Godberson found that he was "starting to fall in love . . . [with] America."

Marianne Lautsch's letters to Hubbard in 1935 make clear her sense of entrancement with the freedom she experienced in the United States. As she exultantly wrote, "I never before suspected that simply a tea for instance in an American home . . . could fill me with so many new ideas. I breathed deeply this new air!"[245] Several weeks later, she wrote cryptically to Hubbard: "There are many things about which I want to talk with you, and which cannot be written. It is not only about those business matters that I am anxious to see you, but much more about other things."[246]

Even exchange students at the very end of the 1930s experienced a transformation in their thinking. Mere days before Hitler precipitated World War II, Otto Schmauss, at Caltech, admitted that he had come to realize that other nations besides Germany had the right to pursue their own interests; likewise, there were other ideas that should be respected, especially when their condemnation was based on limited information.[247] Other students expressed similar sentiments.[248] A college administrator noted in the last days of the German-American exchange that as manifestations of liberal attitudes became increasingly dangerous for German students anticipating repatriation, their vocal enthusiasm for the Third Reich sometimes rang hollow.[249]

The psychological transformation experienced by some of the German exchange students can be summed up in a paragraph written by a student who had returned to Germany after the start of the war in Europe. Anna-Barbara Wojnowska explained to Hubbard the reasons she had acted so arrogantly while studying in the United States the previous year:

> When I look back, I clearly realize that that one year was the happiest of all my life. That will sound strange to someone who met me at the beginning of that year, and with that I come to the point I think is worthwhile to explain to you. If you should happen to meet the new student acting as I did, please, don't feel bad with him, but try to understand that his ways are a mere result of his helplessness in a stage of great changes inside himself, where all his ideas and viewpoints are turned upside down—especially if he comes over with such a fixed "Weltanschauung" as I did. It took me half a year until I was free from all prejudices, until I finally grasped the idea of America, and so fundamentally different from what I had ever heard of. It actually was as if I were entering a new world; it was the moment to begin to like America and grow to love it.[250]

Discussing the letter with Duggan, Hubbard noted, "This letter is proof again that Nazis are influenced in their thought while here and do seem to have some appreciation of America: it seems in a way also a justification for our having kept up the German exchange even through these bad Nazi years!"[251]

Conclusion

The lives of the exchange students in the United States show that German university students in the Nazi era were not simply hordes of fanatical ideologues. Rather, they were individuals shaped by personal experiences, often rooted in traditionally minded families, and instilled with an ethos that predated Nazism. While their reactions to life in the United States varied, it is evident that for most, excluding those chosen to engage in espionage and similar activities, prolonged contact with their American peers sapped some of the energy from their Nazi convictions. Many American values—such as individual liberties, multiethnic harmony, modernism, future-oriented optimism, and anti-militarism—along with the experience of college student life and the myriad, spectacular natural vistas of a continent-sized nation, proved more alluring than the uniform, stultifying, militaristic dictatorship from which they had come.

Pro-Nazism was hardly ensconced in American academia, so with a few exceptions, it would have been a rarity for any of the hundreds of professors who taught the exchange students to praise their steely Nazi enthusiasm. Rather, they were more likely to encourage the students' Americanization or express anger that some of the students' embarrassingly inane propaganda was negatively affecting their school's reputation. Simply put, Nazism had no place in the fundamental decency of American society.

CHAPTER FOUR

Disillusionment, Resistance, Refuge, and Opposition in Exile

> I called her [Irene Gotthelf's] attention to the tremendous amount of research done on testing the intelligence of different races, and that the results of those tests suggested that all races were equally intelligent. She became quite disturbed at such a comparison and seemed convinced that really Germans are a superior race. I suggested to Miss Gotthelf that she has to make a great many adjustments in her attitude if she intended to seek her future progress in this country.
>
> —*G. John Gregory, director, Boston Vocation Bureau*

Among the German exchange students in the 1930s, one might not expect even a moderate questioning of their Nazi convictions. After all, the Reich's selection process for the exchange program was ostensibly designed to identify students based, in part, on their fierce devotion to Nazism. Yet, given the numerous accounts of the German students who fought desperately to remain in the United States at the end of their year of study abroad, it strains credulity to suggest that Nazi fanaticism had fully subsumed the core perspectives of these students. This does not, however, imply that their reasons for wanting to stay—complex and varied as they may have been—were devoid of ideological confusion or doubt.

Some of the German exchange students who sought asylum managed to complete the paperwork and meet the residency requirements for naturalization. In all known cases, the former exchange students who found a way to remain in the United States, through numerous and varied means, eventually became citizens. A number of them claimed that they had opposed Nazism all along and had used the exchange program primarily as a means to escape Germany. While such moral conviction is commendable, it is also exceedingly convenient and not always verifiable. Others, however, experienced profound psychological transformation; their exposure to political and social life in the United States severely challenged, or even shattered, their enthusiasm for the "New Germany." In addition, several of the events that transpired in their homeland while they were abroad made it unlikely that their reception back home would be particularly festive.

As happens during all exchange programs, some of the German students developed strong romantic relationships with Americans during their study abroad. It appears that those who wished to remain in the United States were especially prone to falling in love with an American and in a great hurry to marry. Some of the most interesting refugee cases involved the students who returned to Germany only to have second thoughts about that decision. Reverse, or repatriation, culture shock is a well-documented phenomenon, and it is perhaps especially intense when one has studied in a democratic country only to return home to a dictatorship, and, in the Germans' case, a rapidly radicalizing one.

Young Germans gained prestige and recognition by being accepted into the exchange program, an achievement sometimes noted in the German press and by various other ways. Their arrival and time spent at their host school often attracted media attention, which might well make its way back to German authorities. Students who chose to seek refuge in the United States revealed more than a psychological transformation; in addition, they essentially announced to their acquaintances in the United States as well as family and friends at home that Nazi Germany was a place from which to escape, rather than one to which they wanted to eagerly return.

Undertaking the process of renouncing German citizenship carried significant risks: German authorities would undoubtedly be made aware of it, and becoming a would-be refugee likely invited surveillance by German Nazi Party members then in the United States. Having lived through the 1933 National Revolution and at least several months under the Nazis' tyrannical rule, most potential refugees would have known that their actions could bring unpleasant consequences to their families back home. Failing in their bid to obtain asylum almost certainly meant facing the consequences of their apostasy upon returning to Germany.

Well more than fifty of the exchange students endured the process of obtaining residency and succeeded in staying in the United States, or as in several cases, securing refuge in Britain or a South American country. Others sought to remain in the United States but for various reasons, usually failure

Disillusionment, Resistance, Refuge, and Opposition 129

to secure a residency visa, were unable to achieve this goal. The exchange students who did not return to Germany should thus be regarded among the Nazi regime's "opponents in exile." They publicly and unequivocally rejected Nazism, at great risk both to themselves and to their loved ones. Moreover, several denounced the regime in newspaper interviews or on speaking tours, further endangering themselves in their efforts to undermine support for Hitler in their adopted country.

Rationales to Remain

In the 1930s, only 26,000 Germans per year were allowed to emigrate to the United States. There was no discrete category for refugees as there is today. The waiting list for immigration was long, and the residency permit process was a bureaucratic nightmare. A plethora of official documents had to be presented to consular officials, most involving their own bureaucratic obstacles. Of course, obtaining such documents alerted German authorities of the intention to emigrate. The Nazis welcomed Jews and members of some other groups leaving the country, but not "Aryan" Germans, including students. Typically, prospective immigrants had to find an American to sponsor them financially, usually a relative already living in the United States, or have a guaranteed job waiting for them upon arrival. One also had to provide evidence of sufficient financial resources to buy a ticket for the transatlantic voyage. Transit visas might also be required.[1]

The veracity of the exchange students' explanations for how and why they distanced themselves from Nazism must be carefully weighed. For example, Erwin Wickert had considered himself a master storyteller while studying in the United States. In 2007 *Welt Online* published an interview with him in which he gave a detailed, but dubious account of his activities during the National Socialist era. He claimed that he had never gotten along with his father because the latter was a Nazi and "a convinced anti-Semite." His father supposedly pressured Wickert into joining the SA, and he reluctantly complied; he also "found out later" that his membership was never confirmed. As Wickert told it, his year in the United States taught him "not to generalize, to see both sides of a coin," and that "freedom is the highest good." After learning those fundamental truths, he became "disgusted" with Nazism and in various ways allegedly campaigned against antisemitism. Other students' explanations rang truer.[2]

After arriving in the United States in 1935, Fritz Bartz had told his mentor, Carl Sauer, that he had used the exchange to escape Germany because it was "changing in a way [he] did not like."[3] Sauer, himself a refugee, eventually helped Bartz obtain a research position at Stanford. Fritz Hubertus Scheibe cited the Nazis' obsessive militarization as the reason he sought to obtain a scholarship to the United States and never return home.[4] Some students, among them Ursula Schäfer, later asserted they could not tolerate the "regimentation" of their lives under the Nazis. In Schäfer's case, this was the reason she gave to US officials for her desire to emigrate by means of the exchange program. While at Smith College during her exchange year, however, she demonstrated far more ambivalence about Nazism than she would later claim. Schäfer told a dean at Smith that she "approves of much Hitler has done and disapproves of some." That said, her distaste for Nazism certainly grew during her first semester. Her harsh criticism of the regime during the 1936 Christmas vacation has already been mentioned. After learning about her comments, Rettig pressured her to sign an oath pledging loyalty to Hitler. When she refused, he revoked her DAAD scholarship and ordered her home. At this point, she decided to risk seeking asylum.[5] She applied for a Walter Loewy scholarship, which was designed to help "needy German students," presumably refugees, attend the University of California. German authorities learned of her application, of course, leaving her in further "disfavor with the party." Despite this, her student visa continued to renewed, presumably by the German consul, Fritz Wiedemann, who held that post from 1939 to 1941 and presumably opposed Hitler.

Occasionally, exchange students' parents purportedly played a big role in convincing their children to flee Germany through the exchange. Theodore von Laue went to the United States at the behest of his father, Nobel Prize–winning physicist Max von Laue, who did not want his son "growing up in a country run by gangsters."[6] Ursula Schäfer claimed that she had decided to emigrate while still in Germany, and her mother convinced her that the best way to realize her plan was to "pretend" that she had become a "convert" to National Socialism and act like "a Nazi fanatic." This would put her in good stead to be selected for the exchange program.[7]

Ina and Irene Gotthelf faced an entirely different problem. It was an open secret that under the Nazis' 1935 Nuremberg Laws, the sisters were classified as second-degree *Mischlinge* (one-quarter Jewish), a status that shaped the course of their lives until the end of the war. At IIE, Ruth Hubbard mentioned to the deputy director, Edgar Fisher, that the sisters were Jewish.[8] A December 20, 1941, FBI report described Ina as a "non-Aryan pro-Nazi," citing a June 30, 1940, letter from a "confidential informant" who described Ina as "the only

Disillusionment, Resistance, Refuge, and Opposition 131

Figure 4.1. Irene Gotthelf. Considered one-fourth Jewish, was fiercely loyal to Nazi Germany and engaged in covert operations in the United States; eventually returned home to Germany; sister of Ina Gotthelf. *Legenda* (yearbook), Wellesley College, 1935, 81. Public domain.

non-Aryan Nazi he knew."[9] One observer expressed curiosity at how Ina, despite her Jewish heritage, could find acceptance within German diplomatic circles.[10] Another letter writer speculated that "because she is non-Aryan she could have no future in Germany, hence stays in America."[11]

During World War II, both Gotthelf sisters were interned as enemy aliens. At one of Ina's parole hearings, the board described her as "half Jewish but a rabid Nazi."[12] At a subsequent hearing, in February 1944, the board rather gratuitously pressed her to elaborate on her Jewish ancestry. Ina explained that her grandmother, last name Rosen, had fled Ukraine for Germany during the Russian Revolution, but that all her identification records had been

Figure 4.2. Ina Gotthelf. Considered one-fourth Jewish, engaged in covert operations in the United States, but ultimately chose to remain in America; sister of Irene Gotthelf. *Legenda* (yearbook), Wellesley College, 1932, 64. Public domain.

destroyed.[13] The sisters' Mischlinge classification likely limited their career options in Germany, barring them from public or prominent roles, and possibly hindered their access to higher education.[14] As a result, their half-Jewish mother practically forced them to pursue their college education in the United States and, if possible, to remain there.[15]

Ina had already been immersed in the US educational system before the Nazi era. She attended St. Lawrence University in 1930, Wellesley College in 1931, and Radcliffe College in 1932. In 1934, prior to the Nuremburg Laws, DAAD awarded her an exchange slot to study at Tuft University's Fletcher School of Law and Diplomacy. After her exchange year, Ina returned to Germany and, despite her Jewish ancestry, served as an official hostess for Amer-

Disillusionment, Resistance, Refuge, and Opposition   133

ican VIPs at the 1936 Berlin Olympic Games.[16] By September 1936, both sisters had reentered the United States, Ina obtaining a quota visa for permanent residency from Raymond Geist, the US consul general in Berlin, and Irene arriving on a student visa to attend Wellesley. Irene initiated her naturalization process in December 1938, but delayed following through. Ina similarly began her citizenship application after returning to the United States, but had not completed it by the time of her arrest as an enemy alien on December 10, 1941.[17]

In the late 1930s, both sisters, especially Irene, had exhibited a pronounced dedication to Nazism, taking on various espionage and covert propaganda tasks, possibly as a show of loyalty to Germany. Irene proved most steadfast in her allegiance, though conflicting feelings surfaced. Before going to the United States, Irene had been a "very religious" Confessing Protestant, already hinting of some distance from Nazism.[18] Around 1939, while attending Boston University, she converted to Catholicism,[19] a path not exactly aligned with "working towards the Führer."[20] Following her conversion, she immersed herself in a Catholic academic milieu and sought religious counseling. Her confessor told the Alien Enemy Hearing Board, "Nationalism upset her inner peace and quiet."[21] Irene admitted to the board that although a staunch German patriot, she had reservations about the Reich's treatment of Jewish Germans and the activities of the SS.[22]

By the time of their internment hearings, the sisters' attitudes toward life in Nazi Germany had diverged markedly. Ina expressed a desire to remain in the United States and become a citizen, while Irene requested repatriation, asserting that it was her "duty" to return to Germany and "at least provide comfort" to her mother during the war.[23] She appeared to reconsider by late 1942, perhaps influenced by Ina's decision to stay. By 1944, however, she had resolved again to return to Germany, declaring herself a "loyal German [who] never intends to be anything else" and her hope of marrying someone "100 percent German."[24] She returned home, seemingly determined to prove her loyalty, despite the near certainty of Germany's defeat. Irene was among the last German nationals repatriated, departing on January 6, 1945.[25]

Ina, attempting to explain Irene's seemingly contradictory beliefs, compared them to her own experience of gradual disillusionment. She remarked at a rehearing:

> I went through a whole development. I think there are certain things which they did that were bad. I think the fact that I was away when it happened made

> me think it more ideal than it actually was, for each summer when I went back, I was disappointed . . . My sister is four years younger than I. It is very strange but at each period of our lives, we seem to go through the same development. She is at the stage of her development now that I was four years ago. We don't agree entirely now, but we will eventually.[26]

Ultimately, Ina recognized that the "benefits" of Nazism were illusory when compared to the freedoms, educational opportunities, and hospitality she experienced in the United States. She would spend the rest of her life as a Manhattan socialite.[27]

In contrast, some of the exchange students used evidence of their support for Jewish Germans either to prove they had been against the Nazis even before arriving in the United States, or as justification that they could not safely return Germany, and thus strengthening the legitimacy of their request for US residency. Later, as a naturalized American college professor, Ursula Schäfer claimed she had helped Jews escape Germany before going to the United States. No evidence supporting her assertion has been found. Before Anton-Hermann Chroust left for his year in the United States, he had been appointed student leader of the exchange students by Rudolf Hess, deputy Führer of the Nazi Party. All Chroust's actions during his subsequent leadership position in the United States suggested he was a fanatical Nazi. Yet, after getting into trouble with Kurt Von Tippelskirch, the purportedly non-Nazi consul general in Boston, Chroust seemed to have a change of heart, and long overstayed his student visa. He was later interned as an enemy alien during World War II. Only during his internment hearing did he recall that in 1934, while still living in Germany, he had been instrumental in helping a Jewish friend with his legal troubles; for that, he had been interrogated at Dachau.[28] Chroust would remain in the United States, eventually obtaining citizenship, and become a distinguished professor at Notre Dame University.

Horst Janson frequently mentioned his Jewish German mentor, the art historian Erwin Panofsky, as well as his Jewish American wife, as proof that he would make a good American.[29] Werner von Rosenstiel, an exchange student who went back to Germany and then returned to the United States in 1939, used letters to his American girlfriend—in which he expressed his "disgust and shame" over Kristallnacht—to avoid internment after the United States entered World War II in 1941.[30] Ulrich Pohlenz's claims of having helped his Jewish brother-in-law escape Germany are well documented.

Gertrude Achenbach, another refugee student, told colleagues after the war that she was a Jewish refugee and had received her citizenship papers in 1938. Although a heartwarming story, it is entirely untrue. She was an "Aryan" Evangelical Christian, remained a German citizen throughout the war, and only applied for US citizenship in 1945.[31]

Religious beliefs were sometimes used to explain opposition to Nazism. In the mid-1930s, Wilhelm Vauth, one of the exchange students at the Hartford Theological Seminary, made it clear that he had disagreed with Nazi religious policy even before his exchange year. Soon after his arrival at his host school, Vauth encouraged a classmate to read Karl Barth, Dietrich Bonhoeffer, and other leaders of the Confessing Church.[32] Chroust claimed at one of his internment hearings that his Catholic faith prevented him from "discriminating against any race, color, or creed," thus making allegiance to Nazism impossible. Indeed, he asserted that he had suffered persecution in Germany because of this stance.[33] Margildis Schlüter, from a prominent Catholic family, attended a Catholic college in the United States during her exchange year and made clear to the school's president that she was strongly anti-Nazi.[34]

As previously noted, Herbert Sonthoff had been expelled from the SS in 1934, in part because of his devotion to Catholicism. After completing his exchange year, he returned to Germany in July 1936 and applied to a doctoral program under the mentorship of economics and political science professor Jens Jessen, a member of the Mittwochsgesellschaft (Wednesday Club), an intellectual circle known to attract several anti-Nazi participants. Jessen was also obliquely linked to the circle surrounding Carl Friedrich Goerdeler and later became one of the victims of the July 20 purge, after the failed attempt on Hitler's life.[35] In addition, Sonthoff hoped to study with journalism professor Emil Dovifat, a Catholic anti-Nazi who had previously taught Elisabeth Noelle.

Unfortunately, the leader of the University of Berlin's National Socialist German Lecturers' League (NS-Dozentenbund) had been a member of Sonthoff's SS unit and remembered his apostasy. When he heard that Sonthoff was attempting to enroll in a doctoral program there, he informed the university authorities of Sonthoff's SS expulsion, which Sonthoff had neglected to mention in his application.[36] His request to enroll was denied.[37] Bernhard Harms, a colleague of Jessen and an acquaintance of Sonthoff, had also fallen into disfavor with the regime due to his efforts to protect Jewish colleagues. Still, Harms attempted to mollify the prorector at the University of Berlin, who had jurisdiction over the matter. Harms acknowledged that Sonthoff was guilty of an "inner untruthfulness, a Catholic mentality, astonishing immaturity, lack of education, and sophomoric ambition." Sonthoff had, however, promised to repent and reform his behavior and should therefore be given a chance to prove himself a changed man, Harms argued. The appeal failed.[38] Afterward, Sonthoff often claimed that he had rejected German academia because it lacked "freedom from intellectual imposition and restraint." It seems rather more likely that he left German academia because it rejected him because of the scandal surrounding his expulsion from the SS.[39]

Some of the exchange student refugees implicitly or explicitly argued that they should be allowed to remain in the United States due to their anti-Nazi activities in Germany prior to leaving for the United States. Ulrich Pohlenz maintained that he would make an excellent American citizen, given that he had been "persecuted for leading the opposition to the Nazi movement" while a "professor of sociology" at the University of Hamburg.[40] Ursula Schäfer later told American colleagues that she had participated in a "strike" against the Nazification of her university. The SA punished her, she claimed, by forcing her to run for three hours.[41] One might wonder how, with such a record, she was allowed to represent the Third Reich abroad, especially after a Gestapo investigation into her background. She neglected to mention her anti-Nazi heroics during an FBI interview to determine her eligibility to remain in the United States. Chroust, after deciding he wanted to remain, swore that he had always been a good Social Democrat at heart.[42] He also cited his family's anti-Nazism as evidence that he, too, had always been opposed to Nazism. His parents and his sister, all of whom had been professors in Germany, were lifelong liberals, for which they had been dismissed from their posts.[43]

Elisabeth Noelle asserted that she had joined the NSDStB Study Group for Women (Arbeitsgemeinschaft National Sozialistischer Studentinnen des NSDStB) only to obtain a scholarship to the United States; her position as a "cell leader" was allegedly an accident on the part of the authorities, whom she feared contradicting.[44] After the war, she described herself as something of an anti-Nazi rebel. In the spring of 1937, Adolf Wagner, gauleiter of Munich, visited her study group, expecting its members to fawn over him. Instead, a heated debate broke out between Wagner and Noelle. She asserted a different interpretation of some point in Nazi ideology that incensed him. He yelled at her, "Don't *you* have your own ideas!" His face flushed, he stormed from the meeting. Wagner apparently inquired about Noelle at the University of Munich, learned of her selection for the impending exchange, and in no uncertain terms ordered the head of Munich's AKA to pull the award. Her American sorority responded that if she could not come, the scholarship would

Disillusionment, Resistance, Refuge, and Opposition   137

lapse that year. Nevertheless, it was likely Noelle's friendship with the Führer that cooled Wagner's ardor to punish her.[45]

Fraught Returns and Limited Options

In other cases, the decision to seek asylum was not so much ideological as practical, for example, an event occurring after a student's arrival in the United States that made return to Germany hazardous. Chroust's "epiphany" that he wanted to remain in the United States was entirely self-serving. The irritation he had caused the Foreign Ministry and the Nazi Party certainly induced him to radically reimagine himself as a refugee in America, rather than a Nazi with a bright future ahead of him in Germany. Thus, in the spring of 1936, Chroust began his campaign to establish his pro-American, anti-Nazi credentials. Several months later, Ulrich von Gienanth, the SS-SD head of German exchange students in the United States, visited Chroust at Harvard and tried to talk him back into the fold. He was promised a job at the German Library of Information. Chroust warily declined the offer.[46] At that point, he was ordered to return to Germany without delay, or, it was implied, he could forget about a career in academia.[47] Chroust continued to delay his repatriation until his German passport was set to expire. Although he no longer had a justifiable reason to remain in the United States, in the end, the German consul general in Boston, von Tippelskirch, reluctantly renewed it, only doing so after a row with the Roscoe Pound, the pro-Nazi dean of the Harvard Law School, who promised that Chroust had no intention of returning to Germany but needed a valid passport to obtain permanent residency. The consul had been eager to rid the US-based German diplomatic corps of the constant embarrassment of Chroust's bizarre behavior.[48]

Chroust spent the next three years in limbo, hanging around Harvard with no job, no money, and no scholarly productivity. By the start of World War II, in September 1939, Herbert Scholz had replaced von Tippelskirch in Boston. Scholz informed Chroust that the Reich's patience was finally at an end; he could either return to Germany and join his military outfit or look forward to his forced repatriation and severe repercussions for his past behavior. According to Chroust, Scholz even suggested that his anti-Nazi actions could warrant the death penalty.[49] As one might expect, Scholz's letter got Chroust's attention. Wisely, instead of taking Scholz up on the offer, Chroust became a fervently patriotic American in all but his visa status.[50]

Erika Hanfstaengl also sought to remain in the United States for practical reasons: her prominent family fell out of favor back home. Her father, Eberhard Hanfstaengl, was director of the Nationalgalerie (Germany's National Gallery of Art). Ernst Hanfstaengl, her uncle, was a well-known Nazi associated with Hitler since the early 1920s, who then defected in 1937. Around the same time, Erika's father lost his job, ostensibly because of an imprudent interest in "degenerate art," which had attracted Goebbels' attention. Erika, then at Wheaton College, in Illinois, became "most anxious" to permanently remain in the United States.[51] She was ultimately unsuccessful, however, and returned to Germany to pursue an ultimately controversial career as an art appraiser due to her assistance in the "Nazi stolen art" program.

As noted, there were few means to legally enter the United States as a permanent resident in the 1930s and 1940s. Several exchange students managed to obtain residency without much trouble. One student had close relatives in the United States who helped her get an immigrant visa.[52] Since he had been born in Russia, Horst Janson was also eligible for one of the many unfilled immigration slots for Russians.[53] Most were not so lucky, however, and after their exchange year, they remained in the United States, citing dubious legal justifications while trying to bolster their pursuit of asylum through various strategies.

A surprising number of the exchange students wed Americans and used their marriage as the pretext to remain in the United States. In a letter to IIE's Ruth Hubbard, one of the exchange students noted in January 1939 how surprising it was that so many German students had fallen in love with Americans, but added, "It seems extraordinary how many are really doing something about it—I know of quite a few cases. It needs a great deal of courage to consider a thing like that in these days."[54] At least fourteen exchange students are known to have married Americans.[55] Surely, something more than romantic attachment got some of them to the altar. From the start of war in late 1939 until 1943, when the United States began rehearings for interned Germans, thus raising the possibility of their release (or parole, as officially termed), a group of exchange students seeking refuge made their way to the altar as brides and grooms.

After returning to the United States on the verge of the breakout of the Second World War, Sonthoff wrote in a letter to his friend Norbert Berger, "I can't imagine marrying here at present—an American girl, I mean, unless she had grown up in Europe."[56] Sonthoff apparently had second thoughts about his spousal requirements when the FBI began interning German nationals after Pearl Harbor. He married an American woman with no connections to Germany.[57] Anton Chroust married Elizabeth Redmond in March 1941. She

Disillusionment, Resistance, Refuge, and Opposition   139

had attended school in Germany for a time, and her family had strong and on-going German connections.[58] Once DAAD officials discovered Ulrich Pohlenz's efforts to help his Jewish brother-in-law escape Germany, they canceled his exchange scholarship.[59] Pohlenz held a German diplomatic passport, which the German government could revoke at any time, resulting in his immediate deportation. IIE helped him obtain a temporary student visa to postpone his return.[60] Pohlenz soon found himself in love with an American at Tulane University whom he barely knew; he married her several months after their first meeting. One witness suggested that Pohlenz's bride married him mainly because of his physical attractiveness.[61] His wife immediately applied for his permanent residency based on their marriage. Soon thereafter, Pohlenz left for California to continue his education, while his wife remained at Tulane. It is unclear whether they ever saw each other again.[62] Soon after Werner von Rosenstiel escaped Germany in 1939 and reentered the United States illegally, he married his American girlfriend from his student exchange days.[63] Horst Janson married his Jewish American girlfriend in 1941.[64]

Several of the student refugees claimed that after their exchange year, they had protected other refugees, or indeed the American people, from Nazi machinations. Sonthoff told the FBI that while working at the US Embassy in Berlin in 1939, von Gienanth and Heinrich Rocholl, both former exchange students then in the SD, had offered him money to steal documents on Jewish Germans who had emigrated to the United States.[65] Chroust reported to the Internment Board that he had told von Gienanth in 1936 that he would never work for him "or his people," adding that he had "declared war on the New Germany"; that he had shielded several German refugee students from Nazi agents in the late 1930s; and that he had applied to become a special agent with the FBI in August 1941, based on his knowledge of German espionage in the United States.[66] Former exchange students in the United States during the war but without permanent residency were particularly eager to enlist in the US Army to prove their loyalty to their prospective adopted country as well as denounce Germany in the harshest terms.[67]

Many students ultimately ran into bureaucratic or psychological obstacles that led them to relinquish hopes of asylum. Some returned to Germany out of fear for their families there if they remained in the United States.[68] Gustav Blanke went so far as to use his personal contacts to meet with a US senator from Wisconsin and plead for help. The war broke out amid his efforts, and an officer representing the German military, along with his secretary, paid Blanke a visit to give him a ticket for a Japanese steamship destined for Germany via the Pacific. Once at home, he was to immediately report for military duty. Blanke refused to accept the ticket, explaining that he had applied for US residency. The officer ordered the secretary not to record Blanke's comment and retorted, "This man knows what 'guilt by association' means, and he has two brothers at the front. Note only that I have given him the ticket. That's it. Heil Hitler!" After that unpleasant encounter, Blanke decided it would be best to return to Germany.[69]

In certain cases, it is unclear why a student opposed the Nazi regime, sought to remain in the United States, or in fact obtained residency. Their desire to remain was, nevertheless, manifest. In 1938 Martin Burmeister became desperate to obtain a visa to return to the United States. Hubbard suggested that he go to the US Consulate in Berlin and tell Consul General Geist, "confidentially, just what the situation is" and also proposed that he request a visitor's visa and try to find a job.[70] Another student told Hubbard that his greatest desire was to remain in the United States, but he was apparently willing to live anywhere else but Germany.[71]

There is no evidence that Gerhard Lüdtke necessarily sought to remain in the United States, but while at Colgate University during 1938–39 he became fiercely anti-Nazi and expressed his views even to other Germans. Lüdtke's oppositional comments became so frequent that his friends, as well as one of the professors, urged caution, telling him that if his remarks made it back to German authorities, he might regret it upon returning home. Lüdtke responded with a shrug, "as if to say that those were his views and there was nothing he could do about it." On another occasion, a Colgate professor aboard a ship returning from Germany ran into Lüdtke. Again, he seemed "very indiscreet in his remarks about the government in Germany, to such an extent in fact that he was not at all popular with the other exchange students who were on the boat at the time."[72]

Repatriated, but Americanized

Many of the students could not reasonably hope to remain in the United States and thus returned home, but their Americanization was evident. It was not uncommon for former exchange students, after repatriation, to gather when their host school had a football game against an archrival and listen to it on shortwave radio. Sometimes alumni of the rival schools listened together, cheering for "their" team.[73] German authorities increasingly frowned upon such behavior by the end of the 1930s.

Naturally, some of the repatriated students exhibited stronger signs of

Americanization than others. An American exchange student in Germany in the spring of 1939 reported to Hubbard that Werner Schroedter had become practically an American. Interestingly, Schroedter would soon find himself back in the United States, working for the German diplomatic service; he eventually remained in the United States.[74] Marianne Lautsch rather ostentatiously attempted to maintain some of her Americanisms after she returned home. For example, while at a typical German restaurant with friends, she ordered water, butter, and salad. In response, her waiter brought her a beer glass filled with water, a large slab of butter, and lettuce with vinegar. Lautsch had left $10 at Oberlin College for a friend to mail her Post Toasties or Corn Flakes throughout the year.[75]

Repatriation culture shock was common for the more Americanized students. They tended to write to their American friends or mentors and express a longing for their lives in the United States. A month after Lautsch's return, Hans Gatzke, once back home, wrote Hubbard, "I'm not the only one who is having quite a hard time (getting readjusted to life in Germany—RH). Marianne Lautsch, who I met a few weeks ago, doesn't get along too nicely either. And Günther Kiersch, who is studying in Munich too and who lives just a few houses down the street from where I live, feels similarly."[76] A few months later, in 1936, Gatzke wrote Hubbard that Kiersch found that "America has changed his attitude towards German affairs very much."[77] Gatzke's next letter to Hubbard was a "pathetic," abject wish to "take the next ship back to the U.S.A." Tyler Dennett, president of Williams College, had thought it somewhat cruel to bring German students such as Gatzke to the United States only to then force them to return to Germany.[78] Gatzke undertook a dangerous letter-writing campaign pleading with Williams College and IIE officials to allow him to come back to Williams in particular and the United States in general. They did, and Gatzke would become a renowned American historian.

A letter Lucie Hess wrote to her host school after repatriation demonstrates a clear case of reverse culture shock. In the letter, she bemoans the European tendency to disparage the United States without ever having lived there. Had they done so, they would shake off their "superiority complex" and open their minds to American culture. They would realize that Americans were better grounded than Europeans. Furthermore, Americans had a more authentic spirituality than did Germans at that time:

> Somehow or other you live closer to God—and I think that is why we cannot help taking so deep a liking for you and your country. Perhaps America is really

"God's own country," not only because of its wealth and the richness of its natural resources, not only because of the beauty of its landscape, but in a deeper sense—because of its people. To live a whole year in a thoroughly spiritual atmosphere—I do not think that you can ever perceive how much this means to a German of these times.[79]

In Hess's case, a devotion to her host college seems to have been a critical factor in her Americanization. She admitted in a letter, "There is not a day that I do not think of Agnes Scott College ... and there is always a little longing ... Yet I know that I can be a good Agnes Scotter and loyal to the beloved Alma Mater even when in another country and very 'far from the reach of her sheltering arms.' "[80] Another exchange student wrote to Hubbard that her year in the United States had made her "really open-eyed" about Germany and spoke of feeling "homesick" for the United States.[81] Leopold Christiansen wrote to Rensselaer Polytechnic Institute that after returning to Germany, it took him some time to reacclimate to his "surroundings and circumstances."[82] Hubbard traveled to Germany in 1935, during which many former German-American exchange students met with her. She later remarked to a colleague, "I know from experiences this summer that the readjustment our students must make when they return is very difficult sometimes."[83] Duggan made much the same observation to another academic critical of the exchange.[84]

As one would expect, the repatriated exchange students discovered that their fellow Germans did not welcome overly eager praise of the United States. Trouble continued to haunt Werner von Rosenstiel after he returned to Germany. Being a newly appointed law clerk in 1939 required that he attend a two-month legal training camp that drilled the students on Nazi legal doctrine, ideology, and physical exercise. One night, the campers asked von Rosenstiel about American life. During a discussion about football games, he taught his comrades the University of Kansas rally cry: "Rock, shock, jay hawk. Kay, yoo-hoo." The campers took up chanting the cry, and for this insult to German culture, the official report on von Rosenstiel's behavior noted that "he had seen too much" and was "unreliable." Gerhard Brecher, the last German exchange student to return to Germany, in July 1941, claimed that he was under constant Gestapo surveillance. That Brecher had brought his new American wife with him when he returned to Germany surely deepened their suspicions.[85]

Herbert Sonthoff returned to Germany in July 1936, after completing his exchange year. He was disheartened not only by his academic setbacks, but

Disillusionment, Resistance, Refuge, and Opposition   143

also by the increasingly oppressive hold the Nazis had gained over German society while he was in America. During the next three years, Sonthoff developed a quasi-mentee relationship with the anti-Nazi Emil de Haas, secretary general of the Carl Schurz Vereinigung. De Haas got Sonthoff work at the association's office and dispatched him to guide Americans on the Carl Schurz Tours.[86] While conducting his tours, Sonthoff fell into the habit of "very recklessly" criticizing the Nazi regime.[87] Numerous witnesses later testified that Sonthoff's unabashedly vocal anti-Nazism, while still in Germany, was shocking.[88] Sonthoff also vehemently refuted criticism of the United States. Because of this, he was "more or less ostracized" by many of his associates. This reached its peak when, on the recommendation of de Haas, Sonthoff worked as a training instructor for exchange students heading to the United States.[89] During his lectures, Sonthoff expressed such laudatory opinions about the United States that he was fired.[90]

De Haas once again stepped in to rescue Sonthoff, this time, as it turned out, once and for all. As the Nazi regime's antisemitic policies drove increasing numbers of Jewish Germans to seek refuge in the United States, the workload at the US Consulate in Berlin exploded. Traditionally, local Germans were hired for clerical support, but General Consul Geist seemed to forever be hiring and firing German employees, because their Nazi enthusiasm led them to mistreat potential emigrants, or they were involved in espionage at the consulate. In early 1938, Geist needed another German clerk and was determined to find a trustworthy non-Nazi for the job. Thus, it is telling that he turned to de Haas for a recommendation.[91] De Haas suggested Sonthoff, who accepted the position, which primarily involved drafting reports on contemporary German issues.[92]

After a year and a half at the consulate, Sonthoff suddenly appeared in New York with an immigration visa, just days before the outbreak of World War II. For years afterward, he was shadowed by suspicions of espionage, as he remained evasive about how he had managed to return to the United States under such precarious conditions.[93] Documents from the FBI and the Immigration and Naturalization Service suggest why. On August 4, 1939, Geist had granted Sonthoff a leave of absence specifically to apply for American citizenship in New York and issued him a non-preference, German quota immigration visa (Q2759) to do so. In an unusual move, Geist also communicated directly with INS at the Port of New York, confirming Sonthoff's status as a consular employee who would be arriving in New York to apply for citizenship.[94] Sonthoff arrived in New York as a prospective permanent resident on August 31, 1939.[95]

During the war and later, when Sonthoff applied for an intelligence position with the federal government in the early 1950s, the FBI interviewed several of his former consulate colleagues, including Rosemarie Lochner and Carolus F. Schenke, to learn about the unusual circumstances of Sonthoff's immigration visa. Lochner and Schenke's accounts appear to have been influenced by jealousy and personal animosity. Lochner, who had been romantically involved with Sonthoff from 1939 to 1943, accused his consulate superior, Geist, of being a homosexual who had also been romantically entangled with Sonthoff, claiming that this had complicated her own relationship with him.[96] Sonthoff, in turn, dismissed her allegations as jealousy, though he acknowledged being Geist's "constant companion."[97] Schenke, meanwhile, pointedly remarked to the FBI that, like Sonthoff, "several of the male employees had taken advantage of their connection with the American consul to come to the United States and obtain citizenship."[98] Schenke's remarks were tinged with resentment, as he had obtained his own visa but with considerably greater difficulty than Sonthoff.[99]

To counter the suspicions Sonthoff adopted the guise of an American superpatriot. Two months after his return to the United States, he published an article in the *Atlantic* about his last day in Germany.[100] Perhaps partly apocryphal, the article tells of a final visit to an anti-Nazi official who worked at a "semi-governmental agency," most likely de Haas. Sonthoff's friend applauds his decision to escape: " 'You are going,' he said, 'and you ought to go. Tell them over there that Germany will become again what she once was—not a firstclass military power, but stronger in science, philosophy, and poetry than ever. National Socialism is just an interlude, dark and terrific, but there will be a new dawn. They think I'm a Nazi and therefore I can and must stay— there must be people ready for the change when it comes.' " Given the *Atlantic*'s wide circulation, it is almost inconceivable that German authorities remained unaware of the article.[101]

From the June 1940 until September 1942, Sonthoff went on a speaking tour with a lecture management company. His talks, delivered throughout New England, centered on the evils of Nazism.[102] He admitted to Hubbard that proving to American authorities that his anti-Nazism was irrefutable had been one of the reasons he did the tour. This was especially essential, he told her, since he did not have a Jewish "appearance," which led to questions about the reasons for his return to the United States.[103] Curiously, despite applying

Disillusionment, Resistance, Refuge, and Opposition   145

for US citizenship in November 1939, Sonthoff later told the FBI that he had felt it necessary to renew his German passport at the consulate in Boston in May 1940.[104]

Sonthoff's friend Werner von Rosenstiel also returned to the United States under suspicious circumstances. As he explained it, the German army had chosen him to interrogate English-speaking Allied prisoners in 1939 in the advent of war. He requested a final, one-month visit to Britain to "polish" his English. Oddly enough, the request was granted. He was, somehow, able to leave Britain for the United States, and arrived in New York City as an illegal alien.[105]

Remaining in the United States did not necessarily lead to a happy life for the former exchange students. Sonthoff and Ulrich Pohlenz wandered between careers and residences, and in Pohlenz's case, sometimes names.[106] Several of the students eventually committed suicide.[107]

In a few cases, former exchange students took an active role in efforts to undermine Hitler's regime. Sonthoff's involvement with German opposition circles remains, like much of his life, somewhat ambiguous. After returning from his exchange year in the United States, Sonthoff became connected to the "Siemer-Wirmer Catholic opposition group."[108] His primary link to this circle was his friend Hermann Siemer. Laurentius Siemer, Hermann's cousin and a Dominican priest, had also contributed to the resistance by protecting its members and engaging in various opposition activities.[109] Both Siemers were under Gestapo surveillance.[110]

After settling in the United States, Sonthoff inexplicably maintained a friendly correspondence with Hermann Siemer. In one letter, Sonthoff fondly mentioned their mutual friend, Otto Wirmer, another Catholic opposition figure under Gestapo surveillance.[111] Otto's brother Josef Wirmer was slated to become justice minister in Carl Friedrich Goerdeler's anticipated post-Hitler government.[112] After the July 20, 1944, assassination attempt on Hitler, how-ever, Joseph Wirmer was executed because of his oppositional activities.[113] Had the Gestapo bothered to open the letters to Hermann Siemer from Sonthoff, a very outspoken anti-Nazi refugee in the United States, it is likely the Siemer-Wirmer opposition group would have counted themselves lucky only to have been imprisoned in a concentration camp. Such a discovery could even have unraveled the major anti-Nazi networks as early as 1940, four years before the July 20 attempt.

Another former exchange student, Adolf Henning Frucht, served as a cou-rier for the Goerdeler circle. After growing tired of the group's carelessness about concealing their actives, Frucht joined the Wehrmacht as a doctor.[114] Sigismund von Braun, the brother of aerospace engineer Wernher von Braun, attended the University of Cincinnati during the 1933–34 academic year. After returning to Germany, he began a career in the Foreign Ministry, and in 1943, was appointed secretary of Germany's legation to the Vatican. Von Braun and his superior at the embassy, Albrecht von Kassel, rejected the Nazis and envisioned a peaceful, post-Hitler German commonwealth integrated into Europe and governed by Germans rather than foreign occupiers.[115] Both men were distantly linked to the Kreisau circle, another leading opposition group in Germany.[116] The Kreisau and Goerdeler circles were well aware of each other.[117]

Another former exchange student in the Foreign Ministry, Georg von Lilienfeld, later asserted involvement in resistance activities at the ministry and in the army, reportedly through the Goerdeler circle. His claim rests solely on a single, vague CIA document, however, leaving its veracity open to question.[118]

Conclusion

The majority of the German exchange students were likely struck by the cognitive dissonance between what they had been instructed to expect in the United States and what they actually encountered. Some may have adopted psychological defensive mechanisms to ease the conflict in their minds— perhaps discounting America's advantages, playing on their own notions of honor and loyalty, or resolving that they could not bear to leave behind the unique world they had built in Germany. Naturally, there were also exchange students entirely focused on achieving their career goals and unconflicted in their loyalty to their native country (if not necessarily to its government). In several cases, students sought refuge in the United States for reasons other than psychological dissonance. Some claimed to have been masquerading as Nazis all along in order to use the exchange program to escape the Third Reich. A few male students were apparently anxious to avoid serving in the Wehrmacht. For one reason or another, several exchange students had provoked the wrath of German authorities back home, and therefore felt trepidation about returning.

On another level were students so profoundly affected by their lives in the United States that they tried to remain there. They came to identify more with American society than with Nazi Germany back home. In essence, they left Germany for their exchange year as Nazis, but ended their exchange year as culturally American. The effort necessary to achieve that result in practice

Disillusionment, Resistance, Refuge, and Opposition 147

was daunting. To embark on becoming a permanent resident of the United States, one had to be willing to risk failure, with the knowledge that the consequences back in Germany would likely be catastrophic. If they succeeded in remaining in the United States, they also willingly exposed their families to a Gestapo investigation, at the least. They must have also realized that successfully remaining in the United States presented them with a variety of professional obstacles they would not have otherwise faced in Germany.

That so many of the exchange students were willing to risk these hardships, and even greater ones, is a testament to the superficiality of their Nazification. That such superficiality was not detected—and such students were not eliminated from further consideration for a study abroad program in a liberal democracy—suggests that the Nazification of the traditional branches of German government was not ironclad. The ultimate results of this ideological deficiency had there been no war to radicalize and further constrict German society are questions that can never be answered.

The exchange students inclined to question Hitler's regime were hardly the only ones who studied in the United States. As Germany's military aggression became ever more blatant, the Third Reich's foreign policy toward the United States shifted away from facilitating the penetration of Nazi ideas in America and toward fostering the isolationist movement there, and otherwise improving Germany's position if military conflict with the United States ensued. This provided an excuse for the SS-SD and other political entities to further subvert the exchange program and fill exchange slots with students ordered to conduct espionage in the United States. The foolish assumption that they could gain knowledge useful to Germany outside of normal academic channels, let alone subvert Americans to act as agents of the Reich, would have fatal consequences for the exchange program.

CHAPTER FIVE

Propaganda and Espionage Missions

We must have scouts like hungry, sharp-eyed ravens sitting on all the
world's political fences.

—*Karl Haushofer, pro-Nazi geographer and espionage director*

Can anyone seriously believe that the faith of American students in
their own national institutions and in Democracy as a form of government is so weak that it is likely to be undermined by even two hundred
German students scattered among the hundreds of colleges and universities of the United States? Is it not more likely that those German
students living . . . in the atmosphere of freedom will be influenced in
favor of our way of life?

—*Stephen Duggan to Walter Wilcox, September 24, 1937*

The German exchange students can be categorized as a "traditional" cohort
and an "espionage" cohort. For a number of reasons, German espionage missions in the United States were disastrous. In essence, the Germans relied on
almost randomly chosen, poorly trained, and sometimes unmotivated agents,
most of them from Germany. As was typical for the Third Reich's governmental structure, there was a multitude of covert operations sponsored by a be-
wildering array of traditional and Nazi organizations. They tended to burden
their operatives with assignments from different espionage operations which
all too often worked at cross-purposes; eagerly devised absurd, amateurish
missions to score espionage coups vis-à-vis their competitors in the German covert operations realm; and severely misunderstood the German American community's mindset.[1] Unsophisticated German exchange students were

thrown into this mix, sometimes against their will. In only one type of mission—often employing exchange students—did the Nazis succeed: intimidation of putative opponents. The Nazis were determined to prevent German exiles from openly disparaging the Nazi regime, and were increasingly zealous in investigating possible liberalization of German exchange students.

Covert propaganda, intimidation, espionage, and sabotage operations are here encompassed by the term *covert operations*. These varied in goals and intensity according to German-American and geopolitical relations over the course of the decade preceding the fall of the Reich. The structures of German covert operations remained remarkably unchanging, as did the roles the exchange students played in them. These operations became elements in the German Nazi–Soviet Communist Cold War being fought sub rosa in the United States.

With the deprivations of the Versailles Treaty ranking foremost, German students in the German-American exchange program had been expected since its inception during the Weimar Republic to engage in overt propaganda. While the basic structure of this propaganda did not change after Hitler took power, the focus shifted from foreign to domestic affairs as Americans expressed consternation at the ravages Nazism was wreaking on German society. Especially after the 1938 Sudetenland crisis, the likelihood of war in Europe sharply increased. At that time, propaganda focused on the promotion of American isolationism, and espionage was oriented toward the acquisition of American military technology. Often, it was irrelevant if an agency had experience in such activities; their possible fruits were nonetheless compelling. Once again, as in so many aspects of the Third Reich's political life, the result was a chaotic rush of German organizations into covert propaganda and espionage. They had to establish a network of agents, middlemen, and information transmittal systems, and quickly at that, lest their political rivals crowd them out. Conveniently, there already existed a network of ostensibly committed German Nazis in America who could assist in carrying out these activities: German exchange students. Further, for German organizations that had little understanding of American society, it was easy to imagine that German-Americans were potentially a massive base of collaborators. These grandiose assumptions were illusory. College students with little or no training in espionage or covert propaganda could not possibly function effectively as part of an intelligence network. Even those specifically chosen for this work lacked essential training. In addition, German Americans were no more willing to assist the Third Reich than other Americans were.

Nazi Covert Propaganda

The welter of overlapping and seemingly ad hoc propaganda efforts by various Reich entities or individuals in the United States was noted by Friedrich Auhagen, a Nazi propagandist and former professor in the United States. Auhagen had extensive knowledge of espionage networks run by Herbert Scholz, the German consul general in Boston after 1938 and a high-ranking SS officer, as they were close friends.[2] Auhagen claimed that Nazi propaganda in America "was left virtually to amateurs, ideological sectarians and extremists, by business concerns with an ax to grind, such as I.G. Farben and the Mascena [sic] works; cultural groups, such as the Volksbund für das Deutschtum im Ausland; individual lecturers and writers such as Colin Ross; Professor [Friedrich] Schönemann and others . . . However, there was no concerted policy, nor coordination of individual efforts. Generally, the left hand didn't know what the right hand was doing."[3]

Almost immediately after Hitler took power in Germany, Rudolf Hess, the Reich's deputy Führer, and Ernst Bohle, gauleiter of the Nazi Party Foreign Organization, were eager to exploit the approximately 20 million Americans of German descent. Consequently, in 1933 they funded the Friends of the New Germany, an organization that promoted antisemitism and engaged in various outrageous antics that only served to stoke public anger, such as assaulting designated enemies, organizing pro-Nazi demonstrations, and attempting to take control of German American cultural organizations. To assist in these efforts, English-language propaganda materials were printed in large quantities in Germany for American audiences. DAAD published *News in Brief* to highlight its own activities. Bales of these publications were stuffed into unmarked packages, loaded onto German passenger ships, and offloaded in US ports, primarily in New York, Boston, and Los Angeles. Money and espionage paraphernalia came by the same route. A Nazi agent on the ship would pass off the materials to designated couriers, who would transport them to the Friends, German American Bund, or German diplomatic posts as instructed.[4] In return, the courier picked up espionage materials headed for Germany.[5] On occasion, students might stay overnight at houses belonging to members of the Friends or Bund.[6] In 1935 Ulrich von Gienanth, as a Propaganda Ministry official, set up the German Library of Information in New York City, and staffed it with exchange students, along with employing other German nationals. The "library" became Germany's premier propaganda center, from which a flood of pro-German literature was mailed out around the United States.[7] German exchange students frequently served as couriers, under the supervision of von Gienanth. The students may not have known what was in the packages they delivered.

Word of such activities reached Columbia University professor Franz Boas, a Jewish German émigré often regarded as the founder of American anthropology. Given his status, and because he taught at the alma mater of IIE director Stephen Duggan, Boas took an early lead against German exchange student propaganda. In June 1933, he informed Duggan that a number of exchange students were active anti-Jewish propagandists.[8] Duggan attempted to avoid the issue, explaining that the exchange students had been warned not to engage in such activities, but Boas knew how to get Duggan's attention: he reported the matter to the chairman of the House Immigration Committee, Rep. Samuel Dickstein.[9] With the problems caused by the Friends of the New Germany in addition to Boas' complaints, Dickstein in June 1934 launched an investigation through a new "Special Committee on Un-American Activities Authorized to Investigate Nazi Propaganda and Certain Other Propaganda Activities," co-chaired by Rep. John William McCormack, and informally known as the McCormack-Dickstein Committee (and in 1937, because of political changes, as the Dies Committee). From its inception, the committee sought to prove that hundreds of Nazi propagandists, with millions of dollars in German funding, had flooded the United States with propaganda. Dickstein also intended his investigation to cover all "200" American colleges that sponsored German exchange students; the actual number was about half that. The Anti-Defamation League, working in conjunction with the American Jewish Committee, as well as the Los Angeles Jewish Community Committee presented much of the evidence regarding exchange student machinations.[10] Many of the students' activities, however, were technically not illegal. The only tidbit potentially outside the law involved a thirdhand account that the Friends of the New Germany had requested that DAAD send an exchange student in physics to the United States for "a few little jobs."[11] Nevertheless, because of Dickstein's investigations, Congress passed the Foreign Principal Registration Act of 1938, which required those operating on behalf of foreign governments to disclose that fact to the federal government. The Dickstein/Dies committee was almost immediately succeeded by the House Un-American Activities Committee, which, while periodically holding hearings regarding Nazi activities in the United States, increasingly turned its attention to investigating Communist activities. Thus, German exchange students were always under some kind of government scrutiny, although it was not very effective in impeding Nazi operations.

Recruiting Student Spies

Various exchange students, along with other German agents, were assigned to intimidate any German nationals or refugees in the United States who might embarrass the Reich, as well as covertly investigate suspected liberal leanings of previous or current suspect exchange students. It appears that the German Student Union worked closely with the SD (Sicherheitsdienst)—one of Germany's two official intelligence organizations, the other being the Abwehr (military intelligence)—to carry out these tasks. The union was in a sense a feeder of college students into SD careers. The student union recruited operatives by posting notices at universities encouraging "trustworthy" students who were already Nazi Party members and had proven their dedication to "the cause," to apply for "special" exchange slots. In these cases, academic accomplishments were inconsequential. Applicants did not need to concern themselves with knowing a foreign language, as such skills were important "only to linguists." What mattered was finding recruits with "political instincts," capable of "distinguishing friend from foe, real from unreal." The author of these guidelines snidely remarked that the local student union foreign affairs offices had to take great care in selecting the right students: it was not simply a chore that could be fobbed off to "office secretaries."[12] At least in 1938 and the period thereafter, student operatives were provided with diplomatic visas when possible, no doubt to avoid landing in an American jail on espionage charges. These operatives were often loaned out to whichever covert organization needed someone in the United States suitable for a mission at hand. If one of their reports appeared to be especially interesting, it might have the distinction of working its way up the Nazi organizational chain of command to reach Hess or Heinrich Himmler.[13] While spying, they frequently found themselves also tasked with helping in covert propaganda campaigns.[14]

Albert Einstein became one of the exchange students' first targets for intimidation.[15] The Nazis found him objectionable on many grounds: as a liberal, a pacifist, an anti-Nazi activist, a Jew, and a refugee.[16] In early 1933, Einstein received "warnings and threatening letters," apparently from exchange students; he feared that some "hysterical" German students might attack him.[17] Four years later, Einstein denounced Hans-Werner Gensichen and another German student as alleged spies.[18] In one instance, Dettlof von Simson, a graduate student at Washington University in St. Louis, denied the Nazis' mistreatment of Jews during his local lecture rounds praising the "New Germany." Indeed, so blatant was von Simson's propagandizing that a dean at his school complained that the university was "constantly embarrassed" by von Simson, who had been "a source of perpetual irritation."[19] In what would seem to be an unusually vicious attack, von Simson gave a speech in early 1934 at Maryville College, also in St. Louis, and during the question-and-answer period, a Jewish German refugee, Professor Peter Olden from nearby St. Louis University, dared challenge von Simson's rosy picture. After the presentation, von Simson privately threatened Olden, telling him that "if he valued the welfare of his family in Germany as well as his own, he had better give some satisfactory explanation" for his criticism of the speech.[20] On another occasion, the Social Democratic German refugee Gerhart Seger told an audience that he knew of many cases in which German students (and professors) had spied on German refugees. In one instance, the head of the German Department at one college asked Seger if they could speak alone, "in the dark." When Seger expressed his discomfort with such an odd request, the department head explained the reason: two German students on his campus were watching him constantly. He understood the reason: any public expression of anti-Nazi sentiments would have unpleasant consequences for his family back in Germany.[21] Another émigré faculty member at Connecticut College wrote Ruth Hubbard at IIE that she did not like the college's German exchange student because she was "afraid of the very thing I am trying to escape. You know what I mean."[22] Professor George Danton of Oberlin College became convinced that the exchange students were watching his German refugee colleagues and any vocal American opponents of Nazism.[23] Around 1940, Carl Joachim Friedrich, a refugee academic who more than anyone else could be considered the "father" of German-American student exchanges, gave interventionist lectures about the dangers of Nazi Germany. Irene Gotthelf, one of the committed German espionage students, attended these events and very likely took detailed notes to pass on to Scholz at the Boston consulate.[24] She made her displeasure with Friedrich's remarks clear to him and everyone else in attendance.[25]

Not all the exchange students, of course, were willing to undertake such work. Von Gienanth ordered Horst Janson, at Harvard, to spy on Karl Viëtor, a professor who had written letters of recommendation for exchange candidates and who ultimately became a refugee. Janson apparently refused and was himself subsequently blacklisted by von Gienanth.[26] Ursula Schäfer also refused to spy on refugees.[27] Both Janson and Schäfer would soon become refugees themselves. Werner von Rosenstiel described in detail his experience as a target of such operations. While an exchange student, von Rosenstiel visited German American organizations around Cleveland, as was expected. In one instance, he was at a German American choral group performance, and one of the members had just recently returned from a visit to Germany. He enthusiastically noted the changes. For example, in Rothenburg he saw an enormous sign by the road that read, "Jews not wanted here." Another member asked von Rosenstiel what he thought about it, and, without thinking, he replied that it was awful. A couple of days later, von Rosenstiel received a telephone call from a fellow exchange student at nearby Oberlin College warning him that whatever he had done, it must have been something "very, very stupid." She explained that the German consul in Cleveland had received a report about the incident and had asked her to investigate von Rosenstiel's loyalties. Von Rosenstiel immediately thought to himself, "My God, I have put my head in a noose," and soon found an excuse to stop by the consulate and emphasize his faith in the Führer, presumably resolving his predicament.[28] DAAD deputy director Georg Rettig received reports on the students, undoubtedly through the exchange students who had been willing to spy on the others. In one case, Jenni Karding, an exchange student newly returned to Germany, stopped by the DAAD office, where she encountered Rettig. His only comment to her was, "I hear you have become quite Americanized." It was not intended as a compliment.[29]

By the late 1930s, there were so many current and former exchange students and refugees at Harvard that refugee intimidation, student ideological investigations, and assorted espionage activities required a veritable espionage circle of its own. At various times, von Gienanth, himself a former exchange student at Johns Hopkins University, or another student, Karl Arndt, inquired about the activities of quite a few of the other exchange students, including Anton-Hermann Chroust, Horst Janson, Ernst Lampe, and Rudolf Ullman.[30] Chroust spied on Lampe at one point. Ironically, after Chroust decided to remain in the United States, he tried to help Lampe avoid being spied on by another student.[31] In October 1939, Anneliese von dem Hagen was assigned to look into Herbert Sonthoff's sudden, and unexpected, reappearance at Harvard.[32] Sonthoff published an anti-Nazi article in *The Atlantic* under his own name, but this would not have alerted von dem Hagen to his presence in the United States. She had visited Sonthoff in September, but his article came out two months later. Rather, German authorities must have known of Sonthoff's escape from the Reich soon after it occurred. It is easy to imagine that in trying to find out what he was up to—and assuming Sonthoff would welcome a visit from the very student he had suggested for the exchange several years before—von dem Hagen was sent to investigate. It is unclear which German organization would have undertaken this investigation. One might expect the job to fall under the purview of the SD's foreign intelligence branch, but one should also not be shocked to learn that the SD only became aware of Sonthoff being in the United States several years later, after Germany and the United States were at war. On the other hand, the German Consulate in Boston had learned of Sonthoff's presence in the city by December 1939. Quite thoughtfully, considering that Scholz was a "mastermind" of Nazi espionage, and Sonthoff had become an outspoken anti-Nazi refugee, Scholz nevertheless invited him to the consulate's Christmas party and revalidated his passport in May 1940.[33]

IIE received a number of reports detailing these intimidation and ideological investigation activities. In the spring of 1936, IIE received a letter from a Williams College student informing it that the German exchange student on their campus, Ernst Wilhelm Foerster, a "dyed-in-the-wool-Nazi," had been "quietly trying to find out to what extent his predecessor [Hans Gatzke] had been won over to a liberal outlook. The implications are not pleasant."[34] Indeed, the Gestapo searched Gatzke's apartment after his return to Germany. It is unclear whether this stemmed from Foerster's report or Gatzke's letter-writing campaign to Williams College begging to return to the United States.[35] Similar reports abound in IIE, FBI, and Department of Justice files.[36]

Espionage Free-for-All

With Germany's reorganization of its military in 1935, and Hitler's increasingly ambitious goals thereafter, German espionage in the United States became a growth industry. That year von Gienanth returned to the United States as a freshly trained SD intelligence operative. In addition, he had been commissioned as a lieutenant in the Abwehr, likely to supplement his SD espionage work.[37] With ties to virtually every German organization involved in espionage, his status as a former exchange student at Johns Hopkins University and the added responsibility of overseeing the exchange students, it is hardly surprising that von Gienanth added them to the Nazi espionage machine in the United States, as had already occurred in a number of other countries.[38]

The exchange students also served the Nazi Party Foreign Organization (Auslands-Organisation) in a similar capacity. Given the organization's extraordinarily widespread clientele, Ernst Bohle, its leader, decided to jump into the espionage business himself, using the organization as a sort of espionage field office, passing on information gathered to other intelligence organizations.[39] German organizations' requests for intelligence were sent to the appropriate Foreign Organization's regional leader (*Landesgruppenleiter*); in the United States, this was the vice consul in New York City, Friedhelm Draeger.[40] The Foreign Organization's Cultural Affairs Division, devoted to academics abroad, also had a certain degree of oversight regarding the exchange students in the United States.[41] This is hardly surprising, given that the Foreign Organization had a say in which candidates were selected for the exchange.[42] The German students were required to report to Draeger upon their arrival and to submit information as requested to him, sometimes using von Gienanth as a go-between.[43]

Karl Haushofer used his Institut für Geopolitik at the University of Munich as an intelligence hub. Haushofer, a famous geographer and advocate of Germany's Lebensraum, had been one of Hess's mentors at the school. Haushofer's career flourished after Hess's appointment as the Führer's deputy.[44] Books, articles, and radio broadcasts popularized Haushofer's geopolitical theories. Given Haushofer's prominence and his intellectual flair, SD-Ausland eagerly sought his advice on various intelligence matters.[45] Haushofer's most notable publication, the *Zeitschrift für Geopolitik*, boldly did not attempt to hide its espionage-tinged contents.[46] Several of the German exchange students wrote articles for the *Zeitschrift* that suggest its function: Georg Baare-Schmidt, in "Alaska—Land der Zukunft: Die Strategische Bedeutung" (Alaska—land of the future: Its strategic significance) analyzed the state in the context of military strategy.[47] Klaus Mehnert, a German exchange student in the late 1920s who had returned to the United States to teach at the University of Hawaii and the University of California, Berkeley, in the 1930s, contributed "Problem XIX," an analysis of the US military's 1937 maneuvers at Pearl Harbor. With no doubt, great exaggeration, a United States naval intelligence officer later declared that Mehnert's article provided the foundation for the Pearl Harbor attack plan.[48] Mehnert was also an Abwehr spy, livening up his academic career in the United States with additional espionage activities as well as covert propaganda.[49] In the summer of 1941, when Mehnert's activities were discovered, he found it expedient to visit China.[50] Haushofer's *Weltpolitik von Heute* (1934) fired the imagination of Eugen Lahr, leading to his interest in studying in the United States.[51] In his application for the exchange program, he explained that he enthusiastically taught Haushofer's principles to his SA company. After his exchange year, Lahr eventually returned to the United States as a full-fledged Abwehr espionage agent.[52]

Perhaps the most intriguing member of the Haushofer ring was Fritz Ermarth, an exchange student at Harvard in the early 1930s who identified as a Social Democrat. He remained in the United States after Hitler took power in Germany and taught government at the University of Oklahoma from 1936 to 1940. Ermarth also joined the Federal Union, an organization otherwise known as the Association to Unite the Democracies, which pursued a global federated union of democratic states. He told IIE's Hubbard that he looked forward to participating in an anti-Nazi propaganda campaign in Germany.[53] Yet, as later reported in the Office of Strategic Services (OSS) documents immediately after the war, Ermarth simultaneously engaged in Nazi propaganda activity under the guidance of the German consul in St. Louis.[54] He continued to visit Germany before the United States entered the war, and while there in 1939 to 1940 he socialized with Haushofer and his family. In letters later discovered by the FBI, Ermarth reported back to his host regarding American public opinion about the war in Europe and offered to help Haushofer, if possible.[55] While this might seem a minor transgression, it was not considered so at the time. Haushofer wrote back chastising Ermarth for being so explicit in a letter sent by mail, which might come back to haunt him, as in fact, it ultimately did.[56]

Albrecht Haushofer followed in his father's footsteps, becoming associated with the University of Berlin, among other organizations, as well as taking several government positions. Alfred Kienzler, an exchange student at the University of Cincinnati, was one of Albrecht Haushofer's doctoral students. While at Cincinnati, Kienzler worked on a dissertation on the geography of the St. Lawrence River while carrying out a much different task: acquiring military secrets related to his dissertation topic, specifically locating possible points for illegal transit between Canada and the United States. The German consul general in Cleveland, Karl Kapp, described as "an especially industrious diplomat/spy," supported Kienzler in his mission. Gustav Blanke, one of the last German exchange students in the United States, assisted the FBI in catching Kienzler while he was transporting propaganda materials, concealed under his luggage, to the German American Bund.[57]

After von Gienanth's arrival in the United States in the Propaganda Ministry's employ, exchange student operatives became increasingly important in military espionage. Requests for such assistance came from the SD, the Nazi

Party Foreign Organization, the Institut für Geopolitik, and the Abwehr and were parceled out by von Gienanth (now the SD *Hauptreferent*, the highest-ranking SD intelligence officer in the United States), SD operatives at the German consulates (especially in Boston, New York, and Cleveland), and Rettig. The student operatives usually kept in close contact with von Gienanth or with other espionage agents operating out of local German consulates.[58] Von Gienanth instructed exchange students in espionage during the student exchange assemblies in September in Germany, and during their subsequent voyage to the United States—altogether lasting less than a month.[59] These two or three-week informal espionage and covert propaganda training sessions were unlikely to turn college students into wily spies. Such carelessness was typical of the Reich's US operations. Regardless, von Gienanth bragged to associates that he was proud that his "eager [exchange student] soldiers" made "wonderful spies."[60]

The SD's role was to protect the Nazi Party and the state through domestic and foreign intelligence gathering, which the Gestapo would act upon if it involved "criminal activity." Its Section VI dealt with foreign intelligence. The Abwehr, the German military's intelligence arm, had been set up in the first years of the Weimar Republic. The SD and Abwehr were intense competitors that worked together only when essential, if then. Both stepped up their espionage activities in the United States around 1936.[61] The Abwehr was the largest employer of then-current and former exchange student operatives. This is not surprising, given the agency's extensive espionage networks in the United States and Mexico, as well as its substantial funds; the networks in Mexico focused more on the United States than on Mexico itself. Vice Admiral Wilhelm Canaris headed the Abwehr from 1936 to 1944. Colonel Hans Piekenbrock, in charge of Abwehr I Amt Ausland (intelligence gathered from neutral and adversarial countries), gave managerial approval to major espionage actions in the United States, although Canaris might also get involved in major intelligence operations. In 1937 Canaris chose Nikolaus Ritter, a captain in the Luftwaffe, to serve as chief of Air Force Intelligence under Piekenbrock. Ritter was also responsible for US operations and thus functioned as the "handler" for German spies in the United States. His brother Hans functioned as the paymaster for German spies in Mexico City.[62] Most of their operational nodes were in the German Embassy and its consulates around the United States, as well as the embassy in Mexico City. The Foreign Ministry constantly objected to these arrangements because they interfered with their mission and were likely to be more successful at destroying what was left of German relations with the United States than obtaining useful intelligence.[63]

The Abwehr has a well-earned reputation among historians as one of the least effective espionage agencies of any of the World War II belligerents.[64] It was none too picky about who it employed to achieve its aims in the United States. Ernst Bohle, the gauleiter of Nazis outside of Germany, complained in one of his postwar interrogations that the Abwehr focused more on recruiting individuals who would be in the right place at the right time than for their suitability for the tasks assigned.[65] Subagents were often just German citizens in a target country who might conceivably be able to obtain the information sought in the course of their normal activities. They frequently included scientists, academics, technical experts, businessmen, and exchange students. Such haphazard means of obtaining intelligence were, in part, a consequence of the Reich's lack of espionage coordination. Many exchange student operatives were employed as couriers. Since both the SD and the Propaganda Ministry might employ the same couriers as part of their activities, it is usually not possible to determine which agency employed a particular courier for a particular mission.

As noted earlier, the exchange students also acquired espionage information on their own. Such information was generally openly available and of limited value. Indeed, the German consuls in the United States, attending a January 1940 meeting, disdainfully expressed their amazement that it was so easy to acquire "espionage" intelligence that no special agents were necessary and would only run the risk of discovery and adverse political consequences. As Los Angeles General Consul Georg Gyssling reported to the Foreign Ministry, his office could simply subscribe to a variety of open sources, such as newspapers and published reports. Gyssling had long compiled and sent back information on American shipbuilding and aircraft production using this method. Further, a consular employee need only drive near manufacturing plants and observe the number and type of aircraft being produced. Much the same was being done for shipbuilding. German "agents" could easily find ship schedules, tour the docks to assess the type and quantities of materials being transferred, and so on. Less honestly, the consuls also wrote letters pretending to be representatives of Allied military purchasing offices, requesting information directly from the manufacturers and even being invited to visit the plants. The FBI knew all along of such activities, but before Pearl Harbor, these acts were not illegal and so, again, no action was taken.[66]

The Follies of German Espionage

Exchange students were involved in the two major German espionage rings in the United States, the Rumrich ring, in operation from about 1936 to 1938, and the Duquesne ring, active from 1938 to the summer of 1941. The Rumrich ring had ties to two established espionage groups in the United States, the William Lonkowski and Ignanz Griebl circles (*Nebenstelle*). To accomplish his various missions, Guenther Rumrich, a pro-German ex-army sergeant, developed a habit of impersonating military and government officials to obtain sought-after information. With growing audacity, in early 1938 he even attempted to impersonate the US Secretary of State, Cordell Hull. In a hushed, "secret" call to the State Department's Passport Office in New York City, Rumrich claimed to be in New York incognito and ordered the Passport Office to deliver the blank passports to an "undersecretary of state" who was part of the secret mission. The clerk who took the telephone call recognized the absurdity of the order and notified his superiors. Rumrich was caught in a trap involving his scheme. British intelligence assisted the FBI in identifying him as a principal in a German espionage ring in the United States. During his interrogation, Rumrich agreed to turn state's evidence and provided sufficient information to destroy the entire German intelligence network in the United States. As this was one of the FBI's first counterintelligence cases, the agency made serious rookie mistakes, however, essentially letting some of the spies go, which attracted a scathing public response. Still, Hoover was able to manipulate the episode to justify expanding and reorganizing the FBI to better deal with such espionage cases. Although the Germans obtained military information from these spies, it ultimately provided no serious benefit in terms of German military preparations.[67]

As the United States became ever more involved in the war, Canaris warned against undertaking aggressive covert operations there, knowing that there was less to gain from them than from the Americans' attention remaining elsewhere. Hermann Göring, however, overruled him.[68] Consequently, the exchange student operatives supposedly became the core of the exchange program in the United States; the "normal" exchange students were apparently valued primarily as camouflage.[69] As IIE recognized, the German government was now granting diplomatic passports to quite a few exchange students, rather than obtaining the usual student visas from the US government. This allowed them to remain in the United States after the end of the academic year and made it more difficult for the US government to expel them. DAAD's excuse for this odd procedure was that obtaining student visas was "taking too long."[70] For example, Robert Eggert, an SS member who attended Dickinson College during the 1938–39 school year, began work at the German Embassy on a diplomatic passport some months later, engaging in covert operations.[71]

During this time, the so-called Duquesne ring grew to become Germany's largest ever espionage operation in the United States. Frederick Duquesne was a well-known South African adventurer and anti-British spy for Germany during World War I. At that time, he became acquainted with Wilhelm Canaris and Nikolaus Ritter. Duquesne eventually settled in New York City and obtained US citizenship. After Ritter contacted him in December 1937, he agreed to resume his espionage activities for the Germans, this time against his adopted country. The Duquesne ring, however, was in reality the Ritter ring. The FBI chose to name the group of German spies arrested in 1941 the Duquesne ring due to Duquesne's name recognition, rather than any centrality to what was in fact Ritter's spy ring. Most of the information the ring produced was fairly prosaic; in addition to shipping records, the Abwehr received various photographs and blueprints of airplanes and weapons.[72] Regardless, the Germans made no real technical advances with this information. This includes the Norden bombsight plans the ring obtained; as it turned out, the bombsight was not all that accurate under real-world conditions. The entire "ring" was unraveled because William Sebold, an American born in Germany and working as a double agent for the FBI, secured the names of his fellow Abwehr agents. All 32 German agents were arrested in June 1941.[73]

The Duquesne ring operated during the "golden era" of German exchange student espionage. Von Gienanth was, of course, intimately involved, being friends with one of the agents, Max Blank, and acquainted with all of them.[74] They were all aware of von Gienanth's position in the SS hierarchy. After the FBI apprehended one of the agents, Else Weustenfeld, she told them that she feared von Gienanth would have her executed.[75] During the roundup, the FBI caught one of the former exchange students, Eduard Pestel, with a complete set of maps of New York City harbor as well as microscopes, a rather unusual collection, except for the fact that the microscopes were used to read microdots (documents reduced to the size of periods), a method the Germans commonly employed to render documents practically invisible. Fortunately for Pestel, he was in the United States on a diplomatic passport and thus was only expelled, rather than imprisoned.[76] Von Gienanth had to protect another former exchange student involved in the ring, Eugen Lahr, by hiding him in the German Embassy.[77]

Figure 5.1. Anneliese von dem Hagen, ca. 1938. Coerced into covert activities by Georg Rettig of the German exchange program; interned in the United States during World War II and died shortly afterward. Early IIE Photos, 1930s. Courtesy of the Institute of International Education.

Other exchange students were also caught in the espionage network between the United States and Mexico. Anneliese von dem Hagen, an espionage courier, collected intelligence in the United States and passed it off to contacts in Mexico City. Her involvement in espionage seems partly as punishment for her hostile relationship with Rettig. In 1937 Herbert Sonthoff, one of von dem Hagen's friends, suggested she apply for the German-American exchange. Given her excellent connections, she was awarded an exchange slot. Rettig apparently found it difficult to find a college willing to accept her for the 1938–39 academic year. Yet, very much out of character, he pleaded with IIE to find her a place at any American college, and insured that she received a diplomatic visa from the German government.[78] Rettig had apparently decided to

Propaganda and Espionage Missions   163

force her to assist the Duquesne ring. Ultimately, von dem Hagen was accepted by the Texas State College for Women, much to its eventual regret. Her relationship with Rettig was strained at best. According to an FBI interrogation, she protested against Rettig's order to engage in propaganda activities in the United States. This earned her a stern scolding. but she was allowed to proceed to Texas. In exchange for graciousness on his part, Rettig squeezed von dem Hagen for her assistance in espionage, especially because her school was relatively close to the Mexican border. Seemingly on Rettig's orders, von dem Hagen was often away from campus, visiting German American communities in the Dallas–Fort Worth area and Houston. Although financially destitute, she bought hundreds of dollars of photographic equipment and film. Her new hobby seems to have occupied much of her time in the fall of 1938. However, she made the mistake of having her prints developed by a photography shop directly across from her college, obliviously asking the proprietor to make sure her photographs came out "perfect." Her photographs turned out to include such subjects as Randolph Field and Kelly Field near San Antonio, Texas; industrial plants; government buildings; and ships. Some were aerial shots. All of it was intelligence typically sought by the Abwehr.[79] Von dem Hagen also took an unusual interest in petroleum facilities, such as the Mid-Continent Oil Company's fields in Texas. At some point in the fall of 1938 or spring of 1939, she began taking trips to Mexico City. Meanwhile, she grew increasingly nervous about her activities. In early December 1938, she may have noticed a front-page article in her school's newspaper headlined "Goes to Trial in Espionage Case," reporting an incident involving a group of young German adults getting caught taking photographs of military installations in the US Canal Zone and promptly being arrested and tried.[80]

In February 1939, soon after Rettig was publicly excoriated for attempting to use German exchange students as spies, Erika Mann, the anti-Nazi daughter of the Noble Prize–winning writer Thomas Mann, gave speeches around the country accusing German students of being "Hitler's 'secret agents.'" She told audiences that the students had been chosen for their allegiance to Nazism and trained for two years to spread lies about the Third Reich.[81] Von dem Hagen panicked when she learned about Mann's comments. She frantically brought the article to the attention of her mentor, Rebecca Switzer, the head of the college's foreign language department, and swore that she was not "very guilty." As Switzer told Hubbard, von dem Hagen emphasized that Germany was her home and that she wanted to return there; therefore she "had to do and say certain things [and be] . . . very, very careful to do what

[Rettig] told her," or, von dem Hagen added, he could make life difficult for her. Switzer noted that von dem Hagen was "very much afraid" of him. Rettig likely threatened to destroy von dem Hagen's anticipated career in journalism if she didn't perform the tasks he assigned her.

Apparently due to this peculiar episode, and growing rumors about von dem Hagen's photographs, the Texas Women's College asked IIE to send her back to Germany immediately. Learning of the college's decision, von dem Hagen told Switzer that she actually intended to spend some time in Dallas. Given that she had a diplomatic passport, her status at school was technically inconsequential. "In the end," Switzer wrote, "I looked her straight in the face and said, 'Anneliese, I want you to be careful. Do you understand what I am saying?' She looked worried and replied, 'Yes, I understand, and I promise you to do nothing I do not have to do, but I have to do some things.'" After leaving her host college, von dem Hagen began auditing courses at Southern Methodist University, where she almost immediately attempted to create an underground Nazi "club." Her travels around Texas and Mexico are actually quite easy to explain: she followed the classic path of an Abwehr espionage agent and a covert propagandist. Duggan felt forced to warn other schools that she was a possible "fifth columnist."[82]

Mexico was an important locus of Abwehr espionage against the United States and hosted a veritable circle of exchange student spies.[83] German exchange students operated in Mexico as ancillary agents of the Duquesne ring. The case of Karl Max Weber is perhaps the most illustrative.[84] Weber completed his exchange year in 1933–34 at the University of Denver. After returning to Germany to complete a doctorate, he worked in the field of propaganda journalism. In 1936 Weber began a career reporting on international financial affairs for the Eildienst für Außenhandel und Auslandswirtschaft, a German financial news wire agency. Three years later, the agency assigned him to Mexico. This move occurred just as the Abwehr I Wirtschaft (economic intelligence) was setting up an economic espionage network there, under the control of Georg Nicolaus, the head of a spy ring in Mexico. The Nicolaus circle was tasked with obtaining intelligence related to Mexico's petroleum industry, as war had recently broken out.[85] Because of Weber's economic information gathering, and because he was repeatedly returning to the United States for medical treatment, the Abwehr saw an opportunity to utilize Weber's services.[86]

Weber lived in Mexico under the guise of an inconspicuous *Eildienst* correspondent while conducting espionage activities in Mexico and the United

Propaganda and Espionage Missions   165

States, working in the guise of a journalist, a tactic used by other exchange students as well.[87] On one of his excursions to the United States, Weber clumsily attempted to suborn William Bockhaker, a former classmate from the University of Denver then working as an engineer for a Los Angeles aircraft company. Weber suggested to Bockhaker that since his parents were from Germany, he should feel an obligation to aid the Reich by handing over details of his company's aircraft production secrets. In return, Bockhaker would not only feel proud to have helped the Fatherland but would also receive a handsome monetary gift for his troubles. Unsurprisingly, Bockhaker immediately reported the exchange to the FBI, which then used him as a counterespionage agent to gain insight into Weber's activities in the United States and Mexico. Once again, the Germans misunderstood the impact that acculturation had on German immigrants and their descendants. They assumed that the German Americans they attempted to bribe felt a deep fealty to the Reich. Rather, with rare exceptions, those approached inevitably informed the FBI of the attempts to enlist their services.[88]

Weber sent the Abwehr messages through Sebold in New York and through the German Embassy in Mexico City.[89] Weber's coded messages annoyed Berlin by carelessly including extraneous information; the Abwehr knew that transmissions always ran the risk of being decoded by the United States. They were right. The FBI gained a wealth of information about the operation of the Nicolaus ring because of Weber's amateurish indiscretions.[90] Indeed, the German Embassy in Mexico made it clear that it thought Weber was more a liability than an asset.[91] No doubt to the embassy's relief, in the summer of 1941 the FBI pressured the Mexican government to expel Weber.[92] He was manifestly reluctant to give up his lucrative and exciting espionage work in Mexico, and in letters to the *Eildienst*, bemoaned his expulsion, complaining that no one seemed to appreciate the seriousness of his medical conditions (tropical illnesses), his self-sacrificing and tireless work on behalf of the Reich, or his unstinted cooperation with the German Embassy in Mexico City. Not heeding his protests, the embassy bundled him off to Japan. There his fortunes did not improve, as no one was eager to employ him. Eventually, the German Embassy in Japan took pity on Weber, and agreed to employ him at minimum pay in Beijing or Saigon to report on financial affairs.[93]

There were quite a few other former exchange students in Mexico, but their motives are unclear. In 1940 the president of Lafayette College, William Mather Lewis, expressed his concern to IIE that Lafayette's last German exchange student, Heimfried Wiebe, had told his friends he would not immediately be going back to Germany, but intended to stay in Mexico. Hubbard hastened to assure Lewis that Wiebe and the other exchange students who had left for Mexico were simply stranded due to the war and sought new adventures. Lewis remained unconvinced that the explanation was quite so simple.[94]

Ina Gotthelf and her sister Irene provide excellent examples of this tangled web of military intelligence and covert propaganda. With considerable exaggeration, both women were described by an FBI agent as "dangerous . . . resourceful and intelligent . . . bold and daring in issuing propaganda."[95] Both sisters were certainly on very intimate terms with German officials in Boston, New York, and Washington and engaged in numerous disquieting activities in the Northeast. In the late 1930s, Ina Gotthelf was in the United States, working toward her PhD and at the same time, taught at several private schools near Boston. Her open pro-Nazism, however, tended to get her fired. At Lasell Junior College, Gotthelf had allegedly taught her younger pupils the "Horst Wessel Lied," because, she told them, there was going to be a big parade in Boston one day, and they would have to sing it.[96] Witnesses told the FBI that she frequently went to Boston Harbor to "greet" ships from Germany. Despite the vagaries of secondhand sources, the assistant chief of staff of the Eastern Defense Command reported to the FBI a conversation regarding Ina Gotthelf that he had with Walter A. De Bourg, the Swiss Legation counselor. De Bourg claimed that she was on intimate terms with several leading German military figures and knew a great deal about naval vessels in general, an observation also made by others.[97]

Irene Gotthelf was even less successful in espionage. In the mid-1930s, she was a student at Wellesley College and teaching at Boston-area private schools while working on her master's degree.[98] In one case, she passed along propaganda literature to a theology professor at Boston University to distribute to his students. Flustered by her gesture, he called the material "insidious propaganda." At one of her teaching positions, a Catholic high school near Boston, each week she gave two of her students, Nancy and Adele Chauvenet, packages addressed to the German Aviation and Propaganda Ministries and had the sisters take the materials to German ships in Boston Harbor. The little girls told their parents about their "secret assignments," prompting the inevitable FBI investigation.[99] Such was Nazi espionage in the United States.

The Duquesne arrests, which began in June 1941, infuriated the German diplomatic corps. Hans Thomsen, the ultimately anti-Nazi German chargé d'affaires, sent a series of vehement cables to the Foreign Ministry announc-

Propaganda and Espionage Missions 167

ing the FBI's progress in wrapping up the ring and the subsequent trials. In one dispatch, he succinctly mirrors this study's view of Nazi espionage in the United States:

> In addition to the propaganda damage that the discovery of this ring is causing us here, we are also ridiculed, because, as with Rumrich, Hoffmann, Schlüter, etc., who were arrested for espionage in 1938, most of these spies are petty, unintelligent busybodies who sometimes used conspicuous and clumsy methods and had already been under surveillance by the FBI for the past two years. The American government will exploit their trial to further the war psychosis against Germany.[100]

Rather late in the day, von Gienanth made his Hollywood debut, in a manner of speaking. In the last weeks of the war, 20th Century Fox released *The House on 92nd Street*, a feature film loosely based on the Duquesne fiasco. The film's plot revolves around an American college student used by the Nazis in their attempt to obtain American plans for the atomic bomb. *The House on 92nd Street* featured J. Edgar Hoover and actual FBI agents and highlighted von Gienanth's role in Nazi espionage. It premiered in September 1945, immediately after the end of the war, and won the Academy Award for best Original Motion Picture Story.[101]

As if Abwehr I (active espionage) had not caused enough damage to Germany's reputation in the United States, Abwehr II (sabotage) had also sent several sabotage agents to the United States beginning in 1940, including exchange students. Walter von Hausberger case's is perhaps the most illustrative.[102] Von Hausberger had numerous American connections as well as dual German and American citizenship. Because of this, the Abwehr believed he would make an excellent spy and sent him to espionage school. He was then shipped back to the United States to carry out the usual low-grade espionage activities, such as tracking ships in the New York and Boston harbors. He was also supposed to get in touch with German Americans thought to be sympathetic to the Reich and train them as saboteurs, if and when they received the order. In preparation for such an occasion, von Hausberger stockpiled bomb-making equipment and counterfeit dollars in his New York apartment. The mission proved to be a dismal failure.

Von Hausberger showed up at the German Embassy, explained who he was, and tried to get more money for his mission. When the embassy accused the Abwehr of risking German-American relations for such ridiculous enterprises, the intelligence agency claimed not to know who von Hausberger was.

Almost simultaneously, another Abwehr agent, codenamed Julius Bergmann, showed up at the embassy, with embassy officials having no idea who he was either; although it was noted that Bergmann had a wooden leg. Looking into this disturbing pattern, Thomsen learned of other Abwehr agents operative in the United States, among them Konstantin von Maydell, ostensibly in the United States as a documentary filmmaker,[103] whom Thomsen judged to be yet another "completely unsuitable busy-body." He complained to Berlin, "If my main task is to prevent the entry of the United States into the war by the means at my disposal, and to cultivate the few valuable relations that we still have here, these Abwehr agents have almost destroyed any chance of success. This activity is the surest way to actively bring America to the side of our enemies and destroy the last vestiges of sympathy for Germany. I cannot see any political or military benefits in it."[104]

The Abwehr responded to Thomsen's outbursts with both confusion and consternation. Its officials claimed that they had not given anyone orders for sabotage, nor did they intend to; they did, however, have "sleeper" sabotage agents in the United States, but had not activated any of them. As to Bergmann, they had never heard of him. Most probably, they speculated, he was a "provocateur." They did know von Maydell, but thought he had left the United States long ago.

Several days later, the Abwehr wrote back that it had figured out that Bergmann was, in fact, Georg Busch, one of its agents sent to the United States a year and a half earlier as a "Jewish refugee" with instructions to "protect German interests" there.[105] Busch was reconciled to being recalled home, his mission doomed to failure anyway because his subagents were, as he put it, "useless chatterboxes."[106] After this episode, Thomsen sent von Gienanth around the United States to warn the thirty Abwehr agents known to be in the country to have no contact whatsoever with German diplomatic posts. Thomsen apparently did not know about von Gienanth's own espionage activities.[107] In the end, Abwehr operations in the United States were more reminiscent of the Keystone Cops than credible threats to American democracy.

Von Hausberger was actually done in by Herbert Sonthoff. During their long association with US-centered activities in Germany, von Hausberger and Sonthoff had become well acquainted in the late 1930s. After Rosemarie Lochner and Sonthoff temporarily reunited in the United States, in 1939, she mentioned to Sonthoff that she had seen von Hausberger in New York. Sonthoff realized that given the outbreak of war, von Hausberger could only be in the United States on some type of illegal mission. Sonthoff then devised a plot to use both Lochner and von Hausberger to his own advantage: by tipping off the FBI that they were probably espionage agents.[108] He manipulated Lochner into convincing von Hausberger that she was eager to get involved in German espionage as well. Given they were both dual German and American citizens, the suggestion must have appeared completely natural. At Sonthoff's behest, Lochner spent several months playing counterespionage agent, although she had no sympathy with von Hausberger's mission. Once she insisted that she was no longer interested in playing the game, Sonthoff contacted the FBI and turned them both in as individuals "dangerous to the welfare" of the United States.[109] In the meantime, the FBI picked up von Hausberger, charged him with espionage, and released him, pending trial. Convinced his mission was doomed, and given that he had found it "impossible" to recruit German Americans for pro-German sabotage operations,[110] von Hausberger fled to Germany while free on bail.

The United States Turns the Tables

President Roosevelt well knew that German espionage and covert propaganda operations in the United States bordered on the absurd, but as a brilliant politician, he publicly connected his political opponents with malevolent German activities in the United States. Most notably, in his May 26, 1940, fireside chat on national defense, Roosevelt told the American people that there was a "Trojan horse," a "fifth column" of saboteurs, spies, foreign agents, propagandists, and traitors bent on provoking national discord and sowing confusion and panic to weaken the United States in the face of a Nazi war machine that was rolling across Western Europe and on its way to American shores. Roosevelt connected these "traitors" to isolationists, who expressed their opposition to his policies through appeals that blatantly played to the emotions.[111] Roosevelt's ominous insinuations had their intended effect. After the speech, polls showed that 70 percent of Americans believed that the Nazis were preparing to launch a Fifth Column campaign of frightening proportions and were worried that Nazis lived in their own neighborhoods.[112] Several months after Roosevelt's speech, William Donovan, the de facto lead US intelligence officer of the time, and Edgar Mowrer, a prominent journalist, published a series of articles, inevitably accompanied by a statement certifying them as officially government sanctioned. One of the articles, with perhaps only the slightest exaggeration, was titled "Nazi Germany Declared World-Wide Conspiracy to Rule Whole Universe." It included the subheading "Students Bear Watching" and warned that "German exchange students, carefully schooled in espionage and propaganda, collected no end of information in Switzerland."[113] The implication was obvious.

If anything, the "Brown Scare" benefited the FBI's Hoover even more than Roosevelt. Hoover's obsessive thirst for public acclamation could be assuaged, in part, by breaking up espionage rings, and encouraging widespread media coverage of the arrest and trial of the spies.[114] Beginning around 1939, American citizens inundated the FBI with a veritable tsunami of Fifth Column complaints. The bureau received 175 "tips" on espionage from 1933 to 1938; in 1938 the number climbed to 250; in 1939 it soared to 1,615; by May 1940, the FBI was overwhelmed by 2,871 such claims.[115] Simultaneously, the FBI received a relatively large number of "tips" about the unusual number of German students still in the United States. Hoover was quick to take advantage, alerting the House Appropriations Committee that because the FBI was so lacking in manpower, hundreds of these leads could not be followed up.[116] His tactic worked, and the FBI's budget exploded, increasing seven times over between 1938 and 1945.[117]

As discussed in the introduction, the American media also stood ready to profit from the new fears of domestic subversion. Publishers rushed to get into bookstores such titles as *The Brown Network* (1936), *Secret Agents against America* (1939), *Armies of Spies* (1941), *Total Espionage* (1941), and *Sabotage: How to Guard against It* (1942).[118] Public fear of German students was a subset of fifth columnist fears. John Roy Carlson's *Under Cover* (1943) was the most important book addressing this theme. It accused the exchange students of being propagandists and von Gienanth of being the "spy paymaster" and head of the Gestapo in the United States, all, of course, valid accusations.[119]

Hollywood was even more perceptive of the Nazi menace. In 1939 producers finally ignored Gyssling's threat that any anti-Nazi movie would lead to the end of their royalties in Germany. From 1939 through 1941, the US motion picture industry released five films about German spies and fifth columnists at work in the United States.[120] From 1942 to 1944, Hollywood produced eight additional films in this genre.[121] Ulrich Pohlenz served as a technical advisor for one of the films and played a "Nazi" in four others.[122]

After Hitler declared war on the United States, on December 11, 1941, German nationals who remained in the United States were immediately classified as enemy aliens and arrested. Those students still in the country in the 1940s found that their "charm" and good looks might now be held against them.[123] In 1942 an administrative official at Harvard informed the FBI that an associate dean suspected Herbert Sonthoff of being a spy because of "his general

Figure 5.2. Ulrich Pohlenz, 1944. Was warned against returning to Germany after trying to rescue his Jewish brother-in-law; remained in the United States; here dressed as an SS officer for an American film. Dorothy Watson, "Ex-Nazi, Still Listed as 'Enemy,' Awaits Induction," *Hollywood Citizen News*, March 10, 1944.

appearance" and his apparent inability to "look a person straight in the eye." As such, they were unsure whether to grant him his PhD.[124] A professor at the University of Georgia opined in 1943 that Sonthoff "could be very dangerous if he were engaged in any espionage activity because of his fine personality, his intelligence, self-control and his ability to speak the English language flawlessly."[125] One of the FBI agents wrote in his report that Sonthoff was "a very nice appearing man." It was not meant as a compliment; the implication was that Sonthoff might have been using his good looks to further his anti-American activities.[126] While teaching at Swarthmore College in the later war years, Sonthoff reported having "a hard time of it" because of people's suspicions that he was a Nazi.[127]

Ulrich Pohlenz seems to have been accused of espionage by almost everyone he met. While at Tulane in 1939, Pohlenz's neighbors believed him to be a Nazi spy because he never wanted to discuss his past in Germany. Several months later, he showed up at the University of California, Berkeley, to check on the results of his transfer application. He noted an uncomfortable reserve among the staff he encountered. The chair of the scholarship committee told Pohlenz that there was a misspelling of the Latin abbreviation for one of the degrees on his CV, which raised suspicion about Pohlenz being a "secret agent." While resentful, Pohlenz wrote Hubbard that he understood "the fear of German spies in this country very well." Hans A. Morgenthau, an American international relations scholar born in Germany, had known Pohlenz in Lawrence, Kansas. He told the FBI that he thought Pohlenz was a spy, although based on what evidence he neglected to say. Several years later, in 1944, Pohlenz was an American soldier stationed at Camp Fannin, Texas. A doctor there reported that he believed that Pohlenz might be a German agent, again giving no reason. Similarly, a Red Cross social worker at the camp noted that Pohlenz took much too long to write telegrams to a "Mr. Hofheins"; on another occasion, Pohlenz appeared anxious that no one hear the contents of one of his messages regarding a "Hotel Berlin." Ernest Hofheins was a friend who had introduced Pohlenz to his future wife, and *Hotel Berlin* was a film in which Pohlenz was about to play a small role. The FBI obtained a copy of Pohlenz's telegrams only to discover that these suspicious messages were, in fact, a request that his mail be delivered to him at Camp Fannin, along with "three one-pound boxes of Erna candy." Perhaps because Pohlenz was hounded around the United States due to his German origins, he found it hard to settle down and pursue a career thereafter.[128]

Conclusion

The extensive but clumsy German efforts at propaganda, espionage, and sabotage failed to achieve any meaningful advantage for the Reich. German covert propagandists and spies were seemingly chosen at random, with very little preparatory training. The German intelligence agencies used espionage to obtain information of insignificant value, thus risking exposure for little potential reward. The exchange student operatives, however, in at least some cases, succeeded in unnerving German refugees. In such instances, subtlety and secretiveness were not deployed as assets; simply making it clear that one was devoted to the Nazi "cause," and antagonistically observing refugees may have been enough to discourage some anti-Nazi activities.

The true beneficiaries of German espionage and covert propaganda were not the Nazis, but President Roosevelt, who used exaggerated fifth columnist concerns to build support for intervention, and the FBI's Hoover, who manipulated the public's preoccupation with fifth columnists to transform the bureau into an intelligence behemoth. Americans' fears of German espionage and sabotage also dogged the refugee exchange students, making their adjustment to life in the United States that much more difficult.

The German state was divided between Nazi and traditional governmental organizations, many of which were deeply caught up in brutal power struggles. Hitler generally lacked interest in the United States as well as traditional diplomacy and soft power institutions. Thus, it appeared that any German organization that wanted to try its knack for espionage found the United States a true Wild West, and could enter the arena of uncoordinated, poorly thought-out, and frenetic contests to exploit the country, which they believed to be ripe for subversion, given its open society, massive German American population, and large number of German nationals living there for one reason or another. They spread covert propaganda to encourage American antisemitism, sympathy for the "New Germany," and isolationist sentiment. Simultaneously, they competed for espionage coups that might grab the attention of the Führer, who would grant them more power as a reward. As such, they stumbled over each other in their endeavors, using any tool at their disposal, to the point that their activities became caricatures of professional covert operations. Using naïve, untrained, and sometimes unwilling German exchange students to accomplish these ends was perhaps the most foolish of their tactics. Furthermore, Americans were not just unwilling to assist them, but responded with such antagonism that their machinations were easily exposed. These expensive and resource-consuming activities did not benefit Germany; rather, they ended up being a gift to the FBI, the interventionists, and the anti-Nazi media. The Nazis thought that they could dissuade the United States from entering World War II and obtain valuable military technology in the bargain. Instead, they helped push the United States into a war which left Germany in ruins.

CHAPTER SIX

Consequences of the Nazi-Era German-American Exchange

We all had and have . . . the duty to think about guilt and complicity.
—Gustave Blanke, German-American exchange student

The most important effect of the German-American exchange was not to Germany's benefit so much as it was to the United States. After World War II, former non-Nazi German exchange students—and those who had chosen them, mentored them, and protected them—deliberately sought to transmit America's version of liberal democracy to what would now truly become a "new" Germany. They by and large succeeded. At the same time, former exchange students uninterested in Americanizing Germany sought nevertheless to leverage their American résumé to survive, if not flourish, in West Germany. They, too, were often successful. As the historian Udi Greenberg has noted, the Americans so quickly lost interest in suppressing the remnants of Nazism in West Germany—instead turning their attention to the menace of Soviet communism and dominating Western Europe—that they employed former Nazis regardless of their past sins.[1]

The United States benefited from the German-American exchange in a very different way at home: dozens of former exchange students embarked on careers in the United States. The transfer of "intellectual capital" from Germany to the United States, as represented by the former exchange refugees, symbolizes the much larger brain drain that depleted German academic, scientific, and technological life, while enriching that of the United States.

Work in Wartime

Of the repatriated students whose prewar activities are known, most used their American experience to advance their careers. A few of the exchange students during the Third Reich held US-related jobs. After returning home, Georg von Lilienfeld joined the Nazi Party and was assigned to the American Desk at the Foreign Ministry, in charge of overseeing Americans in Germany involved in pro-Nazi propaganda activities for his ministry.[2] Dietrich Ahrens oversaw Americans employed by the Propaganda Ministry (with the Foreign Ministry and the Propaganda Ministry competing for control over foreign propaganda).[3] For several years Elisabeth Noelle wrote for *Das Reich*, a journal closely associated with the Propaganda Ministry, severely criticizing the United States in a few of her articles.[4] Hans Rupp served as an expert (*Hauptreferent*) for Anglo-American Law at the Kaiser Wilhelm Institute for Foreign and International Law in Berlin.[5]

After Britain and France declared war on Germany, on September 3, 1939, at least sixteen male former exchange students joined the Wehrmacht as junior officers, another translated English for the Luftwaffe.[6] Other former exchange students were engaged in weapons research. In World War II, about one-third of Wehrmacht junior officers from the program were killed, including Martin Mohrdiek, Erwin Neumann, and Wilhelm Vauth.[7] In contrast, it appears that none of the German exchange students who remained in the United States died in the conflict.

Hans Werner Roepke reimagined his wartime military experiences after the war's conclusion. In a letter to a former classmate, subsequently related to the *Middlebury College News Letter* and reported in an article, Roepke explained that he had been a field artillery captain and had fought on the Russian front. Immediately after the war, he worked for the US military in Germany but was arrested because of a passing exchange with "an acquaintance" sought by "American counterintelligence." In prison, he psychologically became "an American in an American prison camp." Eventually, his Americanophile and "pro-democratic" bona fides were recognized, leading to his release. He then worked for the US War Department, followed by employment with an American insurance company in West Germany. Throughout this time, he sought to return permanently to the United States. Roepke wrote his Middlebury correspondent that he had gained "a sense of American values and fairness" during his exchange year. Middlebury alumnae, the article's author wrote, "can well pause and be proud of its part in this story." The article concluded, "This class member has proved to be an outstanding example of loyalty to and interest in Middlebury, as well as a strong and valid argument for the program of international exchange students in our colleges."

The author's comment on Roepke's hope of returning to the United States reads perhaps as deeply ironic: it would be best if Roepke did not relocate to the United States because, as the author put it, he was "the type of German that all of us wish would stay in Germany to rebuild Germany along the democratic lines so greatly needed."[8] Perhaps the Middlebury contributor intuited a disingenuousness in Roepke's account.

Roepke had, in fact, been a "captain" in the war, with the rank of *Hauptsturmführer* in the Waffen-SS Wiking Division. In 1943 he was assigned to command the British Free Corps: a minuscule group of two dozen men, at most, from Britain and its empire who were recruited from POW camps to serve in one of the many burgeoning foreign units of the Waffen-SS. After the war, he worked for the US military in various jobs requiring knowledge of English and was then arrested and imprisoned. Unlike the Middlebury account, however, Roepke was not simply a "distant acquaintance" of a suspicious figure. According to US authorities, Roepke led a Nazi underground movement attempting to reestablish the Reich by using biological weapons of mass destruction against the occupying forces.[9]

In Germany, as the war progressed, several of the former exchange students served in the military and conducted war-related scientific research. Henning von Dobeneck received an army deferral to continue research with Hans Fischer, a Nobel Prize–winning biochemist at the University of Munich.[10] Nevertheless, he was eventually conscripted and surrendered to the French in North Africa.[11] Others, apparently never called to active duty, rode out the war employed in military research projects, which undoubtedly benefited from their studies in the United States. Ulrich Jetter developed weapons for the Kaiser Wilhelm Institute for Metal Research.

Some former exchange students worked in Germany's soft power apparatus during the war. Elisabeth Noelle caught Goebbels' attention when she was writing for *Das Reich*, and was offered a job conducting public opinion research at the Propaganda Ministry. She later claimed that she had been unable to take the position due to a "serious illness" at that time as well as allegedly rejecting the offer on "conscientious grounds."[12] As noted, Georg von Lilienfeld worked at the Wilhelmstrasse, the Reich's Foreign Ministry. He was interrogated in Washington in May 1947, in preparation to turn state's evidence against several American pro-German propagandists. In the interview, he claimed that when Germany declared war against the United States, he had advised his American charges to leave Germany. He then "resigned" his position, "due to his respect for the US." The course of his subsequent wartime career remains shrouded in mystery; he may have been in the German armed forces, or he may have remained in the foreign diplomatic service.[13]

Erwin Wickert was a master at combining his US experience and related skills with imagined wartime memories. Once the war broke out, Wickert used his various Nazi contacts to secure a position writing foreign propaganda in the Foreign Ministry's Cultural Office. This led to his appointment as a radio attaché for the German Consulate in Japanese-occupied Shanghai, where he was responsible for overseeing the establishment and operation of a German propaganda radio station. There he supposedly insisted on a format intertwining objective news programs with American popular music. In that spirit, Wickert objected to a Nazi official reading a speech by Hitler during the station's English-language program, a transgression that purportedly led to demands that he be fired. A clique of former exchange students in the Foreign Ministry's Radio Division, anti-Nazis all, came to his aid. Wickert was merely transferred to Tokyo to serve as a radio attaché at the German Embassy.[14] Klaus Mehnart was also in the area, working in Japanese-controlled China as a pro-Nazi propagandist.[15]

Some former exchange students became involved in wartime activities against the Western Allies and their moral principles. According to an FBI postwar report, Gerold von Minden engaged in "economic warfare" against the United States during the conflict.[16] Several former exchange students took part in Holocaust atrocities. As Das Amt emphasized, work for the Foreign Ministry often might not have been innocuous. Working at the German Embassy in Paris, Kurt Weege played a role in authorizing the deportation of Jews from France.[17] Bruno Weber became an SS Hauptsurmführer and director of the Hygiene Institute of the Waffen-SS and Auschwitz Police, at Auschwitz-Birkenau. The Hygiene Institute was ostensibly responsible for hygienic, medical, and bacteriological lab work for the SS. As its leader, Weber had a close personal and professional relationship with Josef Mengele. Both men engaged in numerous crimes against humanity, including inhumane experiments. British forces captured Weber in the summer of 1946 and extradited him to Poland to face murder charges before the Polish Commission for the Investigation of War Crimes. Weber's ultimate fate is unclear. Some sources report that he died from kidney disease, while others claim that he committed suicide in confinement.[18] After Wilhelm Burmeister left DAAD, in 1941, he was also involved in the Holocaust, leading the Central Department of the Reichskommissariat Ostland. The commissariat's civilian administration assisted in the murder of Jews in the east, expulsion of some of the non-Germanic peoples, "Germanization" of those judged racially worthwhile, and resettlement of ethnic Germans in the territory.[19]

Struggles to Remain

Hitler's incomprehensible declaration of war against the United States on December 11, 1941, unleashed severe consequences for the German exchange students who had remained in the United States after the exchange program ended in 1939. Those who had not completed the naturalization process were arrested as enemy aliens and immediately interned. Many were paroled shortly thereafter, among them Fritz Lilge, Ulrich Pohlenz, Herbert Sonthoff, and Theodore von Laue.[20] On the other hand, those judged to have participated in pro-Nazi activities before the war, such as Anton-Hermann Chroust and the Gotthelf sisters, Irene and Ina, spent several years in jail.[21]

The male former exchange students considered enemy aliens appeared particularly eager to enlist in the US Army, sometimes desperately so. Ulrich Pohlenz is the quintessential example. In an ostentatious quest to serve his new country, Pohlenz wrote a number of important figures asking for help, including President Roosevelt. He swore his willingness to fight to the "last breath" for his adopted homeland.[22] His appeal was finally granted in 1943. Apparently finding the life of a private disagreeable, he suggested that he would be better placed in the US Army Strategic Services as an expert on Nazi Germany.[23] His offer was not accepted.[24] Chroust, his fanatic Nazi leadership over the German exchange students now explained away, also struggled mightily to be released to enlist in the US military, but was denied.[25] Herbert Sonthoff "appeared very anxious to get into the army," but, in this case, his enemy alien status prevented it.[26] On the other hand, Horst Janson, after being reclassified as a Russian immigrant, given his birth in St. Petersburg, registered for the draft in October 1940 and used this as evidence of his loyalty to the United States.[27] Werner von Rosenstiel actually served in both the Wehrmacht (after his repatriation) and the US Army (after his return to the United States to seek asylum). As von Rosenstiel tells it, however, he scored so high on the Army General Classification Test that it raised concerns that he might be a spy.[28] Once this complication was satisfactorily resolved, von Rosenstiel was commissioned as a lieutenant and assigned to work on legal matters; he had earned a JD degree from Fordham after his return to the United States.[29]

As the war progressed, the former exchange students who remained in America often denounced Germany in the harshest terms. Early on, Sonthoff told his landlady on several occasions that "in his opinion, Germany should be destroyed."[30] Several years later, Private Pohlenz told a reporter that he hoped "to puncture—with a bayonet, preferably—some of the Nazi ego which he helped to inflate when he was a Storm Trooper propagandist."[31] In various letters to an old Harvard friend written before Pearl Harbor, Chroust opined that it was no time for the Allies to use "half-hearted measures" against Germany. He worried that the American people were not conscious of the danger Hitler posed to the United States. After all, he wrote, "We are the last hope of all democracies. And we cannot let them down, for we would let down ourselves."[32] Chroust penned these private letters after deciding to try to remain in the United States and then used them to prove his loyalty to the country during his internment and deportation hearings. In 1940 he got into the habit of publicly declaring his hope that the Allies win the war.[33] One of the judges adjudicating his internment case sardonically remarked, "I have heard over five hundred [internment and repatriation] cases and that is the first time I have heard of a Nazi Party member saying that he wanted England and Russia to beat his own country."[34]

Fritz Lilge wrote a letter to his soon-to-be wife in which he noted that the British Royal Air Force (RAF) had just bombed Cologne five times and, so far as he was concerned, that "made it five times better for him" in light of his newfound pro-Allied sentiments. She was with him when a radio news announcement indicated that the RAF was sending one hundred bombers over Germany. Lilge blurted, "The quicker they do it the better."[35] Hans Richter was also outspoken in his condemnation of Hitler and the Nazis, who he described as "idiots" in many of the lectures he gave in central Michigan during the war. He was also a prominent speaker at a 1942 Allied Youth conference.[36]

Several of the former exchange students who fought for Germany resumed their American stay unexpectedly—as POWs.[37] Two of the former exchange student POWs, due to their apparent anti-Nazi inclinations and scholarly knowledge, were allowed to teach college-level courses to other, similarly pro-American German POWs.[38] Gustav Blanke, captured while serving in Rommel's Afrika Korps, taught American studies and American democracy courses for German POWs while interned at Fort Concordia, Kansas, and Fort Kearney, Rhode Island. Hans Henning von Dobeneck lectured on chemistry while a POW at Fort Concordia.[39] The historian Konrad Jarausch believes that these efforts to build a cadre of pro-American apostles of democracy succeeded.[40]

Occupation and Americanization

Throughout 1945, as the Allies continued to capture German territory, the severe need for trustworthy German intermediaries became more apparent. Of the nearly 100,000 occupation force administrators stationed in the American zone, most could not speak German and lacked the professional skills necessary to maintain a semblance of modern civilization in their devastated zone.[41] The American occupiers compounded their problems by initiating a vast "de-Nazification" program in the zone. The Nazis had required a large portion of German officials to join the party after May 1, 1937, or lose their jobs.[42] This meant that during the occupation, most of them were removed from office for being former party members, making it increasingly difficult to manage the American zone and, hence, highlighting the desperate need for German employees.[43]

Somewhat like native elites in European colonies, the "Americanized" former exchange students and the exchange "associates," the German program administrators and associated academic and professional volunteers, could function as mediators. They had an association with the dominant power, the United States, due to their familiarity with its language, people, and culture, and some also held American citizenship; at the same time, their connections to their native land were critically important for the occupation administration. The postwar situation allowed them to parlay their exchange experience into highly sought after jobs. At least four former exchange students eventually worked for US occupation authorities.[44] Several other former exchange students worked for the British occupation authorities.[45] One of them, Gertraut Fiek, told IIE's Ruth Hubbard that in her opinion, "the only thing worthwhile struggling for was the restoration of fundamental human rights."[46] Fritz Ermarth returned to Germany in 1945 and began working for the US occupation authorities as an editor for the US-sponsored Südwestrundfunk. During this period, American forces found Ermarth's correspondence with Karl Haushofer, the German Lebensraum advocate and Rudolf Hess mentor, in the latter's office. Ermarth then committed suicide.[47]

In the immediate postwar period, even those guilty of war crimes managed to manipulate the chaotic situation in Germany to their benefit. Erika Hanfstaengl had quite amazing luck in this regard. During the war, Hanfstaengl worked for the Cultural Office of the South Tyrolean Commission in the Trieste region (Kulturkommission der Südtiroler Umsiedlungskommission) while the city was under German occupation. This organization cataloged artwork, generally Jewish-owned, for shipment from Trieste to Germany. Apparently, her knowledge of these operations was so valuable that US occupation officials employed her to essentially do the opposite after the war. She assisted Americans at the Munich Central Collecting Point, tasked with collecting art in the American zone that had been stolen by the Nazis or lost. Building on her credentials as an art expert for the US government, after the occupation she worked as an art historian for the Bavarian State Painting Collection.[48]

A few of the former exchange students aided the United States during the postwar trials of German Nazis and American traitors. After the war, Dietrich Ahrens, who worked in the Propaganda Ministry, was brought back to the United States to serve as a witness for the prosecution of his former American staff members, such as Douglas Chandler, the most important of the pro-Nazi American radio broadcasters working in Germany during World War II.[49] Given Werner von Rosenstiel's expertise in both German and American law, he returned to Germany to write legal briefs and translate documents for the Americans at the Nuremberg Trials.[50] Sigismund von Braun, having worked in the German Foreign Ministry, was a witness for the prosecution at the Nuremberg Trials and served as a legal advisor in the defense of Ernst von Weizäcker, the highest-ranking civil servant in the Third Reich's Foreign Ministry, in the Wilhelmstrasse Trial.[51] In May 1947, Georg von Lilienfeld returned to the United States to assist in the prosecution of the American propagandists he had previously supervised. For this, he was granted permanent residency.

The first leaders of the postwar Americanization process were not the former exchange students, but their elders—the people who had selected the exchange students or had otherwise been involved in the prewar German-American exchange. While generalizations are impossible, the careers of the non-Nazi exchange program associates often followed some recognizable patterns. A strong contingent had become prominent in the field by the late Weimar era; most were noted national conservatives. At some point, they fell into disfavor with the Nazis because of their overly cosmopolitan inclinations, apparent hesitancy to fully accede to Nazi demands, or Jewish ancestry. Some went into exile in the United States; others remained in Germany and sought to placate the regime or at least not attract its attention.

Carl Joachim Friedrich was fortunate in having established his career in the United States before the Nazis came to power. He thus avoided the wave of refugee Jewish German and leftist academics who fiercely competed for academic employment in the US, beginning in 1933. He had joined the Harvard University faculty as a professor of government in 1936. At the same time, he was intimately involved with efforts to resettle Jewish German exiles in the United States. Friedrich later gained attention as a fierce interventionist. As such, he served on the executive board of the Council for Democracy, an influential pro-interventionist organization. During the war, he helped establish and direct the School of Overseas Administration, to train military officers for administrative positions in the anticipated future US occupation zone. Immediately after the war, Friedrich took a position as a de-Nazification official with the American military government in West Germany and eventually became a representative of General Lucius Clay, military governor of the US Occupation Zone. Friedrich then assisted in drafting German state constitutions and the Basic Law, which would become the German Federal Republic's constitution. Friedrich also taught at the University of Heidelberg while retaining his position at Harvard.[52]

Quite a few of the former exchange students and officials had worked for the Weimar Republic, the Third Reich, as well as the Federal Republic. After his dismissal from DAAD in 1935, Georg von Fritsch served in the legal bureau of the Wehrmacht High Command, eventually achieving the rank of ministerial councilor. In the postwar period, he held various high-level governmental positions and was selected to be the first commissioner for human rights (*Wehrbeauftragte*) for the Bundeswehr. He never took up his new post, however, because he died soon after his appointment.[53] After the war, August Fehling, the anti-Nazi scientist involved in selecting exchange student candidates for the program, was appointed ministerial councilor for science and higher education for the Schleswig-Holstein Ministry of Education and Cultural Affairs. In the 1950s, he became one of West Germany's leading advocates for American science policy, an approach aimed at remodeling German applied scientific research along American lines.[54]

Many leading German academics of Jewish ancestry resumed their academic careers while in exile in the United States. The renowned historian Hans Rothfels serves here as an example. Because of his Jewish ancestry, he was arrested and beaten by the Gestapo in 1938 during Kristallnacht, which resulted in his accepting teaching positions in Britain and the United States, where he took a professorial chair at the University of Chicago in 1946. While at Chicago, he began publishing treatises praising the heroism of Hitler's conservative opponents. In 1951 Rothfels returned to Germany and joined the faculty of the University of Tübingen. Thereafter, he attempted to promote the "American perspective" to his students.[55]

Arnold Bergsträsser, one of the creators of DAAD's prewar ideology, was a radical conservative German nationalist and anti-communist, though with strong cosmopolitan interests. When the Nazis took power, Bergsträsser had already established close ties to the United States, including working with the Rockefeller Foundation in an advisory capacity. He continued to mentor several Jewish students into 1934. His own part-Jewish ancestry elicited harassment, and the Nazis revoked his teaching certification in 1936. He then emigrated from Germany to the United States, eventually landing at the University of Chicago.[56] Bergstrasser's political philosophy changed during his exile. He came to reject militarism, and hoped liberal democracy would return to Germany once the Nazi regime ended. He returned to Germany in 1954 and made a name for himself as a leading pro-American apologist. He ultimately accepted the chair of political science at the University of Freiburg, where his work focused on applying American methodologies to German political science. His promotion of American studies carried him to the pinnacle of academic honors. He entered Chancellor Konrad Adenauer's circle and was appointed to head West Germany's UNESCO mission. In part because of Bergstrasser's Western-oriented political science scholarship, and his overall influence in the fledgling republic, his work became the foundation of the social sciences curriculum in West Germany's schools.[57]

As conditions stabilized in West Germany in the 1950s, some of the former exchange students also sought to foster American principles in their work. After the war, Oskar Bezold became managing editor of the *Westdeutsche Allgemeine Zeitung*, where he established a compulsory training course to improve the journalistic techniques of the editorial staff, he said, "on the basis of the knowledge I gained in American schools of journalism."[58] Claus Holthusen resumed his career as a trainee in the German judicial system after the war, fighting for the application of democratic principles.[59]

After the war, it appears that some of the people involved in the German-American exchange experienced a growth in religiosity. Wilhelm Burmeister, managing director of DAAD from 1934 to 1941, joined the Council for Christian-Jewish Cooperation (Gesellschaften für Christlich-Jüdische Zusammenarbeit) in 1963.[60] Ulrich von Gienanth, the peripatetic SS-SD manager of the German students in the United States from the mid-1930s, became active after the war in the International Christian Leadership, an organization that sought to attract political and economic leaders to its ranks. Ulrich von

Gienanth's wife, Karin von Gienanth, was a principal member of the German branch of the organization and hosted Americans traveling in West Germany on Christian missions.[61]

Several former exchange students continued to be active in exchange programs between the United States and Germany. Marianne Lautsch remained in Germany after her repatriation and, after the war, became involved in the German Language and Culture Summer Program with Indiana University. Lautsch was also a noted activist on women's issues and international relations. For her contributions to German-American relations, and her other accomplishments, the Federal Republic awarded her the Bundesverdienstkreuz First Class in 1976.[62] Ina Gotthelf lived the life of a New York City socialite after the war and was particularly devoted to German-American relations and promoting German culture in the United States.[63]

A number of the former exchange students rose to the highest levels of the German diplomatic service. This is perhaps unsurprising given that many had been selected as exchange students due to their interest in a foreign country, their academic achievement, and their ambition. In general, they neither offered "tenacious resistance to the plans of the Nazi rulers," as a West German Foreign Ministry brochure, "Foreign Policy Today" (*Auswärtige Politik Heute*), put it in 1979, nor, with a few notable exceptions, were they likely involved in the rapacious "looting, robbery, persecution and mass murder" as *Das Amt* suggested.[64]

Generally, the former exchange students who pursued diplomatic careers received American blessings to advance in their careers. After the end of the war, Sigismund von Braun returned to Germany and was duly arrested and interned because of his membership in the Nazi Party. An investigation concluded that he had "supported clerical and other offices in hiding people persecuted for religious, political, and racial reasons and [obviated] their deportation, taking high personal risk" and was therefore cleared of any connection to Nazism. Soon thereafter he worked as a civil servant for the state of Rhineland-Palatinate. Several years after the creation of the Federal Republic, he rejoined the Foreign Ministry, serving as chief of protocol, ambassador to France, observer to the United Nations, and Foreign Ministry state secretary.[65] Although Georg von Lilienfeld obtained permanent residency in the United States in exchange for his postwar testimony, his desire to continue in the German diplomatic corps continued unabated. At some point, American authorities determined that von Lilienfeld was "closely associated with the opposition group in the Foreign Office and the Army" and had assisted in the German surrender in Italy at war's end. Cleared of any wrongdoing, he returned to West Germany in 1951 to assume a post in the Foreign Ministry's Press and Information Office and later became chief of the North American desk. According to the CIA, von Lilienfeld had a "high regard" for the United States and for Americans. He eventually served as West Germany's ambassador to Spain and to Iran.[66] Erwin Wickert returned to Germany from Japan in 1947, was briefly interned, and then worked in the broadcasting industry. In 1955 he joined the diplomatic service, eventually becoming West Germany's deputy ambassador to Great Britain, followed by ambassadorships to Romania and later China.[67]

Quite a few of the former exchange students who returned to Germany pursued careers in academia or research. After Gustav Blanke returned in 1945, he developed American studies programs at several universities. He also helped found the German Association for American Studies (Deutsche Gesellschaft für Amerikastudien) in 1953.[68] According to Blanke, those who joined the association "professed their commitment to the West and to German policy towards the West."[69] American observers acclaimed *Der amerikanischer Geist* (The American spirit) (1956), one of his best-known books. Ralph Lewis, a sociologist at the US State Department, noted that it quickly became the second most popular book about the United States being read in West Germany. Lewis praised the book's "American flavor." It used quotations from famous Americans to illustrate such concepts as liberty, unity, and democracy.[70]

Hans Rupp's career flourished after the war. After holding the position of undersecretary for universities in the Württemberg-Baden Ministry of Culture, he was elected as a Social Democrat to the Constituent Assembly of the state of Württemberg-Hohenzollern. He remained active as a legal theorist, which led to his election as a judge of the Federal Constitutional Court (Bundesverfassungsgericht), a position he held from 1951 to 1975. Rupp also taught briefly at several German universities and as a visiting professor at the University of Michigan and the University of Chicago.[71] In 1959 Fritz Bartz was appointed chair of geography at the University of Freiburg and also taught at the University of California, Berkeley, and the University of Minnesota as a guest professor.[72]

Elisabeth Noelle became the most prominent social scientist to emerge from the German-American exchange program, bringing American survey research methods to Germany.[73] She cofounded the Allensbach Institute for Public Opinion Research (Institut für Demoskopie Allensbach) in 1947, which grew to become West Germany's most prominent conservative-leaning public opinion research center. She also published academic works on polling theories and taught several times as a visiting professor at the University of Chicago. In the 1990s, Leo Bogart and Christopher Simpson wrote articles highlighting her strong connections with Nazi organizations in the 1930s and 1940s, especially the Ministry of Propaganda, and claimed that her public opinion theory was fundamentally influenced by her experience as a Nazi propagandist. Due to the controversy that ensued, Noelle lost her visiting professorship at Chicago.[74] After the war, Ulrich Jetter resumed a career in atomic physics at the Stuttgart University of Applied Sciences (Technische Hochschule Stuttgart). He is best known for the Jetter cycle, a means to sustain a nuclear fusion chain reaction. In 1951 he returned to the United States as a cultural exchange fellow. Oddly, he radically changed his profession at about that time, going to work for Elisabeth Noelle's Allensbach Institute.[75]

After the war, Adolf Henning Frucht was one of the few former exchange students, of which we know, who lived in East Germany. Frucht elected to live in East Berlin to assist with its medical crisis and became a professor of physiology at Humboldt University. In the 1960s, as a consequence of his research, he learned about the Warsaw Pact's Alaska Plan, designed to incapacitate American personnel operating the early warning missile system in the Aleutian Islands. Frucht passed the information on to the CIA and was then denounced by an informant. East German authorities arrested him for treason in 1967. Frucht served ten years in prison, until being exchanged for a Chilean communist spy.[76]

Brain Drain and Institutional Transformations

It is widely accepted that the relative positions of Germany and the United States in scientific discoveries and technological innovations shifted definitively during the Nazi era. Because of the Nazis' persecution of intellectuals due to their ethnicity or political views, many moved permanently to the United States. Further, immediately after the war, the United States virtually commandeered scientists from Germany, seeking their expertise in developing military-related technologies as the Cold War took shape.[77] The German physicist Carl Friedrich von Weizsäcker attributed Germany's sharp decline in intellectual achievement to this "loss of intellectual substance."[78] Indicative of this brain drain, more German former exchange students are known to have entered the professoriate or engaged in scientific research in the United States (17) than in Germany (12). In the United States, Gertrude Achenbach earned a PhD from Princeton University in 1948 and continued researching and teaching Renaissance Italian and Christian art at Princeton University and at Rutgers University.[79] Horst "Peter" Janson became an internationally renowned art historian and a professor of the history of art at New York University.[80] Hans Gatzke received a PhD in history from Harvard University. From 1947 to 1964, he taught at Johns Hopkins University and, from 1965 to 1986, at Yale. His student exchange host school, Williams College, named a professorship in modern European history for Gatzke.[81] Ursula Schäfer earned a doctorate in 1949 from the University of California, Berkeley, focusing on the Age of Exploration, colonial Mexico, and the history of science. She taught at various colleges before concluding her career at the University of Arizona. In 1990 she received the Distinguished Service Award from the Conference on Latin American History, the first woman to be so honored.[82] Theodore von Laue received a PhD degree from Princeton during the war and then taught at several prestigious institutions, eventually being appointed to a chair for European history at Clark University, in Massachusetts.[83] Von Laue had converted to Quakerism after arriving in the United States, where his convictions led him to champion the anti-Vietnam War movement at Washington University, in St. Louis, and to participate in the march to Selma, Alabama, led by Rev. Martin Luther King Jr. He later became active in the nuclear disarmament movement.[84]

In 1946, Anton-Hermann Chroust became a professor of law, philosophy, and history at the University of Notre Dame.[85] Hans Richter taught religion and philosophy at Alma College in Michigan.[86] Fritz Lilge received a PhD in education from Harvard University in 1941 and then taught at Berkeley, becoming a full professor.[87] Herbert Sonthoff earned a PhD from Harvard and eventually became director of professional education at the Stevens Institute.[88] Fritz Tiller received a PhD at Yale and became a professor of German at the United States Military Academy.[89] Rainer Schickele held a number of academic and diplomatic positions, finally settling down at the University of Tennessee.[90] Arthur Ippen taught hydraulic engineering at MIT.[91] Gerhard Brecher pursued a medical research career at several universities.[92] In the 1990s, Werner von Rosenstiel taught a course on human rights and war crimes at the University of South Florida. In 2004 he received an honorary doctorate from the University of Cincinnati, where he had studied as an exchange student.[93]

While Helene Mayer lived most of her life in the United States after Hitler took power, she agreed to represent Germany on the women's fencing team at the 1936 Berlin Olympics, as Germany's only "Jewish" athlete. She won the silver medal in this event. Her Nazi salute during the awards ceremony generated substantial controversy. Mayer returned to the United States after the Olympics but spent the last months of her life in West Germany.[94] She is generally considered one of the foremost women athletes of the twentieth century.

It is also important to consider the import of the institutional transformations that followed the end of the German-American exchange. The onset of World War II brought vast changes to DAAD's leadership along with degeneration of its global network, as only countries allied with Germany or certain friendly nonbelligerent states continued to participate in DAAD exchanges. In 1941 a Nazi student leadership organization, the German Student Association for Foreigners (Deutschen Studienwerks für Ausländer), gained much of the power that DAAD had held over the student exchanges. Burmeister left DAAD as a result. Gustav Scheel became president of DAAD, with Werner Braune, former head of the Foreign Student Leadership Office, replacing Burmeister.[95]

The Institute of International Education, after almost twenty years of stable leadership and administrative processes, experienced rapid changes during the war. The institute's trend toward expanding exchanges with non-European countries strengthened during the war, when oceanic travel was impossible. Furthermore, the US government began its own formalized soft power cultural efforts in Latin America in July 1938, with the US Department of State establishing a Division of Cultural Relations. One of its primary missions, shared with other federal government organizations created in the next several years, was to counter Nazi Germany's soft power efforts in Latin America, which built upon the millions of German descendants in the region. In 1941 IIE began administering its first federally funded exchange, with Latin American students.

Stephen Duggan retired from the IIE directorship in 1946. His son, Lawrence Duggan, had been groomed for just such work, and was chosen to replace his father. Lawrence Duggan represented a generation of far-left intellectuals now out of step with the times, much as his father's Wilsonian internationalism had been anachronistic in the preceding decades. Tragically, only two years before Stephen's death, he learned that Lawrence had "fallen" to his death from his office in IIE headquarters, ten days after being questioned by the FBI over suspicions of being a Soviet spy. In the 1990s, these accusations were found to be true.[96]

The Educational and Cultural Relations Division of the US Office of Military Government in Germany began the first postwar educational study programs for Germans in 1947. Ruth Hubbard, who had managed the German-American exchange at IIE before the war, organized the program.[97] Initially, its organizational structure resembled that of the prewar exchange: American private and religious organizations contributed funding; fraternities, sororities, and the American universities provided housing; and the universities also waived tuition.[98] The State Department-housed US High Commission for the Occupation of Germany inherited the program in 1949, reorganized it as a government program, and continued it until 1956. Hundreds of German college students studied in the United States under its auspices.[99]

Several months after the establishment of the Federal Republic of Germany in 1949, Hubbard, the rector of the University of Bonn, and several state education and culture ministers reconstituted DAAD.[100] Soon thereafter, former DAAD scholarship recipients instituted a new scholarship in honor of Adolf Morsbach, DAAD's first managing director.[101] Responsibility for drafting DAAD's new charter fell primarily to August Fehling, as a high official in the Ministry of Education of Schleswig-Holstein and the Conference of the Ministers of Culture of the German Länder (*Länder*, referring to the federal states). He also served as its first postwar deputy chair.[102] A former German-American exchange student, Fritz Hubertus Scheibe, served as DAAD's secretary general from 1955 to 1979.[103]

In the early post–World War II years, various German committees chose the German exchange students; American authorities in Germany had to declare them "free of Nazism" before final acceptance.[104] The German selectors applied criteria remarkably similar to those of the Weimar and Nazi eras, with the exception, of course, of any association with Nazism. Candidates were still expected to show social and political "awareness." While academic achievement certainly factored prominently in the selection process, the committees also heavily emphasized choosing students judged to represent "the best type of German": usually from elite backgrounds; physically fit and attractive; with a strong interest in extracurricular activities; of good character and with appropriate political attitudes; and a pleasant personality. Leadership qualities were prized.[105] Since the student exchange selection committees during the Third Reich did not always note a candidate's ideological fervor, in some cases it would have been almost impossible to tell if a student's essay explaining why they wished to study in the United States and the qualitative evaluations of the recommendation committees were from the Weimar era, the Third Reich, the postwar American occupation, or the early Federal Republic.

American government officials extensively surveyed the opinions of postwar German exchange students. In general, they responded in a remarkably similar way to those from the Third Reich. Prewar negative and positive American stereotypes remained almost entirely intact. Critical remarks were often strongest upon arrival in the United States. Some of the German exchange students complained about the American penchant for materialism, worship of technology, cultural superficiality, ignorance of the wider world, anti-intellectualism, egalitarianism, and emphasis on collegiate social life rather than academic study. Some noted that the United States preached the wonders of democracy, and yet they observed glaring racial and religious inequalities and a lack of concern for social justice. The most notable difference in postwar attitudes was the propensity of German exchange students in the United States to become highly defensive when asked about Nazism, which they tended to downplay in favor of the "old German" archetype beloved by Duggan: the Germany of literature, classical music, philosophy, and traditional academic culture. Over the course of their time in the United States, however, there usually came to appreciate the "freer and more humane" American way of life. This included social informality, optimism, personal happiness, and "zest for life." By the end of their exchange year in the United States, there tended to be a notable decline in the exchange students' nationalism in favor of a more cosmopolitan attitude, a greater degree of independence of thought and opinion, greater tolerance, and more flexibility. Some assimilated quickly into American life and were shocked when they returned home to perceive West Germans as too narrowminded and (rather surprisingly) militaristic. On the flip side, the adoption of American mannerisms, or overexuberance for the American way of life, tended to alienate their compatriots, who disdained the students' ostentatious Americanization.[106]

Thus, while neither the Germans' propaganda nor their espionage operations had any effect on the United States, the Americanization of so many "Nazi" exchange students did. These young Germans were selected as the future elite of Germany; this part of the Nazis' plan succeeded, though not quite as intended. The majority of the former exchange students were savvy enough to use their newfound knowledge of American culture for their own benefit. Those able to remain in the United States often ascended to leading positions in academia, overcoming seemingly impossible odds, as in the case of Anton-Hermann Chroust. Therefore, instead of benefiting Germany's intellectual life, their knowledge and skills benefited the United States. This exemplifies the stream of German intellectuals to the United States, helping make it the world's academic, scientific, and technological superpower.[107]

Those Germans who had participated in managing the German-American student exchange or who played some other role in it perhaps had a greater effect on the development of West Germany. A dozen or more of these exchange associates either remained in Germany but became Americanized to some extent or returned to Germany after the war. They set about Americanizing the Bonn Republic in their respective fields. Although they only constituted a small fraction of the German-born "Americanizers" after World War II, they illustrate the general path of so many others. Therefore, it is the height of irony that the Third Reich, which had invested so much money and resources in the exchange program, not only failed to benefit from it but ultimately helped the United States and led to the Americanization of Germany. Even in this realm, the United States bested the Third Reich in their relationship.

Conclusion

> Most of our boys are soldiers now, but whenever we write each other, there is much talk about America.
>
> —*Anna-Barbara Wojnowska,*
> *German exchange student at Knox College*

> Sometimes my stay in the U.S. seems to be like a dream which was never real or will never be real . . . You are optimistic in hoping that someday we shall sit at the same table again [at the International House, Chicago]. I wish it could be possible, but I do not see any possibilities as far as I am concerned . . . Give my regards to those who remember me still.
>
> —*Albert Ickler, Wehrmacht officer, 1941*

The experiences of 270 German exchange students in the United States during the 1930s and 1940s may initially seem like a relatively minor historical subject, but their stories offer insight into some of the most interesting historical issues involving Nazism in Germany and the United States. Furthermore, by analogy, these experiences provide a lens through which to examine a relevant issue in American higher education today—the responses of young elites shaped by an authoritarian regime when immersed in a liberal democracy.

All the German exchange students had experienced life under the liberal democracy of the Weimar era. Most of the German administrators associated with international student exchange program belonged to the traditional German elite, in particular those officials who worked for DAAD, the Germany Foreign Ministry, and the Education Ministry as well as members of Germany's professoriate. These officials were largely nationalists with conservative values, who abhorred the Versailles Treaty and yearned for Germany to regain its lost territories, its position among the Great Powers, and most of all, its self-respect. Like virtually all Germans, they felt desperate and helpless amid the Great Depression, which for Germany was its second economic disaster in a decade. The inability or unwillingness of the opposing political parties in the Reichstag to take dramatic steps to overcome these multitudinous crises frustrated them. The attitudes, concerns, and known political affiliations of this cohort sufficiently intersected with the Nazis' immediate goals such that Hitler's government did not initially dismiss most of them from their positions. Over time, however, the Nazi regime purged their ranks with ever-increasing thoroughness, removing anyone who deviated from official ideology or was of Jewish ancestry. Some officials from the Weimar era managed, however, to manipulate the chaotic, bureaucratic nature of the new dictatorship and survive, allowing them to continue to influence the course of events for years to come.

To the extent possible, non-Nazi officials advanced those students most like them: members of the *Bildungsbürgertum*—the conservative, highly educated, and financially secure—many of whom had already traveled abroad, studied foreign languages and cultures, and perhaps regarded the typical Nazi with disdain. Parallels between them and the Swing Youth (*Swingjugend*), well-off German youths passionate about swing dancing and also imitating the behaviors of the British upper class, were apparent.[1] In most cases, these German students focused more on achieving personal goals than those of the state. The pervasive Nazi attitude that commitment to Nazi activities was more important than the attainment of professional knowledge was naturally antithetical to most college students' goals.[2] Further, the pragmatic goals of student organizations at universities became increasingly lost as, typical of the Nazi's Kafkaesque bureaucracy, these groups became focused more on turf battles than on developing appealing new activities to further the students' Nazification.

Those officials willing to advance non-Nazi students feared attracting attention, because doing so could result in dismissal from their positions or worse. Assisting non-Nazi students to leave for the United States or to remain there constituted relatively mild acts of opposition, given the possibility that Nazi zealots might discern their tactics and punish them. Notably, Foreign Ministry officials often were involved in such cases. Foreign Ministry "traditionalists," usually holdovers from the Weimar Republic, believed that official methods and goals prior to the National Socialists takeover were more beneficial to German cultural diplomacy than those adopted by the Nazis. Remarkably, during the Third Reich, several of the eight most important German diplomatic officials in the United States actively worked against the Nazis at some point. This perspective of the Foreign Ministry being less Nazified than other departments, which coincides with the discoveries of many other scholars in the past decade, may be a result of newly found archival sources, as well as documents that reflect the private, rather than public, statements of such individuals regarding the Reich.

Cultural Misunderstandings

The continued domination of the student exchange culture and program by traditionalists and their intellectual (or actual) progeny was sure to be challenged by the politically well-connected, amoral, opportunistic Nazis who formed the new German elite. Thus DAAD was purged of its traditional leadership in the second half of 1934 and staffed with radical Nazis. As many as half of the students who left Germany for the United States in 1933 and 1934 never returned, which made getting the German-American exchange under control a Nazi priority; the radicals therefore inserted themselves directly into the exchange selection process wherever possible. An increasing number of the exchange students were SS members or Nazi student leaders who were rammed through the selection process. The bureaucratic incompetence and competitive struggles of Nazi officialdom, however, impeded the full Nazification of the exchange program. DAAD eventually became subject to the dictates not just of the Foreign Ministry or the Education Ministry, but also of the Propaganda Ministry, the Nazi Party Foreign Organization, the SS, the University Foreign Affairs Offices, the German Student Union, and the National Socialist German Students' League. This exemplified the tendency toward "polycratic" control in Nazi Germany.

Favorable views of the United States did not suddenly disappear after the Nazis took power. The historian Detlef Junker suggests that before World War II, Americans counted among the Germans' "favorite foreigners."[3] A public lecture by one of the German exchange students at St. Lawrence University, New York, illustrates this. She observed that different demographic groups in Germany viewed the United States positively: "The child . . . thinks of America as a world of Indians, and the works of Cooper are widely read . . . The young woman thinks of America in terms of Hollywood, clothes, sports, and freedom. The working-man . . . thinks of it as a place where the laborer is much better off than in Germany."[4]

Along with the influence of sympathetic non-Nazi officials involved in the exchange, a number of other reasons explain why so many students opposed to Nazism, or with the potential to become opposed, made it through the obstacles placed in the way of the regime's less zealous supporters. DAAD came under a great deal of pressure to fill the numerous exchange student slots in the United States reserved for German students. If the Nazis made ideological criteria too stringent to fill them, it meant a lost opportunity for the Reich to impress Americans with yet more paragons of the "New Germany." It also would be a loss for the Reich in that it represented one more missed opportunity to transfer useful knowledge from the United States to Germany. Furthermore, the German academics involved constantly emphasized the importance of the students having to be academically strong for the American schools to accept them. For certain selection committee members, this provided an excellent excuse to push forward students with excellent academic credentials, as opposed to those with less stellar intellectual achievements but stronger evidence of Nazi fanaticism.

The Gestapo, also subject to Nazi bureaucratic confusion, rivalry, and incompetence, was not ideally suited to weeding out non-Nazis from numerous presumably intelligent and wily college students. The state of modern technology made thorough background investigations prohibitively labor intensive. Also, the Gestapo tended to be more reactive than proactive when it came to ferreting out enemies of the state.[5] Determining the degree of an exchange candidate's Nazi fervor was not likely at the top of its list of priorities. Investigating an exchange candidate's past for the Gestapo was akin to expending resources to head off a somewhat unlikely crime, rather than pursuing the overwhelming number of tips regarding crimes against the state already purportedly committed. It appears that in most cases, the Gestapo simply deferred to the judgment of university and DAAD representatives on the selection committees to expose politically unreliable elements, thus putting the onus on those organizations if trouble arose. In turn, DAAD officials demanded that the student associations look into candidates' backgrounds before moving them forward in the selection process. Thus any embarrassing failures in the selection could simply be attributed to sloppy work on their part. For this reason, even by the late 1930s, approximately 10 to 15 percent of the German students chosen to study in the United States never returned home, but eventually became American citizens.

All the students selected for the various exchange programs were required to take an "area studies" course. According to the propaganda presented to them, the American concept of freedom was simply the glorification of rootlessness, chaos, and a perverse adulation of criminals. Political corruption, party machines, demagoguery, radicalism, plutocratic influence, and class warfare formed the basis of American democracy. Americans' much vaunted freedom of the press was really a mirage, because Jewish big business interests controlled the media.[6] The propaganda dispensed in these courses, the Nazis believed, would facilitate Americans' conversion to their worldview. The German instructors who had studied in the United States might have been too Americanized themselves to swallow what they taught, and in any case, those who developed the propaganda had little understanding of the United States.

German officials themselves often failed to understand American psychology and culture. Ulrich von Hassell, Germany's ambassador to Italy, noted that the Americans and Hitler "spoke such an entirely different language that an understanding between them was almost impossible."[7] Americans such as IIE's Stephen Duggan, who dealt with German authorities, clearly recognized this disconnect. Duggan noted in his autobiography,

> It is frequently stated that the Germans have been very unsuccessful in understanding the psychology of other peoples. This has been particularly true of the Nazis. Neither Hitler nor Goebbels had been abroad nor was aware of what the probable attitude of foreigners would be toward the kind of speeches and actions that had won success for the Nazis in Germany. This was even more true of the group of secondary leaders of the Nazis. Their attention had been concentrated upon winning control of Germany . . . It was when the [propaganda] activity was undertaken here that I became convinced of the apparent inability of the Germans to comprehend the psychology of foreign peoples.[8]

Those designing propaganda training for the exchange students also believed that their messages would be most effective if aimed at an academic audience. Modern German culture had a strong tradition of an academic elite derived from the Bildungsbürgertum that enjoyed prestige and influence far beyond its American counterpart.[9] Furthermore, many of the managerial-level functionaries in propaganda organizations, and DAAD, held doctorates. It is entirely likely that their contact with Americans was largely limited to academic circles. Indeed, it appears the Germans believed that academics and the highly educated had an outsized influence on American public opinion, which was a fundamental misreading of American culture. Germans who had taught in the United States had been immersed in an academic environment, which did not necessarily mirror the America outside the ivory tower.

The Nazis at DAAD mistakenly assumed that German students' charisma would ease acceptance of their propaganda messages, but they misunderstood the American concept of charisma. To them, charisma and political leadership were one and the same. In contrast, American college students translated charisma as social popularity. Many regarded the German exchange students as charming, good looking, exotic, and cosmopolitan, and they generated interest on those bases. Such charismatic students were usually welcomed as individuals, not as representatives of a fascist regime. In short, the Nazis selected the exchange students because they represented a propagandistic image of Nazi Germany, but Americans perceived them as "cool kids." Generally, the less they addressed the politics of their home country, the more popular they were.

Americans tolerated the presence of Nazi German students on American college campuses to a surprising degree. This was because they regarded the students more as young, attractive Europeans, and not so much as Nazis, at least until Germany's aggression against neighboring countries in 1938. The Institute of International Education's leadership, as well as most American college administrators, indulged the German students' expression of their political views as representatives of the Reich. Indeed, IIE strongly encouraged exchange students to explain their government's positions if asked.

Although Reich officials had coached the students well in this respect, the resulting propagandistic speeches proved to be dismal failures. The students unexpectedly ran into an unbreachable barrier to the allure of foreign ideologies formed by American students' attachment to the lure of campus life, and also their focus on academics as the key to a rare professional job during the Great Depression; Americans' general lack of interest in foreign affairs; ingrained liberal democratic ideals; a multiethnic society (though flawed); respectfulness toward foreign visitors; and American educators' encouragement of students to think creatively, critically, and independently. On top of that, the seemingly insane dictatorships that had enthralled otherwise admirable peoples at the time and the awkwardness of the Germans' propaganda did not help matters. Indeed, many Americans felt insulted by the students' lies, distortions, evasions, and excuses. The response of Americans subject to such propaganda only worsened as the Nazi regime radicalized.

This does not, however, mean that Americans had no interest in learning about the exchange students' views on their homeland and its politics. Some

Americans were curious about German culture apart from political considerations, as they might have been about any other culture. Later in the decade, others might have become interested in the Reich's domestic and foreign policies. In situations where controversial issues arose, many Americans reacted with civility, once an abiding trait of American culture. The exchange students sometimes misunderstood their courteous response as a sign of ideological agreement.

The German students were exposed to an educational experience radically different form the one they knew from home. Suddenly immersed in the world of their American peers, many became swept up in a whirlwind of social activities, sporting events, and dating. They enjoyed myriad personal freedoms that no longer existed in their own country and they might never have experienced. Some of the German students used the opportunity to defy the Nazi authorities assigned to watch over them while in the United States.

Most of the exchange students found themselves impressed by the freedom and encouragement of personal growth, camaraderie, and vibrant social life on American college campuses. Political or ideological matters, when they came up at all, were freely debated. The state's total lack of concern about one's opinion came as a shock to some of the students experiencing life in a liberal democracy for the first time. What were intelligent college students from Nazi Germany to think when confronted with the contrast between what they were instructed about America and what they actually encountered?

The students' year abroad provided an opportunity to interact, probably for the first time, with German refugees, African Americans, Jewish Americans, and other "non-Aryans." In many instances, the exchange students were, again, surprised at how their perception of these groups clashed with Nazi orthodoxy. The United States was a heterogeneous nation, with dozens of ethnic, religious, and political groups as well as various subcultures. With the glaring exception of people in the Jim Crow South, the groups generally tolerated one another.

While political party affiliations and class differences sometimes led to bitter political contests, a fundamental agreement about the virtues of democracy and (relative) ethnic tolerance held the disparate peoples of the United States together. According to Nazi ideology, such a nation should not have existed. Americans' political animosities usually centered on domestic issues, rather than foreign affairs (with the possible exception of the Soviet Union). Pacifism was the most popular and passionate movement concerned with foreign issues of the era. If anything, the German students appeared to fall remarkably in line with the American isolationist version of pacifism popular among American college students.[10]

As the year abroad progressed, the exchange students developed their own relationships to American society. They often saw America through a "pro-American" or "anti-American" lens.[11] Their complaints almost inevitably reflected the traditional, haughty disdain for America's plebian, childish culture, compared to the refined sophisticated, millennia-old civilizations of Europe. The informal nature of Americans, and the indifference to a student's family status, led some of the German students to bemoan the lack of deference to which they were accustomed. Their anti-American sentiments appear more consistent with the views of the pre-Nazi Bildungsbürgertum than the distinctly anti-intellectual, race-based warrior ideology of Nazism.

The majority of the exchange students enjoyed their year in the United States without experiencing an existential crisis brought on by living there. Almost all of them benefited in some way from the knowledge and skills they gained. Yet, most certainly never imagined attempting to remain in their host country. The incentives to return home were tremendous: entire lives, up to the exchange year, had been lived in Germany. Having taken part in a study abroad program itself conferred a degree of prestige on top of the academic or cultural benefits. Surely many retained their faith in the New Germany, at least to an extent. Of course, some students were simply indifferent to American culture; as they had intended, they focused on their studies much more than on their social lives in preparation for careers back home. This perspective seemed especially common among students in the natural sciences, technology, and medicine and those anticipating a career in the foreign service.

Some German students likely conceded the authenticity of certain American virtues, but found them not as compelling, overall, as the Nazi-German values they held. To justify holding positive feelings about another country, in this case the United States, a conflicted student might lessen their distress by highlighting the flaws in American society while downplaying those of the Third Reich—that is, by adopting the tactic of choice-supportive bias, a tendency to overly validate a desired course of action while simultaneously denigrating the rejected course. Similarly, the exchange student might recognize some desirable traits in American life but find psychological solace in cognitive inertia or belief perseverance, the resistance usually felt to changing a deeply held set of beliefs. For example, the student might decide that more fundamental values, such as honor, patriotism, and allegiance to family and community, overrode attraction to a foreign culture. "My country, right or wrong," an old adage quoted by one of the German students, encapsulates this sentiment.[12] The saga of Fritz Brandi, a German exchange student at Furman University, is an excellent example of this attitude. Brandi so thoroughly enjoyed his time in the United States that he lined up a job on Wall Street and was considering remaining permanently in the country. The Sudetenland crisis erupted, however, and everyone assumed Germany would soon be at war with its traditional adversaries once again. Brandi had to choose: remain in United States as a German emigrant or go home and "do my duty as a German." He chose the latter. Even so, as his ship left the skyline of New York behind, "tears almost got in my eyes because now my year in the U.S.A. was definitely over."[13]

On a more prosaic level, an exchange student might have felt that they could not bear forgoing the family, friends, community, and culture back home. The anxiety of an imagined permanent "exile" could prove overwhelming, regardless of emergent doubts about Nazism. Most the German exchange students were probably not blind to the disjunction between what the Nazis taught about the United States and what they themselves had observed and experienced. They often naively concluded that the German people had simply been misinformed about the United States and that brought out a determination to "set the record straight" once they returned home.

The exchange year more strongly affected other exchange students. Those whose behavior became more "liberalized," or "Americanized," often initially felt a cognitive dissonance between what they had expected to find in the United States and their actual, positive experiences. This often led to a degree of disillusionment with Nazism. In the end, dozens of students found themselves in an existential crisis that could only be resolved by accepting the new reality revealed about life in the United States. Unfortunately, they also faced obstacles to remaining there that would deter all but the most determined. US immigration laws were exceptionally restrictive and the authorities usually had little sympathy for asylum seekers.[14] Further, an immigrant applicant had to present a number of official documents from their home country, which none of the exchange students had in advance. Requesting them would alert officials back home to the student's intention to seek asylum in the United States.

As with the exchange program officials who had willingly provided these students the opportunity to escape Germany, even if for only a year, the decision to seek refuge in the United States represented a form of active opposition to the Nazi state. The Reich dedicated financial and personnel resources to selecting and training exchange students for the privilege of participating in the exchange; they were expected to represent the Nazi regime in their host countries and present a positive image of the New Germany. Such paragons of Nazism refusing to return home humiliated the Reich, sending a public message to the host country and to Germans back home that even individuals who had been carefully chosen for their loyalty to the New Germany might abandon it if given the opportunity. Thus, students who attempted to remain in the United States surely could imagine the consequences of failing to do so. Thus, exchange students who sought refuge in the United States, in fact, engaged in "opposition in exile."[15] After returning home, several German exchange students exhibited signs of reverse culture shock. They had come to identify with American culture so much that their return to Germany elicited anxiety, depression, or fear. Some of these Americanized students attracted close surveillance and stood the chance of having their careers irreparably destroyed. Several made their way back to the United States by means so remarkable as to attract lasting suspicions by the FBI.

Espionage Efforts and the End of the Exchange

After the SS and the Third Reich's intelligence services gained control of DAAD, the students selected were frequently radical Nazis expected not only to present the German view to colleges and local communities, but to also engage in covert operations. Thus, by the late 1930s, the German students sent to the United States could be divided into two groups: a cohort more in line with traditional student exchange objectives and a cohort using the student exchange for much more dubious activities.

Many of the most prominent books of the past decade focusing on German-American relations in the 1930s and 1940s claim that Nazi Germany managed to successfully spread covert propaganda, promote fascist organizations, steal American military secrets, sabotage US industrial activity, and nearly undermine American democracy. The evidence presented in this study argues otherwise. In only one area did the exchange students' covert operations succeed: in identifying and intimidating anti-Nazis, especially other exchange students. While such espionage activities certainly provoked anxiety in the target groups, no evidence suggests that they countered the influence of anti-Nazis in terms of American public opinion. The expected results, or consequences, were forthcoming only when student "covert operatives" sent negative reports to German authorities about repatriated German exchange students accused of manifesting overtly pro-American or anti-Nazi sympathies.

As many scholars and observers have pointed out, the Nazis were especially eager to promote antisemitism in the United States. Certainly, the antisemitism common there prevented Jewish Americans from competing on an equal basis with their fellow Gentile citizens in many endeavors. There were, however, limits to such discrimination, especially compared to antisemitism in Europe, above all in Nazi Germany. American antisemitism did not compare to the virulence of its Nazi German counterpart.[16] By 1938 Nazi Germany's increasingly brutal antisemitic practices negatively affected conditions for German students in the United States. Americans' tolerance of these representatives of the Reich gave way to antagonism. After news of Kristallnacht, in November 1938, American colleges cancelled their participation in the exchange with alacrity. IIE's unwavering toleration of the German exchange students became increasingly questioned as the 1930s progressed. The ever-fewer institutions willing to accept German students often warned IIE that the prevailing atmosphere might shock a German exchange student. The only accomplishment of the German exchange students in the United States who promoted antisemitism was to embarrass their own government.

The Nazis' covert operations involving the exchange students were amateurish, uncoordinated, haphazard, and futile. Most of the "espionage agents" had little or no appropriate training. So many German organizations and individuals engaged in espionage in the United States that even the professional spy agencies had trouble figuring out who was who. German diplomats, constantly frustrated by such antics, knew full well that the ultimate effect on US-German relations would be disastrous. Indeed, the attempt to gain military information through suborning German Americans working in key military industries typically failed, as these Americans were often eager to prove their loyalties to the United States and therefore reported such attempts to the FBI.

As revelations of Nazi activities in the United States elided with growing pressure toward war with the Third Reich, German espionage only succeeded in providing FBI director J. Edgar Hoover with opportunities to increase his own power as head of America's counterespionage agency. Likewise, President Franklin Roosevelt took advantage of German activities to further his case that the Nazis were a menace to Americans and had to be crushed in Europe as well as the United States. In effect, the Germans' espionage was not only unsuccessful, it achieved the exact opposite of what was intended.

After the outbreak of World War II in September 1939, most German exchange students returned home. It is impossible to determine the fate of all of them thereafter; such information is seldom found in American or German archives. Extant records suggest that most males who returned to Germany served as Wehrmacht officers. About a quarter of them died in action. Several former exchange students became involved in perpetrating the Holocaust, while several others became involved with resistance circles. A few of the former exchange students returned to the United States under the rather less welcoming status of a POW. A few also joined the US Army.

After the fall of the Third Reich, former exchange students in Germany adroitly used the experience of their exchange year, such as their English-language and intercultural skills, to navigate the postwar and Cold War worlds to their own advantage. Overwhelmed American occupation authorities employed dozens of former exchange students, asking few questions about their past association with Nazism.[17] Germans in general wanted to forget about the war and rebuild their lives. Thus, the former exchange students in Germany rapidly resumed their carriers in foreign affairs, science, medicine, academia, business, religious institutions, and journalism. Many rose to the pinnacle of their profession. Their prewar pasts as exemplars of the new Nazi elite all but forgotten.

"Remigrants"—former exchange students and German academics associated with the exchange who fled the Third Reich for the United States but returned to Germany after the war—as well as Americanophile Germans who remained in the Reich obtained leading positions in West German society from the end of the war and into the 1950s. Naturally, where possible the Americans sought to elevate the careers of "pro-American" Germans with the goal of leaving them in charge of the country after US occupation authorities left. Initially, these privileged positions remained in the hands of the older generation of exchange program associates. A decade after the war, the former exchange students themselves, now well established in their professions, took on this role. Many of them sought to promote West Germany's evolution as a democratic, tolerant, and self-reflective state, much as they remembered the United States.[18] The sectors of West Germany most strongly affected by their conscious application of "American" principles were its constitutional development; educational, scientific, academic and research institutions; journalism; and science and technology. Some of the former exchange students obtained leading positions in the postwar German exchange program, including the secretary-generalship of DAAD. A number of them in foreign affairs sought to emphasize their supposed Americanization, manufacturing mendacious backstories about their years under Nazism.

Certain elements underlying the Weimar-era student exchange starting around 1930 carried over into the Third Reich and into the 1950s, such as selection of students for their nationalistic convictions and the students' willingness to serve Germany as propagandists. Some criteria for selection also remained the same, among them an emphasis on charm, attractive physical appearance, leadership skills, and elite family backgrounds. Outlooks from the Weimar era generally related to traditional Bildungsbürgertum culture survived from the first half of the twentieth century and beyond. If presented this continuity without the political context, one might not be able to identify whether some of the German exchange students had been chosen in the Weimar era, the Third Reich, or postwar West Germany.

Although the German-American student exchange program failed in propagandizing a congenial view of Nazi Germany, and information obtained through espionage was inconsequential, the endeavor required the Nazis to divert significant financial and human resources to the massive undertaking. The exchange program also allowed dozens of highly talented German students to obtain asylum in the United States. They may have come to America as "Nazis," but they ended their lives as Americans. The careers of these refugee students exemplify part of the great flow of intellectual capital from Nazi Germany to America. German science and scholarship never fully recovered from the blow, which conversely positioned the United States as the world's foremost scientific and technological power to this day.[19]

Shortly after the end of the German-American exchange, the students who had returned to Nazi Germany sent one last message to the outside world. A sense of longing for the good times back in the United States permeated the 1940 newsletter for former exchange students, the *Heimatrundbrief*, in contrast to their current life in the wartime "Greater German Reich." In the introduction, the editors wrote,

> Many of you will read [this] perhaps in a garrison in Poland, perhaps in a pill-box at the Westwall. We hope, however, that it will bring to all of you joy and help in keeping alive the memory of those times when a whole continent was ours to roam in, when our secondhand cars traveled over the wide roads of the U.S.—today in the snows of the Alleghenies, tomorrow in the shade of the Royal Palms of Florida; the times when the wild rhythm of metropolises captivated us, as did the silent loneliness of deserts and prairies; the times when our songs rang out, now over the bluish green surfaces of quiet Rocky Mountain lakes, now over the expanses of the Pacific gleaming in the sun. It was a year

full of unbridled joy in life, but also full of cares and struggles. Indeed, work and joy, knowledge and experience, but ultimately growth and maturity—that is what America has been to us.

The *Heimatrundbrief* included the most pro-American articles written by the exchange students from 1936 to 1938. It also listed the former exchange students from that period who had been killed in the war. Many, many more would die soon thereafter.

Perhaps the most thought-provoking point of *Nazis in the New World* is summed up in a casual observation by Kurt Leidecker, a Rensselaer professor, relaying the contents of the *Heimatrundbrief* to the school's student newspaper while the war raged in Europe. He noted, in passing, that the *Heimatrundbrief*'s introduction was signed by the editors.

There was no "Heil Hitler."[20]

NOTES

Introduction

Epigraph. Lilge, *Abuse of Learning*, 164, quoting Julius Ebbinghaus's inaugural speech as the new rector of the University of Marburg, September 25, 1945.

1. The terms used in this book are similar to those in the scholarship on the Third Reich: *Nazi* and *radical Nazi*—those fully committed to Nazi ideology and practice; *moderate Nazis*—Germans who agreed with some aspects of National Socialist ideology but had reservations about others; *non-Nazi*—those with reservations more profound than moderate Nazis' concerns; *anti-Nazi*—those who objected to Nazism, even if they did not engage in direct opposition to the party. *Nazi* also refers to anyone who represented the Third Reich abroad. On these terms, also see Kershaw, *Nazi Dictatorship*, 118n28, 120.

2. Hitler used this expression. See Noakes, *Government, Party, and People in Nazi Germany*, 33n36; Breit, "Culture as Authority," 137.

3. See Gallagher, *Nazis of Copley Square*; Ross, *Hitler in Los Angeles*; Rosenzweig, *Hollywood's Spies*; Hart, *Hitler's American Friends*; Maddow, *Prequel*; Tate, *Hitler's Secret Army*; Watson, *Nazi Spy Pastor*; Usdin, *Bureau of Spies*; Whiting, *Hitler's Secret War*; and Jeffreys-Jones, *Nazi Spy Ring in America*.

4. Gallagher, *Nazis of Copley Square*, 227–29.

5. Ross, *Hitler in Los Angeles*, 2, 4.

6. Hart, *Hitler's American Friends*, 16–17.

7. Ross, *Hitler in Los Angeles*, 290, 307–8; Hart, *Hitler's American Friends*, 4, 11, 20.

8. Hart, *Hitler's American Friends*, 11.

9. Olson, *Those Angry Days*, 312–19, 325–26, 379–80, 385–90; Breitman and Lichtman, *FDR and the Jews*.

10. Doerries, "Transatlantic Intelligence," 67.

11. For a discussion of Coughlin's influence on the quasi-fascist movement in the United States, see Hart, *Hitler's American Friends*, 18–22, 68–70. The intersection of Coughlin's ideology with Nazism is also discussed in Gallagher, *Nazis of Copley Square*, 8–13, 36, 84–98, and 110.

12. Mullen and Vials, *U.S. Antifascism Reader*, 10; Gallagher, *Nazis of Copley Square*, 1–3, 8, 17.

13. NARA RG 65. FBI. CRS. Class 65. 2904. German Espionage Activities. 1351. Ulrich Von Gienanth File. FBI Report, November 21, 1939.

14. Gallagher, *Nazis of Copley Square*, 9, 223–24, 230; Ross, *Hitler in Los Angeles*, 250–51, 324–25, 331; Hart, *Hitler's American Friends*, 8–9, 17, 85.

15. Hart, *Hitler's American Friends*, 17.

208   *Notes to Pages 4–7*

16. "Students Veto American Haven for Jews." Students were asked, "Should the United States offer a haven in this country for Jewish refugees from central Europe?" To this, 31.2 percent responded yes, and 68.8 percent said no, whereas in terms of their sympathy, "It was clear from the coast to coast returns that students as a whole would like to see the United States help oppressed German minorities in some way, some suggesting the offering of homes in U.S. possessions."

17. On student empathy, see Puckett, "Reporting on the Holocaust," and Medoff, "Retribution Is Not Enough." On fear of professional competition (along with outright antisemitism) as well as sympathy for Jewish refugees, see Leff, "Combating Prejudice."

18. Breitman and Lichtman, *FDR and the Jews*, 164–71; Bartrop, *Evian Conference*, 1–5; Afoumado, *Indésirables*; Friedman, *No Haven for the Oppressed*; Rosenbaum, *Waking to Danger*, 6. For an example of the internment of Jewish refugees as enemy aliens, see Lansen, "Victims of Circumstance." During the war, Jewish refugees were often interned as enemy aliens in locations, including Jamaica and Egypt, reflecting widespread but misplaced security concerns. This situation also provided cover for espionage: for instance, Herbert Behr's case illustrates how Germany's covert agents exploited refugee statuses to infiltrate the United States. Gross, "The U.S. Government Turned Away Thousands of Jewish Refugees."

19. Rosenzweig, *Hollywood's Spies*, 114; Seidman, *Transatlantic Antifascisms*, 141. On prejudiced American perceptions of Jews, including refugees, see Bendersky, *The Jewish Threat*; on American perceptions of antisemitism as a "foreign" import, see Lansen, "Dissension in the Face of the Holocaust."

20. Rosenzweig, *Hollywood's Spies*, 114.

21. CSUNA URB. CRC-1. Ness Report to Lewis, April 10, 1936, 3.

22. Sirois, *Zwischen Illusion und Krieg*, 38; Junker, *Kampf um die Weltmacht*, 2.

23. Jonas, *United States and Germany*, 227.

24. Sirois, *Zwischen Illusion und Krieg*, 38.

25. Reuther, *Ambivalente Normalisierung*, 77.

26. NARA RG 65. Class 65. 2904. 1351. Ulrich von Gienanth File. Report, November 21, 1939, in Foxworth to Hoover, April 6, 1940; Ross, *Hitler in Los Angeles*, 273–78, 301–2.

27. Hart, *Hitler's American Friends*, 207.

28. Hart, 207.

29. Ross, *Hitler in Los Angeles*, 248 and 255, and also see 34, 92, 266, 284, 288, 290, 303. Naval intelligence and the Los Angeles County Sheriff's Department also allegedly failed to recognize the Nazi menace (211).

30. Ross, 266, 283–84. Maddow, *Prequel*, 208 and 211, also mentions government officials, including postal inspectors, who failed to act because, they said, no laws had been broken. Hart, in *Hitler's American Friends*, tends to be less critical of the FBI's response to such threats.

31. Gallagher, *Nazis of Copley Square*, 183.

32. Maddow, *Prequel*, xxix, 325. Maddow mentions Gallagher, Hart, and Ross as particularly inspirational in her analysis of fascist threats in the United States.

33. Maddow, xxix, 125.

34. Maddow, 88, 121–25, 151, 211. For a parallel assessment, see Ross, *Hitler in Los Angeles*, 284.

35. Maddow, *Prequel*, 107–8, 160.

36. Maddow, 167–68.

37. Maddow, 169, quoting Gallagher (with no primary source cited) on how the press described the Christian Front plotters.

38. PA AA. R 101.855. Pol. I M 28.Nordamerika. Gyssling to Dieckhoff, November 4, 1941. For additional examples, see chapter 5, in this volume.

39. Gallagher, *Nazis of Copley Square*, 147 and 150, where Scholz is called "a true master of spy craft."

40. NARA RG 65. FBI. CRS. Class 65. 2904. 1351. Von Gienanth File. Jones Reports January 8, 1941, and November 25, 1941; NARA RG 65. FBI. CRS. Class 65. 2904. 4414. Scholz File; NARA RG 60. DOJ. CRS. Class 146. 32. 2-49-424. Kurt Ludwig File.

41. Hart, *Hitler's American Friends*, 206.

42. Vasey, *Nazi Intelligence Operations in Non-occupied Territories*, 114–17; "Memorandum, Re: Ludwig Case"; Federal Bureau of Investigation, "Ludwig Spy Ring"; Mowry, "Cryptologic Aspects of German Intelligence Activities," 24–25.

43. Batvinis, *Origins of FBI Counterintelligence*, 164, 199, 204, 223, 232–63.

44. Gallagher, *Nazis of Copley Square*, 152–54.

45. Vasey, *Nazi Intelligence Operations in Non-occupied Territories*, 124–30, 148–49.

46. Vasey, 124–30. This result was similar to a later German sabotage scheme, Operation Pastorius, launched in 1942.

47. Ross, *Hitler in Los Angeles*, 287–91; Maddow, *Prequel*, 257–58.

48. For examples of German diplomatic staff warning their government not to commit sabotage, see Frye, *Nazi Germany and the American Hemisphere*, 41, 95–96; NARA RG 65. FBI. CRS. Class 65. 2904. 53615. EBF 99. "RETTICH"; PA AA R 101.855. Pol. I M 28. Nordamerika. Thomsen to von Weizsäcker, May 21, 1940.

49. Naval History and Heritage Command. "German Espionage and Sabotage"; Federal Bureau of Investigation, "Nazi Saboteurs and George Dasch." It is also worth noting that the Hercules explosion on September 12, 1940, predated the Lend-Lease Act by about six months, during a period when US aid to Britain was escalating but had not yet become a decisive factor in the conflict.

50. Ryerson, *Hazards on the Home Front*; Regis, *When Our Mothers Went to War*, 66; Kersten, *Labor's Home Front*, 166, 175–76; Petersen, "Occupational Safety in Time of Haste," 408–9; Hepler, "And We Want Steel Toes Like the Men," 689–90. On the causes of industrial accidents in the United States in World War II, as well as some statistics regarding such issues, see "More Deadly Than War," 66–71, 148. For examples of munitions plant catastrophes in Germany before and after the war, see "Burgomaster of Reinsdorf Tells How Explosion Spread Disaster," 3; "Reich Mourns Blast Dead," 6, for the 1935 Reinsdorf disaster; and "In Memory of the Victims of the 1943 and 1948 Explosions," for the 1943 and 1948 I.G. Farben explosions. Analogously, the United States saw, for example, the 1926 Lake Denmark explosion, and the 1947 Texas City explosion. Winston, "1926 Lake Demark Explosion"; United States, Department of Defense, "Explosive Accident Summary."

51. United States, Department of Defense, "Explosive Accident Summary," 118.

52. BASF, "In Memory of the Victims of the 1943 and 1948 Explosions."

53. United States, Department of Defense, "Explosive Accident Summary." Among the explosions were those at the Hirschhagen munitions plant on May 25, 1943; April 10, 1943; June 2, 1944; August 14, 1944; February 25, 1945; and March 31, 1945. There were other such disasters at Hirschhagen for which fatality counts are not available. The Allies never bombed the Hirschhagen plant. Heine, "Geschichte einer Sprengstofffabrik." A tank car being overfilled on a very hot day on July 29, 1943, caused the explosion at the I.G. Farben plant, in Ludwigshaften.

54. Gallagher, *Nazis of Copley Square*, 151, 175.

55. NARA RG 238. Bohle interrogation, July 26, 1945.

56. Wighton, Lahousen, and Peis, *Hitler's Spies and Saboteurs*, 22.

57. For examples of Canaris self-sabotaging covert missions as a tool against Hitler, see "Fritsch, Werner von," 367–68; Paterson, *Hitler's Brandenburgers*, 57–58; Bryden, *Fighting to Lose*.

210   Notes to Pages 9–13

58. CSUNA URB. CRC-1. Ness to Lewis, April 10, 1936, 2.

59. Ribuffo, *Old Christian Right*, xiii, 4–5, 178–215, 228, 237–41.

60. Ross, *Hitler in Los Angeles*, 195–96, and also see also 331.

61. On German exchange student covert agents, see Spivak, *Secret Armies*, 84, 118–19, and 130–31.

62. "Spivak Returned to Jail," 2.

63. Haynes, Klehr, and Vassiliev, *Spies*, 161–67, 476.

64. John Roy Carlson is a pseudonym for Avedis Boghos Derounian.

65. Gallagher, *Nazis of Copley Square*, 56, 71–72, 89–90, 121, 138, 144–45, 160, 219, 221; Maddow, *Prequel*, 267–71.

66. On German exchange students, see Carlson, *Under Cover*, 192.

67. Ribuffo, *Old Christian Right*, 190–92.

68. Gallagher, *Nazis of Copley Square*, 215–16.

69. Rollins, *I Find Treason*, 205.

70. Maddow, *Prequel*, 150–51, referring to Leon Turrou, *Confessions of a Nazi Spy* (1939).

71. Norwood, *Third Reich in the Ivory Tower*, 34, 61–62, 67, 97, 102, 164.

72. Piller, *Selling Weimar*, 129, 206, 371–73, 336.

73. Institute of International Education, *Seventeenth Annual Report of the Director*, 5–6.

74. BArch (Koblenz) SL. ZSG 137. 636K. Friedrich Stieve to Auswärtiges Amt, April 3, 1936.

75. Adam, *Germany and the Americas*, 7; IIE. HF. Criticism of American-German Student Exchange. IIE Answers and Suggestions, 1936–38. Duggan to Wilcox, September 24, 1937.

76. See Kershaw, *Hitler, the Germans, and the Final Solution*.

77. Schneppen, "Ämter und ihre Vergangenheit im "Dritten Reich," 93–94.

78. See Benz, *Im Widerstand*; Eley, "Hitler's Silent Majority?" no. 2, 389–425, and no. 3, 550–83; Pine, *Life and Times in Nazi Germany*; Kershaw, *Nazi Dictatorship*; Tuchel, *Vergessene Widerstand*; Gellately, *Backing Hitler*; and Jacobsen, "Zur Rolle der Diplomatie im Dritten Reich," 92.

79. Balfour, *Withstanding Hitler*, 61.

80. Ringer, *Decline of the German Mandarins*, 251.

81. Hitler was quite aware of this tactic. See Caplan, *Government without Administration*, 169.

82. Von Hassell, MacRae, with Ameskamp, *Alliance of Enemies*; Döscher, *Auswärtige Amt im Dritten Reich*; Heideking and Mauch, *USA und deutscher Widerstand*; Hill, "National-Conservatives and Opposition to the Third Reich before the Second World War"; Hoffmann, *Beyond Valkyrie*; Hoffmann, *Widerstand-Staatsstreich-Attentat*; von Klemperer, *German Resistance against Hitler*; Mauch, *The Shadow War Against Hitler*; Scholtyseck, *Robert Bosch und der Liberale Widerstand gegen Hitler*.

83. Conze, Weinke, and Wiegeshoff, *Das Amt und die Vergangenheit*, 5.

84. See Schulte and Wala, *Widerstand und Auswärtiges Amt*; and Hürter and Mayer, *Auswärtige Amt in der NS-Diktatur*. For more information on the controversy, see Becker, " 'Historikerstreit' Reloaded?" 47–71; Schneppen, "Vom Jagdtrieb historischer Ermittler," 593–620.

85. CSUNA URB. CRC-1. Lewis to Livingston, December 4, 1933.

86. NARA RG 60. DOJ. CRS. Class 146. 13. 2-36-4. Chroust File. Chroust Reconsideration, July 15, 1944.

87. Caplan, *Government without Administration*, 192.

88. See Schneppen, "Ämter und ihre Vergangenheit im "Dritten Reich," 97. Döscher, *Auswärtige Amt im Dritten Reich*, 66, expressed the same concept as "waiting and holding out."

Notes to Pages 13–16   211

89. Caplan, *Government without Administration*, 159.

90. "Nazi Consulate Aide Here Beaten to Death in Home," 1, 4; Batvinis, *Hoover's Secret War*, 21–22; CSUNA URB. CRC-2. Roos to Klein, January 11, 12, 13, 1940; CSUNA URB. CRC-2. Marshall to Klein, February 29, 1940; CSUNA URB. CRC-2. Klein to Roos, March 2, 1940; CSUNA URB. CRC-2. Roos to Klein, March 7, 1940; Ross, *Hitler in Los Angeles*, 126.

91. Sylvia Taschka finds that Hans-Heinrich Dieckhoff, the German ambassador to the United States, had reservations about Nazism, but did not act on them. See Taschka, *Diplomat ohne Eigenschaften?*, 214; Reginald Phelps characterized Baron Kurt von Tippelskirch, the German consul general in Boston from 1927 to 1938, as a "non-Nazi," but he does not provide a specific source for this claim. Phelps, "Thomas Mann, LL. D., Harvard, and the Third Reich," 66.

92. Numerous books discuss "Bébé" Thomsen, a well-known socialite at the time. See, for example, Solomon, *Such Splendid Prisons*. On US-German Foreign Ministry dealings here, see CIA. L Peis File: Thomas Thacher to Wm J. Donovan, September 5, 1941; Malcolm R. Lovell to Donovan, September 11, 1941; Donovan to W.S. Stephenson, September 15, 1941; Lovell to Donovan, September 25, 1941; Lovell to Donovan, October 10, 1941; Lovell to Donovan, October 28, 1941; Donovan to Roosevelt, October 30, 1941; Lovell to Donovan, November 5, 1941; Lovell to Donovan, November 6, 1941; Lovell to Donovan, November 9, 1941; Donovan to Roosevelt, November 13, 1941; Donovan to J. Edgar Hoover, December 1, 1941; Lovell to Donovan, December 12, 1941; Lovell to Donovan, December 16, 1941; Lovell to Donovan, March 2, 1942; Donovan to John L. Sullivan, April 1, 1942; James R. Murphy to Dulles, July 17, 1942; Lovell to Allen Dulles, July 19, 1942; Allen Dulles to James Murphy, July 24, 1942.

93. CSUNA URB. CRC-2. German Consuls Meeting, January 11, 12, 13, 1940.

94. Blanke, *Vom Nazismus zur Demokratisierung Deutschlands*, 51. See chapter 6, in this volume, for more on Blanke.

95. Weber, *Hitler's First War*, 322–26; Hoerlin, *Steps of Courage*, 201–2; Langer, *A Psychological Analysis of Adolph Hitler*, 57, 81. Later in the war, Berlin posted Wiedemann to Tianjin, China, where he is known to have helped Jewish refugees from Germany. University of Aberdeen, "Steps of Courage."

96. Julius Klein, "To Whom It May Concern," December 16, 1947. Accessed January 1, 2023. https://www.fold3.com/image/311346468/. The Los Angeles Jewish Community Committee was an autonomous associate organization of the Anti-Defamation League / American Jewish Congress working group against Nazism in the United States.

97. CSUNA URB. CRC-2. Roos to Klein, January 24, 1940; CSUNA URB. CRC-2. Roos to Klein, February 5, 1940; CSUNA URB. CRC-2. Roos to Klein, February 19, 1940; CSUNA URB. CRC-2. Roos to Klein, March 2, 1940; CSUNA URB. CRC-2. Roos to Klein, March 7, 1940; Ross, *Hitler in Los Angeles*, 67, 223, 331.

98. Ross, *Hitler in Los Angeles*, 331–32.

99. Ross, 218.

100. The terms *opposition circles* and *resistance circles* are used interchangeably, as members often belonged to both those circles aimed primarily at post-Nazi planning and the ones directed mainly at removing Hitler from power. Metternich and the Mazal Holocaust Collection, *Purgatory of Fools*, 105; MacDonogh, *A Good German*, 164; Cooper, *Patrick Leigh Fermor*, 87; Sams, "Adam von Trott zu Solz: Early Life and Political Initiatives in the Summer of 1939," 13, 73.

101. PA AA. RZ 507. 64227.27. "Betätigung deutscher Studenten im Ausland," October 28, 1935.

102. Laitenberger, *Akademischer Austausch und auswärtige Kulturpolitik*, 182.

103. Hoffman, *History of the German Resistance*, 33.

104. Kempner, "Vernetzung des Herrn von Twardowski am 11. August 1947."

212 *Notes to Pages 16–19*

105. Hürter and Mayer, *Auswärtige Amt*, 13.
106. Laitenberger, *Akademischer Austausch und auswärtige Kulturpolitik*, 185.
107. Weinreich, *Hitler's Professors*, 9.
108. Ericksen, *Complicity in the Holocaust*, 1, 23, 125, 230–31.
109. Remy, *Heidelberg Myth*, 239.
110. Benz, *Im Widerstand*, 22.
111. Works suggesting that a considerable number of academics were not so enamored of the Nazis include Sims, "Intellectuals in Crisis"; Sims, "Unsettling History"; Witkop, "Remembering Heinrich Wieland"; Nagorski, *Hitlerland*; Kroll, " . . . Gott schütze unser liebes Deutsches Volk!"; Goldschmidt, "Freiburger universitäre Widerstand"; Grüttner, "Die 'Säuberung' der Universitäten."
112. Rothfels, *German Opposition to Hitler*; Ritter and Fitzsimons, "The German Professor in the Third Reich."
113. Wagner, "Forschungsförderung auf der Basis eines nationalistischen Konsenses," 183. There were prominent exceptions. On the latter, see Bialas and Rabinbach, *Nazi Germany and the Humanities*, 3–5.
114. Ericksen, *Complicity in the Holocaust*, 62, 139.
115. Ritter and Fitzsimons, "The German Professor in the Third Reich," 249–51.
116. Fülbier, "Digging Deeper," 380.
117. Connelly and Grüttner, *Universities under Dictatorship*, 84–85.
118. Scholtyseck and Studt, "Einleitung," 3. For similar remarks, see Grüttner, "Nationalsozialistiche Wissenschaftler," 164; Ritter and Fitzsimons, "The German Professor in the Third Reich," 249; Bollenbeck, "Humanities in Germany after 1933," 11. Otto D. Tolischus, a prominent American journalist for the *New York Times* then living in Germany, also reported on this phenomenon. He claimed that only 25 percent of academics were Nazis. Tolischus, "Nazis in Struggle with Professors," 15.
119. Shrivastava, "Survival of the Mandarin Tradition in German Universities," 80–88, 92, 95, 104, 108, 296; Ritter and Fitzsimons, "The German Professor in the Third Reich," 244–45, 250.
120. Goldschmidt, "Freiburger universitäre Widerstand," 143–58; Thomsett, *German Opposition to Hitler*, 215.
121. There are a plethora of examples. To name a few, see IIE. AF: Richey File. "First Semi-Annual Report," February 10, 1935; Palmer File. Report, ca. spring 1934; Boyle O'Reilly Rocking File. "Report no. 2 to the Institute of International Education in Connection with the American German Exchange" [ca. spring 1934]; FBI. RMD. RIDS. CRS. Class 61. 7578. Bureau of Internal Revenue. BIR Report, July 1, 1944, 59–60, observations of John Hallowell, an American exchange student at Heidelberg University for the 1935–36 school year.
122. Likewise, Jacobsen, "Rolle der Diplomatie im Dritten Reich," 190, noted that party officials were hardly in a position to judge the performance of German diplomats.
123. One of the American exchange students in Germany took note of this dynamic. See IIE. AF. Richey File. Richey. "First Semi-Annual Report," February 10, 1935.
124. Remy, *Heidelberg Myth*, 20.
125. Fülbier, "Digging Deeper," 379–80.
126. Remy, *Heidelberg Myth*, 14–15, 19–20, 22, 47, 124, 139, 141–45, 193, 207.
127. Eriksen, *Complicity in the Holocaust*, 31, 34, 36, 40–41.
128. Giles, "German Students and Higher Education Policy," 331.
129. BArch (Licht.) NS38/2478. "Memorandum," October 20, 1933; PA AA. RZ 507. 64225. 27. Deutsche Studentenschaft to Oster, "Niederschrift"; University of Munich Archives Zsg. II-14. Bd. 01. "Protokoll"; BArch (Koblenz) SL. ZSG 137/13. Bd. 11. Scurla to Laitenberger, September 18, 1973; PA AA. RZ 507. 64227. 27. "Bericht über die Tagung."

Notes to Pages 19–27   213

130. Giles, *Students and National Socialism,* 136.

131. Giles, "Rise of the National Socialist Students Association," 174.

132. Giles, 180.

133. Albrecht and Romberg, *Widerstand und Exil,* 86, 96.

134. See Jarausch, *Deutsche Studenten,* 169; Grüttner, *Studenten im Dritten Reich,* 254; Ritter and Fitzsimons, "The German Professor in the Third Reich," 248, 251–52.

135. IIE. AF. Richey File. "First Semi-Annual Report," February 10, 1935; Furgason, "Student Life in Germany," 5–6; "Pitt Exchange Student Back from Study in Land of Hitler," 12.

136. NARA RG 65. FBI. CRS. Class 65. 2904. 28452. Herbert Sonthoff File. Manning Report, February 4, 1943. Sonthoff to Hermann Siemer, February 6, 1940 and July 31, 1940.

137. CIA. "Source of Black Report no. 52, no. 14, November 28, 1944."

138. "Josef Wirmer," Kartellverbandes katholischer deutscher Studentenvereine.

139. Wonschik, *Briefe aus Bautzen II,* 19.

140. See Nolan, *Transatlantic Century.*

141. Doering-Manteuffel, "Deutsche Weg nach Westen," 23–39.

142. Greenberg, *Weimar Century.*

143. For example, see Snyder, *Bloodlands,* a remarkable work that emphasizes the similarity of Hitler and Stalin's policies in their treatment of Eastern Europe.

144. See Nolan, *Visions of Modernity.*

145. Wala, "Gegen eine Vereinzelung Deutschlands," 311.

146. In the latter instance, there was no "continuity" in the strictest sense of the term since the German-American student exchange ceased from spring 1939 to the late 1940s.

147. Junker, "Continuity of Ambivalence," 256; Nolan, "Anti-Americanism," 95; Füssl, *Deutsch-amerikanischer Kulturaustausch im 20. Jahrhundert,* 97.

148. For more on this concept, see Pedersen, *Five Stages of Culture Shock*; Welsh, "Long Term Effects of Reverse Culture Shock," 35; Szkudlarek, "Reentry—A Review of the Literature," 3–8.

149. Benz, *Im Widerstand,* 11.

150. Nolan, "Anti-Americanism," 90–91.

Chapter 1 · Nazi Infiltration of the Student Exchange

Epigraph. IIE. HF. Criticism of American-German Student Exchange. IIE Answers and Suggestions, 1936–38. Stephen Duggan to Walter Wilcox, Cornell University, Sept 24, 1937.

1. Gienow-Hecht, "Anomaly of the Cold War," 13–14, 40, 54; Kramer, "Is the World Our Campus?," 800.

2. Sims, "Intellectuals in Crisis," 258, cites an example of such maneuvering: German historians during the Third Reich faced scrutiny not only by the university rector, but also by the Ministry of Education, the Ministry of the Interior, the Ministry of Propaganda, the Gestapo, and the local gauleiter. Given the inevitability of a clash ongoing between the leaders of any number of these organizations at any given moment, it was possible to claim allegiance to whomever was most convenient.

3. Levine, "Baltimore Teaches, Göttingen Learns," 788.

4. Duggan, "American-German Student Exchange," 46–74.

5. Halpern," Institute of International Education," 104.

6. YUL. The Inquiry Papers (MS 8); Brooks, "Apostle of Internationalism," 64–73.

7. FBI. RMD. RIDS. FBI. CRS. Class 61. 7578. BIR Report, 4.

8. McMurry and Lee, *Cultural Approach,* 56–57; Füssl, *Deutsch-amerikanischer Kulturaustausch,* 61.

9. Harrington, *German Cosmopolitan Social Thought,* 128.

10. BArch (Koblenz). SL ZSG 137. 137/6. Bd. 4: Von Gienanth, Ulrich (I and II). Vogt

214   *Notes to Pages 27–31*

address; von Gienanth, Ulrich (I and II). Program of Exchange Student Summer Camp, September 3–5, 1932.

11. See, for example, "State Delegates Hear German Student's Talk," 4; Kersten, "Why the Youth of Germany Demands Political Changes," 4.

12. FBI. RMD. RIDS. CRS Class 61. 7578. Lynch Report, March 28, 1944.

13. BArch (Koblenz). SL ZSG 137/13. Bd. 11. Scurla to Laitenberger, September 12, 1973. Several of the exchange students made similar comments regarding Morsbach's seeming lack of Nazi enthusiasm.

14. Two young Jewish women were in the 1933 cohort sent to the United States. Most likely, they were Ina and Irene Gotthelf, daughters of a Russian woman likely of Jewish ancestry and an "Aryan" German. See FBI. RMD. RIDS. CRS Class 61. 7578. BIR Report, 30.

15. PA AA. RZ 507. 64227.27. "Betätigung deutscher Studenten im Ausland," October 28, 1935.

BArch (Licht.) NS38/2478. DAAD to DSt Ostpolitik, August 15, 1933.

16. Impekoven, *Alexander von Humboldt-Stiftung*, 653.

17. BArch (Koblenz) SL ZSG 137/13. Bd. 11. Scurla to Laitenberger, September 14, 1973.

18. PA AA. R 64225. Deutsche Studentenschaft to Oster, "Niederschrift."

19. BArch (Koblenz) SL ZSG 137/13. Bd. 11. Laitenberg to Scurla, September 6, 1973; FBI. RMD. RIDS. CRS. Class 61. 7578. BIR Report, 22; FBI. RMD. RIDS. CRS Class 61. 7578. Seeman Report, December 13, 1944; PA AA. RZ 507. 27. 64228. 27. Burmeister to Auswärtiges Amt, February 5, 1936, enclosure, 10–11.

20. Kenny, *History of the Rhodes Trust,* 391.

21. Strobel, "Wehrbeauftragte."

22. FBI. RMD. RIDS. CRS. Class 61. 7578. Snyder Report, May 19, 1944; FBI. RMD. RIDS. CRS. Class 61. 7578. Lynch Report, March 28, 1944; FBI. RMD. RIDS. CRS. Class 61. 7578. Fritz Lilge File. Brusch Report, June 27, 1944; FBI. RMD. RIDS. CRS. Class 61. 7578. Davidson Report, September 7, 1944.

23. Impekoven, *Alexander von Humboldt-Stiftung*, 97.

24. BArch (Koblenz) SL ZSG 137/13. Bd. 11. Scurla to Laitenberger, September 12, 1973.

25. Impekoven, *Alexander von Humboldt-Stiftung*, 179n689.

26. Impekoven, 179n689.

27. BArch (Koblenz) S.L. ZSG 137/13. Bd. 11. Scurla to Laitenberger, September 18, 1973.

28. Impekoven, *Alexander von Humboldt-Stiftung*, 184.

29. PA AA. RZ 507. 64226. 27. Aufstellung des Personals des DAAD, March 31, 1935.

30. BArch (Koblenz) S.L. ZSG 137/13. Bd. 11. Scurla to Laitenberger, September 18, 1973. Nazis entering the civil service and losing their ideological elan was something Hitler worried about. See Caplan, *Government without Administration*, 169.

31. Ulich, "Education in the Nazi Reich," 108.

32. Maria Hermkes Schlüter specifically asked that the letter she wrote Facht with this information be destroyed because of the very unpleasant consequences that would ensue were it to fall into the wrong hands. IIE. AF. Schlueter File: Elizabeth L. Facht to Duggan, April 26, 1938; Elizabeth Facht to Hubbard, April 28, 1938; Hubbard to Grace C. Dammann, May 2, 1938; Zacharias, "Johannes Schlüter."

33. IIE. AF. Schlueter File. Grace C. Dammann to Duggan, January 26, 1940.

34. Brantz, "German-American Friendship," 242.

35. PA AA. RZ 514. 80313. Richter to Führ, July 14, 1934.

36. Institute of International Education, *News Bulletin of the Institute of International Education*, no. 14, 16.

37. Deutscher Akademischer Austauschdienst, *Deutsche Akademische Austauschdienst 1925 bis 1975*, 25.

Notes to Pages 31–34   215

38. Impekoven, *Alexander von Humboldt-Stiftung*, 130.

39. Emil de Haas, from the Carl Schurz Vereinigung, substituted for Morsbach as the lead tour guide.

40. "Americans' 'Host' Put in Nazi Prison," 3.

41. Impekoven, *Alexander von Humboldt-Stiftung*, 177.

42. Von Gienanth, "Lebenserringung," Von Gienanth Family Documents, 11; UJA Best. U Abt. II Nr. 19 Bl. 1. Richtlinien für die Arbeit der Akademischen Auslandstellen, ca. March 8, 1935, 1.

43. Jacobsen, *Nationalsozialistische Außenpolitik*, 19.

44. The SD was charged with "monitoring" SS and Nazi Party members, and by the late 1930s, all Germans as well as foreign public opinion on Germany. The Gestapo used its information to make arrests.

45. Von Gienanth, "Lebenserringung," 11.

46. PA AA. RZ 507. 27. 64225. 27. Von Massow to Oster, October 10, 1934.

47. NARA RG 65. FBI. CRS. Class 65. 2904. 55597. George [*sic*] Rettig File. Longstreth Report, November 14, 1945.

48. UHA. Rep 5/1. Akademische Auslandsabteilung der Universität [Heidelberg] to the Pressestelle des Badenischen Staatsministeriums, March 27, 1934.

49. NARA RG 65. FBI. CRS. Class 65. 2904. 55597. Rettig File. Longstreth Report, November 14, 1945.

50. NARA RG 65. FBI. CRS. Class 65. 2904. 55597. Rettig File. Longstreth Report, November 14, 1945.

51. FBI. RMD. RIDS. CRS. Class 61. 7578. Sonthoff File. Manning Report, April 30, 1943. Julien Bryan to Sonthoff, March 4, 1938; FBI. RMD. RIDS. CRS. Class 61. 7578. Sonthoff File. Manning Report, June 18, 1943.

52. FBI. RMD. RIDS. CRS. Class 61. 7578. BIR Report, 22.

53. "Transfer Student from Germany Is Entered at Bates," 1.

54. IIE. HF. Criticism of American-German Student Exchange. IIE Answers and Suggestions, 1936–38. G[ünther] H[ans] Grueninger to Hubbard, March 24, 1939.

55. NARA RG 65. FBI. CRS. Class 65. 2904. 55597. Rettig File. Longstreth Report, November 14, 1945.

56. From a December 1936 decree from the German Minister of Education. See *Deutsche Wissenschaft, Erziehung und Volksbildung*, 184; BArch (Licht.) NS nr. 38/2082 fol. 1. Deutsch Studentenschaft, Hauptamt für Grenzland und Außenpolitik Auslandamt to Auslandsämter. Rundschreiben C 9 1933/34, November 10, 1933.

57. NARA RG 65. FBI. CRS. Class 65. 2904. 55597. Rettig File. Longstreth Report, November 14, 1945.

58. "Gemeinschaftslager des Deutschen Akademischen," 28–30.

59. FBI. RMD. RIDS. CRS. Class 61. 7578. Axis Exchange Students File. Davidson Report, September 7, 1944.

60. IIE. HF. Criticism of American-German Student Exchange. IIE Answers and Suggestions, 1936–38. Duggan to Walter Wilcox, September 24, 1937; FBI. RMD. RIDS. CRS Class 61. 7578. Davidson Report, September 7, 1944.

61. Adam, *Germany and the Americas*, 7; IIE. HF. Criticism of American-German Student Exchange. IIE Answers and Suggestions, 1936–38. Duggan to Walter Wilcox, September 24, 1937.

62. Institute of International Education, *Seventeenth Annual Report of the Director*. 5–6.

63. BArch (Koblenz) S.L. ZSG 137. 639K. German Embassy Washington to Auswartiges Amt, August 30, 1935.

64. BArch (Koblenz) S.L. ZSG 137. 636K. Friedrich Stieve to Auswartiges Amt, April 3, 1936.

216   Notes to Pages 34–38

65. PA AA. RZ 514. 27. 80313. Karl Bertling to Hans Dieckhoff, March 19, 1934. Three years later, Dieckhoff would succeed Luther as German ambassador to the United States. Samuel Dickstein, a Democratic congressional representative from New York, was instrumental in founding the Special Committee on Un-American Activities in 1934 and used the committee to investigate suspected pro-fascist and pro-Nazi groups in the US. The remark here implies that Bertling was aware that Dickstein was a closet Communist.

66. FBI. RMD. RIDS. CRS. Class 61. 7578. BIR Report, 9.

67. FBI. RMD. RIDS. CRS. Class 61. 7578. Davidson Report, September 7, 1944.

68. PA AA. RZ 507. 64227. 27. Von Fritsch to Auswartiges Amt, July 6, 1935.

69. FBI. RMD. RIDS. CRS. Class 61. 7578. BIR Report, 27.

70. Laitenberger, *Akademischer Austausch und auswärtige Kulturpolitik*, 87–89.

71. NARA RG 65. FBI. CRS. Class 65. 2904. 1351. Von Gienanth File. Jones Report, November 29, 1941.

72. FBI. RMD. RIDS. CRS Class 61. 7578. BIR Report, 25.

73. NARA. RuSHA. SS Officer Personnel Files. A3343 SSO 012A. 8365. SS Officer Dossier. Ulrich von Gienanth. Von Gienanth joined the SS rank as *gefreiter* (corporal), was promoted to *unterstrumführer* (second lieutenant) in 1935, and by 1938 had eventually advanced to *obersturmführer* (first lieutenant).

74. BArch (Koblenz) SL ZSG 137/6. Bd. 4. Von Gienanth, Ulrich (I and II). Von Gienanth to Morsbach, August 3, 1932; BArch (Licht.) R 8088. 1064. [Apparently a meeting of the DAAD Presidium], July 17, 1933; University of Munich Archives. Zsg-II. Nr. 14. Bd. 03. "Die Entwicklung der Deutschen Akademischen Auslandstelle München von 1934–1938." November 4, 1938. Von Gienanth seems to have been rather proud of his SS status. He even told Ruth Hubbard about some "apparently gruesome details" of his SS work in Germany.

75. NARA. Roll no. A3343 SSO-012A. SS Officer Dossier. Ulrich von Gienanth.

76. Salinas, *Strategy, Security, and Spies*, 148.

77. NARA RG 65. FBI. CRS. Class 65. 2904. 1351. Von Gienanth File. Jones Report, November 29, 1941.

78. NARA RG 65. FBI. CRS. Class 65. 2904. 1351. Von Gienanth File. Jones Report, November 5, 1941, and March 28, 1942.

79. Joachim von Ribbentrop, who became foreign minister soon after von Gienanth's transfer, was a sometime ally of Heinrich Himmler, and allowed Gestapo agents to be placed at embassies. This, of course, was consistent with von Gienanth's other duties. Kimmich, *German Foreign Policy*, 17.

80. Rogge, *Official German Report*, 44–5; FBI. RMD. RIDS. CRS. Class 61. 7578. Davidson Report, September 7, 1944.

81. FBI. RMD. RIDS. CRS. Class 61. 7578. BIR Report.

82. "Prof. Hans Grueninger Appointed Adviser"; UHA. B-0689/1 RA. "Antrage der Auslandsabteilung." A letter sent by Grueninger to Hubbard suggests that they were on good terms, and Grueninger was at pains to emphasize that he did not want his role in exchanges with Germany "misinterpreted": IIE. HF. Germany: Rettig File—on German Student "Spies," 1939–40. G[ünther] H[ans] Grueninger to Hubbard, March 24, 1939. Ironically, the Nazis would abolish German fraternities in 1936.

83. Given the name of the program, one might expect it to have been managed by the Carl Schurz Vereinigung. The association, however, does not appear to have been involved with it; the program is not mentioned in its records. The money for the program may have come from the Alexander von Humboldt Stiftung in Berlin. NARA RG 65. FBI. CRS. Class 65. 2904. 55597. Rettig File. Longstreth Report, November 14, 1945.

84. Chall, *Statewide and Regional Land-Use Planning in California*.

85. IIE. AF. Habermann File. Wilhelm Burmeister to Duggan, June 14, 1938.

Notes to Pages 38–44   217

86. IIE. AF. Habermann File. Duggan to Wilhelm Burmeister, May 16, 1938.

87. FBI. RMD. RIDS. CRS. Class 61. 7578. Davidson Report, September 7, 1944.

88. IIE. HF. Germany: Rettig File. Memorandum, Hubbard to Fisher and Duggan, December 5, 1938.

89. IIE. HF. Germany: Rettig File. Memorandum, Hubbard to Fisher and Duggan, December 5, 1938.

90. NARA RG 65. FBI. CRS. Class 65. 2904. 55892-1. Circular Letter no. 1, in Cimperman Report, June 12, 1945.

91. IIE. HF. Germany: Rettig File. Eunice Schenk to Hubbard, January 7, 1939.

92. Federal Bureau of Investigation. File no. 65–1819. "Closing by Germany of the New York Office." See Jonas, *United States and Germany*; Beck, *Hitler's Ambivalent Attaché*, 112; Fromm, *Blood and Banquets*, 122.

93. "On Capitol Hill," 2.

94. NARA RG 65. FBI. CRS. Class 65. 2904. 55597. Rettig File. Longstreth Report, November 14, 1945.

95. IIE. AF. Lilge File. Hubbard to Lilge, May 10, 1939.

96. Füssl, *Deutsch-amerikanischer Kulturaustausch*, 100–101.

97. Duggan, Professor at Large, 183–84.

Chapter 2 · Recruitment and Training

Epigraph. BArch (Koblenz) SL. ZSG 137. 639K. Richard Sallet to Goebbels via Auswärtiges Amt, June 4, 1936.

1. Bielenberg, *Past Is Myself*, 26.

2. Sonthoff, "Campus Unknown to European Students," 1.

3. BArch (Koblenz) SL. ZSG 137. 635K. Luther to Auswärtiges Amt, April 2, 1936.

4. FBI. RMD. RIDS. CRS. Class 61. 7578. Janson File. Pieper Report, February 26, 1944.

5. UMA. 305a/8617. Georg Fohrer, Exchange Student Application, 1937.

6. The IIE archives contain examples of the forms, e.g., IIE. AF. Harms File. Bewerbung; IIE. AF. Kossak File. Bewerbung; "Nazis to Multiply Students Abroad," 9.

7. FBI. RMD. RIDS. CRS. Class 61. 7578. Lilge File. Brusch Report, June 27, 1944.

8. IIE. AF. Von dem Hagen File. Memorandum by Hubbard, May 24, 1940.

9. Rodgers, *Mencken*, 425. Lüdtke would go even further than his mentor in his disdain for the regime.

10. FBI. RMD. RIDS. CRS. Class 61. 7578. Herbert Sonthoff File. Lynch Report, March 28, 1944.

11. Noelle-Neumann, *Erinnerungen*, 45, 94.

12. Benedikt, *Emil Dovifat*, 10–15.

13. FBI. RMD. RIDS. CRS. Class 61. 7578. Ursula Schäfer File. Crane Report, May 6, 1944; "Max Dessoir," 241.

14. FBI. RMD. RIDS. CRS. Class 61. 7578. Davidson Report, September 7, 1944; Heschel, *Moral Grandeur and Spiritual Audacity*, xii. Hans Rothfels, a leading German historian, was a friend of Masur and often served on the DAAD selection committee before he, too, emigrated to the United States.

15. FBI. RMD. RIDS. CRS. Class 61. 7578: Tull Report, January 24, 1944; Herbert Sonthoff File. Lynch Report, March 28, 1944; IIE. AF. Scholl File; IIE. AF. Achenbach File. Bewerbung; Füssl, *Deutsch-amerikanischer Kulturaustausch*, 100.

16. FBI. RMD. RIDS. CRS. Class 61. 7578. Snyder Report, May 19, 1944.

17. FBI. RMD. RIDS. CRS. Class 61 7578. Hoover to SAC, June 30, 1943.

18. IIE. AF. Von dem Hagen File. Memorandum by Hubbard, May 24, 1940; FBI. RMD.

218 *Notes to Pages 44–47*

RIDS. CRS. Class 61. 7578: Conroy Report, November 27, 1943; Tull Report, January 24, 1944. The FBI interviewer added that one of the former exchange students, Anneliese von dem Hagen [Backhus], enigmatically "admitted a rather close acquaintanceship" with Friedrich Schönemann, a professor at the University of Berlin who was one of the first American studies experts in Germany.

19. IIE. AF. Foerster File. Lebenslauf; IIE. AF. Gatzke File. Lebenslauf, February 11, 1934.

20. FBI. RMD. RIDS. CRS. Class 61. 7578. Ursula Schäfer File. Crane Report, May 6, 1944; IIE. AF. Hörhager File. Bewerbung; IIE. AF. Weber File. "German Student Explains Aims of Youth Movement"; "Karl Herrmann, Exchange Student," 1; Steinacher, *Hans Steinacher*, 482; Blanke, *Vom Nazismus zur Demokratisierung*, 28; King, "Foreign Countries Well Represented"; IIE. AF. Von Schwerin File. Ruth Büttner, March 31, 1937. Many of the male exchange students, such as Heinz Rudolph, had leadership roles in both the Hitler Youth and later the SA. IIE. AF. Rudolph File. Bewerbung.

21. They included Kurt Weege and Wolfgang Hupe, one of the few exchange students with a Nazi Party membership card. IIE. AF. Weege File. Bewerbung; IIE. AF. Hupe File. Bewerbung.

22. BArch (Koblenz) SL. ZSG 137. 635K. Rettig to the Auswärtiges Amt, May 7, 1936 Among the exchange students, Wolfgang Hupe had been a party member since 1931; Kappelt, *Braunbuch DDR*, 97. Ulrich Pohlenz was accused of being a member of the Nazi Party, but this seems doubtful; "An Exchange Student." Otto Schmauss was also a party member; IIE. AF. Schmauss File. Bewerbung.

23. UJA. U. Abt. II, Nr. 18. Akademische Auslandsstelle: Studium deutsche Studenten im Ausland betr. 1928–38. Application form for exchange: fol. 114.

24. FBI. RMD. RIDS. CRS. Class 61. 7578. BIR Report, 27.

25. IIE. AF. Giesing File. Bewerbung.

26. IIE. AF. Schat File; IIE. AF. Reissinger File. Bewerbung.

27. IIE. AF. Lahr File. Bewerbung. Unfortunately, the Carl Schurz Vereinigung has not attracted the scholarly attention it deserves. The most important work devoted to it is Brantz, "German-American Friendship," 229–51.

28. Kleine, "Interview of von Rosenstiel"; IIE. Schlueter File. Fisher to Sister Eugenia, April 4, 1938; IIE. AF. Gilde File. Memorandum, June 10, 1940; FBI. RMD. RIDS. CRS. Class 61. 7578. Conroy Report, November 27, 1943.

29. PA AA. RZ 507. 64225. 27. Mitteilungen des Deutschen Akademischen Austausch-dientes, early February 1934; PA AA. RZ 507. 64227. 27. "Betätigung deutscher Studenten im Ausland," October 28, 1935.

30. UJA. U. Abt. II, Nr. 19, Akademische Auslandsstelle, 1935–44. DAAD Rundschreiben Nr. 35, to Akademische Auslandsstelle, November 2, 1938.

31. UJA. U. Abt II, Nr. 2, Bl. 301r. "Auslese der Austauschstudenten für das nächste Jahr." DAAD to AKAs, November 4, 1935.

32. PA AA. RZ 507. 64225. 27. Mitteilungen des Deutschen Akademischen Austausch-dientes, early February 1934.

33. BArch (Licht.) NS 38/2642. Kosmehl. Aktennotiz: Gerda Trojandt.

34. BArch (Licht.) NS 38/2642. DSt Aussenamt to Tech, September 4, 1934; BArch (Licht.) NS 38/2642. DSt Aussenamt to Lehmann, September 14, 1934; BArch (Licht.) NS 38/2642. Lehmann, to DSt Aussenamt, September 15, 1934.

35. BArch (Licht.) NS 38/2494. Werhahn and Hagert, "An die Aussenämter," November 29, 1934.

36. BArch (Licht.) NS 38/2494. Leiter Deutsche Studentenschaft Aussenamtes to Akademische Auslandsstelle, December 19, 1934.

Notes to Pages 47–50   219

37. BArch (Licht.) NS 38/2507. Gauschulungsreferent to Reichsführung der Deutschen Studentenschaft, August 16, 1935.

38. BArch (Licht.) NS 38/2507. [Hellmuth] Weiss, no recipient, [ca. 1934].

39. BArch (Licht.) NS 38/2507. Kreis Ausland to Peter Wecker, September 23, 1935.

40. BArch (Licht). NS 38/2644: Hauptamtsleiter II (Aussenamt Kreis Ausland) to Piwko (Amtsleiter, Aussenamt Kreis Ausland), June 14, 1935; Hauptamtsleiter II (Aussenamt Kreis Ausland) to Piwko (Amtsleiter, Aussenamt Kreis Ausland), June 23, 1935; Piwko (Amtsleiter, Aussenamt Kreis Ausland) to the University of Kiel's Foreign Office, May 27, 1936; Piwko (Amtsleiter, Aussenamt Kreis Ausland) to the University of Kiel's Foreign Office, June 1936; University of Kiel to Piwko (Amtsleiter, Aussenamt Kreis Ausland), September 6, 1936; Piwko (Amtsleiter, Aussenamt Kreis Ausland) to the University of Kiel's Foreign Office, September 9, 1936.

41. Dahrendorf, *Society and Democracy in Germany*, 84.

42. UJA. U. Abt. II. Bl. 301r. Nr. 11, Akademische Auslandsstelle, a.z. 1004, 1928–43. DAAD to AKAs, April 9, 1935, fol. 181.

43. For example, one of Frederic Lilge's professors wrote to Morsbach about him, "In appearance he could hold his own, without being striking looking in any way." IIE. AF. Lilge File. W. H. Wells to Adolph Morsbach, no date; Hall, "German Exile Reviews 'Nazi Propaganda Methods' in U.S.," 64. Among the typical examples, Ingeburg Oesterlin was described as "attractive" ("German Girl Coming to University to Continue Studies in Chemistry," 3), and Hans Ulrich Weiss was called a "charming . . . smiling, handsome young man" ("Society," 2); NARA RG 65. FBI. CRS. Class 65. 2904. 28452. Herbert Sonthoff File. Smith Report, November 20, 1942; IIE. AF. Lilge File. Bewerbung. W. H. Wells to Adolph Morsbach, no date; IIE. AF. Kossack File. Jane Daddow to Bernice Drown Cronkhite, February 16, 1938; IIE. AF. Kipper File. Mary Coolidge to Fischer, March 15, 1938; IIE. AF. Ingeborg Jung File, Hubbard, Memorandum, February 23, 1940. Numerous other such comments can be found in the IIE files.

44. FBI. RMD. RIDS. CRS. Class 61. 7578. Conroy Report, November 27, 1943.

45. Noelle-Neumann, *Erinnerungen*, 50. As Noelle-Neumann relates it, around the spring of 1937 she led her NSDStB Women's Working Group (Arbeitsgemeinschaft National Sozialistischer Studentinnen des NSDStB) on an excursion to Obersalzberg, where they enjoyed gazing at Hitler's Eagle's Nest resort from its lower entrance. As it so happened, Hitler was entering the elevator at the time and stopped to shake hands with some of his admirers. He then noticed Noelle and invited her to tea. During her refreshments with the Führer, he took her arm, led her to view the mountains toward Salzburg, Austria. He bemoaned, "I often wonder if, like Moses, I'll see the Holy Land, but never reach it."

46. NARA RG 60. DOJ. CRS. Class 146. 13. 2-16-21. Irene Gotthelf File. Gotthelf, Irene. Reconsideration of Hearing. Chief of the Review Section. March 29, 1944.

47. "Memories of Tufts."

48. Duggan, "American-German Student Exchange," 46.

49. IIE. AF. Lilienfeld File. Hubbard to Ingrid Dybwad, Re: von Lilienfeld, March 16, 1934.

50. FBI. RMD. RIDS. CRS. Class 61. 7578. BIR Report, 52, 54. The letter was written on June 16, 1932, before the Nazis took power. It is interesting to note that a Treasury Department official investigating IIE mentioned Hubbard's observation in his report to stress that racism influenced the selection of American exchange students as well. Ironically Dybwad was half Jewish, and thus might not have fit Hubbard's racial model, suggested by her characterization of various student populations in the New York area.

51. Wells College requested an exchange student of "good social background." IIE. HF. Fellowships for German students in the US, 1937–38. Hubbard to Adolph Morsbach, December 7, 1932.

220 Notes to Pages 50–54

52. FBI. RMD. RIDS. CRS. 61. 7578. BIR Report, 7, 13.

53. BArch (Licht.) NS 38/2627. Sofortprogramm der Aussenämter, November 15, 1934.

54. UJA. U. Abt. II, Nr. 19. DAAD to Akademische Auslandsstelle,. Rundschreiben Nr. 108, "Auslese der Austauschstudenten für das nächste Jahr," November 4, 1935.

55. BArch (Licht.) NS 38/2487. DSt Aussenamt to Reichsministerium für Wissenschaft, March 19, 1936.

56. IIE. AF. Achenbach File. Fleissner to Scholz, July 16, 1936.

57. BArch (Licht.) 38/2627. Werhahn and Hagert, "An die Aussenämter," November 29, 1934.

58. NARA RG 65. FBI. CRS. Class 65. 53615. EBF 99. "RETTICH."

59. FBI. RMD. RIDS. CRS. Class 61. 7578. Conroy Report, November 27, 1943.

60. BArch (Licht). NS 38/2644. Studentenschaftsführer, September 6, 1936; BA L NS 38/2644. Kreisführer des Kreises Ausland, Auslandsamt SDSt, to K. Schütze, DSt Kiel University, September 9, 1936.

61. BArch (Licht.) NS 38/2494. Leiter der Studentenschaft und Leiter des Aussenamtes, "Persönliche Beurteilung des Kameraden Otto Müller," January 3, 1936.

62. FBI. RMD. RIDS. CRS. Class 61. 7578. BIR Report, 7.

63. BArch (Licht.) R 8088/1064. [Apparently meeting of the DAAD Presidium], July 17, 1933.

64. PA AA. RZ 507. 64225. 27. Mitteilungen des Deutschen Akademischen Austauschdientes, early February 1934.

65. FBI. RMD. RIDS. CRS. Class 61. 7578. Ursula Schäfer File. Crane Report, May 6, 1944.

66. FBI. RMD. RIDS. CRS. Class 61. 7578. Janson File. Pieper Report, February 26, 1944.

67. NARA RG 65. FBI. CRS. Class 65. 2904. 55597. Rettig File. Longstreth Report, November 14, 1945.

68. NARA RG 65. FBI. CRS. Class 65. 2904. 55597. Rettig File. Longstreth Report, November 14, 1945; NARA RG 65. FBI. CRS. Class 65. 53615. EBF 99. "RETTICH," and "Note on Austausch Dienst [sic] in U.K. by Source Dictionary"; FBI. RMD. RIDS. CRS. Class 61. 7578. Conroy Report, November 27, 1943.

69. BArch (Licht.) 137/13. Scurla to Laitenberger, September 14, 1973; Fleck, *Etablierung in der Fremde*, 58. See also Mertens, "Anmerkungen zur NS-Wissenschafts- und Forschungspolitik," 232–33.

70. Von Twardowski, *Anfänge der deutschen Kulturpolitik*, 29; Gross, *Export Empire*, 226–27; Barbian, *Politics of Literature in Nazi Germany*, 102–3.

71. Paulus, *Vorbild USA?*, 207.

72. Syga, "Philanthropic American Foundations, 3–5; Fleck, *Etablierung in der Fremde*, 58; Mertens, "Einige Anmerkungen," 232–33.

73. Kenny, *The History of the Rhodes Trust*, 393.

74. The Goerdeler circle was a group of conservative civilians associated with Carl Friedrich Goerdeler, who supported General Ludwig Beck's anti-Hitler objectives in 1938. Goerdeler continued to be active against the Nazis until his arrest in August 1944. He was executed several months before the end of the war. Fest, *Plotting Hitler's Death* 160–61.

75. Bonhoeffer, Green, Kelly, and Reuter, *Dietrich Bonhoeffer Works*, 12:167–68; Goldschmidt, "Freiburger universitäre Widerstand, 143–58.

76. Ritter and Fitzsimons, "German Professor," 244–45, 250–51; Benz, *Im Widerstand Größe*, 83.

77. Boyer, "Chicago and the World of Higher Education in the Late Nineteenth Century"; Rabinbach and Bialas, introduction to *Nazi Germany and the Humanities*, xxxii.

78. Landeshauptstadt Hannover, "Empfehlungen Beirat 'Namensgebende Persönlichkeiten' Tischvorlage zur GOK am 1. Oktober 2015," 7.

Notes to Pages 54–58 221

79. BArch (Licht.) 137/13. Scurla to Laitenberger, September 14, 1973.

80. FBI. RMD. RIDS. CRS. Class 61. 7578. BIR Report.

81. FBI. RMD. RIDS. CRS. Class 61. 7578. BIR Report.

82. NARA RG 65. FBI. CRS. Class 65. 2904. 9438. Berle to Hoover, July 30, 1940.

83. "Exchange Student Is Pleased," 1.

84. Press, "Size of Campus," 1.

85. IIE. AF. Strasmann File. Bewerbung.

86. FBI. RMD. RIDS. CRS. Class 65. Annaliese von dem Hagen File. Albert Carlblom Report, June 7, 1940.

87. FBI. RMD. RIDS. CRS. Class 61. 7578. BIR Report, 13–14, 49.

88. "Foreign Student Receives Degree," 1.

89. "And Now—," 2.

90. "Men Invited to Address," 3.

91. NARA RG 65. FBI. CRS. Class 65. 9438. Berle to Hoover, July 30, 1940.

92. IIE. AF. Elisabeth Hühnlein File.

93. BArch (Koblenz) SL. ZSG 137. 638K. Listen von Austauschstudenten 1931/32 und später (DAAD-Auswahl). Handwritten notes on the document indicate the considerable indebtedness of one applicant's parents. It is unclear how DAAD obtained such information; Laitenberger, *Akademischer Austausch und auswärtige Kulturpolitik*, 182.

94. PA AA. RZ 507. 64225. 27. Metzger to [recipient not indicated], February 23, 1934.

95. FBI. RMD. RIDS. CRS. Class 61. 7578. BIR Report, 29; Kramer, "München ruft!," 157.

96. FBI. RMD. RIDS. CRS. Class 61. 7578. BIR Report, 29.

97. FBI. RMD. RIDS. CRS. Class 61. 7578. BIR Report, 12.

98. FBI. RMD. RIDS. CRS. Class 61. 7578. BIR Report, 29.

99. Albrecht and Romberg, *Widerstand und Exil, 1933–1945*, 89.

100. IIE. AF. Ickler File. Bewerbung and Ickler to Hubbard, February[?], 1939[?].

101. Ickler to Hubbard, February[?], 1939[?].

102. UMA. 305a/8617. Abschrift zu WU 971/39. Dr. Adams, DAAD, to Education Ministry, November 22, 1938. Hans Richter obtained his MA in theology from the Princeton Theological Seminary in 1939. He apparently never returned to Germany.

103. UMA. 305a/8617. Abschrift zu WU 971/39. Dr. Adams, DAAD, to Education Ministry, November 22, 1938.

104. Leiper, "Dear Homelanders"; Gensichen, "My Pilgrimage in Mission," 167.

105. Hockenos, *Church Divided*, 207; Herman, *It's Your Souls We Want*, 166; Leiper, "Dear Homelanders"; Barnett, Green, and Huber, *Dietrich Bonhoeffer Works*, 492; Matthews, "My Pilgrimage in Mission," 18; Reynolds, *Against the World*, 239.

106. Correspondence from Michigan, "News of the Christian World," 886.

107. Gensichen, "My Pilgrimage in Mission," 167.

108. Gensichen, 167; Scherf, *Evangelische Kirche und Konzentrationslager*, 117–18.

109. NARA. RG 65. FBI. CRS. Class 65. 2904. German Espionage Activities. 28452. Herbert Gunther Sonthoff. 100-10760. Manning Report, June 18, 1943.

110. NARA. RG 65. FBI. CRS. Class 65. 2904. German Espionage Activities. 28452. Herbert Gunther Sonthoff. 100-10760. Manning Report, June 18, 1943.

111. FBI. RMD. RIDS. CRS. Class 121. 31988. 52.27450. Sonthoff File, Report of Loyalty, July 24, 1951; "Gemeinschaftslager des Deutschen Akademischen Austauschdienstes," 28–30.

112. UBA Z.DI:977 Ka.031 Inhalt 14 Sonthoff. Leiter der Personalstelle, N.S. Dozantenbund to. Riedior, January 6, 1938.

113. NARA. RG 65. FBI. CRS. Class 65. 2904. German Espionage Activities. 28452. Herbert Gunther Sonthoff. 100-10760. Manning Report, June 18, 1943. For more on ancestral proof, see Ehrenreich, *Nazi Ancestral Proof*.

222   *Notes to Pages 58–62*

114. UBA Z.DI:977 Ka.031 Inhalt 14. Herbert Sonthoff. Leiter der Personalstelle, N.S. Dozantenbund to Riedior, January 6, 1938; UBA Z.DI:977 Ka.031 Inhalt 14 Sonthoff. Betr. Herbert Sonthoff, Berlin, January 11, 1938; NARA RG 65. FBI. CRS. Class 65. 2904. 28452. O'Connor Report, June 10, 1943. Lochner affidavit, May 29, 1943.

115. NARA. RG 65. FBI. CRS. Class 65. 2904. German Espionage Activities. 28452. Herbert Gunther Sonthoff. 100-10760. Manning Report, June 18, 1943.

116. FBI. RMD. RIDS. CRS. Class 61. 7578: Tull Report, January 24, 1944; Janson File. Pieper Report, February 26, 1944.

117. IIE. AF. Kossack File. Jane Daddow to Bernice Drown Cronkhite, February 16, 1938. Viëtor left Germany in the summer of 1937. Kossak wrote her exchange application about six months later.

118. IIE. AF. Kossack File. Berwerbung. Thomas Wolfe's "I Have a Thing to Tell You" (*New Republic*, March 1937) condemned the treatment of Jews in Germany. Kossack's "personal statement" was written around mid-January 1938.

119. FBI. RMD. RIDS. CRS. Class 61. 7578. Janson File. Pieper Report, February 26, 1944; IIE. AF. Ickler File. Ickler to Hubbard, February 1939 [?]; IIE. AF. Kossack File. Recommendation letter for Luzie Kossack from Karl Viëtor, professor of Germany philology and director of the German seminars, University of Giessen; IIE. AF. Schlueter File. Hubbard to Maria Schlüter-Hermkes, May 10, 1938; IIE. AF. Pohlenz File. Memorandum, March 22, 1939; IIE. AF. Pohlenz File. Hubbard: Memorandum, March 14, 1939.

120. IIE. AF. Wössner File. Bewerbung.

121. IIE. AF. Wiemers File. Bewerbung.

122. IIE. AF. Hörhager File. Bewerbung.

123. IIE. AF. Kipper File. Bewerbung.

124. IIE. AF. Giesing File. Bewerbung.

125. "Kiwanians Hear Munich Student," 1.

126. Sanborn, "Fraulein Oesterlin Finds American People," 2.

127. IIE. AF. Weber File. Bewerbung.

128. IIE. AF. Ickler File. Bewerbung.

129. Hausmann, "English and Romance Studies," 358.

130. IIE. AF. Lindenmeyer File. Bewerbung.

131. IIE. AF. Bischoff File. Bewerbung.

132. IIE. AF. Holthusen File. Bewerbung.

133. IIE. AF. Von dem Hagen File. Hubbard, "Memorandum," to Duggan and Fisher, May 24, 1940.

134. Email communication, Ursula Dibbern Baare-Schmidt to the author, January 15, 2014.

135. BArch (Licht.) NS 38/2628. Referent Schmidt, Aussenamt/Kreis Ausland, to the Aussenamtsleiter of the DSt Würzburg, March 2, 1936; BArch (Licht.) NS 38/2082. "Dienstanordnung des Aussenamtes der Deutschen Studentenschaft."

136. FBI. RMD. RIDS. CRS. Class 61. 7578. Seeman Report, December 13, 1944.

137. FBI. RMD. RIDS. CRS. Class 61. 7578. BIR Report, 16a; Goepel, "150 Austauschstudenten nehmen Abschied," 1–2, 8.

138. FBI. RMD. RIDS. CRS. Class 61. 7578. BIR Report, 16a.

139. FBI. RMD. RIDS. CRS. Class 61. 7578. Snyder Report, May 19, 1944.

140. FBI. RMD. RIDS. CRS. Class 61. 7578. Herbert Sonthoff File. Lynch Report, March 28, 1944.

141. FBI. RMD. RIDS. CRS. Class 61. 7578. Herbert Sonthoff File: Lynch Report, March 28, 1944; Snyder Report, May 19, 1944.

142. BArch (Licht.) NS 38/2478. Reichsstudentenführung / Nationalsozialistischer Deutscher Studentenbund. "Memorandum," October 20, 1933; BArch (Licht.) NS 38. 2082.

Notes to Pages 62–66 223

Deutsch Studentenschaft, Hauptamt fuer Grenzland und Aussenpolitik Auslandamt to Auslandsämter, Rundschreiben C 9 1933/34, November 10, 1933.

143. BArch (Licht.) NS 38. 2082. "Dienstanordnung des Außenamtes der Deutschen Studentenschaft." Grundsätze.

144. BArch (Licht.) NS 38/2627. Werhahn and Hagert, "An die Aussenämter," November 29, 1934.

145. PA AA. RZ 507. 64227. 27. "Betätigung deutscher Studenten im Ausland," October 28, 1935.

146. UJA. U. Abt. II, Bl. 301r. Nr. 11. "Niederschrift über die 4. Arbeitstagung der Akademischen Auslandstellen am 22. und 23. Oktober 1934 im Humboldt-Haus, Berlin," 6, 8, 9.

147. BArch (Licht.) NS 38/2642. Lehmann to DSt Aussenamt, September 15, 1934; BArch (Licht.) NS 38/2644. Kreisführer des Kreises Ausland Kieler Deutsch Studentenschaft, September 9, 1936; BArch (Licht.) NS 38/2627. Werhahn and Hagert, "An die Aussenämter," November 29, 1934.

148. PA AA. RZ 507. 64227. 27. "Betätigung deutscher Studenten im Ausland," October 28, 1935.

149. Krammer, "München ruft!" 143.

150. "Kurzer Tätigkeitsbericht des Aussenpolitischen Amtes der NSDAP."

151. Wickert, *Mut und Übermut*, 183; UJA. U. Abt. II, Nr. 11, Bl. 262-6. "Amerika-Deutschland," 4; Wickert, "Bild des grossen Mannes in den Vereinigten Staaten," 4–8.

152. FBI. RMD. RIDS. CRS. Class 61. 7578. Snyder Report, May 19, 1944; FBI. RMD. RIDS. CRS. Class 121. 31988. 4409. Sonthoff, Civil Service Commission application, September 25, 1951; FBI. RMD. RIDS. CRS. Class 121. 31988. 52.27450. Sonthoff File, Report of Loyalty, July 24, 1951; "Gemeinschaftslager des Deutschen Akademischen Austauschdienstes," 28–30.

153. "Students Vote on Olympics in Berlin."

154. Maier, "Deutsche Studenten im Auslande," 146–47.

155. FBI. RMD. RIDS. CRS. Class 61. 7578. Conroy Report, November 27, 1943.

156. BArch (Licht.) NS 38/2478. Auslandsamt to Reichsbund für Sicherheit, October 20, 1933.

157. PA AA. RZ 507. 64227. 27. "Betätigung deutscher Studenten im Ausland," October 28, 1935.

158. UHA. B-0689/1 RA. Generalia: Verkehr mit dem Ausland, 1934–37. Amtsblatt des Reich, December 24, 1936; BArch (Licht.) NS 38/2478. Auslandsamt to Reichsbund für Deutsche Sicherheit, October 20, 1933; NARA RG 65. FBI. CRS. Class 65. 2904. 55597. Rettig File. Longstreth Report, November 14, 1945.

159. BArch (Licht.) NS 38/2653. Referent, Kreis Ausland, to DSt Goethe Universität, July 3, 1935.

160. FBI. RMD. RIDS. CRS. Class 61. 7578. BIR Report, 15–16.

161. IIE. AF. Achenbach File. Fleissner to Scholz, July 16, 1936.

162. PA AA. RZ 507. 64226. 27. Luther to Auswartiges Amt, May 14, 1935.

163. PA AA. R 64228. Sallet to Goebbels, "Deutsch-Amerikanischen Studentenaustausch," June 4, 1936; PA AA. Washington RAV 171 18/64. Sallet to Auswartiges Amt, September 19, 1935.

164. BArch (Koblenz) SL. ZSG 137. 635K: Luther to Auswartiges Amt, April 2, 1936; Stieve to Auswartiges Amt, April 3, 1936.

165. PA AA. RZ 507. 64226. 27: Luther to Auswartiges Amt, May 14, 1935; New York General Consulate to AA. "Auslanderstudien in Deutschland und Frankreich," January 28, 1935; von Tippleskirch to Luther, June 3, 1936; Sallet to Goebbels, "Deutsch-Amerikanischen Studentenaustausch," June 4, 1936; PA AA. RZ 507. 64229. 27. Burmeister to Auswartiges Amt, August 20, 1936.

224   *Notes to Pages 66–73*

166. BArch (Koblenz) SL. ZSG 137. 636K. Luther to Auswartiges Amt, June 5, 1936.

167. "Muskingum College Fraulein," 2. Gerhard Gräfe managed the exchange for German students coming directly out of secondary school, such as Boursé.

168. PA AA. RZ 507. 64227. 27. "Betätigung deutscher Studenten im Ausland," October 28, 1935.

169. BArch (Licht.) NS 38/2487. Leiter der Hochschulgruppen Lausanne, to the Landesleiter der D.St. in der Schweiz, January 20, 1936.

170. BArch (Licht.) NS 38/2487. DSt Aussenamt to Riese, January 18, 1936.

171. BArch (Licht.) NS 38/2487. DSt Aussenamt to Reichsministerium für Wissenschaft, March 19, 1936.

172. Von Braun, *Flüchtlinge Gäste*, 13–55.

173. "Gemeinschaftslager des Deutschen Akademischen," 28–30.

174. This handshaking was likely inspired by a similar ceremony for teenage boys when inaugurated into the Hitler Youth. Pine, *Education in Nazi Germany*, 101.

175. FBI. RMD. RIDS. CRS. Class 61. 7578. BIR Report, 12.

176. Burmeister, "Deutsche Geist," 772; Englert, "Ansprache zum Abschied," 773–74.

177. FBI. RMD. RIDS. CRS. Class 61. 7578. Herbert Sonthoff File. Lynch Report, March 28, 1944; G[räfe], "Lager der Austauschstudenten," 432; "Austauschstudenten und -lehrer in Neustrelitz," 777.

178. IIE. HF. Criticism, 1936–38. Duggan to Walter Wilcox, September 24, 1937. Wilcox set up the committee anyway, apparently sometime in late 1938. FBI. RMD. RIDS. CRS. Class 61. 7578. BIR Report, 23.

179. FBI. RMD. RIDS. CRS. Class 61. 7578. Conroy Report, November 27, 1943; Blanke, *Vom Nazismus zur Demokratisierung*, 21–23.

180. PA AA. RZ 507. 64227. 27. "Betätigung deutscher Studenten im Ausland," October 28, 1935.

181. No doubt the fact that both Hess and Bohle were born in the British Empire (Egypt and South Africa, respectively), suggested their involvement with Nazi Party members outside of Germany.

182. PA AA. RZ 507. 64228. 27. Luther to Auswätiges Amt, December 5, 1935.

183. NARA RG 60. DOJ. CRS. Class 146. 13. 2-36-4. Chroust File. Chroust Hearing Board Recommendation, February 11, 1942.

184. PA AA. RZ 507. 64228. 27. Luther to Auswätiges Amt, December 5, 1935.

185. NARA RG 60. DOJ. CRS. Class 146. 13. 2-36-4. Chroust File. Chroust Hearing Board Recommendation, February 11, 1942; NARA RG 60. DOJ. CRS. Class 146. 13. 2-36-4. Chroust File. Alien Enemy Repatriation Hearing, January 24, 1946.

186. NARA RG 60, DOJ. Class 146. 13. 2-36-4. Chroust File. Alien Enemy Repatriation Hearing, January 24, 1946.

187. IIE. AF. Lilienfeld File. "Memorandum, RE: Anton Hermann Chroust," January 2, 1942.

188. NARA RG 60. DOJ. CRS. Class 146. 13. 2-36-4. Chroust File. Alien Enemy Repatriation Hearing, January 24, 1946.

189. FBI. RMD. RIDS. CRS. Class 146. 13. 2-36-4. Chroust File. 65-1582. Whaley Report, August 21, 1944; NARA RG 60. DOJ. CRS. Class 146. 13. 2-36-4. Chroust File. Alien Enemy Repatriation Hearing, January 24, 1946.

190. FBI. RMD. RIDS. CRS. Class 61. 7578. Snyder Report, May 19, 1944. Other reports mention that Ulrich von Gienanth was with the students in December 1934. These reports were, however, compiled a decade after the fact and were not as detailed as Jenni Karding Moulton's account. FBI. RMD. RIDS. CRS. Class 61. 7578. Sonthoff File. Manning Report, June 18, 1943; PA AA. RZ 507. 64228. 27. Luther to Auswätiges Amt, December 5, 1935.

Notes to Pages 73–88   225

191. NARA RG 60. DOJ. CRS. Class 146. 13. 2-36-4. 65–1582. Chroust File. Deitchler Report, January 8, 1942.

192. NARA RG 60. DOJ. CRS. Class 146. 13. 2-36-4. 65–1582. Chroust File. Deitchler Report, January 8, 1942.

193. PA AA. RZ 507. 64228. 27. Luther to Auswätiges Amt, December 5, 1935. According to Reginald Phelps, Tippelskirch was opposed to Nazism. See "Thomas Mann," 65–68.

194. FBI. RMD. RIDS. CRS. Class 65. 33035. Boston Office file no. 65–1582. Report by J. R. Foley, January 30, 1941, in appendix, Rees, "Roscoe Nathan Pound and the Nazis," 1313–47; Phelps, "Thomas Mann," 65–68.

195. PA AA. RZ 507. 64228. 27. Von Twardowski to Hess, December 24, 1935.

196. PA AA. RZ 507. 64228. 27. Luther to Auswätiges Amt, December 5, 1935.

197. NARA RG 60. DOJ. CRS. Class 146. 13. 2-36-4. Chroust File. Alien Enemy Repatriation Hearing, January 24, 1946.

198. PA AA. RZ 507. 64228. 27. Von Tippleskirch to Luther, June 3, 1936.

199. PA AA. RZ 507. 64228. 27. Kunisch to Auswartiges Amt, April 15, 1936; PA AA. RZ 507. 64228. 27. Von Tippelskirch to Chroust, May 25, 1936.

200. PA AA. RZ 507. 64228. 27. Luther to Auswätiges Amt, December 5, 1935; PA AA. RZ 507. 64228. 27. Kunisch to Auswartiges Amt, April 15, 1936; PA AA. RZ 507. 64228. 27. Von Tippelskirch to Chroust, May 25, 1936.

201. NARA RG 60. DOJ. CRS. Class 146. 13. 2-36-4. Anton Hermann Chroust File. Janson [Second] Affidavit, May 29, 1944.

202. Gellately, *Gestapo and German Society*, 213.

Chapter 3 · Brave New World

Epigraph. IIE. AF. Rudolph File. Rudolph to Hubbard, May 6, 1937.

1. UHA. B-0689/1 RA. Generalia: Verkehr mit dem Ausland, 1934–37; BArch (Licht.) NS 38/2478. Auslandsamt to Reichsbund für Sicherheit, October 20, 1933.

2. NARA RG 60. DOJ. CRS. Class 146. 13. Chroust File. Janson, Second Affidavit. May 29, 1944.

3. IIE. AF. Von dem Hagen File. Von dem Hagen to Hubbard, October 26, 1938.

4. Scott, "Muskingum College Fraulein," 2.

5. Von Wistinghausen, "German Political Situation," 2.

6. "Conference of Youth in Pasadena," 20.

7. See in particular, Norwood, *Third Reich in the Ivory Tower.*

8. Singh, "Two Foreign Visitors Write of Nazi Rule," 37. Hitler was never a mason.

9. Hershfield, "Ilse Wiegand Gives Her Views."

10. Noelle, "An Open Letter."

11. Traun-Strecker, "German Universities Today," 2.

12. IIE. AF. Wickert File. Wickert to American-German Exchange, December 7, 1935.

13. Elliot, "Ilse Dunst," 3; Dunst, "Letter to the Editor," 2–3. The account of Dunst's interview prompted criticism and ridicule on the part of Barnard students. See, for example, Vidair, "Letter to the Editor."

14. Dunst, "Letter to the Editor," 2–3.

15. "Students Speak on Nazi Regime."

16. Gassert, *Amerika im Dritten Reich*, 186.

17. Noelle, "An Open Letter."

18. Priwer, "Nazi Exchange Students," 353–61. Traun-Strecker, "German Universities Today," conveyed somewhat the same attitude, but added, "An educator of the young generation must first of all have the confidence of this young generation." Ergo, since Jewish professors did not have the confidence of young Nazis, they had to go.

226   *Notes to Pages 89–93*

19. IIE. AF. Zwicker File. Zwicker to Duggan, July 5, 1936.
20. IIE. AF. Zwicker File. E. H. Lindley to Duggan, July 6, 1936.
21. Henning von Dobeneck, "Open Answer," 2.
22. Henning von Dobeneck, "Open Answer," 2.
23. "Georgia Student Ardent Hitlerite."
24. Van Paassen and Wise, *Nazism*, 243.
25. "Students Vote on Olympics in Berlin," 1, 6.
26. Freiling, "Germany: Post-War and Present."
27. IIE. AF. Foerster File. Bewerbung, Lebenslauf.
28. IIE. AF. Lautsch File. Gesuch von Marianne Lautsch. November 14, 1933. See Lautsch and Herbig, *F. A. D. Kroschenen*.
29. Crow, "Miss Helga Prym, 6.
30. Traun-Strecker, "German Universities Today," 2.
31. IIE. HF. Criticism of American-German Student Exchange. IIE Answers and Suggestions 1936–38. Hubbard to J. F. Brown, Department of Psychology, University of Kansas, May 27, 1937, quoting Brown's letter.
32. IIE. AF. Thiele File. Francis Thomson to Fisher, January 26, 1938; IIE. AF. Roepke File. Paul D. Moody to Duggan, May 11, 1938; IIE. AF. Wojnowska File. Fisher to Hubbard, November 17, 1943; IIE. HF. Criticism of American-German Student Exchange. IIE Answers and Suggestions 1936–38: 9062. Name unreadable, "For the Goldenrod Student Paper," Nebraska State Teachers' College, April 12, 1939, on Albert Ickler; 9062. Hubbard to J. F. Brown, May 27, 1937.
33. Duggan, *A Professor at Large*, 175.
34. FBI. RMD. RIDS. CRS. Class 61. 7578. BIR Report, 32, 38–41.
35. IIE. HF. Fellowships for German Students in US, 1937–38. Erich Sauer, April 7, 1938.
36. IIE. AF. Schmauss File. Otto Schmauss, Annual Report, "German Exchanges in California Institute of Technology for the Year 1938/39," ca. August 16, 1939.
37. IIE. AF. Schröder File. Elijah Swift to Fisher, March 26, 1938.
38. For an invocation of this explanation, see Werner, "I Was Proud of America." 19.
39. "Last Year's Exchange Student," 3.
40. Jacobson, "An Open Letter," 2.
41. Jacobson, 2; IIE. AF. Kubitz File. Carl Scheve to Hubbard, Re: Hans Werner Kubitz, November 19, 1934; IIE. AF. Rein File. Dean Nye to Douglass, November 11, 1936.
42. "Carleton Girl," 1.
43. "Miss Edeltraut Proske Tells of German System," 3. Proske eventually remained in the United States. "Mrs. Barrett Plans to Lead Open Road Trip to Europe," 5.
44. Williams, "Big Apple and Hot Dogs Impress German Student," 1.
45. See, for example, IIE. AF. Roepke File. Paul D. Moody to Duggan, May 11, 1938; IIE. AF. Kubitz File. Carl Scheve to Hubbard, Re: Hans Werner Kubitz, November 19, 1934; IIE. AF. Rein File. Dean Nye to Douglass, November 11, 1936.
46. IIE. HF. Fellowships for German Students in US, 1937–38. T. R. Powell to Fisher, March 8, 1938.
47. IIE. HF. Comments on German Students. Letters from Colleges and Universities, 1938–39. IIE AF. Hess File. James McConaughy to Fisher, November 17, 1938.
48. "German People Don't Want War," 4.
49. Huck, "To the Editors," 2, 4.
50. IIE. AF. Closterhalfen File; IIE. HF. Fellowships for German Students in US, 1937–38. Joseph Brewer to Fisher, March 10, 1938.
51. IIE. HF. Comments on German Students Letters from Colleges and Universities, 1931–36. Report on Herbert Beyer. February 29, 1936.

Notes to Pages 93–101   227

52. IIE. AF. Brandi File. Fisher to Student Bureau, Re: Furman University, February 6, 1938.

53. IIE. AF. Mueller File. Benjamin Goldman to Duggan, December 16, 1937.

54. IIE. AF. Habermann File. J. Edgar Park to IIE, May 9, 1938.

55. Kramer, "München ruft!" 173.

56. IIE. AF. Richey File. "Extract from Report of Homer G. Richey," [ca. Spring 1934].

57. See Haugh, "Intercultural (im)politeness and the Micro-Macro Issue."

58. Dennery, "French Economist's Visit," 10.

59. Merritt, *Democracy Imposed*, 38.

60. Orr, "Unclassified Comment," 5.

61. IIE. AF. Hütter File. Theo Hueter to Hubbard, May 13, 1938.

62. FBI. RMD. RIDS. CRS. Class 61. 7632. Frederick Ernst Auhagen, American Fellowship Forum. Cohle Report, June 16, 1941.

63. Levine, *American College and the Culture of Aspiration*, 123.

64. Levine, 207.

65. According to Lee, *Campus Scene*, 66.

66. IIE. AF. Kipper File. Jane to Hubbard, April 22, 1938.

67. IIE. AF. Pfeiffer File. W. H. Freeman to Duggan, May 17, 1938.

68. BArch (Licht.) NS 38/2625. Bruno Wehner to Gerhard Gräfe, November 10, 1933.

69. Scott, "Muskingum College Fraulein," 2.

70. "There Is a Difference," 4.

71. See, for example, *Cornellian*, 1937, 352; *Cornellian*, 1938, 228; *Cornellian*, 1939, 406.

72. "Parade of Opinion," 4.

73. BArch (Licht.) NS 38/2082. Theo Claussen Letter.

74. IIE. AF. Roepke File. Paul Moody to Duggan, May 11, 1938.

75. For the most prominent claim that considerable numbers of denizens of the American ivory tower were sympathetic to Nazism, see Norwood, *Third Reich in the Ivory Tower*.

76. IIE. AF. Roepke File. Paul Moody to Duggan, May 11, 1938.

77. Frye, *Nazi Germany and the American Hemisphere*, 41.

78. Pentlin, "German Teachers' Reaction to the Third Reich," 236.

79. IIE. AF. Kubitz File. Ben Cherrington to Douglass, February 21, 1935.

80. "Williams Does Not Want German Students," 13; Boardman, "Trustees Scrap German Exchange Student Policy," 1–2.

81. Foerster, "Youth in Danger," 10–12.

82. IIE. AF. Foerster File. Foerster to Hubbard, May 19, 1936; Farnsworth Fowle to Fisher, May 8, 1936.

83. IIE. AF. Foerster File. Paul Birdsall to Douglass, February 4, 1936.

84. IIE. AF. Mueller File. Benjamin J. Goldman, to Duggan, December 16, 1937; Richard Gutstadt to Alvin Johnson, December 17, 1937; Alvin Johnson to Duggan, December 20, 1937; Duggan to Hans Dieckhoff, December 23, 1937; Duggan to Alvin Johnson, December 23, 1937; Duggan to Rees Edgar Tulloss, December 23, 1937; Hans Dieckhoff to Duggan, January 1, 1938; Benjamin Goldman to Duggan, January 14, 1938; E. L. to Duggan, January 14, 1938; Rees Edgar Tulloss to Duggan, January 31, 1938; Duggan to Benjamin Goldman, February 16, 1938.

85. Vidair, "Letter to the Editor," 2, 5.

86. Jacobson, "An Open Letter," 2.

87. Margolin, "Mr. Margolin Objects," 1.

88. Moore, *Know Your Enemy*, 71, 75.

89. Brandi, "Dear Hornet!," 3.

90. Fischer, "Open Letter to Fritz Brandi," 3.

91. IIE. AF. Habermann File. Wilhelm Burmeister to Duggan, June 14, 1938.

92. IIE. AF. Kipper File. Jane Daddow to Hubbard, April 22, 1938.

228   *Notes to Pages 101–104*

93. IIE. AF. Habermann File. Wilhelm Burmeister to Duggan, April 9, 1938.

94. Goodrich, "Two Times," 2; "Dictators 'Taken Apart' by Students," 36; IIE. AF. Baare-Schmidt File. H.G. Baare-Schmidt to Hubbard, May 31, 1938; IIE. AF. Schröder File. Wilhelm Burmeister to Duggan, June 14, 1938; FBI. RMD. RIDS. CRS. Class 61. 7578. BIR Report, 39.

95. IIE. HF. Germany: Rettig Files. On German Student "Spies." 1939–40.

96. IIE. AF. Borchers File. Ernest H. Wilkins to Duggan, April 5, 1939.

97. "Nazi Mistreatment," 2.

98. IIE. AF. Habermann File. Park to IIE, May 9, 1938.

99. IIE. AF. Frucht File. Helene Wurlitzer to Duggan, June 15, 1938.

100. IIE. HF. Fellowships for German Students in US, 1939–40. C. W. Prettyman to Fisher, February 27, 1939.

101. "Students Speak on Nazi Regime."

102. Lucas, *American Higher Education: A History*, 211.

103. Thelin, *History of American Higher Education*, 161.

104. Levine, *American College and the Culture of Aspiration*, 123.

105. Lucas, *American Higher Education*, 211.

106. Lucas, 119.

107. Thelin, *History of American Higher Education*, 178.

108. IIE. AF. Brandi File. Fisher to Student Bureau, Re: Furman University, February 6, 1938; IIE. HF. Fellowships for German Students in US, 1937–38. Wittenberg College, December 3, 1936. Report regarding Gerhard Koeppen; IIE. HF. Fellowships for German Students in US, 1937–38. Wittenberg College; Report on Theodore Heuter, May 16, 1938; Iowa State College, April 7, 1938. Report on Erich Sauer; Prof. C. E. Gates, Colgate University, to Fisher, January 7, 1938. Report on Hans-Georg Baare-Schmidt; Furman University, March 7, 1938, report regarding Hella von Schwerin. Also see IIE. HF. Fellowships for German Students in US, 1937–38. Hans Joachim Grauert, Post Graduate Medical School, Columbia University, New York January 13, 1937; Paul Jahn, Wesleyan University, Connecticut, February 15, 1937; IIE. HF. Comments on German Students. Letters from Colleges and Universities, 1936–37. RSI [no RSI given. ca. 6.2.20. 313. HF. 9-22]. Comments on German Students. Letters from Colleges and Universities, 1936–37. [Ursula Engler] Lilian Stroebe to Duggan, February 16, 1937; IIE. HF. American-German Student Exchange Committee on Selection, 1931–35; IIE. AF. Geulen File. Hubbard to Gerhard Gräfe, March 16, 1938; IIE. HF. Fellowships for German Students in US, 1937–38. Fletcher School of Law and Diplomacy, February 28, 1938. Report on Rolf Harri Hoppe.

109. IIE. AF. Naumann File. Clarence Shedd to Elizabeth Barney, February 23, 1935.

110. IIE. HF. Fellowships for German Students in US, 1937–38. Annemarie Closterhalfen File. Mary E. Schiltz to Douglass, October 13, 1937, and for similar remarks, H. Casey, March 7, 1938.

111. IIE. AF. Sarnow File. Esther Metzenthin to Hubbard, March 16, 1937; IIE. HF. Fellowships for German Students in US, 1937–38. Gertrude H. Dunham to Douglass, March 12, 1937.

112. IIE. AF. Lahr File. Andrew Louis to Hubbard, April 24, 1936.

113. IIE. AF. Lilienfeld File. Halford L. Hoskins to Douglass, March 19, 1935.

114. IIE. HF. Fellowships for German Students in US, 1937–38. Roy. B. Thomsen to Fisher, March 1, 1938. [Re: Erich Sauer]; IIE. HF. Comments on German Students. Letters from Colleges and Universities, 1938–39. C. W. Gates to Fisher, January 7, 1938. [Re: Hans-Georg Baare-Schmidt].

115. IIE. AF. Dibbern File. Hanna Hafkesbrink to Duggan, December 6, 1937.

116. IIE. AF. Rein File. Dean Nye to Douglass, March 15, 1937; IIE. AF. Dibbern File. Hanna Hafkesbrink to Duggan, December 6, 1937.

Notes to Pages 104–108   229

117. IIE. AF. Ickler File. Wilhelm Pauck to Fisher, May 11, 1939.

118. The reaction to Annemarie Closterhalfen serves as a typical example. IIE. HF. Fellowships for German Students in US, 1937–38. Closterhalfen File. H. Casey, March 7, 1938.

119. For example, see IIE. AF. Köster File. Wallace W. Atwood to Duggan, May 6, 1938; IIE. AF. Kossak File. Jane Daddow to Bernice Drown Cronkhite, February 16, 1938.

120. IIE. AF. Lilienfeld File. Hubbard to Ingrid Dybwad, March 16, 1934.

121. See, for example, IIE. AF. Kubitz File. Carl Scheve to Hubbard, November 19, 1934; IIE. HF. Fellowships for German Students in US, 1937–38. 7112. University of Georgia, February 15, 1937, referencing Peter Wecker; NARA RG 65. FBI. CRS. Class 65. 2904. 28452. Herbert Sonthoff File. Smith Report, November 20, 1942.

122. AF. Köster File. Wallace W. Atwood to Duggan, May 6, 1938.

123. IIE. AF. Endlich File. Hubbard, Memorandum re: Anna Maria Endlich; IIE. AF. Hoppe File. Hubbard to Fisher [RE: Rolf Harri Hoppe], January 3, 1938; IIE. HF. Comments on German Students. Letters from Colleges and Universities, 1938–39. Virginia Thomas to Fisher, March 7, 1938; IIE. HF. Criticism of American-German Student Exchange. IIE Answers and Suggestions 1936–38. Joseph Brewer to Duggan, November 22, 1937; IIE. AF. Goy File. Morse Cartwright to John C. Patterson, September 22, 1939.

124. Kramer, "München ruft!" 173.

125. IIE. HF. Fellowships for German Students in US, 1937–38. Tulloss to IIE, December 3, 1937.

126. Kleine, "Interview of Werner von Rosenstiel." The text of this quotation has been slightly shortened.

127. Mann and Mann, *Escape to Life*, 249.

128. McBane, "German Exchange Student Finds American College Life Surprising," 1.

129. Kramer, "München ruft!" 173.

130. "Edeltraut Proske," 3.

131. BArch (Licht.) NS 38/2082. Theo Claussen Letter [to his friends; no date or further information given].

132. Dornbach, "Da kann kein Blizzard," 18.

133. Wickert, "Anschlagsaeule," 18; similarly, see BArch (Licht.) NS 38/2082. Theo Claussen Letter.

134. Blanke, *Vom Nazismus zur Demokratisierung Deutschlands*, 27.

135. IIE. AF. Godberson File. Godberson to Hubbard, March 17, 1938.

136. IIE. AF. Gilde File. "National Feuds Forgotten"; IIE. AF. Kienzler File. F. K. Kruger to Fisher, September 29, 1939.

137. McBane, "French and German Students Find Mutual Friendship," 1.

138. IIE. AF. Rudolph File. Duggan to Herbert Scholz, January 4, 1937.

139. Hörhager, "Schlagt Dickinson!" 26.

140. Hörhager, 26.

141. "In This Corner with Gregory," 4. Furman did, in fact, beat the University of South Carolina.

142. "Last Year's Exchange Student," 3.

143. Wickert, "Anschlagsaeule," 18.

144. "Exchange Student Describes Impressions," 3.

145. See, for example, IIE. AF. Kuhne File. Kuhne to Hubbard, June 18, 1935.

146. Bigell, "Fear and Fascination," 128–48.

147. Jetter, "Gedanken über ein Land der Technik," 8–11.

148. "Freiheit im Mittelwestern."

149. "Ernst Mahr Describes Trip," 3; Priwer, "Nazi Exchange Students," 365.

230 *Notes to Pages 108–112*

150. FBI. RMD. RIDS. CRS. Class 61. 7578. Snyder Report, May 19, 1944.

151. Huehnlein, "Floridafahrt," 8–9.

152. Huehnlein, 8–9.

153. Scott, "Muskingum College Fraulein," 2; IIE. AF. Boursé File. Mary E. Sharp to IIE, September 25, 1939. When World War II broke out, Boursé wanted to remain in the United States as a student. As this proved impossible, she left for Mexico City. Toward the end of the war, the FBI informed Hubbard that she was in Spain. I do not know if she ever returned to Germany. IIE. AF. Kaessbohrer File: Boursé and Kaessbohrer to Duggan, September 22, 1939; Boursé and Kaessbohrer to Hubbard, September 22, 1939; Hubbard to Eduard Pestel, October 4, 1939; Heimfried Wiebe to Hubbard, October 14, 1939; Hubbard to Boursé and Kaessbohrer, October 16, 1939; Hubbard, Memorandum, March 26, 1940; Hubbard, Memorandum, March 9, 1944.

154. "[Notice on 'Miss Elizabeth (*sic*) Noelle']," 358.

155. IIE. AF. Jahn File. Jahn to Hubbard, December 31, 1936.

156. FBI. RMD. RIDS. CRS. Class 61. 7578. Davidson Report, September 7, 1944.

157. Blanke, *Vom Nazismus zur Demokratisierung Deutschlands*, 38–39.

158. IIE. AF. Habermann File. Fisher to Miriam Carpenter, March 21, 1938. On Habermann, see "Over the Tea Cups," *Wheaton News*, January 15, 1938, referenced in Habermann File. Miriam Carpenter to Hubbard, January 19, 1938.

159. Stroebe, "Teaching of German at Vassar," 26.

160. "Carleton Girl from Germany," 1.

161. "Freiheit im Mittelwestern."

162. Häring, "Julian," 34–37.

163. Weege, "Sing-Sing," 12–13.

164. Blanke, *Vom Nazismus zur Demokratisierung Deutschlands*, 37.

165. Blanke, 63.

166. AF. Blanke File. Blanke to Hubbard, May 3, 1940.

167. IIE. AF. Blanke File. Joyce [?] M. Bachelor [?] to IIE, ca. 1940.

168. Kleine, "Interview of von Rosenstiel."

169. IIE. AF. Wolf File. Wolf to Hubbard, June 10, 1936; IIE. AF. Hütter File. Theo Hueter to Hubbard, May 13, 1938; "German Gives Views on D-Son," 1; Wickert, "American Way of Life," 3: Hellmann, *Mit dem DAAD in die Welt*, 33–38.

170. Mann and Mann, *Escape to Life*, 249.

171. Mann and Mann, 249–52. This episode apparently took place in late 1938 or early 1939. I have not been able to identify this particular student supposedly from Leipzig. It is conceivable that his hometown was purposefully misidentified to prevent the Nazis being able to easily track him down.

172. Priwer, "Nazi Exchange Students," 353–61. Noelle, "Two Languages to Learn," 17–18. After returning home, Noelle portrayed her American experience quite differently to her German readership. She claimed that American women in college were only concerned with popularity, fashionableness, sex, and college athletics. Wealthy girls' desire to attend college had a lot more to do with escaping boring small town life than it did with scholarship. See Noelle, "'College Girls' in Amerika," 30.

173. IIE. AF. Lenkeit File. Carl Rogers to Duggan, May 24, 1938.

174. IIE. AF. Goy File. Donald Stevenman to IIE, September 24, 1939.

175. Brecher, *Brecher's Odyssey*, 29.

176. Blanke, *Vom Nazismus zur Demokratisierung Deutschlands*, 35.

177. IIE. AF. Godberson File. Godberson to Hubbard, March 17, 1938.

178. Kreisberg, "German Exchange Student," 1.

Notes to Pages 113–119 231

179. IIE. AF. Boehr File. Memorandum. RE: Werner Boehr, January 20, 1939.

180. See Lusane, *Historical Experiences of European Blacks*; Kesting, "Black Experience during the Holocaust"; Hitler, "Nation and Race," *Mein Kampf*, 1:286, on Latin America and race.

181. Wickert, *Mut und Übermut*, 140–41.

182. Lazenby, "Some Contributions of the Negro," 7–11.

183. Blanke, *Vom Nazismus zur Demokratisierung Deutschlands*, 33.

184. [Notes on students' activities], *Rundbrief deutscher Austauschstudenten in den U.S.A.* 5, no. 2 (December 1935): 17.

185. Woessner, "'Dunkle' Erinnerungen," 4–5.

186. BArch (Licht.) NS 38/2082. Theo Claussen letter.

187. IIE. AF. Prym-von Becherer File. Prym-Becherer to Hubbard, August 22, 1939.

188. Wickert, *Fata Morgana*, 31.

189. Woessner, "'Dunkle' Erinnerungen," 4–6.

190. Mahlin, "The Student Exchange System (with Apologies to Lincoln)," 172; "Freiheit im Mittelwestern," 58; Waagen, "How Do You Like America?" 28–29, 40.

191. Mohrdiek, "Paradoxie Amerika," 12–13.

192. UJA. U. Abt. II. Nr. 11. Bl. 266. "Amerika-Deutschland," 2.

193. Kleine, "Interview of von Rosenstiel." It is not surprising that automobile ownership in the United States seemed remarkable to the exchange students. In 1933 there was one automobile per 3.5 people in the United States, but only one car per 90 people in Germany. Gillingham, *Industry and Politics*, 71.

194. See, for example, "Freiheit im Mittelwestern," 58.

195. UJA. U. Abt. II. Nr. 11. Bl. 266. "Amerika-Deutschland."

196. Bezold, "Herrgott—Amerika!," 38–39.

197. BArch (Licht.) NS 38/2625. Bruno Wehner to Gerhard Gräfe, November 10, 1933.

198. Ducas, "German Girl Admires American Parents," 1.

199. Scheibe, "Was an der Universität arbeiten bedeutet," 29; IIE. AF. Baare-Schmidt File. Baare-Schmidt to Hubbard, May 31, 1938.

200. Wickert, "American Way of Life," 33–38.

201. Scott, "Muskingum College Fraulein," 2.

202. Kennedy, "André Siegfried"; Rubin and Rubin, *Hating America*, 144–56.

203. Schäfer, "Kleiner Triumph im grossen Amerika," 14–15. Schäfer's critique of American women's fashion relative to her own is essentially a textbook example of the Nazis' couture ideology. See Pine, *Education in Nazi Germany*, 125.

204. Schäfer, "Kleiner Triumph im grossen Amerika," 14–15.

205. For more on this topic, see Aly, *Hitler's Beneficiaries*; Baranowski, *Strength through Joy*; Wiesen, *Creating the Nazi Marketplace*.

206. IIE. AF. Sievers File. Sievers to Hubbard, October 20, 1934.

207. Junker, "Continuity of Ambivalence," 263.

208. Wickert, *Fata Morgana*, 29.

209. Wickert, *Fata Morgana*, 30.

210. Mohrdiek, "Paradoxie Amerika," 12–13; Wickert, *Fata Morgana*, 13.

211. Wickert, *Fata Morgana*, 13–15.

212. Jetter, "Gedanken über ein Land der Technik," 8–10.

213. Dornbach, "Amerika. Individualismus und Individualitaet," 5–7.

214. Von Lilienfeld, "Amerika im Umbruch," 5.fr.

215. Von Lilienfeld.

216. Sonthoff, "Anpassung?" 1–3.

232   *Notes to Pages 119–125*

217. IIE. HF. 9-22. Comments on German Students, Letters from Colleges and Universities, 1938–39. Walter H. Freeman to Fisher, February 10, 1939.

218. IIE. HF. 9-22. Comments on German Students. Letters from Colleges and Universities, 1938–39. Mildred Moore to Fisher, March 30, 1939.

219. IIE. AF. Schröder File. Elijah Swift to Fisher, March 26, 1938.

220. IIE. AF. Schröder File. Duggan to Mary Jean Simpson April 20, 1938.

221. Schrey, "Amerikanische Geist," 252.

222. Mohrdiek, "Paradoxie Amerika," 12–3.

223. Schrey, "Amerikanische Geist," 255–7.

224. Heimböckel, "Zivilisation auf dem Treibriemen," 50.

225. Bezold, "Herrgott—Amerika!" 38–9.

226. Scheibe, "Was an der Universität arbeiten bedeutet," 29.

227. "Kleine Liebe zu Amerika," 56–57.

228. Martin, *The Nazi-Fascist New Order*, 209, 272.

229. "German Gives Views on D-Son."

230. IIE. AF. Von Schwerin File. Von Schwerin to Hubbard, September 14, 1938.

231. IIE. HF. Criticism of American-German Student Exchange IIE Answers and Suggestions, 1936–38. Duggan to Walter Wilcox, September 24, 1937.

232. "Hess Nephew Was Student at Wesleyan," 1. Regardless of the claim in the article, I have found no evidence that Gerhard Hess was related to Rudolf Hess, deputy führer of the Nazi Party. See also IIE. AF. Schaper File. Letter from William F. Roertgen, February 8, 1938.

233. IIE. AF. Simon File. Mildred Fairchild to Hubbard, February 22, 1937.

234. IIE. AF. Habermann File. J. Edgar to IIE, May 9, 1938.

235. IIE. AF. Ungemach File. John Mackay to Duggan, May 13, 1938.

236. IIE. AF. Lebsanft File. C.G. Shatzer to Douglass, March 20, 1935. See also, "Hess Nephew Was Student at Wesleyan."

237. IIE. HF. Criticism of American-German Student Exchange. IIE Answers and Suggestions 1936–38. A. B. Faust to Duggan, December 27, 1937.

238. NARA RG 65. FBI. CRS. Class 65. 2904. 3017. Franz Pohlenz File. Weingarten Report, February 18, 1943.

239. "German Student Exchange Seen Plan to Spread Naziism," 1.

240. PA AA. RZ 507. 64227. 27. Borchers to Auswartiges Amt, November 27, 1935.

241. IIE. AF. Von Schwerin File. Von Schwerin to Hubbard, September 14, 1938.

242. IIE. AF. Kerkhof File. Kerkhof to Hubbard, September 2, 1936.

243. IIE. AF. Diffenbacher File. Diffenbacher to Hubbard, December 2, 1935.

244. IIE. AF. Godberson File. Godberson to Hubbard, May 24, 1938 [received date stamp]; IIE. AF. Hütter File. Hütter to Hubbard, May 13, 1938.

245. IIE. AF. Lautsch File. Lautsch to Hubbard, January 16, 1935.

246. IIE. AF. Lautsch File. Lautsch to Hubbard, February 9, 1934.

247. IIE. AF. Schmauss File. Dr. Otto Schmauss, Annual Report, "German Exchanges in California Institute of Technology for the Year 1938/39," ca. August 16, 1939.

248. IIE. AF. Baare-Schmidt File. Baare-Schmidt to Hubbard, May 31, 1938; "German Gives Views on D-Son." See, for instance, the caption for Eike Dornbach, in *The Gold* (1936), Beloit College's yearbook: "His presence on the campus as an exchange student has been as much of a treat for us as for Eike. We've known him as an intelligent, alert, cordial and most democratic young man."

249. IIE. AF. Ickler File. Assistant Director IIE [Fisher] to Nebraska State Teachers College, April 28, 1939.

250. IIE. AF. Wojnowska File. Wojnowska to Hubbard, November 14, 1940.

251. IIE. AF. Wojnowska File. Wojnowska to Hubbard, November 14, 1940.

Notes to Pages 129–133   233

Chapter 4 · Disillusionment, Resistance, Refuge, and Opposition in Exile

Epigraph. NARA RG 60. DOJ. CRS. Class 146. 13. 2-16-21. Irene Gotthelf File. Reconsideration of Hearing. Chief of the Review Section, March 29, 1944. Gregory Affidavit, January 23, 1942.

1. Leff, *Well Worth Saving*, 3–4, 83.
2. Kulke, "Ein undiplomatischer Diplomat und die Freiheitsliebe."
3. Williams, *To Pass on a Good Earth*, 70.
4. Alder, *Spuren in die Zukunft*, 30.
5. IIE. AF. Schäfer File. Memorandum, Hubbard, March 30, 1937.
6. Ropp and Little, "In Memoriam."
7. FBI. RMD. RIDS. CRS. Class 61. 7578. Ursula Schäfer File. Crane Report, May 6, 1944.
8. IIE. AF. Kipper File. Comment by Ruth Hubbard, written on a letter from Mary L. Coolidge to Fisher, March 15, 1938.
9. NARA RG 60. DOJ. CRS. Class 146. 13. 2-51-385. Ina Gotthelf File. Reconsideration Memorandum, March 27, 1944.
10. NARA RG 60. DOJ. CRS. Class 146. 13. 2-51-385. Ina Gotthelf File. Reconsideration Memorandum, March 27, 1944.
11. NARA RG 60. DOJ. CRS. Class 146. 13. 2-51-385. Ina Gotthelf File. Reconsideration Memorandum, March 27, 1944.
12. NARA RG 60. DOJ. CRS. Class 146. 13. 2-51-385. Ina Gotthelf File Reconsideration Memorandum, March 27, 1944.
13. NARA RG 60. DOJ. CRS. Class 146. 13. 2-51-385. Ina Gotthelf File. Alien Enemy Rehearing, February 15, 1944.
14. Benecke, "Between Exclusion and Compulsory Service," 224, 234–49.
15. NARA RG 60. DOJ. CRS. Class 146. 13. 2-51-385. Ina Gotthelf File. Alien Enemy Rehearing, February 15, 1944.
16. "Chapter and Alumni News," *Key* 54, no. 1 (1937): 53.
17. NARA RG 60. DOJ. CRS. Class 146. 13. 2-51-385. Ina Gotthelf File. "Report in the Case of Ina Gotthelf," February 23, 1944; Fox, *America's Invisible Gulag*, 27; NARA RG 60. DOJ. CRS. Class 146. 13. 2-16-21. Irene Gotthelf File: Alien Enemy Hearing Board, Washington, DC, January 30, 1942; Alien Enemy Hearing Board, April 10, 1942, including FBI report [Irene Gotthelf] April 10, 1942; Alien Enemy Repatriation Hearing, December 20, 1943; Irene Alexandra Gotthelf et al. to Francis Biddle, December 3, 1942; Irene Gotthelf File. G.S. Studebaker Report, January 5, 1942; [Summary of Reasons for Internment]. Re: Irene Alexandra Gotthelf. Summary by J.J.B., December 10, 1941; Petition for Repatriation, Irene Alexandra Gotthelf, May 20, 1942; Irene Gotthelf to Adolph Schiavo, January 3, 1943. Quite interestingly, Ina Gotthelf had been secretly informally engaged to Josias von Rantzau, who was discussed in the introduction to this book; Keiper, "Rantzau, Josias von," 570.
18. NARA RG 60. DOJ. CRS. Class 146. 13. 2-51-385. Ina Gotthelf File. Alien Enemy Rehearing, February 15, 1944.
19. NARA RG 60. DOJ. CRS. Class 146. 13. 2-16-21. Irene Gotthelf File. Alien Enemy Repatriation Hearing, December 20, 1943. "To Whom It May Concern." A. J. Burggraff, May 5, 1943.
20. The phrase comes from Ian Kershaw, "'Working Towards the Führer': Reflections on the Nature of the Hitler Dictatorship," *Contemporary European History* 2, no. 2 (July 1993): 103–18.
21. NARA RG 60. DOJ. CRS. Class 146. 13. 2-16-21. Irene Gotthelf File. Alien Enemy Repatriation Hearing, December 20, 1943. "To Whom It May Concern ." A. J. Burggraff, May 5, 1943.

234 *Notes to Pages 133–137*

22. NARA RG 60. DOJ. CRS. Class 146. 13. 2-16-21. Irene Gotthelf File. Reconsideration of Hearing. Chief of the Review Section, March 29, 1944.

23. NARA RG 60. DOJ. CRS. Class 146. 13. 2-16-21. Irene Gotthelf File. Alien Enemy Unit, Repatriation Requestion Request. January 25, 1944.

24. NARA RG 60. DOJ. CRS. Class 146. 13. 2-51-385. Ina Gotthelf File. Reconsideration Memorandum, March 27, 1944.

25. NARA RG 60. DOJ. CRS. Class 146. 13. 2-16-21. Irene Gotthelf File: Report of Alien Enemy Irene Alexandra Gotthelf, January 8, 1945; In the matter of Irene Alexandra Gotthelf, Alien Enemy, Francis Biddle, February 13, 1945.

26. NARA RG 60. DOJ. CRS. Class 146. 13. 2-51-385. Ina Gotthelf File. Alien Enemy Rehearing, February 15, 1944.

27. NARA RG 60. DOJ. CRS. Class 146. 13. 2-51-385. Ina Gotthelf File. Reconsideration Memorandum, March 27, 1944. NARA RG 60. DOJ. CRS. Class 146. 13. 2-51-385. Ina Gotthelf File. "Report in the Case of Ina Gotthelf," February 23, 1944; Keiper, "Rantzau, Josias von," 570; "Kesseler, Ina."

28. NARA RG 60. DOJ. CRS. Class 146. 13. 2-36-4. Chroust File. Chroust First Hearing. January 20, 1942; NARA RG 60. DOJ. CRS. Class 146. 13. 2-36-4. Chroust File. Chroust Hearing Board Recommendation, February 11, 1942; NARA RG 60. DOJ. CRS. Class 146. 13. 2-36-4. Chroust File. Chroust to Alien Enemy Control Unit, Review Section, [after September 16, 1942].

29. NARA RG 60. DOJ. CRS. Class 146. 13. 2-36-4. Chroust File. Janson [First] Affidavit, June 1, 1942.

30. Kleine, "Interview of von Rosenstiel."

31. "Coor, Gertrude Marianne Achenbach."

32. Stob, Summoning Up Remembrance, 139.

33. NARA RG 60. DOJ. CRS. Class 146. 13. 2-36-4. Chroust File. Chroust First Hearing. January 20, 1942.

34. IIE. AF. Schlueter File. Grace C. Dammann to Duggan, January 26, 1940.

35. "Jessen, Jens."

36. UBA Z.DI:977 Ka.031 Inhalt 14 Sonthoff. Leiter der Personalstelle, Betrifft: Ihre Anfrage über den assistentenbewerber Sonthoff, January 6, 1938.

37. UBA Z.DI:977 Ka.031 Inhalt 14 Sonthoff. Betr. Herbert Sonthoff File. Unknown to University Rector, January 11, 1938.

38. UBA. Z.DI:977 Ka.031 Inhalt 14. Herbert Sonthoff File. Prof. Dr. Bernhard Harms, to Prorektor, March 10, 1938.

39. NARA RG 65. FBI. CRS. Class 65. 2904. 28452. Sonthoff File. Ylitalo Report, June 29, 1942.

40. "Former K.U. Student Signs Contract," 5.

41. FBI. RMD. RIDS. FBI. CRS. Class 61. 7578. Schäfer [Lamb] File. Crane Report, May 6, 1944.

42. NARA RG 60. DOJ. CRS. Class 146. 13. 2-36-4. Chroust File. Foley Report, January 16, 1942.

43. NARA RG 60. DOJ. CRS. Class 146. 13. 2-36-4. Chroust File. Foley Report, January 16, 1942.

44. Noelle-Neumann, *Erinnerungen*, 51.

45. Noelle-Neumann, 51.

46. NARA RG 60. DOJ. CRS. Class 146. 13. 2-36-4. Chroust File. Chroust to Alien Enemy Control Unit, [after September 16, 1942].

Notes to Pages 137–139   235

47. PA AA. RZ 507. 64228. 27: Luther to Auswätiges Amt, December 5, 1935; Kunisch to Auswartiges Amt, April 15, 1936; von Tippelskirch to Chroust, May 25, 1936; Tippleskirch to Luther, June 3, 1936; Luther to Auswartiges Amt, June 10, 1936.

48. NARA RG 60. DOJ. CRS. Class 146. 13. 2-36-4. Chroust File. Chroust to Alien Enemy Control Unit, [after September 16, 1942]. Many of the Department of Justice officers involved in Chroust's hearings during the war noted Pound's unusually fierce attachment to Chroust. This apparently had something to do with Pound's pro-Nazism, Chroust's hospitality when Pound visited him in Germany in 1934, and Chroust's successful efforts to help Pound obtain an honorary degree from the University of Berlin that same year. It is unknown whether Pound's solicitous attachment to Chroust was simply avuncular or if he was afraid of embarrassment if Chroust revealed Pound's pro-Nazism and "Nazi" university degree. NARA RG 60. DOJ. CRS. Class 146. 13. 2-36-4. Chroust File. Deitchler Report, January 8, 1942; Norwood, *Third Reich in the Ivory Tower*, 56–7; Rees, "Nathan Roscoe Pound and the Nazis."

49. NARA RG 60. DOJ. CRS. Class 146. 13. 2-36-4. Chroust File. Chroust to Alien Enemy Control Unit, [after September 16, 1942].

50. NARA RG 60. DOJ. CRS. Class 146. 13. 2-36-4. Chroust File. Painter to Cooley, April 12, 1942.

51. IIE. AF. Hensel File. IIE to Mary Smallwood, May 5, 1938.

52. IIE. AF. Gilde File: H. G. to Hubbard, June 10, 1940; Memorandum, November 4, 1940. Her brother lived on Long Island.

53. FBI. RMD. RIDS. CRS. Class 61. 7578. Janson File. Report by Joseph J. Pieper, February 26, 1944.

54. IIE. AF. Hütter File. Hütter to Hubbard, January 20, 1939. Carl Rogers, who mentored several of the German students, also noticed that students who seemed to be "Americanizing" often tended to become engaged to or marry American women while in the United States. IIE. AF. Lenkeit File. Carl Rogers to Duggan, May 24, 1936.

55. Among those known to have married are Gerhard Brecher, Anton-Hermann Chroust, Fritz Ermarth, Hans-Joachim Grauert, Horst Janson, Hermann Lacher, Fritz Lilge, Ulrich Pohlenz, Edeltraute Proske, Ursula Schäfer, Ulrich Ernst Volkmar Solmssen, Herbert Sonthoff, Kathe Dorothea Strauss, and Werner von Rosenstiel. Brecher, *Brecher's Odyssey*, 1; IIE. AF. Rein File. Hubbard, Memorandum, March 29, 1937; IIE. AF. Lacher File. Hubbard, Memorandum, June 16, 1939. Lacher married the daughter of the dean of women at the University of Georgia. He had to go to Cuba to get his immigrant visa; FBI. RMD. RIDS. CRS. Class 61.7578. Hans-Joachim Grauert File. Crane Report, June 5, 1943; IIE. AF. Grauert File. Memorandum by Hubbard. April 24, 1937; FBI. RMD. RIDS. CRS. Class 61. 7578: Ursula Schäfer [Lamb] File. Ellerin Report, November 6, 1944; German Exchange Students. Seeman Report, December 13, 1944; IIE. AF. von Lilienfeld File. Memorandum. Hubbard, September 25, 1941; NARA RG 60. DOJ. CRS. Class 146. 13. 2-36-4. Chroust File. Chroust Hearing Board's Recommendation, February 11, 1942.

56. FBI. RMD. RIDS. CRS. Class 61. 7578. Sonthoff File. John J. Manning Report, February 4, 1943. Sonthoff to Norbert Berger, August 6, 1941.

57. Court of Common Pleas, Delaware County, PA. March 1949 Session. Hearing no. 1324. Naturalization of Herbert Gunther Sonthoff, May 10, 1949.

58. NARA RG 60. DOJ. CRS. Class 146. 13. 2-36-4. Chroust File. Alien Enemy Repatriation Hearing, January 24, 1946.

59. IIE. AF. Pohlenz File. German Consulate [?] to Pohlenz, March 29, 1939.

60. IIE. AF. Pohlenz File. Fisher to J. H. Wagner, April 7, 1939.

61. IIE. AF. Pohlenz File. Secretary, Student Bureau, University of Kansas City, to Hubbard, January 16, 1940; NARA RG 466. 3.4. March 1949 thru July 1950. Alien's Personal History and Statement. Order no. 3651-A. Franz Ulrich Pohlenz, April 20, 1942.

236 *Notes to Pages 139–143*

62. NARA RG 65. FBI. CRS. Class 65. 2904. 3017. Pohlenz File: Mrs. Pohlenz, Statement, June 12, 1942; Franz Pohlenz File. "Police Check," February 4, 1943.

63. Kleine, "Interview of von Rosenstiel."

64. FBI. RMD. RIDS. CRS. Class 61. 7578. Janson File. Pieper Report, January 12, 1944.

65. FBI. RMD. RIDS. CRS. Class 61. 7578. Sonthoff File. Manning Report, April 30, 1943. Rocholl had worked at the embassy after his US exchange year but was fired after being caught attempting to steal confidential files. Larson, *In the Garden of Beasts*, 226–27.

66. NARA RG 65. FBI. CRS. Class 65. 2904. 33035. Anton-Hermann Chroust File. Foley Report, January 30, 1941; NARA RG 60. DOJ. CRS. Class 146. 13. 2-36-4. Chroust File. Chroust to Alien Enemy Control Unit, [after September 16, 1942].

67. On this, see chapter 6, in this volume.

68. FBI. RMD. RIDS. CRS. Class 61. 7578. Jansen File. Pieper Report, February 26, 1944.

69. Blanke, *Vom Nazismus*, 75.

70. IIE. HF. Burmeister File. Martin Burmeister to Hubbard, February 17, 1937; Hubbard to Martin Burmeister, March 1, 1937.

71. IIE. AF. Brinkman File. Brinkman to Hubbard, February 19, 1939.

72. FBI. RMD. RIDS. CRS. Class 65. 1379. Von dem Hagen [Backhus] File. Cunningham Report, May 4, 1940. Similarly, two 1934-35 academic year exchange students, Ulrich Lebsanft, at Wittenberg College, and Elizabeth Borgwardt, at the University of Vermont, widely made it clear that they were "adamantly" anti-Nazi. NARA RG 65. FBI. CRS. Class 65. 2904. 28452. Sonthoff File. Ylitalo Report, June 29, 1942.

73. Schroeder, "Zwischenvölkische Aufgaben des Rundfunks," 17.

74. IIE. AF. Trittelvitz File. Roderic Davidson to Hubbard, February 5, 1939; FBI. RMD. RIDS. CRS. Class 61. 7578. BIR Report.

75. IIE. AF. Lautsch File. John Holt to Hubbard, October 6, 1935.

76. IIE. AF. Kirsch File. Hans Gatzke to IIE, November 28, 1935.

77. IIE. AF. Kirsch File. Hans Gatzke to Hubbard, January 27, 1936.

78. IIE. AF. Foerster File. Tyler Dennett to Douglass, January 13, 1936.

79. "What Exchange Students Think of Us," 30.

80. "What Exchange Students Think of Us," 30.

81. IIE. AF. Kerkhof File. Hilde Kerkhof to Hubbard, September 2, 1936.

82. "Christiansen, German Student Writes of American Auto Trip," 1.

83. IIE. HF. Germany Successful 1930–31, 1934. Hubbard to John Holt, November 13, 1935.

84. IIE. HF. Criticism of American-German Student Exchange. Duggan to Walter Wilcox, September 24, 1937.

85. Brecher, *Brecher's Odyssey*, ix.

86. UBA. Z.DI:977 Ka.031 Inhalt 14 Sonthoff. Lebenslauf, ca. December 1937.

87. NARA RG 65. FBI. CRS. Class 65. 28452. Sonthoff File. Skelly Report, April 6, 1943.

88. NARA RG 65. FBI. CRS. Class 65. 28452. Sonthoff File. O'Connor Report, January 11, 1944.

89. FBI. RMD. RIDS. CRS. Class 61. 7578: Sonthoff File. Manning Report, April 30, 1943 Julien Bryan to Sonthoff, March 4, 1938; Jenni Karding [Mrs. William Moulton] File. Snyder Report, May 19, 1944.

90. FBI. RMD. RIDS. CRS. Class 61. 7578. Sonthoff File. Manning Report, June 18, 1943; FBI. RMD. RIDS. CRS. Class 121. Loyalty of Government Employees. 31988. 4409. Sonthoff Civil Service Application, September 25, 1951; UBA. Z.DI:977 Ka.031 Inhalt 14 Sonthoff. Leiter der Personalstelle, N.S. Dozantenbund to Riedior, January 6, 1938. Something similar apparently happened to another former exchange student. He had lectured to Ursula Schäfer's preparatory exchange class in the typical American college fashion, but not long after emigrated to

Notes to Pages 143–145   237

the United States. FBI. RMD. RIDS. CRS. Class 61. 7578. Schäfer [Lamb] File. Davidson Report, September 7, 1944.

91. FBI. RMD. RIDS. CRS. Class 61. 7578. Sonthoff File. Manning Report, April 30, 1943. Sonthoff to Bryan, February 2, 1938; FBI. RMD. RIDS. CRS. Class 61. 7578. 100–9400. Jenni Karding [Mrs. William Moulton] File. Snyder Report, May 19, 1944; FBI. RMD. RIDS. CRS Class 65. 28452. Sonthoff File. Lynch Report, March 7, 1944.

92. FBI. RMD. RIDS. CRS. Class 61. 7578. Sonthoff File. Manning Report, April 30, 1943.

93. FBI. RMD. RIDS. CRS. Class 121. 31988. 4409. Sonthoff File. Civil Service Commission Application, September 25, 1951; FBI. RMD. RIDS. CRS. Class 121. 31988. Sonthoff File. Mulhern Report, November 10, 1951; NARA RG 65. FBI. CRS. Class 65. 2904. 28452. Sonthoff File: Danner to Special Agent in Charge, Boston, July 29, 1940; Breed Report, August 25, 1941; Ylitalo Report, June 29, 1942; Callister Report, May 24, 1943; Callister Report, December 2, 1943.

94. FBI. RMD. RIDS. CRS. Class 121. 31988. Sonthoff File. Mulhern Report, November 10, 1951; NARA RG 65. FBI. CRS. Class 65. 2904. 28452. Sonthoff File. Lipe Report, June 23, 1942.

95. FBI. RMD. RIDS. CRS. Class 121. 31988. Sonthoff File. Mulhern Report, November 10, 1951.

96. NARA RG 65. FBI. CRS. Class 65. 2904. 28452. Sonthoff File: R. B. Hood to Hoover, June 29, 1943; Smith Report, November 20, 1942; FBI. RMD. RIDS. CRS. Class 61. 7578. Sonthoff File. J. F. Sears to Hoover, December 17, 1942; FBI. RMD. RIDS. CRS. Class 121. 31988. Sonthoff File. Report [Author's Name Redacted], September 22, 1951.

97. FBI. RMD. RIDS. CRS. Class 61. 7578. Sonthoff File. J. F. Sears to Hoover, December 17, 1942.

98. FBI. RMD. RIDS. CRS. Class 121. 31988. Sonthoff File. Mulhern Report, November 10, 1951.

99. FBI. RMD. RIDS. CRS. Class 121. 31988. Sonthoff File. Mulhern Report, November 10, 1951.

100. Sonthoff, "Last Hours in Germany," 687–88.

101. Given the clues in Sonthoff's article, anyone familiar with his life in Germany after his exchange year could have deduced that Emil de Haas was the anti-Nazi friend. Sonthoff had a penchant for risking the safety of others for his own advantage.

102. FBI. RMD. RIDS. CRS. Class 121. 31988. Sonthoff File. Manning Report, October 12, 1951.

103. NARA RG 65. FBI. CRS. Class 65. 2904. 28452. Sonthoff File. Ylitalo Report, June 29, 1942.

104. FBI. RMD. RIDS. CRS. Class 61. 7578. Sonthoff File. Manning Report, June 18, 1943.

105. Kleine, "Interview of von Rosenstiel."

106. Pohlenz changed his name perhaps half a dozen times, including adopting Peter and Frank as first names. Janson also went by the name Peter.

107. IIE. AF. Ruch File. Memorandum. Hubbard, November 9, 1944; von Braun, *Flüchtlinge Gäste*, 11; Stob, *Summoning Up Remembrance*, 180; Blanke, *Vom Nazismus*, 53; IIE. AF. Von Minden File. "Faculty Member of Alma College Disappears," 2; Episkopos, "Importance of Fritz Ermarth"; IIE. AF. Buch File. Buch to Hubbard, May 20, 1940.

108. Riebling, *Church of Spies*, 143–44.

109. Blesgen, *Financiers, Finanzen und Finanzreformen*, 100.

110. Conze, Kosthorst, and Nebgen, *Jakob Kaiser*, 60, 105; Neumann, *Theodor Tantzen*, 351; Groothuis, *Im Dienste einer Überstaatlichen Macht*, 80; Kuropka and Austing, *"Um Den Karren Wieder Aus Dem Dreck Zu Holen . . ."*, 84, 101; Ditscheid, "German Resistance" [Father Laurentius Siemer].

111. NARA RG 65. FBI. CRS. Class 65. 28452-11. Sonthoff File. Manning Report, February 4, 1943. Sonthoff to Hermann Siemer, July 31, 1940.

112. Boehm, We Survived, ix; Wistrich, Who's Who in Nazi Germany, 80.

113. Conze, Kosthorst, and Nebgen, *Jakob Kaiser*, 60, 105; Neumann, *Theodor Tantzen*, 351; Groothuis, *Im Dienste einer Überstaatlichen Macht*, 80; Kuropka and Austing, *"Um Den Karren Wieder Aus Dem Dreck Zu Holen . . ."*, 84, 101; Ditscheid, "German Resistance."

114. Wonschik, *Briefe aus Bautzen II*, 8, 14–32.

115. CIA. "Source of Black Report no. 52, no. 14, November 28, 1944."

116. "Albrecht von Kessel"; von Klemperer, *German Resistance against Hitler*, 215.

117. Manvell, *Men Who Tried to Kill Hitler*, 64–65.

118. CIA. "Biographic Report: George von Lilienfeld, FRG, Ambassador-Designate to Iran." American Embassy, Bonn, to Department of State, July 26, 1968.

Chapter 5 · Propaganda and Espionage Missions

Epigraphs. Philipp Gassert, *Amerika im Dritten Reich: Ideologie, Propaganda und Volksmeinung, 1933–1945* (Stuttgart: Franz Steiner, 1997), 145; IIE. HF. Criticism of American-German Student Exchange, 1936–38. Duggan to Walter Wilcox, September 24, 1937.

1. For support on the contention that German espionage in general was ineffective, see Vasey, *Nazi Intelligence Operations*, 12, 16, 83, 112; Breitman et al. *U.S. Intelligence and the Nazis*, 94, 103, 106, 447.

2. FBI. RMD. RIDS. CRS. Class 61. 7632. Frederick Ernst Auhagen File. Memorandum for the File, August 28, 1940; Hoover to Earl J. Connelley, May 12, 1941.

3. FBI. RMD. RIDS. CRS. Class 61. 7632. Friederich Ernst Auhagen File. Rogge Report, December 11, 1943.

4. Rosenzweig, *Hollywood's Spies*, 30, 73, 93.

5. Farago, *Game of Foxes*, 32.

6. Priwer, "Nazi Exchange Students," 363.

7. Rogge, *Official German Report*, 53. All told, the German government spent the 2024 equivalent of $24 million annually on operating costs solely for US-based propaganda activities. MeasuringWorth.com database, with 1939 as the comparison date.

8. FBI. RMD. RIDS. CRS. Class 61. 7578. BIR Report, 30.

9. FBI. RMD. RIDS. CRS. Class 61. 7578. BIR Report, 30; "Boas, Disclosing Secret Nazi Document"; "Nazi Probe Will Cover 200 Schools."

10. Rosenzweig, *Hollywood's Spies*, 65.

11. "Mr. 'X' at Hearing Details Nazi 'Plot.'"

12. BArch (Licht.) NS 38/2082. Tiesenhausen and Hagert, Rundschreiben C 23/1934. From Auslandamt, Deutsche Studentenschaft, to Auslandämter der Einzelstudentenschaften, March 28, 1934.

13. Archive.org. "Sicherheitsdienst in Luxemburg, 1937–1940"; NARA RG 60. DOJ. CRS. Class 146. 13. 53615. EBF 99. "RETTICH" and "Note on the Austausch Dienst [*sic*] in U.K. by Source Dictionary"; Kahn, *Hitler's Spies*, 98.

14. Archive.org. "Sicherheitsdienst in Luxemburg, 1937–1940."

15. Siebe, *"Germania docet,"* 436.

16. Einstein's experience of anti-Semitism in Germany was so severe, as was his intuition that Hitler would become chancellor of Germany, that he left Berlin for the United States in December 1932, apparently never intending to return.

17. Leber, *Conscience in Revolt*, 160.

18. Gensichen, "My Pilgrimage in Mission," 167–68.

19. FBI. RMD. RIDS. CRS. Class 61. 7578. BIR Report, 29.

Notes to Pages 153–156   239

20. Rosenzweig, *Hollywood's Spies*, 65; "Herr Von Simson Argues," 1 "Herr Von Simson Argues Defense of German Policy," 1; Duquesne, "In Memoriam," 107.

21. "Editor Would Bar German Students," 4; White, *Partridge in a Swamp*, 184.

22. IIE AF. Engelbrecht File. Hanna Hafkesbrink to Hubbard, April 14, 1936. Hafkesbrink was part of a generation of German scholars who emigrated from Germany to the United States for political reasons in the 1930s.

23. FBI. RMD. RIDS. CRS. Class 61. 7578. BIR Report, 45; Danton was a vocal critic of the Nazis. Lauwers-Rechs, "Influence of Nazism and World War II on German Studies," 42.

24. It appears that quite a few people believed that Irene Gotthelf was working for Scholz. NARA RG 60. Class 146. 13. 2-16-21: Irene Gotthelf File. Studebaker Report, January 5, 1942; Mrs. Ronald Cordingley Affidavit, January 24, 1942. Cordingley also claimed that Gotthelf belonged to the Christian Front, but provided no supporting evidence.

25. NARA RG 60. DOJ. CRS. Class 146. 13. 2-16-21. Irene Gottfelf File. Mrs. Ronald Cordingley Affidavit, January 24, 1942.

26. NARA RG 60. DOJ. CRS. Class 146. 13. 2-36-4. Chroust File. Janson [First] Affidavit, June 1, 1942.

27. FBI. RMD. RIDS. CRS. Class 61. 7578. Schäfer [Lamb] File. Crane Report, May 6, 1944. She claimed to have "refused," not by stating as much, but simply by failing to carry out the order.

28. Kleine, "Interview of von Rosenstiel."

29. FBI. RMD. RIDS. CRS. Class 61. 7578. Karding [Mrs. William Moulton] File. Snyder Report, May 19, 1944.

30. NARA RG 60. DOJ. CRS. Class 146. 13. 2-36-4. Chroust File. Chroust Repatriation Hearing, January 24, 1946.

31. NARA RG 60. DOJ. CRS. Class 146. 13. 2-36-4. Chroust File. Chroust Repatriation Hearing, January 24, 1946; FBI. RMD. RIDS. CRS. Class 146. 13. Chroust File. Kelly to Ennis, February 12, 1946.

32. NARA RG 65. FBI. CRS. Class 65. 28452. Sonthoff File. Manning Report, April 30, 1943.

33. NARA RG 65. FBI. CRS. Class 65. 28452. Sonthoff File. Manning Report, April 30, 1943.

34. IIE. AF. Foerster File. Farnsworth Fowle to Fisher, May 8, 1936.

35. Daum, "Refugees from Nazi Germany as Historians," 12.

36. See, for example, FBI. RMD. RIDS. CRS. Class 61. 7578. BIR Report, 44–5; FBI. RMD. RIDS. CRS. Class 61. 7632. Auhagen File. Brightman Report, April 27, 1941.

37. FBI. RMD. RIDS. CRS. Class 61. 7578. BIR Report, 25; NARA RG 65. CRS. Class 65. 1351. Von Gienanth File. Jones Report, November 5, 1941.

38. Archive.org. "Sicherheitsdienst in Luxemburg, 1937–1940"; Laitenberger, *Akademischer Austausch und auswärtige Kulturpolitik*, 229; Mader, *Hitlers Spionage Generale sagen aus*, 360; Jacobsen, *Nationalsozialistische Außenpolitik*, 128; NARA RG 65. FBI. CRS. Class 65. 53615. EBF 99. "RETTICH" and "Note on the Austausch Dienst [sic] in U.K. by Source Dictionary"; Bolliger, *Zeichen der Nationalisierung*, 309.

39. FBI. RMD. RIDS. CRS. Class 61. 7578. Sonthoff File. Thompson Report, June 24, 1945; Browder, *Hitler's Enforcers*, 199.

40. Jacobsen and Smith, *Nazi Party*, 59.

41. Jacobsen, *Nationalsozialistische Außenpolitik*, 136.

42. NARA RG 65. FBI. CRS. Class 65. 53615. EBF 99. "RETTICH."

43. NARA RG 65. FBI. CRS. Class 65. 53615. EBF 99. "RETTICH."

44. See, for example, the discussion on Karl Haushofer and the Academy for Academic

240   *Notes to Pages 156–159*

Research and for the Advancement of German Culture / German Academy Munich (Akademie zur Wissenschaftlichen Erforschung und zur Pflege des Deutschtums / Deutsche Akademie München) in Laitenberger, *Akademischer Austausch und auswärtige Kulturpolitik*, 146; Füssl, *Deutsch-amerikanischer Kulturaustausch*, 99.

45. Archive.org. Interrogation Center. "Intelligence Bulletin," May 22, 1945, no. 1/58.

46. Murphy "Hitler's Geostrategist?," savages the notion that Haushofer was involved in anything that could be called espionage. The article contradicts itself a number of times, however, as on pages 11–12, and 23. Haushofer was involved in much more than Murphy credits him.

47. Baare-Schmidt, "Alaska," 723–29.

48. Zacharias, *Secret Mission*," 193. Also of note, Friedrich Schönemann praised Mehnert's published account of his exchange year, *Ein deutscher Austauschstudent in Kalifornien*.

49. Mader, *Hitlers Spionage Generale sagen aus*, 41.

50. Zacharias, *Secret Mission*, 193.

51. IIE. AF. Lahr File. Bewerbung.

52. NARA RG 238. Series: Interrogations. Von Gienanth File, October 5, 1945.

53. IIE. AF. Lilienfeld File. Hubbard, Memorandum [RE: Fritz Ermarth], September 25, 1941.

54. FBI. Vault. RG 65. 9106. 55. Weisberg to Sharrier, "Re: "Americans in Communication with German Intelligence Agencies," September 1945.

55. Fritz Ermarth to Karl Haushofer, March 18, 1940, quoted in FBI. Vault. RG 65. 9106. 55. Weisberg to Sharrier, "Re: "Americans in Communication with German Intelligence Agencies," September 1945.

56. Haushofer to Ermarth, October 15, 1940, in FBI. Vault. RG 65. 9106. 55. Weisberg to Sharrier, "Re: "Americans in Communication with German Intelligence Agencies," September 1945.

57. Blanke, *Vom Nazismus zur Demokratisierung*, 48–52; Dolibois, *Pattern of Circles*, 46.

58. NARA RG 60. DOJ. CRS. Class 146. 13. 2-16-21. Irene Gotthelf File. Irene Gotthelf Hearing, January 30, 1942; FBI. RMD. RIDS. CRS. Class 146. 13. Chroust File. Kelly to Ennis, February 12, 1946; NARA RG 60. DOJ. CRS. Class 146. 13. 2-36-4. Chroust File. Cooley to Burling, November 2, 1945.

59. FBI. RMD. RIDS. CRS. Class 61. 7632. Auhagen File. Conroy Report, February 11, 1941; PA AA. RZ 507. 64227. "Bericht über die Tagung"; FBI. RMD. RIDS. CRS. Class 61. 7578. Janson File. Pieper Report, February 26, 1944; FBI. RMD. RIDS. CRS. Class 61. 7578. Schäfer [Lamb] File. Crane Report, May 6, 1944; NARA RG 65. FBI. CRS. Class 65. 28452. Sonthoff File. Manning Report, June 18, 1943; NARA RG 60. DOJ. CRS. Class 146. 13. 2-36-4. Chroust File. Janson [Second] Affidavit, May 29, 1944. IIE. AF. Foerster File. Foerster to Hubbard. November 13, 1935. Von Gienanth went to the 1935 Bad Blankenburg exchange student assembly and the Riverdale Conference immediately thereafter.

60. NARA RG 65. FBI. CRS. Class 65. 2904. 1351. Von Gienanth File. Jones Report, November 29, 1941.

61. Vasey, *Nazi Intelligence Operations*, 9, 32.

62. Federal Bureau of Investigation, "Duquesne Spy Ring."

63. Vasey, *Nazi Intelligence Operations*, 12, 85.

64. CIA: "German Intelligence Service (WWII)," July 1944, 7–8; W.R.E., "The German Intelligence Service and the War," December 1, 1945, 2–3; Craig, *Peculiar Liaisons*, 217.

65. Miller, "Spies in America," 8.

66. PA AA. R 101.855. Gyssling to Dieckhoff, November 4, 1941; CSUNA URB. CRC-2. Klein to Roos, March 2, 1940; Vasey, *Nazi Intelligence Operations*, 14.

Notes to Pages 160–164 *241*

67. Jeffreys-Jones, *Nazi Spy Ring in America*, 144–49.

68. Vasey, *Nazi Intelligence Operations*, 38.

69. FBI. RMD. RIDS. CRS Class 61. 7632. Auhagen File. Conroy Report, February 11, 1941; FBI. RMD. RIDS. CRS. Class 61. 7578. Janson File. Pieper Report, February 26, 1944.

70. FBI. RMD. RIDS. CRS. Class 61. 7578. BIR Report, 48; IIE. AF. Pohlenz File. Fisher to J. H. Wagner, April 7, 1939; FBI. RMD. RIDS. CRS. Class 65. 1379. Anneliese von dem Hagen File. "Annalessia or Annelise von dem Hagen Albrecht," March 14, 1940; IIE. AF. Von dem Hagen File: Hubbard to von dem Hagen, February 14, 1939; Hubbard to Alfons Adams, May 9, 1939; Hubbard Memorandum, August 15, 1941; Hubbard Memorandum, May 24, 1940.

71. NARA RG 65. FBI. CRS. Class 65. 1351. Von Gienanth File. Jones Report, November 29, 1941.

72. Ritter, Wallace, and Barbier, *Cover Name*, 34, 55–56, 82, 107, 192.

73. Gallagher, *Nazis of Copley Square*, discusses the Duquesne ring. In particular, he explains that Duquesne had acquired the plans for the M1 Garand rifle, under consideration by the US Army as a standard issue weapon (155). Duquesne had brought the plans to Sebold's FBI-provided office while agents in the next room watched and recorded the incident. Duquesne criticized the gun in the documents he gave Sebold, noting that it "jams when it heats up," and the gas trap works for about 30 shots, then becomes "erratic." As it turns out, Duquesne was handing over plans for an earlier version of the gun; the army was reviewing an improved one. Archive.org. FBI. "Subject: Frederick Duquesne," March 12, 1985; Keefe, "U.S. Army Ordnance vs. NRA."

74. Rogge, *Official German Report*, 42–43; von Gienanth, "Lebenserringung."

75. NARA RG 65. FBI CRS Class 65. 2904. 1351. Von Gienanth File. Carson to Foxworth, July 23, 1941.

76. IIE. AF. Pestel File: LeRoy Clark to Hubbard, September 26, 1939; Hubbard to Pestel, October 4, 1939; Ray Baker to Hubbard, January 17, 1940; Ray Baker to Hubbard, February 9, 1940; Hubbard, Memorandum, September 30, 1940; Hubbard, Memorandum, October 29, 1940; von Gienanth to Hubbard, June 20, 1941; Hubbard, Memorandum, May 5, 1942.

77. NARA RG 238. Series: Interrogations. Von Gienanth File, October 5, 1945; NARA RG 65. FBI. CRS. Class 65. 2904. 1351. Von Gienanth File. Fletcher to Ladd, December 10, 1945.

78. Her references were Schönemann, who had suggested she apply; Julius Petersen, president of the Goethe Society; Rudolf Sieverts, director of the London branch of DAAD; and Emil Dovifat, professor of journalism at the University of Berlin (and a Catholic anti-Nazi). IIE. AF. Von dem Hagen File: Georg Rettig to Douglass, August 15, 1938; Hubbard to von dem Hagen, February 14, 1939.

79. Vasey, *Nazi Intelligence Operations*, 37.

80. "Goes to Trial in Espionage Case," 1.

81. "Nazis vs. U.S." 4.

82. IIE. AF. Von dem Hagen File: Georg Rettig to Douglass, August 15, 1938; Rebecca Switzer to Fisher, October 11, 1938; Fisher to Rebecca Switzer, February 14, 1939; Rebecca Switzer to Fisher, February 9, 1939; Hubbard to von dem Hagen, February 14, 1939; Rebecca Switzer to Fisher, February 17, 1939; Hubbard to Alfons Adams, July 6, 1939; von dem Hagen to Hubbard, September 21, 1939; Hubbard "Memorandum on Anneliese von dem Hagen Albrecht," October 7, 1939; Rebecca Switzer to Fisher, January 24, 1940; Rebecca Switzer to Fisher, May 23, 1940; Hubbard, Memorandum, May 24, 1940; Fisher to Allen C. Blaisdell, June 4, 1940; Rebecca Switzer to Fisher, June 22, 1940; IIE Memorandum [Hubbard or Fisher], July 24, 1940; von Gienanth to Hubbard, June 20, 1941; Hubbard, "Memorandum: Visit of Mr. Carlbloom [*sic*], Representative of the Federal Bureau of Investigation," August 15, 1941; Hubbard, Memorandum, September 29, 1941; Hubbard, Memorandum, June 5, 1944; Hubbard, Memorandum, March 6, 1945.

FBI. RMD. RIDS. CRS. Class 65. 1379. Anneliese von dem Hagen [Backhus] File: Fallon Report, September 28, 1939; Fallon Report, October 10, 1939; Arterberry Report, November 20, 1939; Paul Report, March 14, 1940; Stevens to New York Office Special Agent in Charge, April 1, 1940; Cunningham Report, May 4, 1940; Calhoun Report, June 29, 1940; Calhoun Report, December 16, 1941; Hoover to Wilkinson, April 22, 1942; Special Agent in Charge, San Francisco, to Hoover, March 15, 1947; Hoover to Special Agent in Charge, San Francisco, June 30, 1943.

83. Batvinis, *Origins of FBI Counterintelligence*, 207.

84. NARA RG 226. 15016. "Report of the Attorney General of Mexico, Re: Persons Engaged in Espionage Activities," April 17, 1942.

85. Naval History and Heritage Command, "German Espionage and Sabotage."

86. PA AA. R 9-I/610. Paul Max Weber File. Weber, Radiotelegram to Abwehr I Wirtschaft, August 29, 1941; Weber to Freiherrn Rüdt von Collenberg, June 24, 1941.

87. Barnes and Barnes, *Nazis in Pre-War London*, 192.

88. There are many cases of German Americans working with the FBI to ferret out German spies in the United States. See Miller, "Spies in America," 65.

89. Archive.org. FBI. "Subject: Frederick Duquesne," March 12, 1985; Keefe, "U.S. Army Ordnance vs. NRA."

90. PA AA. R 9-I/610. Paul Max Weber File. Weber to Keller, August 14, 1941; Klünner to Keller, August 14, 1941, September 19, 1941; Ruedt to "Dahaste" [Deutsche Außenhandelsstelle], September 24, 1941; Weber to Keller, September 1, 1941; Weber to Direktion der Eildienst, September 14, 1941; Wiehl to Keller, September 29, 1942.

91. PA AA. R 9-I/610. Paul Max Weber File. "Dahaste" [Deutsche Außenhandelsstelle], August 9, 1941; Reichstelle für Außenhandel, to Referat R VIII of AA, August 26, 1941.

92. PA AA. R 9-I/610. Paul Max Weber File. Klünner to Auswärtiges Amt, June 18, 1940; Weber to Direktion, Eildienst, June 5, 1941; Klünner to Auswärtiges Amt, July 27, 1941; "Dahaste" [Deutsche Außenhandelsstelle] to Klünner, July 24, 1941.

93. PA AA. R 9-I/610. Paul Max Weber File. Ott to Wiehl, September 29, 1942; Eildienst Memorandum, October 5, 1942; Ref Per H, Auswärtiges Amt to Reichstelle für Außenhandel, November 1942; Berger to Reichstelle für Außenhandel, November 18, 1941.

94. IIE. AF. Wiebe File: Wiebe to Hubbard, October 14, 1939; Lewis to Fisher, June 18, 1940; Hubbard to W. M. Lewis, June 24, 1940; W. M. Lewis to Fisher, June 28, 1940; IIE. AF. Pestel File: Hubbard, Memorandum, September 30, 1940; Hubbard, Memorandum, October 29, 1940; von Gienanth to Hubbard, June 20, 1941.

95. FBI. RMD. RIDS. CRS. Class 61. 7632. Frederick Auhagen File. 523. Memorandum for Clark, September 29, 1943.

96. NARA RG 60. DOJ. CRS. Class 146. 13. 2-51-385. Ina Gotthelf File. Ina Gotthelf Reconsideration, March 27, 1944.

97. NARA RG 60. DOJ. CRS. Class 146. 13. 2-51-385. Ina Gotthelf File. Ina Gotthelf Reconsideration, March 27, 1944.

98. Irene Gotthelf was issued a student visa by the US government but was considered an exchange student by DAAD, although on an unofficial basis, since her sister had already been an exchange student, and DAAD rules only allowed one child per family to go into the exchange program. IIE. AF. Kipper File. Mary Coolidge to Fischer, March 15, 1938.

99. NARA RG 60. DOJ. CRS. Class 146. 13. 2-16-21. Irene Gotthelf File. Irene Gotthelf Hearing, January 30, 1942; NARA RG 60. DOJ. CRS. Class 146. 13. 2-16-21. Irene Gotthelf File. Alien Enemy Hearing Board, April 10, 1942. Since it is quite unlikely that Irene Gotthelf was sending propaganda back to Germany, this was presumably part of an espionage operation.

100. PA AA. R 101.855. Pol. I M 28. Thomsen to von Weizsäcker, July 17, 1941.

101. *House on 92nd Street.*

Notes to Pages 167–172   243

102. Vasey, *Nazi Intelligence Operations*, 16; PA AA. R 101.855. Pol. I M 28: Thomsen to von Weizsäcker, May 21, 1940; Thomsen to von Weizsäcker, May 22, 1940.

103. Craig, *Peculiar Liaisons*, 217.

104. PA AA. R 101.855. Pol. I M 28: Thomsen to von Weizsäcker, May 21, 1940; Thomsen to von Weizsäcker, May 22, 1940.

105. PA AA. R 101.855. Pol. I M 28: Abwehr Division II, "Nr. 626/40 g.Kdos," June 1, 1940; Thomsen to Weizsäcker, June 2, 1940; von dem Heyden-Rynsch to Canaris, June 4, 1940; Weizsäcker to Thomsen, June 10, 1940; Canaris to V.A.A., June 11, 1940; Weizsäcker to von dem Heyden-Rynsch, June 17, 1940.

106. PA AA. R 101.855. Pol. I M 28. Thomsen to von Weizsäcker, May 21, 1940.

107. Rogge, *Official German Report*, 42–43; von Gienanth, "Lebenserringung."

108. NARA RG 65. FBI. CRS. Class 65. 28452. Sonthoff File. Manning Report, February 4, 1943; NARA RG 65. FBI. CRS. Class 65. 2904. 28452. Sonthoff File. Loebl Report, June 28–29, 1943.

109. NARA RG 65. FBI. CRS. Class 65. 2904. 28452. Sonthoff File. Smith Report, November 20, 1942.

110. PA AA. R 101.855. Pol. I M 28. Thomsen to von Weizsäcker, May 21, 1940.

111. Roosevelt, "May 26, 1940: Fireside Chat 15: On National Defense."

112. Breitman, *Berlin Mission*, 215.

113. Donovan and Mowrer, "Nazi Germany Declared World-Wide Conspiracy," 8.

114. Vasey, *Nazi Intelligence Operations*, 76.

115. MacDonnell, *Insidious Foes*, 8.

116. MacDonnell, 178.

117. Theoharis, Poveda, Rosenfeld, and Powers, *FBI: A Comprehensive Reference Guide*, 182.

118. Miller, "Spies in America," 29.

119. Carlson, *Under Cover*, 93, 412–13, 464. For more on Carlson and his book, see the introduction, in this volume.

120. The films are *Confessions of a Nazi Spy* (1939); *I Married a Nazi* (1940); *Dangerous They Live* (1941); *International Lady* (1941); and *All Through the Night* (1942).

121. The films are *Dawn Express* (1942); *Hillbilly Blitzkrieg* (1942); *Let's Get Tough!* (1942); *Phantom Plainsmen* (1942); *Saboteur* (1942); *Air Raid Wardens* (1943); *Ghosts on the Loose* (1943); and *Watch on the Rhine* (1943), for which Pohlenz was employed as a technical advisor.

122. IMDb.com, "Pohlenz, Peter," credits him as follows: as a technical advisor in *Edge of Darkness* (1943), *Watch on the Rhine* (1943), and *Operation Secret* (1952); as a Wehrmacht lieutenant in *Hostages* (1943) and *North Star* (1943); as Reinhard Heydrich in *Hitler Gang* (1944); and as an SS lieutenant in *Hotel Berlin* (1945).

123. NARA RG 65. FBI. CRS. CLASS 65. 2904. 28452. Sonthoff File. Gilligan Report, March 30, 1943.

124. NARA RG 65. FBI. CRS. Class 65. 2904. 28452. Sonthoff File. Smith Report, November 20, 1942.

125. NARA RG 65. FBI. CRS. CLASS 65. 2904. 28452. Sonthoff File. Gilligan Report, March 30, 1943.

126. NARA RG 65. FBI. CRS. CLASS 65. 2904. 28452. Sonthoff File. Breed Report, August 25, 1941.

127. NARA RG 65. FBI. CRS. Class 65. 28452. Sonthoff File. Manning Report, April 30, 1943; IIE. AF. Sonthoff File. Sonthoff to Hubbard, June 28, 1955.

128. NARA RG 65. FBI. CRS. Class 65. 2904. 3017. Pohlenz File. Memorandum for Office in Charge, June 11, 1942. While at the University of California, Berkeley, to apply for a doctoral program, Pohlenz was also disturbed to observe a professor dismissing the complaint of a

Jewish German refugee student because the student neither had money nor "any rights here." IIE. AF. Pohlenz File. Pohlenz to Hubbard, ca. early April 1940; NARA RG 65. FBI. CRS. Class 65. 2904. 3017. Franz Pohlenz File. "Police Check," February 4, 1943; NARA RG 65. FBI. CRS. Class 65. 2904. 3017. Franz Pohlenz File. Memorandum for the Director. Re: Franz Ulrich Pohlenz, June 21, 1944; NARA RG 65. FBI. CRS. Class 65. 2904. 3017. Pohlenz File. Nahrendorf Interview, April 17, 1943.

Chapter 6 · Consequences of the Nazi-Era German-American Exchange

Epigraph. Blanke, *Vom Nazismus zur Demokratisierung*, 8.

1. Greenberg, *Weimar Century*, 17–24; Jarausch, *After Hitler*, 137.

2. CIA. "Biographic Report: George von Lilienfeld, FRG, Ambassador-Designate to Iran." American Embassy, Bonn, to Department of State, July 26, 1968.

3. Lerg, "Amerikanische Rundfunkmacher," 213.

4. Shea, "Nazi Apologist or Noted Scholar?"

5. "Rupp, Hans."

6. IIE. AF. Kipper File. Bewerbung.

7. Hausmann, *Anglistik und Amerikanistik*, 204; IIE. AF. Ruch File. Hubbard, Memorandum, November 9, 1944; von Braun, *Flüchtlinge Gäste*, 11; Stob, *Summoning Up Remembrance*, 180; Blanke, *Vom Nazismus zur Demokratisierung*, 53.

8. "Midd Man Jailed," 1.

9. FBI. RMD. RIDS. CRS. Class 61. 7578. Schäfer [Lamb] File. Crane Report, May 6, 1944; Jewish Virtual Library, "Great Britain & the Holocaust"; "Nazi Underground," 1; "Midd Man Jailed"; Weale, *Army of Evil*, 279–81; Walker, *Traitors.* Roepke is depicted in "The Brits Who Fought for Hitler," season 1, episode 2, of *Revealed.*

10. Oakes, *Encyclopedia of World Scientists*, 235; IIE. AF. Von Dobeneck File. Hubbard Memorandum, October 19, 1943.

11. IIE. AF. Von Dobeneck File. Hubbard Memorandum, October 19, 1943.

12. Bauer, *Geschichter der Zeitgeschichte*, 140.

13. Bergmeier and Lotz, *Hitler's Airwaves*, 85; CIA. "Biographic Report: George von Lilienfeld, FRG, Ambassador-Designate to Iran." American Embassy, Bonn, to Department of State, July 26, 1968; von Eckardt, "Reviving German Propaganda," 13–14.

14. Kulke, "Ein undiplomatischer Diplomat."

15. "Nazi Interned Shanghai," 2.

16. FBI. RMD. RIDS. CRS. Class 61. 7578. BIR Report, 49.

17. Biewer and Blasius, *In den Akten*, 78; Browning, *Final Solution and the German Foreign Office*, 31.

18. Lifton, *Nazi Doctors*, 305; Langbein, *People in Auschwitz*, 354; Auschwitz-Birkenau Memorial and Museum, "New Publication on the Conservation of the Auschwitz SS-Hygiene Institut Documents"; Kłodzinski and Ryn, "Suicide in the Nazi Concentration Camps."

19. Angrick and Klein, *"Final Solution" in Riga*, 302–3, 310, 369, 450; Seckendorf, "Reichskommissariat Ostland."

20. Court of Common Pleas of Delaware Co., PA. March 1949 Session. Hearing no. 1324. Naturalization of Herbert Gunther Sonthoff. May 10, 1949; FBI. RMD. RIDS. CRS. Class 61. 7578. Snyder Report, May 19, 1944; "Federal Agents Detain Theodore von Laue," 1.

21. Fox, *America's Invisible Gulag*, 30, 132–36.

22. IIE. AF. Pohlenz File. Pohlenz to Hubbard, March 3, 1942; Pohlenz to Hubbard, [after March 1944].

23. IIE. AF. Pohlenz File. Pohlenz to Hubbard, March 23, 1944; Frank Ulrich "Peter" Pohlenz to Colonel E. F. Connely, Office of Strategic Services, March 12, 1944.

24. IIE. AF. Pohlenz File. Pohlenz to Hubbard, [after March 1944].

Notes to Pages 179–183   245

25. NARA RG 60. DOJ. CRS. Class 146. 13. 2-36-4. Chroust File. Chroust Repatriation Hearing, January 24, 1946.

26. NARA RG 65. FBI. CRS. Class 65. 2904. 28452. Herbert Sonthoff File: Smith Report, November 20, 1942; Special Agent in Charge [HWS] Report, December 11, 1943, for the enclosure Francis Biddle, Attorney General. "Warrant: To the Director of the Federal Bureau of Investigation. [RE: Herbert Gunther Sonthoff], December 2, 1943.

27. NARA RG 60. DOJ. CRS. Class 146. 13. 2-36-4. Chroust File. Janson [First] Affidavit, June 1, 1942.

28. Kleine, "Interview of von Rosenstiel."

29. "Werner von Rosenstiel Obituary."

30. NARA RG 65. FBI. CRS. Class 65. 28452. 65–1176. Sonthoff File. Gelder Report, February 19, 1941.

31. Johnson, "Ex-Storm Trooper," 4.

32. NARA RG 60. DOJ. CRS. Class 146. 13. 2-36-4. Chroust File. Painter to Cooley, April 12, 1942.

33. NARA RG 60. DOJ. CRS. Class 146. 13. 2-36-4. Chroust File. Chroust Repatriation Hearing, January 24, 1946.

34. NARA RG 60. DOJ. CRS. Class 146. 13. 2-36-4. Chroust File. Chroust Repatriation Hearing, January 24, 1946.

35. FBI. RMD. RIDS. FBI. CRS. Class 61. 7578. 100–13895. Lilge File. Roettling Report, September 24, 1942.

36. "Alma Ex-Nazi Disappears," 2; "Speakers Address Youth Conference," 16.

37. IIE. AF. Ruch File. Hubbard Memorandum, November 9, 1944.

38. The course credits were accepted by some German universities. Weis, "On Behalf of My Comrades," 96.

39. IIE. AF. Von Dobeneck File. Hubbard to Mrs. E. Bado, October 20, 1943; Lt. Col. George V. Eggers, "To Whom It May Concern," September 14, 1945; von Dobeneck to Hubbard, ca. September 27, 1945.

40. Jarausch, *After Hitler*, 133.

41. United States, *Demobilization of Armed Forces: Hearings before the Committee on Military Affairs*, January 16–18, 1946, 344; Baring, "In Der Vergangenheit Nach Zukunftsperspektiven," 126.

42. Trent, "Free University of Berlin," 248.

43. Jarausch, *After Hitler*, 139.

44. Tisch, "Soldier in Hitler's Army Fled to the U.S., Served as Translator in Nuremberg Trials"; IIE. AF. Hoppe File. Rolf H. Hoppe Alumni Information Record–1953[–54]; IIE. AF. Kipper File. Alumni Information Record–1953; "Midd Man Jailed As Underground Leader of Nazis."

45. IIE. AF. Waltz File. Friederike Waltz Bezold to Hubbard, March 22, 1955; "Zeitgenossinnen Inhalt.indd—Stadt Krefeld," 1–8; Grunenberg, "Immer schön die Türen schließen."

46. IIE. AF. Fiek File. Fiek to Hubbard, January 22, 1947.

47. Episkopos, "Importance of Fritz Ermarth."

48. Scheuer, "German Military Art Protection in Italy"; Heftrig, Peters, and Schellewald, *Kunstgeschichte im "Dritten Reich*," 305, 325; Petropoulos, *Artists under Hitler*, 53; Petropoulos, *Art as Politics in the Third Reich*, 56; Lauterbach, "Central Art Collecting Point (1945–1949)"; "Hanfstaengl, Frau Dr. Erika"; Fuhrmeister, "Vom Führerbau zum Central Collection," 96.

49. Lerg, "Amerikanische Rundfunkmacher im Dienste," 213.

50. "Werner von Rosenstiel Obituary."

51. Maguire, *Law and War*, 140.

52. Boxfordurgess, *In Search of the Federal Spirit*, 131.

246 *Notes to Pages 183–188*

53. Strobel, "Der Wehrbeauftragte"; "Fritsch, Georg Freiherr von."

54. Kellermann, *Cultural Relations*, 197–98; Paulus, *Vorbild USA?*, 344–45.

55. Rothfels became in many ways the founder of the study of German contemporary history. He established the Institut für Zeitgeschichte (Institute for Contemporary History), in Munich, and served as coeditor of the *Vierteljahrshefte für Zeitgeschichte*, dedicated to the study of contemporary history. He emphasized the respectability of the German nationalist tradition, but in the 1950s, Rothfels expanded his criticism of Nazism to include its militaristic aggression and its responsibility for the Holocaust. Von Klemperer, "Hans Rothfels," 381–83; Lehmann and Sheehan, *Interrupted Past*, 89, 157.

56. Harrington, *German Cosmopolitan Social Thought*, 128, especially note 158; Blank and Schmidt, "Verletzte oder verletzende Nation?"

57. Paulus, *Vorbild USA?*, 244–45; Strote, "Emigration and the Foundation of West Germany," 425–27, 435, 460, 477, 482–85.

58. Kellermann, *Cultural Relations as an Instrument of U.S. Foreign Policy*, 220.

59. IIE. AF. Hupe File. Hupe to Christie, June 10, 1954.

60. Angrick and Klein, *"Final Solution" in Riga*, 302–3, 310, 369, 450; Seckendorf, "Reichskommissariat Ostland."

61. Sharlet, *Family*, 172–74.

62. Zeitgenossinnen Inhalt.indd"; Grunenberg, "Immer schön die Türen schließen."

63. Fox, *America's Invisible Gulag*, 135–36; Spencer, "Modern Dance"; Obituary: "Ina Kesseler," B8.

64. Conze, Frei, Hayes, and Zimmermann, *Das Amt*, 12, 16.

65. "Gestorben: Sigismund von Braun"; von Braun, *Flüchtlinge Gäste*, 11; von Braun, *Stille Post*.

66. CIA. "Biographic Report: George von Lilienfeld, FRG, Ambassador-Designate to Iran." American Embassy, Bonn, to Department of State, July 26, 1968; Princeton University Archives. Allen W. Dulles Papers. MC019, box 38, folder 15, Biography of Lilienfeld, author unknown.

67. Conze, Frei, Hayes, and Zimmermann, *Das Amt*; Wickert, *Mut und Übermut*, 210–12.

68. IIE. AF. Blanke File. Blanke to Hubbard, December 25, 1946; Strunz, *American Studies oder Amerikanistik?* 102.

69. Paulus, *Vorbild USA?*, 272.

70. Lewis, "Books That Germans Are Reading about America," 247.

71. "Rupp, Hans."

72. Brogiato, "Bartz, Fritz," 119–20.

73. Ash, "Science and Scientific Exchange," 423. Note comments on this phenomenon in O'Shaughnessy, *Selling Hitler*, 3.

74. Buckow, "Allensbach Institute," 32; Bogart, "Pollster & the Nazis," 47–49; Honan, "U.S. Professor's Criticism of German Scholar's Work Stirs Controversy," 8; Shea, "Nazi Apologist or Noted Scholar?"

75. Jetter, "Zeitgenossen der Wasserstoffbombe," 596; Jetter, *Physikalische Blatter*, 199, in McNally, "Nuclear Fusion Chain Reaction," 3.

76. "Adolf-Henning Frucht," 300; Wonschik, *Briefe aus Bautzen II*, 8, 14–32; Hansen and Vogt, "Blut und Geist," 38–39; "Giftwolken," no. 27, July 3, 1978; no. 34, August 20, 1978; no. 39 September 23, 1978; Freeman and Roberts, *Kälteste Krieg*.

77. Paulus, *Vorbild USA?*, 15–17, 356.

78. Bauschiger, "American Reception of Contemporary German Literature," 437–38.

79. "Coor, Gertrude Marianne Achenbach."

80. Russell, "Prof. H. W. Janson Is Dead," 44.

81. "Hans Gatzke, 71, Dies," 10.

Notes to Pages 188–194   247

82. In 1939 Schäfer had married physicist Willis Lamb, who in 1955 won the Nobel Prize in Physics for his work on quantum mechanics. Klein, "Ursula Lamb"; Torodash, "Ursula Lamb," 281–82; University of Arizona Archives, MS 636. Willis E. Lamb, Jr. Papers, 1937–2007. Series VI: Ursula Schaefer Lamb, 1937–1996. Finding Aid.

83. Ropp and Little, "In Memoriam: Theodore H. von Laue"; "Federal Agents Detain Theodore von Laue," 1.

84. Ropp and Little, "In Memoriam: Theodore H. von Laue."

85. University of Notre Dame Archives. Anton-Herman Chroust Papers, 1924–81. Finding Aid.

86. "Faculty Member of Alma College Disappears," 2.

87. University of California (System) Academic Senate, "University of California: In Memoriam: Frederic Lilge."

88. "Administrative Program Established at Stevens," 3.

89. "Dr. Fritz Tiller Memorial," 43.

90. North Dakota State University, Institute for Regional Studies & University Archives, Mss 224. Rainer Schickele Papers Finding Aid.

91. National Academy of Engineering, "Arthur Thomas Ippen," 127–30.

92. Brown, *Footsteps in Science*, 75.

93. "Werner von Rosenstiel Obituary."

94. Mogulof, *Foiled*, 67–79.

95. Because of his participation in the Einsatzgruppen massacres, Braune was sentenced to death and executed in 1951.

96. Weinstein and Vassiliev, *Haunted Wood*, 295ff.

97. Hubbard resumed working for IIE in late 1948, as head of the Western European Division. She retired from IIE in the mid-1950s. In 1957 the Federal Republic of Germany awarded her the Knight's Cross of the German Order of Merit for her work in German-American relations. "Ruth Hubbard Honored"; IIE. AF. Holthusen File. Hubbard to Rolf Harri Hoppe, August 6, 1954.

98. See, for example, the untitled notice, *Union-Bulletin*, 5.

99. Kellermann, *Cultural Relations*, 10; Adam, *Germany and the Americas*, 433.

100. Haase, *Pragmatic Peacemakers*, 120.

101. Füssl, *Deutsch-amerikanischer Kulturaustausch*, 204.

102. Pilgert, *Exchange of Persons Program*, 197–98; Deutscher Akademischer Austauschdienst, "Geschichte–DAAD."

103. "Portrait Ehemalige Geschäftsführer und Generalsekretäre," Deutscher Akademischer Austauschdienst.

104. "[Hermann] Nickel Is First German Exchange Student," 3.

105. Pilgert, *Exchange of Persons Program*, 22–27, 57–58, 61; Kellermann, *Cultural Relations*, 186–87; "German Exchange Student Impressed," 6.

106. Kellermann, *Cultural Relations*, 122–23, 209–15, 221–31; Pilgert, *Exchange of Persons Program*, 71–72.

107. As an illustration, before 1945, Americans won less than half the number of Nobel Prizes as the Germans won (27 vs.57). After the war, Americans won almost six times more Nobels in science as Germans (375 vs. 64).

Conclusion

Epigraphs. IIE. AF. Wojnowska File. Wojnowska to Hubbard, November 14, 1940; IIE. AF. Ickler File. Extract from the International House Association, International Quarterly 5 (Winter 1941).

1. The *Bates Student*, the Bates College newspaper, reported that before going to the

United States, Werner Doehr "had been principally acquainted with British jazz and he may be frequently heard around the campus singing 'The Lambeth Walk' to himself." Williams, "Big Apple and Hot Dogs Impress German Student," 1. "The Lambeth Walk" was popular among the German Swing Youth but particularly reviled by the Nazis because its writer was supposedly Jewish. Cox, "Dance in Nazi Germany."

2. Evans, *Third Reich in Power*, 293–94.

3. Junker, "Continuity of Ambivalence," 256.

4. "Exchange Student Gives German View of America," 2.

5. Gellately, *Backing Hitler*, 72, 191.

6. Gassert, *Amerika im Dritten Reich*, 75.

7. IIE. AF. Habermann File. J. Edgar Park, President, Wheaton College, to IIE, May 9, 1938.

8. Duggan, *Professor at Large*, 175.

9. Sims, "Intellectuals in Crisis," 247; Smith, *Politics and the Sciences of Culture*, 77–78; Rowold, *Educated Woman*, 77; Dahrendorf, *Society and Democracy in Germany*, 86.

10. "Lee, Campus Scene," 48–72.

11. Jacqué, *Constructing America*, 54.

12. Fox, *America's Invisible Gulag*, 27.

13. "Last Year's Exchange Student," 3.

14. United States Holocaust Memorial Museum, "What Did Refugees Need to Obtain a U.S. Visa in the 1930s?"

15. Shain, "War of Governments against Their Opposition in Exile," 341–56.

16. Breitman and Lichtman, *FDR and the Jews*, 316.

17. Lichtblau, *Nazis Next Door*, 9–15.

18. See Berghahn, "Debate on 'Americanization,'" 107–30.

19. Rabinbach and Bialas, *Nazi Germany and the Humanities*, xxvi; Nagel, *Hitlers Bildungsreformer*, 250.

20. Leidecker, "Letter to Editor."

BIBLIOGRAPHY

Abbreviations for archival sources used in the chapter notes are defined below.

BArch (Koblenz) SL	Bundesarchiv Koblenz. Sammlung Laitenberger
BArch (Licht.) NS	Bundesarchiv Lichterfelde. Bestand NS
BArch (Licht.) R	Bundesarchiv Lichterfelde. Bestand R
CSUNA	California State University, Northridge, Archives
FBI. RMD. RIDS. CRS	Federal Bureau of Investigation. Records Management Division. Record/Information Dissemination Section. Central Records System
IIE. AF. RSI	Institute of International Education. Alumni Files. Roll, Side, Index
IIE. HF. RSI	Institute of International Education. Historical Files. Roll, Side, Index
NARA RG	National Archives and Records Administration. Record Group
PA AA	Politische Archiv des Auswärtigen Amts
UBA	University of Berlin Archives
UHA	University of Heidelberg Archives
UJA	University of Jena Archives
UMA	University of Marburg Archives
YUL	Yale University Library

Archival Sources in Germany

Bundesarchiv Koblenz. (BArch Koblenz). ZSG 137. Sammlung Laitenberger (SL). Mikrofilme aus Beständen des Politischen Archivs des Auswärtigen Amtes und des Bundesarchivs

> 635K   Reichsministerium für Wissenschaft, Erziehung und Volksbildung (R 21, R 21 Rep.).

Hans Luther to Auswärtiges Amt, April 2, 1936.
Georg Rettig to the Auswärtiges Amt, May 7, 1936.
Hans Luther to Auswärtiges Amt, June 5, 1936.

636K Deutsche Akademie (R 51).
Friedrich Stieve to Auswärtiges Amt, April 3, 1936.

638K Ausgewählte Quellen (nur Kopien–"DAAD Dokumentation").
Listen von Austauschstudenten 1931/32 und später (DAAD–Auswahl).

639K Politisches Archiv des Auswärtigen Amtes, Bonn.
DAAD.
German Embassy, Washington, to Auswärtiges Amt, August 30, 1935.
Rettig to Auswärtigen Amtes, May 7, 1936.
Personen Quellen (nach Namen A–Z).

Nr. 6, Bd. 4. Von Gienanth, Ulrich (I and II).
Fol. 1.
[Program of Exchange Student Summer Camp], September 3–5, 1932.
Ulrich Von Gienanth to Morsbach, August 3, 1932.
Karl Vogt [address, summer camp for the German exchange students], Köpenick, August 29–September 1, 1931.

Nr. 13, Bd. 11. Scurla, Dr. Herbert.
Laitenberg to Scurla, September 6, 1973.
Scurla to Laitenberger, September 12, 1973.
Scurla to Laitenberger, September 14, 1973.
Scurla to Laitenberger, September 18, 1973.

Bundesarchiv Lichterfelde (BArch Licht.) Bestand NS (NS) 38.
Reichsstudentenführung/Nationalsozialistischer Deutscher Studentenbund

1.2 Reichsleitung der Deutschen Studentenschaft
18. Auslandsamt
1. Allgemeines.
2082. Rundschreiben und Anordnungen der Deutschen Studentenschaft, 1932–37.
Bd. 17, 1933–34.
"Dienstanordnung des Aussenamtes der Deutschen Studentenschaft." Grundsätze.
Theo Claussen Letter to [Friends].
Deutsch Studentenschaft, Hauptamt für Grenzland und Außenpolitik Auslandamt, to Auslandsämter, Rundschreiben C 9 1933/34, November 10, 1933.
Tiesenhausen and Hagert, Rundschreiben C 23/1934. From Auslandamt, Deutsche Studentenschaft, to Auslandämter der Einzelstudentenschaften March 28, 1934.
2478. Auslandsangelegenheiten-Verschiedenes. Bd. 7, September–November 1933.
DAAD to DSt Ostpolitik, August 15, 1933.
Auslandsamt to Reichsbund für Sicherheit, October 20, 1933.

Reichsstudentenführung/Nationalsozialistischer Deutscher Studentenbund, "Memorandum," October 20, 1933.

2487. Auswärtiges Amt und Reichministerium für Wissenschaft, Erziehung und Volksbildung zur Vorbereitung und Prüfung einzelner Studenten für das Studium in der Schweiz, 1935–36.

DAAD to the Deutsche Studentenschaft, Amt für Ostpolitik, University of Jena, August 15, 1933.

Leiter der Hochschulgruppen Lausanne, to the Landesleiter der D.St. in der Schweiz, January 20, 1936.

Deutsche Studentenschaft Aussenamt to Riese, Lausanne, January 18, 1936.

Deutsche Studentenschaft Aussenamt to Reichsministerium für Wissenschaft, March 19, 1936.

2494. Urlaubsanträge von Kandidaten des DAAD für Studienaufenthalte im Ausland, 1935–36.

Werhahn, and Hagert, Rundschreiben, "An die Aussenämter und aussenstellen der Deutschen Studentenschaft," November 29, 1934.

Leiter Deutsche Studentenschaft Aussenamtes, University of Leipzig, to Akademische Auslandsstelle, Breslau, December 19, 1934.

Leiter der Studentenschaft und Leiter des Aussenamtes, "Persönliche Beurteilung des Kameraden Otto Müller," Darmstadt, January 3, 1936.

2505. Zurückgezogene Urlaubsanträge von Studenten für Auslandsaufenthalte. Bd. 3, 1935–35.

2507. Zurückgezogene Urlaubsanträge von Studenten für Auslandsaufenthalte. Bd. 2, 1934–35.

Weiss, no recipient, [ca. 1934].

Gauschulungsreferent, National Sozialistische Deutscher Studentenbund, Studentenbundführung des Gause München-Oberbayern, to Reichsführung der Deutschen Studentenschaft, Kreis Ausland, August 16, 1935.

Kreis Ausland to Wecker, September 23, 1935.

2625. Au-Pair-Stellen in Frankreich und Deutsch-Französischer Studentenaustausch; Anfragen zu Aufenthalten ausländischer Studenten in Deutschland und zu Aufenthalten deutscher Studenten im Ausland, Buchstaben G–R. 1933–34.

Wehner to Gräfe, November 10, 1933.

2627. Austausch von Studenten vom und in das Ausland. Rundschreiben der Deutsche Studentenschaft, Außenamt, Grenzlandamt, Ostmarkenamt, Landdienst. 1934–36.

Sofortprogramm der Aussenämter, November 15, 1934.

2628. Dringlichkeitsbescheinigungen für Studenten zur Mitnahme von Reichsmark in das Ausland durch die Deutsche Kongresszentrale und Berichte von Studentenschaften zum Auslandsstudium. 1936.

Reichsstudentenführung/Nationalsozialistischer Deutscher Studentenbund to Auslandsämter. "Memorandum."

Schmidt to Deutsche Studentenschaft Aussenamtsleiter Würzburg, March 2, 1936.

2642. Urlaubsanträge von Studenten für Auslandsaufenthalte, 1934–37. Bd. 8.

Kosmehl. Aktennotiz: zum Urlaubsgesuch der stud. phil. Gerda Trojandt.

DSt Aussenamt to Tech, September 4, 1934.

DSt Aussenamt to Lehmann, September 14, 1934.

Lehmann to DSt Aussenamt Berlin, September 15, 1934.

2644. Urlaubsanträge von Studenschaften für Auslandsaufenthalte von Studenten sowie Berichte von Studentenschaften über die Studenten, die im Ausland studiert haben, 1934–36.

Studentenschaftsführer, Studentenschaft Universität Kiel, to Auslandsamt Deutsche Studentenschaft, September 6, 1936.

Kreisführer des Kreises Ausland, Auslandsamt Deutsche Studentenschaft, to Kieler Deutsch Studentenschaft, September 9, 1936.

2653. Bestandsaufnahmen der genehmigten und abgelehnten Urlaubsanträge von Studenten für Auslandsaufenthalte, July 1935.

Referent, Kreis Ausland, to Deutsche Studentenschaft, Goethe Universität, July 3, 1935.

Bundesarchiv Lichterfelde (BArch Licht.) Bestand R (R) Norddeutscher Bund und Deutsches Reich (1867/1871–1945)

1064. [Apparently meeting of Presidium of DAAD], July 17, 1933.

2625. Organisation Aufenhalt ausländischer Studenten. R8034 II.

8034. II Reichslandbund.- Presseausschnittsammlung. Politik, Wirtschaft, Kultur (Inland). Außenpolitik, Politik, Wirtschaft und Kultur des Auslands

8088. Reichsverband der deutschen Hochschulen. 7 Auslandbeziehungen, 7.1 Wissenschaftliche Beziehungen mit internationalen und ausländischen Institutionen. Bd. 2, 1933–34.

9362. Deutscher Akademischer Austauschdienst.

9368. Vereinigung Carl Schurz e.V. Bd. 3. Besuch und Betreuung amerikanischer Germanisten in Deutschland, 1938.

Politische Archiv des Auswärtiges Amts (PA AA)

R 9-I. Reichsstelle für den Außenhandel.

610. Weber, Dr. Paul Max. (Portugal, Mexiko, Japan).

Weber to Rüdt von Collenberg, June 24, 1941.

"Dahaste" [Deutsche Außenhandelsstelle], August 9, 1941.

Weber to Keller, August 14, 1941.

Reichstelle für Außenhandel, to Referat R VIII of AA, August 26, 1941.

Radiotelegram to Abwehr I WI, August 29, 1941.

Weber to Keller, September 1, 1941.

Weber to Direktion der Eildienst, September 14, 1941.

Bibliography 253

Klünner to Keller. [Anweisung bezüglich der Handhabung von Berichten über persönliche Angelegenheiten und Übertragungssicherheit] [Directive on the Handling of Reports Concerning Personal Matters and Transmission Security]. Internal telegram with reference to Weber's Telegram of August 14, 1941, September 19, 1941.

Ruedt to "Dahaste" [Deutsche Außenhandelsstelle], September 24, 1941.

Berger to Reichstelle für Außenhandel, November 18, 1941.

Ott to Wiehl, September 29, 1942.

Wiehl to Keller, September 29, 1942.

Eildienst Memorandum, October 5, 1942.

Ref Per H Aüswartiges Amt, to Reichstelle für Außenhandel, November 1942.

R 101.855. Pol. I M 28. Nordamerika.

Thomsen to von Weizsäcker, May 21, 1940.

Thomsen to von Weizsäcker, May 22, 1940.

Abwehr Division II, "Nr. 626/40 g.Kdos," June 1, 1940.

Thomsen to von Weizsäcker, June 2, 1940.

Von dem Heyden-Rynsch to Canaris, June 4, 1940.

Von Weizsäcker to Thomsen, June 10, 1940

Canaris to V.A.A., June 11, 1940

Von Weizsäcker to von dem Heyden-Rynsch, June 17, 1940.

Thomsen to Aüswartiges Amt, July 7, 1941.

Thomsen to von Weizsäcker, July 17, 1941.

Gyssling to Dieckhoff, November 4, 1941.

RZ 507. Hochschulen. 27. Nordamerika.

64225. 27. Studentenaustausch, Allgemeines (DAAD). Hochschulwesen 19. Amerika.

Bd. 4, November 1933–October 1934.

Mitteilungen des Deutschen Akademischen Austauschdientes E.V. an die Akademischen Auslandsstellen den deutschen Hochschulen. n. 15, "Für den engeren Geschäftssbereich der Akademischen Auslandsstellen," early February 1934.

"Für den engeren Geschäftssbereich der Akademischen Auslandsstellen," Nr. 15, 390, AA VIW 1260, early February 1934.

Metzger to [recipient not indicated], February 23, 1934.

Deutsche Studentenschaft to Oster, "Niederschrift über die vertrauliche Besprechung," June 18, 1934.

Von Massow to Oster, "Arbeitstagung der Akademischen Auslandsstellen, eine Tagung der Leiter der Zweigstellen des Austauschdienstes im Ausland," October 10, 1934.

64226. 27. Studentenaustausch, Allgemeines (DAAD). Hochschulwesen 19.

Amerika.

Bd. 5, November 1934-June 1935.

New York General Consulate to Auswärtiges Amt. "Auslanderstudien in Deutschland und Frankreich," January 28, 1935.

Aufstellung des Personals des DAAD, March 31, 1935.

Luther to Auswärtiges Amt, May 14, 1935.

64227. 27. Studentenaustausch, Allgemeines (DAAD). Hochschulwesen 19. Amerika.

Bd. 6, June 1935-December 1935.

Von Fritsch to Auswärtiges Amt, July 6, 1935.

Geschäftsberichte der Alexander von Humboldt-Stiftung. "Bericht über die Tagung der deutschen Austauschstudenten im Turnerschafthaus in Bad Blankenburg vom 31. August–3. September," September 20, 1935.

"Betätigung deutscher Studenten im Ausland," October 28, 1935.

Borchers to Auswärtiges Amt, November 27, 1935.

64228. 27. Studentenaustausch, Allgemeines (DAAD). Hochschulwesen 19. Amerika.

Bd. 7, December 1935–July 1936.

Luther to Auswätiges Amt. December 5, 1935 (with excerpts from Kurt von Tippelskirch to Hans Luther, October 15 and 23, November 12 and 13, 1935).

Von Twardowski to Hess, December 24, 1935.

Burmeister to Auswärtiges Amt, February 5, 1936, enclosure, 10–11.

Kunisch to Auswärtiges Amt, April 15, 1936.

San Francisco Consulate to Luther, May 9, 1936.

Von Tippelskirch to Chroust, May 25, 1936.

Von Tippelskirch to Luther, June 3, 1936.

Sallet to Goebbels, "Deutsch-Amerikanischen Studentenaustausch," June 4, 1936.

Luther to Auswärtiges Amt, June 10, 1936.

64229. 27. Studentenaustausch, Allgemeines (DAAD). Hochschulwesen 19. Amerika.

Bd. 8 August 1936-December 1936.

Burmeister to Auswartiges Amt, August 20, 1936.

64251. 27. Studentenaustausch, Allgemeines (DAAD). Hochschulwesen 19. Amerika. Bd. 33, 1935–37.

RZ 514 Propaganda: kulturpropaganda (Kult gen), 1925–40.

61303. Kult Prop 1. Amerika 1. Deutsche Kulturpropaganda in Nordamerika. Carl Schurz Memorial Foundation und Vereinigung Carl Schurz. Bd. 1, December 1937–December 1938.

Jordan to Rosenberg, April 4, 1933. "Memorandum: Über Deutsche Kulturpropaganda in Nordamerika."

61304. Kult Prop 1. Amerika 1. Deutsche Kulturpropaganda in Nordamerika. Carl Schurz Memorial Foundation und Vereinigung Carl Schurz. Bd. 2, December 1938–January 1942.

80313. Abt. III. Politik 26. Politische und kulturelle Propaganda in den Vereinigten q. Bd. 21, August 1, 1934–August 31, 1934.

"Bericht des Universitätsprofessors Dr. Friedrich Schönemann (Berlin) über seine amerikanische Vortragsreise."

Bertling to Dieckhoff, March 19, 1934.

Richter to Führ, July 14, 1934.

80328. Abt. III. Politik 26. Politische und Kulturelle Propaganda in den USA. "Vereinigung Carl Schurz." Bd. 2, October 1932–December 1934.

Washington RAV 171

18/64. Richard Sallet File.

Sallet to Auswärtiges Amt, September 19, 1935.

Sallet to Goebbels, June 4, 1936.

University of Berlin Archives (UBA)

Z.DI:977 Ka.031 Inhalt 14 Sonthoff.

Lebenslauf, ca. December 1937.

Leiter der Personalstelle, N.S. Dozantenbund der Universitat Berlin to Riedior, Betrifft: Ihre Anfrage über den assistentenbewerber Sonthoff, January 6, 1938.

Betr. Herbert Sonthoff, Berlin, January 11, 1938.

Unknown to University Rector, January 11, 1938.

Harms, to Prorektor, Universitat Berlin, March 10, 1938.

University of Heidelberg Archives (UHA)

B-0689/1 RA. *Rektor, Senat und allg. Verwaltung.* 1918–69, 1918–34.

"Antrage der Auslandsabteilung der Universität Heidelberg and Erhöhung der ihr Badischen Ministerium des Kultus und Unterrichts gewährten Mittel."

Generalia: Verkehr mit dem Ausland, 1934–37. Amtsblatt des Reich und "Vorträge deutscher Dozenten im Ausland, Auslandsreisen von Dozenten und Studenten, Beteiligung von Dozenten an wiss. Institutionen, Mitgliedschaft bei wiss. Vereinen des Auslands, 1934–1937."

Prüssischen Ministerium für Wissenschaft, Erziehung und Volksbildung zu allen Bildungseinrichtungen, December 24, 1936.

Rep 05/1. Akademische Auslandsabteilung der Universität [Heidelberg] to the Pressestelle des Badenischen Staatsministeriums, March 27, 1934.

University of Jena Archives (UJA)

U. Abt. II. Akademische Auslandsstelle der Universität Jena.

Nr. 2, Bd. II: DAAD Rundschreiben 1933–37.

DAAD Rundschreiben 109, November 7, 1935.

Bl. 301r. "Auslese der Austauschstudenten für das nächste Jahr."
DAAD to Akademische Auslandsstelle, November 4, 1935.
Nr. 11. Akademische Auslandsstelle, a.z. 1004, 1928–43.
"Niederschrift über die 4. Arbeitstagung der Akademischen Auslandstellen am 22. und 23. Oktober 1934 im Humboldt-Haus, Berlin."
DAAD to Akas, April 9, 1935, fol. 181.
Bl. 262–6. "Amerika-Deutschland. Die nationalsozialistische Idee im Spiegel der Vereinigten Staaten von Nord-Amerika," ca. late 1933, 4.
Nr. 18. Akademische Auslandsstelle: Studium deutsche Studenten im Ausland betr. 1928–38.
"Amerika-Deutschland." [n.d.]
Application Form for Exchange, fol. 114.
"Gutachten über das Austauschgesuch v. Gerlach, Maz-Ludwif, agr. Nach USA," January 28, 1938.
Nr. 19. Akademische Auslandsstelle, 1935–44. DAAD.
Richtlinien für die Arbeit der Akademischen Auslandstellen, ca. March 8, 1935.
DAAD to Akademische Auslandsstelle, Rundschreiben nr.108, "Auslese der Austauschstudenten für das nächste Jahr," November 4, 1935.
Rundschreiben nr. 35, to Akademische Auslandsstelle, November 2, 1938.

University of Marburg Archives (UMA)

305a/8617. Abschrift zu WU 971/39. Adams to Education Ministry, November 22, 1938.
305a/8617. Georg Fohrer, Austausch Bewerbung, 1937.

University of Munich Archives Zsg-II. Arbeitsbücher (1933–45)

14. Deutsche Akademische Auslandstelle München, 1927–45. Sen. 0030/11a.
Bd. 01. "Protokoll Über die Vorstandssitzung der Deutschen Akademischen Auslandsstelle München e. V," July 3, 1936.
Bd. 03. "Die Entwicklung der Deutschen Akademischen Auslandsstelle München von 1934–1938," November 4, 1938.

Archival Sources in the United States

California State University, Northridge. Special Collections and Archives (CSUNA)

URB. Jewish Federation Council of Greater Los Angeles, Community Relations Committee Collection (CRC).
Part 1 (1921–37). [CRC-1].

Bibliography 257

Subseries C: Informant Files, 1932–37.
    Ness Reports, April 1936. Box 6, folder 24.
    Ness Report to Lewis, April 10, 1936.
    Ness Reports, August 1936. Box 7, folder 6.
Subseries E: Jewish Groups and Individuals, 1931–37.
    Anti-Defamation League/B'nai B'rith. National: Correspondence, December 1933. Box 22, folder 17.
    Lewis to Livingston, December 4, 1933. Box 22, folder 17.
Part 2 (1920–50) [CRC-2].
    Subseries I: News Research Service, Inc. (NRS), 1933–circa 1949.
    Klein, Julius. 1939, 1940. Box 199, folder 44.
    Roos to Klein, January 24, 1940.
    Roos to Klein, February 5, 1940.
    Roos to Klein, "Subject: Recent Meeting of All German Consuls Held at the German Embassy–January 11, 12, 13, 1940," February 19, 1940.
    Marshall to Klein, February 29, 1940.
    Klein to Roos, March 2, 1940.
    Roos to Klein, March 2, 1940.
    Roos to Klein, March 7, 1940.

Court of Common Pleas of Delaware Co., PA. March 1949 Session. Hearing no. 1324

Naturalization of Herbert Gunther Sonthoff, May 10, 1949.

Federal Bureau of Investigation (FBI). Records Management Division (RMD). Record/Information Dissemination Section (RIDS). Central Records System (CRS)

Class 61. Treason
    7578. Axis Exchange Students/German Exchange Students—Internal Security (G).
    Bureau of Internal Revenue, "Student Exchange Between Germany and the United States, July 1, 1944." [BIR Report].
    Albert H Geberich File.
    Donahoe Report, January 7, 1941.
    Hans-Joachim Grauert File.
    Crane Report, June 5, 1943.
    Jenni Karding [Mrs. William Moulton] File.
    Snyder Report, May 19, 1944.
    Horst W. Janson File.
    Kennedy Report, April 7, 1943.
    Hines Report, Report, June 30, 1943.
    Kelley Report, July 9, 1943.
    Pieper Report, January 12, 1944.

258 Bibliography

Tull Report, January 24, 1944.
Pieper Report, February 26, 1944.
Pieper Report, March 29, 1944.
O'Connor Report, June 1, 1944.
Fritz Karl Heinrich Lilge File.
Roettling Report, September 24, 1942.
Brusch Report, June 27, 1944.
Ursula Schäfer [Lamb] File.
Crane Report, May 6, 1944.
Davidson Report, September 7, 1944.
Ellerin Report, November 6, 1944.
Ulrich Ernst Volkmar Solmssen and Kathe Dorthea Solmssen File.
Seemann Report, December 13, 1944.
Herbert Sonthoff File.
Manning Report, February 4, 1943. Sonthoff to Norbert Berger,
July 21, 1941, and August 6, 1941.
Sears to Hoover, December 17, 1942.
Manning Report, February 4, 1943.
Manning Report, April 30, 1943. Julien Bryan to Sonthoff, March
4, 1938.
Manning Report, April 30, 1943. Sonthoff to Bryan, February 2,
1938.
Manning Report, May 29, 1943.
Manning Report, June 18, 1943.
Lynch Report, March 28, 1944.
Thompson Report, June 24, 1945.
Anneliese von dem Hagen [Backhus] File.
Conroy Report, November 27, 1943.
7632. Frederick Ernst Auhagen, American Fellowship Forum—Registration
Act (G).
Memorandum for the File, August 28, 1940.
Conroy Report, February 11, 1941.
Brightman Report, April 27, 1941.
Cohle Report, June 16, 1941.
Memorandum for Clark, September 29, 1943.
Rogge Report, December 11, 1943.
Class 65. Espionage
1379. Anneliese von dem Hagen [Backhus] File.
Fallon Report, September 28, 1939.
Fallon Report, October 10, 1939.
Arterberry Report, November 20, 1939.
Paul to District Director, San Antonio, Texas. "Annalessia or Anne-
lise von dem Hagen Albrecht," March 14, 1940.
Paul Report, March 14, 1940.

Stevens to Special Agent in Charge, New York Office, April 1, 1940.
Cunningham Report, May 4, 1940.
Carlblom Report, June 7, 1940.
Calhoun Report, June 29, 1940.
Fuller Report, August 18, 1940.
Carlblom Report, November 20, 1940.
Calhoun Report, December 16, 1941.
Hoover to Wilkinson, April 22, 1942.
Miller Report, May 11, 1942.
Hoover to Special Agent in Charge, San Francisco, June 30, 1943.
Carlblom Report, October 1, 1943.
Special Agent in Charge, San Francisco, to Hoover, March 3, 1947
Special Agent in Charge, San Francisco, to Hoover, March 15, 1947.
Class 121. Loyalty of Government Employees
31988. Sonthoff File.
52.27450. Report of Loyalty of Applicants and Appointees Investiga-
tion. Attachment to letter, James E. Hatcher to J. Edgar Hoover,
July 24, 1951.
Report [Author's Name Redacted], September 22, 1951.
Manning Report, October 12, 1951.
Mulhern Report, November 10, 1951.
4409. Herbert Gunther Sonthoff. Educational Specialist-Applicant. Mili-
tary Intelligence Research-Applicant, U.S. Civil Service Commission,
Washington, DC, September 25, 1951.
Class 146. War Division. Special War Policies Unit
13. Series: Alien Enemy Litigation.
Chroust File.
Foley Report, January 16, 1942.
Whaley Report, August 21, 1944.
Cooley to Burling, November 2, 1945.
Kelly to Ennis, February 12, 1946.

Herbert Hoover Presidential Library

Manuscript Collections. Wayne S. Cole Papers.
Box 8, Individual Files.
Laura Ingalls.

Institute of International Education Archives (IIE)

I reviewed the unprocessed archive of the Institute of International Education in May
2012. At that time, I identified documents according to the roll, side, and index (RSI)
number on the microfilm. Since then, the collection has been transferred by accession
to the Rockefeller Archive Center, Institute of International Education, Record Group
1: Alumni and Historical Files, 1924–97. The Rockefeller Archive filing system is based

on the institute's Grant Locator cards, so the citations in this book should make it possible to find the cited sources in their new archival home.

Alumni Files (AF)

RSI 2.2.02. 1545. Richard Boyle O'Reilly Rocking File.
RSI 2.2.14. 1557. Lucille Palmer File.
RSI 2.2.20. 1564. Homer G. Richey File.
RSI 2.2.36. 3573. Gustav Heinrich Blanke File.
RSI 4.2.25. 1412. Angelika Sievers File.
RSI 5.2.55. 1746. Hans Gatzke File.
RSI 5.2.56. 1747. Jenna Hanser File.
RSI 6.1.01. 1753. Günter Kirsch File.
RSI 6.1.02. 1754. Hans Werner Kubitz File.
RSI 6.1.03. 1755. Rudolf Kuhne File.
RSI 6.1.04. 1756. Marianna [sic] Lautsch File.
RSI 6.1.05. 1757. Ulrich Lebsanft File.
RSI 6.1.06. 1758. Fritz Lilge File.
RSI 6.1.08. 1761. Kurt Naumann File.
RSI 6.1.10. 1762. Ingeborg Oesterlin File.
RSI 6.1.15. 1767. Herbert Sonthoff
RSI 6.1.17. 1769. Georg [von] Lilienfeld File.
RSI 6.1.18. 1770. Gerold von Minden File.
RSI 6.1.20. 1772. Friederike Waltz File.
RSI 9.1.01. 2033. Irene Boner File.
RSI 9.1.02. 2034. Martin Burmeister File.
RSI 9.1.03. 2035. Ruth Ismene Diffenbacher File.
RSI 9.1.05. 2037. Irmgard Erhorn File.
RSI 9.1.06. 2038. Ernst Wilhelm Foerster File.
RSI 9.1.08. 2040. Max Haug File.
RSI 9.1.10. 2042. Elisabeth Hühnlein File.
RSI 9.1.13. 2045. Ursula Kaufmann File.
RSI 9.1.16. 2048. Eugen Lahr File.
RSI 9.1.18. 2050. Dora Margarete Pfeiffer File.
RSI 9.1.19. 2051. Hermann Reissinger File.
RSI 9.1.21. 2053. Werner Ruch File.
RSI 9.1.23. 2055. Ursula Schäfer File.
RSI 9.1.24. 2056. Otto Wilhelm Schat File.
RSI 9.1.33. 2065. Henning von Dobeneck File.
RSI 9.1.38. 2070. Kurt Weege File.
RSI 10.2.5. 1752. Hildebrand Kerkhof File.
RSI 11.2.45. 1936. Lisabeth Engelbrecht File.
RSI 12.1.01. 2373. Ilse Giesing File.
RSI 12.1.02. 2374. Erika Anna Gilde File.
RSI 12.1.03. 2375. Hans-Joachim Grauert File.

Bibliography 261

RSI 12.1.04. 2376. Hans Heinrich Harald Harms File.

RSI 12.1.06. 3478. Karl Heyers File.

RSI 12.1.07. 2379. Heinz-G. Hintze File.

RSI 12.1.08. 2380. Herbert Hörhager File.

RSI 12.1.09. 2381. Wolfgang Hupe File.

RSI 12.1.1. 2391. Irmgard Rein File.

RSI 12.1.11. 2388. Paul Hugo Jahn File.

RSI 12.1.20. 2392. Hans Roepke File.

RSI 12.1.21. 2393. Heinz Rudolph File.

RSI 12.1.22. 2394. Erika Sarnow File.

RSI 12.1.23. 2395. Robert Scholl File.

RSI 12.1.25. 2397. Erika Simon File.

RSI 12.1.27. 0204. Walter Steines File.

RSI 12.1.28. 2400. Heinrich Thiele File.

RSI 12.1.30. 2402. Wolf Weber File.

RSI 12.1.31. 0229. Peter Wecker File.

RSI 12.1.34. 2406. Erwin Wickert File.

RSI 12.1.35. 2407. Maria Wiemers File.

RSI 12.1.36. 2408. Karl Wolf File.

RSI 12.1.37. 2409. Ilse Maria Wössner File.

RSI 12.1.37. 2410. Dietrich Zwicker File.

RSI 14.2.21. 2688. Ursula Dibbern File.

RSI 14.2.38. 2675. Hans-Georg Baare-Schmidt File.

RSI 14.2.39. 2676. Erika Beseler File.

RSI 14.2.42. 2679. Guenther Bischoff File.

RSI 14.2.44. 2681. Ilse Borchers File.

RSI 14.2.45. 2682. Fritz Brandi File.

RSI 14.2.47. 2684. Hugo Brinkman File.

RSI 14.2.49. 2686. Annemarie Closterhalfen File.

RSI 14.2.53. 2690. Gertraut Helene Elisabeth Fiek File.

RSI 14.2.54. 2691. Paula Fischer File.

RSI 14.2.55. 2692. Adolf Henning Frucht File.

RSI 14.2.57. 2694. Elfriede Geulen File.

RSI 15.1.00. 2695. Godber Godberson File.

RSI 15.1.06. 2701. Marie Luise Habermann File.

RSI 15.1.1. 2706. Friedrich-Theodor Hütter File.

RSI 15.1.2. 2707. Albert Ickler File.

RSI 15.1.7. 2702. Gudrun Hartmann File.

RSI 15.1.7. 2712. Lothar Lenkeit File.

RSI 15.1.9. 2704. Claus Eberhard Holthusen File.

RSI 15.1.10. 2705. Rolf H. Hoppe File.

RSI 15.1.14. 2709. Marie-Luise Köster File.

RSI 15.1.15. 2710. Hermann Lacher File.

RSI 15.1.17. 2732. Hella von Schwerin File.

262 Bibliography

RSI 15.1.18. 2713. Inge Lindenmeyer File.
RSI 15.1.23. 2718. Guenther Mueller File.
RSI 15.1.30. 2725. Gudrun Schaal File.
RSI 15.1.31. 2726. Wolfgang Schaper File.
RSI 15.1.32. 2727. Eva Schröder File.
RSI 15.1.35. 2730. Annemarie Sieger File.
RSI 15.1.36. 2731. Adolf Ungemach File.
RSI 15.1.39. 2734. Ilse Wiegand File.
RSI 18.1.35. 3034. Gertrude Achenbach File.
RSI 18.1.37. 3036. Helga Boursé File.
RSI 18.1.41. 3039. Hildegard Buch File.
RSI 18.1.43. 3041. Werner Boehr File.
RSI 18.1.46. 3044. Anna-Maria Endlich File.
RSI 18.1.48. 3046. Gisela Hensel File.
RSI 18.1.49. 3047. Gerhard Hess File.
RSI 18.1.50. 3048. Ingeborg Jung File.
RSI 18.1.51. 3049. Elisabeth Matilde Kaessbohrer File.
RSI 18.2.53. 3051. Bodo Kienzler File.
RSI 18.2.54. 3052. Hannalene Kipper File.
RSI 18.2.55. 3053. Luzie Kossack File.
RSI 18.2.64. 3062. Eduard Pestel File.
RSI 18.2.65. 3063. Frank Pohlenz File.
RSI 18.2.67. 2934. Helga Prym-von Bercherer File.
RSI 18.2.70. 2749. Margildis Schlueter File.
RSI 18.2.71. 3069. Otto Schmauss File.
RSI 18.2.75. 2073. Eva Strasmann File.
RSI 18.2.76. 2418. Günter Trittelvitz File.
RSI 18.2.78. 2076. Anneliese von dem Hagen File.
RSI 18.2.A03. 3081. Anna-Barbara Wojnowska File.
RSI 21.1.23. 3380. Gerhard Goy File.

Historical Files (HF)

RSI 6.1.1. 278. Education—Germany Foreign Students, 1927–41.
RSI 6.2.1. American-German Student Exchange Committee on Selection, 1931–35.
RSI 6.2.5. 298. 9–7. Fellowships for German Students in US, 1939–40.
RSI 6.2.5. 299. 9–8. Fellowships for German Students in the US, 1937–38.
RSI 6.2.18. 313. Comments on German Students Letters from Colleges and Universities, 1931–36.
RSI 6.2.19. 314. Comments on German Students. Letters from Colleges and Universities, 1936–37.
RSI 6.2.20. 315. Comments on German Students. Letters from Colleges and Universities, 1938–39.
RSI 6.2.25. 318. Criticism of American-German Student Exchange. IIE Answers and Suggestions, 1936–38.

Bibliography   263

RSI 6.2.6. 299. 9–8. Fellowships for German Students in US, 1937–38.

RSI 9.1.21. Germany: Rettig Files–on German Student "Spies," 1939–40.

RSI 10.2.5. 6136. Germany A–Z, 1935.

RSI 10.2.42. Germany Successful, 1930–31, 1934.

RSI [no RSI given. ca. 6.2.20. 313. HF. 9–22]. Comments on German Students. Letters from Colleges and Universities, 1936–39.

National Archives and Records Administration (NARA). Record Group (RG)

Berlin Document Center. Rasse-und-Siedlungs-Hauptamt (RuSHA).
    SS Officer Personnel Files. Microfilm Publication A3343. SSO 012A.
        8365. Ulrich Freiherr von Gienanth File.
Record Group 59 [RG 59]. General Records of the Department of State
    Records of the Department of State Special Interrogation Mission to Germany, 1945–46. M679. Roll 1.
    Ulrich von Gienanth File.
Record Group 60 [RG 60]. Department of Justice (DOJ). Central Records System (CRS).
    Class 100. Domestic Security.
        13895. Fritz Karl Heinrich Lilge File.
            Roettling Report, September 24, 1942.
    Class 146. War Division. Special War Policies Unit.
        13. Series: Alien Enemy Litigation.
            2-16-21. Irene Gotthelf File.
                [Summary of Reasons for Internment]. Re: Irene Alexandra Gotthelf. Summary by J.J.B., December 10, 1941.
                G. S. Studebaker Report, January 5, 1942.
                Reconsideration of Hearing. Chief of the Review Section, March 29, 1944. Gregory Affidavit, January 23, 1942.
                Mrs. Ronald Cordingley Affidavit, January 24, 1942.
                Alien Enemy Hearing Board, Washington, DC, January 30, 1942.
                Alien Enemy Hearing Board, April 10, 1942, including FBI report [Irene Gotthelf] April 10, 1942.
                Petition for Repatriation, Irene Alexandra Gotthelf, May 20, 1942.
                Irene Alexandra Gotthelf et al. to Francis Biddle, December 3, 1942.
                Irene Gotthelf to Adolph Schiavo, January 3, 1943.
                Alien Enemy Repatriation Hearing, December 20, 1943.
                Alien Enemy Unit, Repatriation Requestion Request, Irene Alexandra Gotthelf, January 25, 1944.
                Reconsideration of Hearing. Chief of the Review Section, March 29, 1944.
                Report of Alien Enemy Irene Alexandra Gotthelf, Philip For-

man, Chief, Detention and Deportation Section, January 8, 1945.

In the matter of Irene Alexandra Gotthelf, Alien Enemy, Francis Biddle, February 13, 1945.

2-36-4. Anton-Hermann Chroust File.

Deitchler Report, January 8, 1942.

Foley Report, January 16, 1942.

First Hearing, January 20, 1942.

Hearing Board's Recommendation. Dr. Anton Hermann Chroust, February 11, 1942.

Painter to Cooley, April 12, 1942.

Horst Janson [First] Affidavit, June 1, 1942.

Chroust to Alien Enemy Control Unit, Review Section [after September 16, 1942].

Memorandum to the Chief of the Review Section [RE: Anton-Hermann Chroust], September 25, 1942.

Elizabeth Chroust to Cooley, February 22, 1943.

Horst Janson Second [Affidavit], May 29, 1944.

Horst Janson Affidavit, June 15, 1944.

Reconsideration: Memorandum to Chief of the Review Section [RE: Anton-Hermann Chroust], July 15, 1944.

Alien Enemy Repatriation Hearing. Subject: Anton-Hermann Chroust, January 24, 1946.

2-49-424. Kurt Ludwig File.

2-51-385. Ina Gotthelf File.

Emrich Report, September 9, 1940.

Alien Enemy Rehearing, February 15, 1944.

Alien Enemy Rehearing, February 16, 1944.

"Report in the Case of Ina Gotthelf," February 23, 1944.

Reconsideration Memorandum to Chief of the Review Section. Ina Nina Marina Gotthelf, March 27, 1944.

Reconsideration. Special Board for Parole. March 27, 1944.

Record Group 65 [RG 65]. Federal Bureau of Investigation [FBI]. Central Records System [CRS] Class 65: Espionage.

2020. German Espionage in the United States [also find a copy in Class 65–2904] Report, November 21, 1939, in Foxworth to Hoover, April 6, 1940. [RG 65, box 170, folder 1. "German Activities in the United States"].

2904. German Espionage Activities [boxes 170–171]

557. Irene Alexandra Gotthelf File.

Hanson Report, December 24, 1941.

1351. Ulrich Von Gienanth File.

FBI Report, November 21, 1939

Jones Report, January 8, 1941.

Kelley Report, January 19, 1941.
Kelley Report, February 15, 1941.
Mott Report, February 21, 1941.
Hines Report, April 16, 1941.
Hooper Report, April 23, 1941.
Hooper Report, May 5, 1941.
Madden Report, May 11, 1941.
Carson to Foxworth, July 23, 1941.
Jones Report, November 5, 1941.
Jones Report, November 25, 1941.
Jones Report, November 29, 1941.
Jones Report, March 28, 1942.
Fletcher to Ladd, December 10, 1945.
1582. Anton Hermann Chroust File.
Deitchler Report, January 8, 1942.
3017. Franz Ulrich Pohlenz File.
Memorandum for Officer in Charge, Interview with Mrs. Ruth
Cochran, June 11, 1942.
Mrs. Pohlenz, Statement, June 12, 1942.
"Police Check," February 4, 1943.
Weingarten Report, February 18, 1943.
Nahrendorf Interview, April 17, 1943.
Memorandum for Hoover, June 21, 1944.
4373. Herbert Sonthoff File.
Goodman to Hoover, July 22, 1942.
Johnson Report, January 14, 1944.
Mott Report, March 6, 1944.
Huston Report, April 4, 1944.
Richardson Report, April 5, 1944.
Johnson Report, May 19, 1944.
Norton Report, May 20, 1944.
4414. Herbert W. Scholz File.
9428. Department of State, case no. F-2015-02354.
Geberich to Fletcher, ca. July 3, 1940.
9438. Berle to Hoover, July 30, 1940.
28452. Herbert Gunther Sonthoff File.
Danner to Special Agent in Charge, Boston, July 29, 1940.
Gelder Report, February 19, 1941.
Manning to Hoover, July 21, 1941.
Breed Report, August 25, 1941.
J.F. Sears to Hoover, February 17, 1942.
Lipe Report, June 23, 1942.
Ylitalo Report, June 29, 1942.
Smith Report, November 20, 1942.

J.F. Sears to Hoover, December 17, 1942.

Richardson Report, February 2, 1943.

Manning Report, February 4, 1943.

Manning Report, February 4, 1943. Sonthoff to Hermann Siemer, February 6, 1940.

Manning Report, February 4, 1943. Sonthoff to Hermann Siemer, July 31, 1940.

Norton Report, February 8, 1943.

Callister Report, February 10, 1943.

Smith Report, March 14, 1943.

Gilligan Report, March 30, 1943.

Mott Report, April 1, 1943.

Jones Report, April 3, 1943.

Skelly Report, April 6, 1943.

Smith Report, April 17, 1943.

Manning Report, April 30, 1943.

Mott Report, May 23, 1943.

Callister Report, May 24, 1943.

Manning Report, May 29, 1943.

O'Connor Report, June 10, 1943. Lochner Affidavit, May 29, 1943.

Manning Report, June 10, 1943.

White Report, June 15, 1943.

Manning Report, June 18, 1943.

Loebl Report, June 28–29, 1943.

Smith Report, May 29, 1943.

R. B. Hood to Hoover, June 29, 1943.

Loebl Report, July 7, 1943.

Richardson Report, July 8, 1943.

White Report, July 9, 1943.

Callister Report, December 2, 1943.

Special Agent in Charge [HWS] Report, December 11, 1943.

O'Connor Report, January 11, 1944.

Johnson Report, February 1, 1944.

Lynch Report, March 7, 1944.

Lynch Report, March 28, 1944.

Loyalty Investigation, July 24, 1951.

33035. Anton-Hermann Chroust File.

Foley Report, January 30, 1941.

53615. EBF 99. "RETTICH" and "Note on Austausch Dienst [sic] in U.K. by Source Dictionary."

55597. George [sic] Rettig File [box 36].

Longstreth Report, November 14, 1945.

Bibliography 267

55892-1. Cimperman to Hoover. "Rettig, Georg," June 12, 1945. Including "Circular Letter no. 1."

Record Group 226 [RG 226]. Records of the Office of Strategic Services
15016. "Report of the Attorney General of Mexico, Re: Persons Engaged in Espionage Activities," April 17, 1942.

Record Group 238 [RG 238]. World War II War Crimes Records.
Series: Interrogations, Summaries of Interrogations, and Related Records File Unit.
Bohle, Ernst Wilhelm.
Gienanth, Ulrich von.
Wiedemann, Fritz.

Record Group 242.4 [RG 242.2]. Microfilm Copies of Records of German Ministries, 1833–1945.
Records of the Foreign Office and the Reich Chancellery.
Politische und Kulturelle Propaganda.
Vereinigung Carl Schurz, 1933–36. Microfilm T-120. Rolls 4616, 5177–5179.

Record Group 260 [RG 260]. Records of U.S. Occupation Headquarters, World War II.
Records Relating to Claims for Personal Property ("Claims File"), 1946–51.
1947 boxes.
Grätz-Gyssling.
Julius Klein to Whom It May Concern, December 16, 1947.

Record Group 466 [RG 466]. Records of the Office of the U.S. High Commissioner for Germany.
3.4. Land Commissioner for Hesse.
Legal Affairs Division.
Reading Files of the Chief and Deputy Chief, July 1, 1946–June 25, 1952.
June 1949 File.
March 1949– July 1950.

Archival Sources Online

Archive.org

"Subject: Frederick Duquesne." Section 8, June 25, 1941, p. 839 [p. 238 of section 8]. FBI RG 65. 1819. Duquesne Spy Ring Files. "Duquesne Spy Ring," March 12, 1985. Accessed November 3, 2024. https://archive.org/details/Duquesne /Duquesne%2C%20Frederick%20Section%208/mode/2up?q=%22frederick +Duquesne%22+%22section+8%22

"The Sicherheitsdienst in Luxemburg, 1937–1940," March 1945. Office of Strategic Services X-2. 5825. Ref. RIG-73. German Section. Accessed February

268 Bibliography

10, 2020. https://archive.org/details/GERMANINTELLIGENCESERVICE
WWIIVOL3-0006/page/n3/mode/2up.

CIA. Freedom of Information Act Electronic Reading Room

"Dr. Haushofer." Records of the Mobile Field Interrogation Unit #1. No. 1/58, Reichs Sicherheits Hauptamt [sic], May 22, 1945. German Intelligence Service (WWII). vol. 1, no. 0007. [p. 9] Special Collection. Nazi War Crimes Disclosure Act. Doc. no.

(FOIA)/ESDN (CREST): 519cd819993294098d515d0e. Accessed November 4, 2024. https://www.cia.gov/readingroom/document/519cd819993294098d515d0e.

"German Intelligence Service (WWII)," July 1944, 7–8. Accessed October 16, 2024. https://www.cia.gov/readingroom/docs/GERMAN%20INTELLI GENCE%20SERVICE%20%28WWII%29,%20%20VOL.%201_0003.pdf.

L. Peis File. Donovan Correspondence, 1942–. OSS Collection. Document Number (FOIA)/ESDN (CREST): CIA-RDP13X00001R000100470004-9, July 29, 1943. Accessed November 3, 2024. https://www.cia.gov/readingroom /docs/CIA-RDP13X00001R000100470004-9.pdf.

"Source of Black Report no. 52, no. 14, November 28, 1944." Special Black Reports on Political Attitudes of Religious Leaders/German Catholic Resistance to Hitler. OSS Collection. Doc. no. (FOIA)/ESDN (CREST): CIA RD-P13X00001R000100040001-9, November 4, 1944. Accessed November 3, 2024. https://www.cia.gov/readingroom/docs/CIA-RDP13X00001R00010 0040001-9.pdf.

"Special Black Report no. 81, and appendix IV, March 6, 1945." Special Black Reports on Political Attitudes of Religious Leaders/German Catholic Resistance to Hitler. OSS Collection. Document Number (FOIA)/ESDN (CREST): CIA RDP13X00001R000100040001-9, November 4, 1944. Accessed November 3, 2024. https://www.cia.gov/readingroom/docs/CIA -RDP13X00001R000100040001-9.pdf.

W.R.E. "The German Intelligence Service and the War," December 1, 1945, 2–3. Accessed October 17, 2024. https://www.cia.gov/readingroom/docs/CIA -RDP78-03362A002500070002-3.pdf.

"Biographic Report: George von Lilienfeld, FRG, Ambassador-Designate to Iran." American Embassy, Bonn, to Department of State, July 26, 1968. Special Collection Nazi War Crimes Disclosure Act. Document Number (FOIA) /ESDN (CREST): 519b7f9c993294098d5137e5. Accessed November 3, 2024. https://www.cia.gov/readingroom/docs/LILIENFELD%2C%20GEORG %20VON_0019.

Department of State. Office of the Historian. Historical Documents.

Foreign Relations of the United States Diplomatic Papers, 1939: General, the British Commonwealth and Europe, Vol. 2 (1956).
"Closing by Germany of the New York Office of the German Student Ex-

change Agency at the Request of the American Government. The Advisor on Political Relations (Dunn) to the Acting Secretary of State (Welles)." January 9, 1939. Doc. 550. 800.01B11 Registration German University Service/12. Intelligence Service (WWII). Accessed November 3, 2024. https://history.state.gov/historicaldocuments/frus 1939v02/ch21subch6.

Federal Bureau of Investigation (FBI). FBI Records: The Vault

Harold Weisberg to Leo Sharrier. "Re: "Americans in Communication with German Intelligence Agencies," September 1945. RG 65. Class 100. Domestic Security. 9106-55. Harold Weisberg File. Accessed June 15, 2023. https://vault.fbi.gov/harold-weisberg/harold-weisberg-part-01-of-01/view.

North Dakota State University Libraries, Institute for Regional Studies & University Archives

Mss 224. Rainer Schickele Papers, 2009. Finding Aid. Accessed August 29, 2018. https://library.ndsu.edu/ir/bitstream/handle/10365/322/Mss0224.pdf?sequence=6&isAll wed=y.

Princeton University Archives

MC019. Allen W. Dulles Papers.
Box 38, folder 15. Biography of Georg von Lilienfeld. Accessed August 29, 2019, https://findingaids.princeton.edu/collections/MC019/c00641.

ProQuest History Vault Module: US Military Intelligence Reports, 1911–44

Joseph Roos. "Digest of Report on Meeting of all German Consuls held at the German Embassy—Jan. 11, 12, 13, 1940," 654. In "Behind the Nazi Activities in the United States, First Reports—1933–1934: A Synopsis of the 1933–1934 Investigation and Other Events (1939–1940), compiled by Julius Klein, Lt. Colonel, AMC 33rd Division."

United States Holocaust Memorial Museum

RG-60.1942. Film ID no. 4261. *Carl Schurz Tour of American Professors and Students through Germany in Summer 1934.*

University of Arizona Archives

MS 636. Willis E. Lamb, Jr. Papers, 1937–2007. Series VI: Ursula Schaefer Lamb, 1937–96. Finding Aid. Accessed August 29, 2018. http://www.azarchivesonline.org/xtf/view?docId=ead/uoa/UAMS636.xml#series6.

University of Notre Dame Archives

Anton-Herman Chroust Papers, 1924–81. Finding Aid. Accessed March 3, 2018. http://archives.nd.edu/findaids/ead/xml/chr.xml.

Yale University Library. Manuscripts and Archives (YUL)

The Inquiry Papers (MS 8). Series I. Box 1, folder 18. Duggan, Stephen. Accessed April 7, 2024. https://archives.yale.edu/repositories/12/archival_objects /1377302.

Published Primary Sources

Administrative Program Established at Stevens." *Fitchburg Sentinel* (Massachusetts), May 7, 1963.

"Alma Ex-Nazi Disappears, Leaves Note." *Lansing State Journal*, January 31, 1945.

"Americans' 'Host' Put in Nazi Prison." *New York Times*, July 13, 1934.

"And Now—." *Brown and White* (Bethlehem, PA), September 28, 1937.

"Austauschstudenten und -lehrer in Neustrelitz." *Hochschule und Ausland* 15, no. 3 (October 1937): 777.

Baare-Schmidt, Hans-Georg. "Alaska—Land der Zukunft: Die Strategische Bedeutung." *Zeitschrift für Geopolitik* 15, no. 2 (September 1938): 723–29.

Bezold, Oskar H. "Herrgott,—Amerika!" *Rundbrief deutscher Austauschstudenten in den U.S.A.*, November 3, 1938. In "Abschied." *Heimatrundbrief deutscher Austauschstudenten in den U.S.A.* (1940): 37.

"Big Apple and Hot Dogs Impress German Student." *Bates Student*, October 5, 1938.

Bielenberg, Christabel. *Past Is Myself & the Road Ahead: An Englishwoman in Nazi Germany.* Omnibus ed. London: Transworld Publishers, 2011.

Blanke, Gustav H. *Vom Nazismus zur Demokratisierung Deutschlands: Erinnerungen und Erfahrungen, 1933–bis 1955.* Hamburg: Verlag Dr. Kovač, 1999.

Boardman, Francis. "Trustees Scrap German Exchange Student Policy after 9 Year Existence." *Williams College Record*, May 2, 1936.

"Boas, Disclosing Secret Nazi Document, Asks Probe of German Students in U.S. In Letter to House Immigration Head." *Columbia Daily Spectator* (New York), October 27, 1933.

Brandi, Fritz. "Dear Hornet!" *Furman Hornet* (Greenville, SC), April 22, 1938.

Brecher, Gerhard. *Brecher's Odyssey: Reminiscences of a Doctor: World War II.* Yukon, OK: Pueblo Publishing Press, 1987.

Briffault, Robert. *Europa: The Days of Ignorance.* New York: Charles Scribner's Sons, 1935.

Burmeister, Wilhelm. "Der Deutsche Geist in der Welt der Gegenwart." *Geist der Zeit* 1, no. 15 (January 1937): 1–12.

"Burgomaster of Reinsdorf Tells How Explosion Spread Disaster." *New York Times*, June 14, 1935.

"Carleton Girl from Germany Remembers Customs Back Home." *Carletonian* (Northfield, MN), February 17, 1937.

Carlson, John Roy. *Under Cover: My Four Years in the Nazi Underworld of America—the Amazing Revelation of How Axis Agents and Our Enemies Within Are Now Plotting to Destroy the United States.* New York: E. P. Button & Co., 1943.

Chall, Malca. *Statewide and Regional Land-Use Planning in California, 1950–1980.* Vol. 2, *Berkeley's Academic Community Surveys State and Bay Area: Regional Planning Proposals and Programs, 1940–1982.* Interviews with T. J. Kent, Jr., Victor Jones, and Stanley Scott. Regional Oral History Office, Bancroft Library, University of California, Berkeley, 1981–82.

"Chapter and Alumni News." *Key* 54, no. 1 (1937): 53.

"Christiansen, German Student Writes of American Auto Trip." *Rensselaer Polytechnic*, October 14, 1937.

"Conference of Youth in Pasadena." *Santa Ana Register*, August 17, 1932.

Bibliography

Conze, Eckart, Norbert Frei, Peter Hayes, and Moshe Zimmermann. *Das Amt und die Vergangenheit: Deutsche Diplomaten im Dritten Reich und in der Bundesrepublik*. Munich: Karl Blessing Verlag, 2010.

Cornellian (yearbook). Ithaca, NY: Cornell University, 1937–39.

Correspondence from Michigan. "News of the Christian World." *Christian Century*, 61, no. 6 (June 9, 1944): 886.

Crow, Barbara. "Miss Helga Prym, German Exchange Student, Tells of Life in Germany in Talk with CAMPUS Reporter." *Middlebury Campus*, October 12, 1938.

Dennery, Étienne. "A French Economist's Visit to Western Colleges." *Institute of International Education Extramural Lectures*. Report no. 1. New York: Institute of International Education, 1936.

Deutsche Wissenschaft, Erziehung und Volksbildung 8 (1937): 184.

"Dictators 'Taken Apart' by Students; Il Duce Leads Hitler, Stalin in Vote." *Indianapolis Star*, March 20, 1938.

Dodd, Jr., William E., and Martha Dodd, eds. *Ambassador Dodd's Diary, 1933–1938*. London: Victor Gollangz, 1945.

Donovan, William, and Edgar Mowrer. "Nazi Germany Declared World-Wide Conspiracy to Rule Whole Universe." *Decatur (IL) Daily*, August 22, 1940.

Dornbach, Eike. "Amerika. Individualismus und Individualitaet." *Rundbrief deutscher Austauschstudenten in den U.S.A.* 5, no. 4 (February 1936): 5–7.

———. "Da kann kein Blizzard." *Rundbrief deutscher Austauschstudenten in den U.S.A.* 5, no. 4 (February 1936): 18.

Dowd, Agnes. "Super Patriotism in Education." *News Bulletin of the Institute of International Education* 11 (December 1935): 8–9.

Ducas, Dorothy. "German Girl Admires American Parents." *Tyrone (PA) Daily Herald*, March 31, 1934.

Duggan, Stephen. "The American-German Student Exchange." *American-German Review* (December 1938): 46–74.

Duggan, Stephen. *A Professor at Large*. New York: The McMillan Company, 1943.

Dunst, Ilse. "Letter to the Editor." *Bernard Bulletin* (New York, New York) February 19, 1937.

"Edeltraut Proske Likes Friendly Spirit and Companionship Found at Mt. Holyoke." *Mount Holyoke News*, February 17, 1934.

"Editor Would Bar German Students." *New York Times*, December 19, 1938.

Elliot, Cornelia. "Ilse Dunst, German Exchange Student, Finds Roosevelt's Ideas in Harmony with Hitler's." *Barnard Bulletin*, January 15, 1937.

Englert, Ludwig. "Ansprache zum Abschied der deutschen Austauschstudenten." *Geist der Zeit* 15, no. 3 (October 1937): 773–74.

"Ernst Mahr Describes Trip to Florida with Other German Exchange Students." *Susquehanna* (Selinsgrove, PA), March 3, 1936.

"An Exchange Student." *Lawrence (KS) Journal-World*, March 12, 1946.

"Exchange Student Describes Impressions of America after Vacation Travels South." *Mount Holyoke News*, February 14, 1936.

"Exchange Student Gives German View of America." *Hill News* (Canton, NY), November 4, 1933.

"Exchange Student Is Pleased with Campus Life at Stevens." *Stute* (Hoboken, NJ), October 20, 1937.

"Federal Agents Detain Theodore von Laue '39." *Daily Princetonian*, July 23, 1942.

Fischer, Bernie. "An Open Letter to Fritz Brandi." *Furman Hornet* (Greenville, SC), April 29, 1938.

Foerster, Ernst-Wilhelm. "Youth in Danger." *Sketch* (Williamstown, MA), May 1936.

Bibliography

"Foreign Exchange: Herbert Hoerhager." *Microcosm Yearbook*. Dickinson College, Carlisle, PA, 1936–37, 161. Accessed October 12, 2024. https://archives.dickinson.edu/microcosm/microcosm-yearbook-1936-37.

"Foreign Student Receives Degree." *Stute* (Hoboken, NJ), March 10, 1937.

"Former K.U. Student Signs Contract for Picture 'Hotel Berlin.'" *Lawrence (KS) Journal-World*, December 19, 1944.

"Freiheit im Mittelwestern." In "Rundbrief der deutschen Austauschstudenten in Amerika." *Hochschule und Ausland* 11, no. 9 (September 1933): 58.

Freiling, Paul. "Germany: Post-War and Present." *Bethanian* (Bethany, WV) November 1939.

"Fraulein Schepp Excuses Army." *Oberlin Review*, October 11, 1935.

Fromm, Bella. *Blood and Banquets: A Berlin Diary, 1930–38*. New York: Simon & Schuster, 1943.

Furgason, Waldo H. "Student Life in Germany." *Institute of International Education News Bulletin* 11 (April 1936): 7–8.

———. "Student Life in Germany." *Institute of International Education News Bulletin* 11 (May 1936): 5–6.

"Gemeinschaftslager des Deutschen Akademischen Austauschdienstes in Cöpenick (2.–5. September 1933)." *Hochschule und Ausland* 11, no. 10 (October 1933): 28–30.

"Georgia Student Ardent Hitlerite." *Atlanta Constitution*, October 1, 1933.

"German Enrollment in American Institutions of Higher Learning." *German Quarterly* 7, no. 4 (November 1934): 129–30.

"German Exchange Student Impressed by Friendliness and Open Mindedness in U.S." *Union-Bulletin* (Walla Walla, WA), January 14, 1950, 6.

"German Girl Coming to University to Continue Studies in Chemistry." *Daily Nebraskan* [Lincoln], July 26, 1934.

"German Gives Views on D-Son." *Dickinsonian* (Carlisle, PA), February 28, 1935.

"German People Don't Want War; Says S.C.W. Student; Sustenance Is Big Problem." *Denton (TX) Record-Chronicle*, October 5, 1938.

"German Student Exchange Seen Plan to Spread Naziism [*sic*] in America." *Arizona Republic* (Phoenix, AZ), November 8, 1937.

"German Student Explains Aims of Youth Movement." *Daily Courant* (Hartford, CT), October 28, 1936.

Godberson, Godber. "To the Editorial Director." Correspondence. *Cornell Daily Sun*, February 18, 1938.

Goepel, Kurt. "150 Austauschstudenten nehmen Abschied." *Hochschule und Ausland* 10, no. 9 (October 1931): 1–8.

"Goes to Trial in Espionage Case." *Denton (TX) Record-Chronicle*, December 7, 1938.

Goodrich, Roger B. "Two Times—Nazi Economics." *Colgate Maroon*, February 4, 1938.

G[räfe], G[erhard]. "Lager der Austauschstudenten und Austauschlehrer." *Internationale Zeitschrift für Erziehung* 6, no. 6 (1937): 432.

Hall, Martin. "German Exile Reviews 'Nazi Propaganda Methods' in U.S." *Commonwealth* (McFarland, CA), April 2, 1940.

Häring, Heiner. "Julian." *Heimatrundbrief deutscher Austauschstudenten in den U.S.A.* (1940): 34–37.

"[Hermann] Nickel Is First German Exchange Student since War." *Kingston (NY) Daily Freeman*, September 23, 1947.

"Herr Von Simson Argues Defense of German Policy." *Gong* 6, no. 4 (February 1934): 1.

Hershfield, Ruth. "Ilse Wiegand Gives Her Views on Life in Germany Today." *Barnard Bulletin*, December 10, 1937.

Bibliography 273

"Hess Nephew Was Student at Wesleyan: Gerhard Attended as Exchange in 1938–1939; Recalled." *Hartford Courant*, May 17, 1941.

Hitler, Adolf. *Mein Kampf*. 1925. Translated by Ralph Manheim. Boston: Houghton Mifflin Harcourt, [1943], 1971.

"Hitler a Man of Peace, Student Here Believes." *Ames (IA) Daily Tribune*, April 4, 1934.

Hörhager, Herbert. "Schlagt Dickinson!" *Heimatrundbrief deutscher Austauschstudenten in den U.S.A.* (1940): 26.

The House on 92nd Street. Directed by Henry Hathaway. 20th Century Fox, 1945. 1 hr. 28 min. Released September 10, 1945. Turner Classic Movies, December 1, 2010. Accessed March 18, 2023. https://www.tcm.com/tcmdb/title/78582/the-house-on-92nd-street/#articles -reviews?articleId=359254.

Huck, Peggy. "To the Editors of the Miscellany News." *Vassar Miscellany News*, June 9, 1937.

Huehnlein, Elisabeth. "Floridafahrt." *Rundbrief deutscher Austauschstudenten in den U.S.A.* 5, no. 1 (November 1935): 8–9.

Hurrey, Charles D. "Foreign Students in the United States." *International Law and Relations* 11, no. 9 (March 1937).

"In This Corner with Gregory." *Furman Hornet* (Greenville, SC), November 19, 1937.

Institute of International Education. *News Bulletin of the Institute of International Education*, no. 11 (1930).

———. *News Bulletin of the Institute of International Education*, no. 14 (1936).

———. *Seventeenth Annual Report of the Director*. New York, October 15, 1936.

Investigation of Un-American Propaganda Activities in the United States: Hearings, November 19–December 14, 1938, at Washington, D.C. Washington, DC: Government Printing Office, 1938.

Jacobson, Nicholas Biel. "An Open Letter to the Baron von Dobeneck." *Massachusetts Daily Collegian (Amherst)*, March 19, 1936.

James, William. "Is Life Worth Living?" *International Journal of Ethics* 6, no. 1 (October 1895): 1–26.

Jancik, Vladimir. "Mr. Jancik Adds." *Massachusetts Daily Collegian (Amherst)*, April 9, 1936.

Jetter, Ulrich. "Gedanken Über Ein Land der Technik." *Heimatrundbrief deutscher Austauschstudenten in den U.S.A.* (1940): 8–10.

———. *Physikalische Blatter* 6 (October 1950): 199. In J. Rand McNally, Jr. "Nuclear Fusion Chain Reaction Applications in Physics and Astrophysics." IAEA/SM-170/49. United States Atomic Energy Commission, ca. 1972.

———. "Die Zeitgenossen der Wasserstoffbombe." *Physikalische Blätter* 10, no. 12 (December 1954): 596–600.

Johnson, Alvin. "International Aspects of the University in Exile." *News Bulletin of the Institute of International Education* 9, (November 1933): 12–13.

Johnson, Erskine. "Ex-Storm Trooper, Who Played Nazi Film Roles, Becomes an American G.I." *Miami Daily News-Record*, June 1, 1944.

Jones, Frederick Elwyn. *The Attack from Within: The Modern Technique of Aggression*. London: Penguin Books, 1939.

"Karl Herrmann, Exchange Student, Tells of Life among Undergraduates of Universities in Germany." *Middlebury Campus*, October 13, 1937.

Kersten, Ulrich. "Why the Youth of Germany Demands Political Changes." *New York Times*, March 6, 1932.

King, Eliza. "Foreign Countries Well Represented This Year at Agnes Scott College." *Atlanta Constitution*, September 30, 1937.

"Kiwanians Hear Munich Student." *Chester Times* (Chester, PA), June 7, 1934.

Bibliography

"Kleine Liebe zu Amerika." In "Rundbrief der deutschen Austauschstudenten in Amerika." *Hochschule und Ausland* 11, no. 9 (September 1933): 56–57.

Kreisberg, Ben. "By Lines: An Amiable Chap." *Campus* (Rochester, NY), October 9, 1936.

———. "German Exchange Student Explains Nazi Policies, Declares That Facts Have Been Misrepresented." *Campus* (Rochester, NY), October 9, 1936.

"Kurzer Tätigkeitsbericht des Aussenpolitischen Amtes der NSDAP." Doc. no. 003-PS. Exhibit U.S.A. 603. *Nazi Conspiracy and Aggression*, Vol. 3. Office of the United States Chief Counsel for Prosecution of Axis Criminality. Washington, DC: United States Government Printing Office, 1946. Assessed May 31, 2023. https://stacks.stanford.edu/file/yz849fs7687/yz849fs7687.pdf.

Langer, Walter C. *A Psychological Analysis of Adolph Hitler: His Life and Legend*. Washington, DC: M.O. Branch of Office of Strategic Services, ca. 1943. Accessed October 26, 2024. https://www.cia.gov/readingroom/docs/CIA-RDP78-02646R000600240001-5.pdf.

"Last Year's Exchange Student." *Furman Hornet* (Greenville, SC), October 14, 1938.

Lautsch, Marianne, and Barbara Herbig. *F. A. D. Kroschenen: Ein Spiel vom Arbeitslager*. Berlin: Oesterheld, 1934.

Lazenby, Candler. "Some Contributions of the Negro to American Culture." *Rundbrief deutscher Austauschstudenten im den U.S.A.* 5, no. 4 (February 1936): 7–11.

Leidecker, Kurt F. "Letter to the Editor." *Rensselaer Polytechnic*, January 16, 1940.

Leiper, Henry Smith. Letter to "Dear Homelanders," August 30, 1935. Presbyterian Historical Society. Accessed January 6, 2021. https://digital.history.pcusa.org/islandora/object/islandora:14426#page/1/mode/1up.

"Letters to the Editor." *Barnard Bulletin*, December 14, 1937.

Lilge, Frederic. *The Abuse of Learning: The Failure of the German University*. 1948. Reprint, New York: Octagon Books, 1975.

Mader, Julius. *Hitlers Spionage Generale sagen aus*. Berlin: Verlag der Nation, 1970.

Mahlin, Sibylle. *Montclair State College, La Campana Yearbook, Class of 1933*. Montclair: New Jersey State Teachers College, 1933.

Maier, Georg O. T. "Deutsche Studenten im Ausland." In *Wir Deutsch in der Welt*, edited by Verband Deutscher Vereine im Ausland e.V. NS Schriftums, 141–48. Berlin: Otto Stollberg, 1936.

Margolin, O[scar]. "Mr. Margolin Objects." *Massachusetts Daily Collegian (Amherst)*, March 12, 1936.

Mann, Erika, and Klaus Mann. *Escape to Life*. Boston: Houghton Mifflin, 1939.

McBane, Reed H. "French and German Students Find Mutual Friendship in Campus Work." *Campus* (Rochester, NY), October 4, 1935.

———. "German Exchange Student Finds American College Life Surprising." *Campus* (Rochester, NY), October 12, 1934.

Mehnert, Klaus. *Ein deutscher Austauschstudent in Kalifornien*. Stuttgart: Deutsche Verlags Anstalt, 1930.

———. "Problem XIX: U.S.-Flottenmanöver im Pazifik 1938." *Zeitschrift für Geopolitik* 15 (July 1938): 559–69.

"Memories of Tufts: Donald J. Winslow ('34) Remembers. Before the War." Tufts University Digital Collections and Archives, 2008. Accessed January 1, 2020. https://exhibits.tufts.edu/spotlight/memories-of-tufts/feature/before-the-war.

"Men Invited to Address." *Marysville (OH) Tribune*, March 3, 1934.

"Midd Man Jailed as Underground Leader of Nazis." *Middlebury Campus*, February 27, 1947.

"Mines Student Kiwanis Speaker." *Montana Standard* (Butte), April 12, 1934.

"Miss Edeltraut Proske Tells of German System." *Mount Holyoke News*, October 23, 1936.

Bibliography   275

Mohrdiek, Martin. "Die Paradoxie Amerika." *Heimatrundbrief deutscher Austauschstudenten in den U.S.A.* (1940): 12–13.

"Mrs. Barrett Plans to Lead Open Road Trip to Europe." *Mount Holyoke News,* January 20, 1939.

"Mr. 'X' at Hearing Details Nazi 'Plot.' " *New York Times,* November 15, 1933.

"National Feuds Forgotten." *Birmingham News,* December 22, 1936.

"Nazi Consulate Aide Here Beaten to Death in Home." *New York Times,* December 7, 1939.

"Nazi Interned Shanghai." *Sarasota Herald-Tribune,* October 30, 1945.

"Nazi Mistreatment." *Auburn Plainsman,* March 24, 1939.

"Nazi Probe Will Cover 200 Schools." *Columbia Daily Spectator* (New York), October 30, 1933.

"Nazi Underground: Leaders Captured Bacteria Weapon Reported." *San Bernardino Sun,* February 24, 1947.

"Nazi Writers Ousted as Spies on Refugees, London Papers Reveal." *Jewish Telegraphic Agency,* August 12, 1937.

"Nazis to Multiply Students Abroad." *New York Times,* April 25, 1936.

"Nazis vs. U.S.: It's a War, but Only of Propaganda." *Arizona Daily Star* (Tucson), January 19, 1939.

"New Propaganda by Reich Seen Here." *New York Times,* December 3, 1938.

Noelle, Elisabeth. "An Open Letter." *Columbia Missourian,* February 11, 1938. In Esther Priwer, "Nazi Exchange Students at the University of Missouri. With a Memorandum on American-German Student Exchange." *Menorah Journal* 26, no. 3 (October–December 1938): 358.

———. " 'College Girls' in Amerika." *Deutsche Allgemeine Zeitung,* April 16, 1939.

———. "Two Languages to Learn: German Student Must Know Slang and English to Understand 'Jelling,' 'Cokes,' 'Dates.' " *Key* 55, no. 1 (1938): 17–18.

Noelle-Neumann, Elisabeth. *Die Erinnerungen.* Munich: F. A. Herbig Verlagsbuchhandlung, 2006.

[Notice on "Miss Elizabeth (*sic*] Noelle"). *Columbia Missourian.* January 21, 1938. In Esther Priwer, "Nazi Exchange Students at the University of Missouri. With a Memorandum on American-German Student Exchange." *Menorah Journal* 26, no. 3 (October–December 1938): 358.

Orr, Nancy. "Unclassified Comment." *Kannapolis (NC) Daily Independent,* December 15, 1939.

Orten, Vrest. "Return of the Native." *Rutland (VT) Daily Herald,* May 20, 1936.

"Over the Tea Cups." *Wheaton News,* January 15, 1938.

Oxonian. "Nazis and the Swiss Universities: Propaganda and Espionage." *Manchester (UK) Guardian Weekly,* February 10, 1939.

"Parade of Opinion." *Agonistic* (Decatur, GA), January 18, 1939.

Perros, George P. *Preliminary Inventory of the Special House Committee on Un-American Activities Authorized to Investigate Nazi Propaganda and Certain Other Propaganda Activity.* History, Art & Archives, United States House of Representatives. Modified October 19, 2012. Accessed February 3, 2021. http://history.house.gov/Records-and-Research/Finding-Aids/SpecialPIs/Special-House-Committee-on-Un-American-Activities/.

———. *Preliminary Inventory of the Special House Committee on Un-American Activities Authorized to Investigate Nazi Propaganda and Certain Other Propaganda Activity.* Appendix B: List of Folder Heading of Main Correspondence File: Isabel Thatcher: Third Experiment in International Living; A.S. Lipsius, German Exchange Students at the University of Georgia; Jacob H. Hollander, German Exchange Students [Johns Hopkins]; A. M. Goldish, Activities of a German Student at Marietta College; Mabel DeVries Tanner, on Nazi Propaganda at West Virginia University. History, Art & Archives. United States House of Representatives. Modified October 19, 2012. Accessed February 3, 2021. http://

276 Bibliography

history.house.gov/Records-and-Research/Finding-Aids/Special-PIs/Special-House
-Committee-on-Un-American-Activities/.

"Personalia, 1939–41." *Monatshefte für deutschen Unterricht* 32, no. 7 (November 1940): 343.

Pilgert, Henry P. *The Exchange of Persons Program in Western Germany.* Bad Godesberg: Office of the U.S. High Commissioner for Germany, Historical Division, Office of the Executive Secretary, 1951.

"Pitt Exchange Student Back from Land of Hitler." *Pittsburgh Post-Gazette*, August 7, 1939.

Press, Harry. "Size of Campus, Many Cars Amaze German Student on First U.S. Visit." *Stanford Daily*, October 16, 1936.

Priwer, Esther. "Nazi Exchange Students at the University of Missouri. With a Memorandum on American-German Student Exchange." *Menorah Journal* 26, no. 3 (October–December, 1938): 353–61.

"Prof. Hans Grueninger Appointed Adviser to Foreign Students." Office of Media Relations, DePauw University, October 21, 1948. Accessed March 31, 2018. https://www.depauw.edu /news-media/latest-news/details/20/.

"Professor Scores Newspapers Here." *New York Times*, December 9, 1934.

Rich, Dan. "What European Nation Do You Like Best?" *Carletonian* (Northfield, MN), November 11, 1938.

Ritter, Gerhard, and M. A. Fitzsimons. "The German Professor in the Third Reich." *Review of Politics* 8, no. 2 (1946): 242–54.

Robertallen, Drew Pearson. "The Daily Washington Merry-Go-Round." *Daily Illini* (Champaign), April 13, 1939.

Rogge, O. John. *The Official German Report: Nazi Penetration, 1924–1942.* New York: T. Yoseloff, 1961.

Rollins, Richard. *I Find Treason: The Story of an American Anti-Nazi Agent.* New York: W. Morrow, 1941.

Roosevelt, Franklin Delano. "May 26, 1940: Fireside Chat 15: On National Defense." University of Virginia Miller Center Presidential Speeches. Accessed November 24, 2019. https:// millercenter.org/the-presidency/presidential-speeches/may-26-1940-fireside-chat-15 -national-defense.

Ross, Colin. *Unser Amerika: Der deutsche Anteil an den Vereinigten Staaten.* Leipzig: F. A. Brockhaus, 1936.

Salinas, María Emilia Paz. *Strategy, Security, and Spies: Mexico and the U.S. as Allies in World War II.* University Park: Pennsylvania State University Press, 1997.

Sanborn, Doris. "Fraulein Oesterlin Finds American People 'Take It Easy and Have Good Time." *Lincoln (NE) Sunday Journal and Star*, March 10, 1935.

Schäfer, Ursula. "Kleiner Triumph im grossen Amerika." *Rundbrief deutscher Austausch-studenten in den U.S.A.* 5, nos. 6/7 (April/May 1936): 14–15.

Scheibe, Fritz Hubertus. "Was an der Universität arbeiten bedeutet, habe ich in Amerika gelernt." In *Spuren in die Zukunft.* Vol. 3, *Fakten und Zahlen zum DAAD*, edited by Peter Alter, 29. Bonn: Deutscher Akademischer Austauschdienst, 2000.

Schrey, Heinz-Horst. "Der amerikanische Geist." *Geist der Zeit* 16, no. 2 (February 1938): 252.

Schroeder, Herbert. "Zwischenvölkische Aufgaben des Rundfunks." *Hochschule und Ausland* 13, no. 3 (March 1935): 17–28.

Scott, Joe. "Muskingum College Fraulein Co-Ed Thinks Americans Children Looking for Good Time." *Sunday Times-Signal* (Zanesville, OH), December 11, 1938.

Singh, P. P. "Two Foreign Visitors Write of Nazi Rule." *Columbia Missourian*, November 24, 1937.

"Society." *Atchison (KS) Daily Globe*, February 10, 1937.

Bibliography 277

Sonthoff, Herbert. "Anpassung?" *Rundbrief deutscher Austauschstudenten in den U.S.A.* 5, no. 2 (December 1935): 1–3.

———. "Campus Unknown to European Students; Sonthoff Likes American Ways, Customs." *Red and Black* (Athens, GA), November 8, 1935.

———. "Last Hours in Germany." *Atlantic* (November 1939): 687–88.

"Speaker Lauds Hitler Regime." *St. Joseph (MO) Gazette*, May 25, 1936.

"Speakers Address Youth Conference." *Detroit Free Press*, October 28, 1942.

Spivak, John. *Secret Armies: The New Technique of Nazi Warfare*. New York: Modern Age, 1939.

"Spivak Returned to Jail." *New York Times*, April 2, 1940, 2.

"State Delegates Hear German Student's Talk." *State College News* (Albany, NY), November 4, 1932.

Stroebe, Lilian Luise. *The Teaching of German at Vassar College in Peace and War: A Retrospect, 1905–1943*. Poughkeepsie, NY: Vassar College, 1944.

"The Student Exchange System (with Apologies to Lincoln)." *La Campana: Nineteen Hundred and Thirty-Three*. Montclair: New Jersey State Teachers College, 1933.

"Students Show Keen Interest in Conference." *Bates Student*, February 3, 1932.

"Students Speak on Nazi Regime." *Daily Messenger* (Canandaigua, NY), March 31, 1939.

"Students Veto American Haven for Jews." *Concordian* (Moorhead, MN), December 15, 1938.

"Students Vote on Olympics in Berlin." *Middlebury Campus*, December 4, 1935.

"There Is a Difference." *Sunday Times-Signal* (Zanesville, OH), December 18, 1938.

Tolischus, Otto D. "Nazis in Struggle with Professors." *New York Times*, February 14, 1935.

"Transfer Student from Germany Is Entered at Bates." *Bates Student*, October 3, 1934.

Traun-Strecktr, Littlott. "German Universities Today." *Vassar Miscellany News*, February 21, 1934.

Two Foreign Visitors Write of Nazi Rule." *Columbia Missourian*, November 24, 1937.

Two Germans Begin Studies." *Dickinsonian* (Carlisle, PA), September 27, 1934.

Ulich, Robert. "Education in the Nazi Reich." *Harvard Educational Review* 13, no. 2 (March 1943): 101–18.

"Ulrich Pohlenz, German Exchange Scholar." *Lawrence (KS) Journal-World*, February 11, 1939.

United States. Congress. House. Committee on Un-American Activities. *Investigation of Un-American Propaganda Activities in the United States: Hearings before the Committee on Un-American Activities, House of Representatives, Seventy-Fifth Congress, Third Session, November 19–December 14, 1938, at Washington, D.C.* Vol. 2. Washington, DC: U.S. Government Printing Office, 1938.

———. *Investigation of Un-American Propaganda Activities in the United States: Hearings before a Special Committee on Un-American Activities, House of Representatives, Seventy-Sixth Congress, Third Session on H. Res. 282, Executive Hearings.* Vol. 3, Part 2, Appendix. Washington, DC: US Government Printing Office, 1940.

———. *Investigation of Un-American Propaganda Activities in the United States: Hearings before the Special Committee on Un-American Activities, House of Representatives, Seventy-Sixth Congress, Third Session to Seventy-Eighth Congress, First Session, on H. Res. 282, to Investigate (1) the Extent, Character, and Objects of Un-American Propaganda Activities in the United States, (2) the Diffusion within the United States of Subversive and Un-American Propaganda That Is Instigated from Foreign Countries or of a Domestic Origin and Attacks the Principle of the Form of Government as Guaranteed by Our Constitution, and (3) All Other Questions in Relation Thereto That Would Aid Congress in Any Necessary Remedial Legislation.* Vol. 6. Washington, DC: US Government Printing Office, 1939–43.

———. *Investigation of Un-American Propaganda Activities in the United States: Hearings*

278   Bibliography

before the Special Committee on Un-American Activities, House of Representatives, Seventy-Sixth Congress, Third Session to Seventy-Eighth Congress, First Session, on H. Res. 282, to Investigate (1) the Extent, Character, and Objects of Un-American Propaganda Activities in the United States, (2) the Diffusion within the United States of Subversive and Un-American Propaganda That Is Instigated from Foreign Countries or of a Domestic Origin and Attacks the Principle of the Form of Government as Guaranteed by Our Constitution, and (3) All Other Questions in Relation Thereto That Would Aid Congress in Any Necessary Remedial Legislation. Vol. 6. *Annual Report.* Washington, DC: U.S. Government Printing Office, 1939–43.

[Untitled Notice]. *Union-Bulletin* (Walla Walla, WA), September 28, 1951.

Van Paassen, Pierre, and James Waterman Wise, *Nazism: An Assault on Civilization.* New York: H. Smith and R. Haas, 1934.

Vidair, Vera J. "Letter to the Editor." *Bernard Bulletin (New York, New York),* February 9, 1937.

Von Braun, Sigismund. *Flüchtlinge Gäste: Auf Weltenbummel, 1933–1935.* Frankfurt am Main: Haag und Herchen, 1993.

Von Dobeneck, Henning. "An Open Answer to Mr. N. B. Jacobson." *Massachusetts Daily Collegian* (Amherst), March 26, 1936.

Von Gienanth, Ulrich. "Lebenserringung." Von Gienanth Family Documents.

Von Lilienfeld, Georg. "Amerika im Umbruch." *Rundbrief deutscher Austauschstudenten in Den U.S.A.* 5, no. 2 (December 1935): 5.

———. "Amerikanische Propaganda für das rote Spanien." *Zeitschrift für Politik* 27, nos. 11/12 (November/December 1937): 601–6.

Von Strempel, Heribert. "Confessions of a German Propagandist." *Public Opinion Quarterly* 10, no. 2 (Summer 1946): 216–33.

Von Twardowski, Fritz. *Anfänge der deutschen Kulturpolitik zum Ausland.* Bonn-Bad Godesberg: Inter Nationes, 1970.

Von Wistinghausen, R. "German Political Situation Told by Exchange Student." *The Daily Illini* (Champaign, IL), July 29, 1932.

Waagen, Ludwig. "How Do You Like America?" *American-German Review* 5, no. 2 (February 1939): 28–29, 40.

Weege, Kurt. "Sing-Sing." *Rundbrief deutscher Austauschstudenten in den U.S.A.* 6, no. 1 (January 1936): 12–13.

"What Exchange Students Think of Us." Letter from Lucie Hess to friends at Agnes Scott College, July 5, 1936. *Agnes Scott Alumnae Quarterly* 15, no. 1 (November 1936): 30.

Wickert, Erwin. "American Way of Life oder: Ein denkwürdige Teestunde." In *Spuren in die Zukunft,* Vol. 2, *Fakten und Zahlen zum DAAD,* edited by Peter Alter, 33–38. Bonn: Deutscher Akademischer Austauschdienst, 2000.

———. "Anschlagsaeule." *Rundbrief deutscher Austauschstudenten in den U.S.A.* 5, no. 1 (November 1935): 18.

———. "Das Bild des grossen Mannes in den Vereinigten Staaten." *Heimatrundbrief deutscher Austauschstudenten in den U.S.A.* (1940): 4–8.

———. *Fata Morgana über den Strassen.* Leipzig: Arwed Strauch Verlag, 1938.

———. *Mut und Übermut: Geschichten aus meinem Leben.* Stuttgart: Deutsche Verlags-Anstalt, 1991.

White, Viola Chittenden. *Partridge in a Swamp: The Journals of Viola C. White, 1918–1941.* Edited by W. Storrs Lee. Woodstock, VT: Countryman Press, 1979.

"Williams Does Not Want German Students with 'Certificates of Political Responsibility.'" *New York Times,* May 1, 1936.

Williams, Donald F. "Big Apple and Hot Dogs Impress German Student." *Bates Student,* October 5, 1938.

"Will Make Exchange: Anonymous Donor Sends Check for German Scholarship." *Daily Journal-World* (Lawrence, KS), April 2, 1938.

Woessner, Ilse. " 'Dunkle' Erinnerungen." *Rundbrief deutscher Austauschstudenten in den U.S.A.* 5, no. 5 (March 1936): 4–6.

Wolf, Karl. "To the Editor of the CAMPUS." *Middlebury Campus,* May 27, 1936.

"Young Plan Unjust, Exchange Student Says." *The Daily Illini* (Champaign, IL), July 26, 1932, 2.

Zentralblatt für Jugendrecht und Jugendwohlfahrt, 26 (1934): 166–67.

Zwicker, Dietrich. "Freiheit und Zwang." *Rundbrief deutscher Austauschstudenten in den U.S.A.* 5, no. 1 (November 1935): 12–14.

Secondary Sources

Adam, Thomas, ed. *Germany and the Americas: Culture, Politics, and History. A Multidisciplinary Encyclopedia.* Santa Barbara, CA: ABC Clio, 2005.

"Adolf-Henning Frucht." *Der Spiegel,* January 11, 1993.

Afoumado, Diane. *Indésirables: 1938: La conférence d'Evian et les réfugiés juifs.* Paris: Calmann-Lévy, 2018.

Albrecht, Richard, and Otto R. Romberg. *Widerstand und Exil, 1933–1945.* Frankfurt am Main: Campus Verlag, 1986.

"Alumni/ae News." *Chicago Theological Seminary Newsletter,* Fall 1981, 7.

Aly, Götz. *Hitler's Beneficiaries: Plunder, Racial War, and the Nazi Welfare State.* Translated by Jeffrey Chase. New York: Metropolitan Books, 2007.

Angrick, Andrej, and Peter Klein. *The 'Final Solution' in Riga: Exploitation and Annihilation, 1941–1944.* New York: Berghahn Books, 2009.

Ash, Mitchell G. "Science and Scientific Exchange in the German-American Relationship." In *The United States and Germany in the Era of the Cold War, 1945–1990: A Handbook,* edited by Detlef Junker, 417–24. New York: Cambridge University Press, 2004.

Auschwitz-Birkenau Memorial and Museum. "New Publication on the Conservation of the Auschwitz SS-Hygiene Institut Documents." Accessed October 12, 2024. https://www .auschwitz.org/en/museum/news/new-publication-on-the-conservation-of-the-auschwitz -ss-hygiene-institut-documents,846.html.

Balfour, Michael. *Withstanding Hitler in Germany, 1933–45.* London: Routledge, 1988.

Baranowski, Shelley. *Strength through Joy: Consumerism and Mass Tourism in the Third Reich.* Cambridge: Cambridge University Press, 2004.

Barbian, Jan-Pieter. *The Politics of Literature in Nazi Germany: Books in the Media Dictatorship.* London: Bloomsbury, 2013.

Barclay, David, and Elisabeth Glaser-Schmidt, eds. *Transatlantic Images and Perceptions: Germany and America since 1776.* Washington, DC: German Historical Institute; Cambridge: Cambridge University Press, 1997.

Baring, Arnulf. "In Der Vergangenheit Nach Zukunftsperspektiven Ausschau Halten: Die Vereinigten Staaten Von Amerika und Deutschland 1945–1950 und Danach." *Zeitschrift für Kultur-Austausch* 37, no. 2 (1987).

Barnes, James J., and Patience P. Barnes. *Nazis in Prewar London, 1930–1939: The Fate and Role of German Party Members and British Sympathizers.* Eastbourne: Sussex Academic Press, 2005.

Barnett, Victoria J., Clifford J. Green, and Wolfgang Huber, eds. *Dietrich Bonhoeffer: Indexes and Supplementary Materials.* Vol. 17 of *Dietrich Bonhoeffer Works.* Minneapolis, MN: Fortress Press, 2014.

Bartrop, Paul R. *The Evian Conference of 1938 and the Jewish Refugee Crisis*. New York: Palgrave Macmillan, 2018.

BASF. "In Memory of the Victims of the 1943 and 1948 Explosions." *BASF Global*. Accessed September 17, 2024. https://www.basf.com/global/en/who-we-are/history/explosions-1943-48.

Batvinis, Raymond J. *Hoover's Secret War against Axis Spies: FBI Counterespionage during World War II*. Lawrence: University Press of Kansas, 2014.

———. *The Origins of FBI Counterintelligence*. Lawrence: University Press of Kansas, 2007.

Bauer, Theresia. *Gesichter der Zeitgeschichte deutsche Lebensläufe im 20. Jahrhundert*. Munich: Oldenbourg, 2009.

Bauschiger, Sigrid. "The American Reception of Contemporary German Literature." In *The United States and Germany in the Era of the Cold War, 1945–1990: A Handbook*, Vol. 1, *1945–1968*, edited by Detlef Junker, 432–38. New York: Cambridge University Press, 2004.

Bautz, T. "Schrey, Heinz-Horst." *Verzeichnis der Autorinnen und Autoren unseres Verlages*. Accessed August 25, 2024. https://www.bbkl.de/index.php/frontend/autor?id=1652.

Beck, Alfred M. *Hitler's Ambivalent Attaché: Lt. Gen. Friedrich von Boetticher in America, 1933–1941*. Lincoln: University of Nebraska Press, 2011.

Beck, Earl R. "Friedrich Schönemann, German Americanist." *Historian* 26 (1964): 381–404.

Becker, Manual. " 'Historikerstreit' Reloaded? Eine geschichtspolitische Einordnung der Kontroverse um 'Das Amt und die Vergangenheit.' In *Die Ämter und ihre Vergangenheit im "Dritten Reich": "Horte des Widerstands" oder "verbrecherische Organisationen"?*, edited by Manuel Becker and Christoph Studt, 47–71. Augsburg: Weissner, 2013.

"Beindorff, Fritz." Namensgebende Persönlichkeiten. Tischvorlage zur GOK am 1. Oktober 2015. Empfehlungen des Beirates. 1/32. Wissenschaftliche Betrachtung von namensgebenden Persönlichkeiten, Landeshauptstadt Hannover.

Bendersky, Joseph W. *The "Jewish Threat": Anti-Semitic Politics of the U.S. Army*. New York: Basic Books, 2000.

Benecke, Jakob. "Between Exclusion and Compulsory Service: The Treatment of the Jewish 'Mischlinge' as an Example for Social Inequality Creation in the Hitler-Jugend." *Policy Futures in Education* 17, no. 2 (2019): 222–45.

Benedikt, Klaus-Ulrich. *Emil Dovifat: Ein katholischer Hochschullehrer und Publizist*. Mainz: Matthias-Grünewald, 1986.

Benz, Wolfgang. *Im Widerstand: Größe und Scheitern der Opposition gegen Hitler*. Munich: C. H. Beck Verlag, 2019.

Berghahn, Marion. *Continental Britons: German-Jewish Refugees from Nazi Germany*. Oxford; New York: Berghahn Books, 2007.

Berghahn, Volker R. "The Debate on 'Americanization' among Economic and Cultural Historians." *Cold War History* 10, no. 1 (February 2010): 107–30.

Bergmeier, Horst J.P., and Rainer E. Lotz. *Hitler's Airwaves: The Inside Story of Nazi Radio Broadcasting and Propaganda Swing*. New Haven, NJ: Yale University Press, 1997.

Biewer Ludwig, and Rainer Blasius. *In den Akten, in der Welt: Ein Streifzug durch das Politische Archiv des Auswärtigen Amts*. Göttingen: Vandenhoeck & Ruprecht, 2007.

Bigell, Werner. "Fear and Fascination: Anti-Landscapes between Material Resistance and Material Transcendence." In *The Anti-Landscape*, edited by David E. Nye and Sarah Elkind, 128–48. Amsterdam: Rodopi B.V., 2014.

Blank, Thomas, and Peter Schmidt. "Verletzte oder verletzende Nation? Empirische Befunde zum Stolz in Deutschland." *Journal für Sozialforschung* 33 (1993): 391–415.

Blesgen, Detlef J. *Financiers, Finanzen und Finanzreformen des Widerstandes*. Münster: LIT, 2006.

Boehm, Eric H. *We Survived: Fourteen Histories of the Hidden and Hunted in Nazi Germany.* Boulder, CO: Basic Books, 2009.

Bogart, Leo. "The Pollster & the Nazis." *Commentary,* August 1991, 43–49.

Bollenbeck, Georg. "The Humanities in Germany after 1933: Semantic Transformations and the Nazification of the Disciplines." In *Nazi Germany and the Humanities,* edited by Wolfgang Bialas and Anson Rabinbach, 1–20. London: Oneworld, 2014.

Bolliger, Silvia. *Im Zeichen der Nationalisierung: : Die Haltung der Universität Zürich gegenüber ausländischen Studierenden in der Zwischenkriegszeit.* Vienna: Vandenhoeck & Ruprecht, 2019.

Bonhoeffer, Dietrich. *Berlin, 1932–1933.* Edited by Larry L. Rasmussen. Translated by Claudia D. Bergmann, Peter Frick, and Scott A. Moore. *Dietrich Bonhoeffer Works.* Vol. 12, *Berlin, 1932–1933.* Minneapolis, MN: Fortress Press, 2009. Originally published 1997.

Boxfordurgess, Michael. *In Search of the Federal Spirit: New Theoretical and Empirical Perspectives in Comparative Federalism.* Oxford: Oxford University Press, 2012.

Boyer, John W. "Chicago and the World of Higher Education in the Late Nineteenth Century." In *We Are All Islanders to Begin With.* Vol. 17, part 2. Chicago: University of Chicago, 2021. Accessed October 12, 2024. https://college.uchicago.edu/sites/default/files/documents /Boyer_AR_2021_V4.pdf.

Brantz, Rennie W. "German-American Friendship: The Carl Schurz Vereinigung, 1926–1942." *International History Review* 11, no. 2 (May 1989): 229–51.

Breit, Peter K. "Culture as Authority: American and German Transactions." In *The American Impact on Postwar Germany,* ed. Reiner Pommerin, 621–42. Providence, RI: Berghahn Book, 1995.

Breitman, Richard. *The Berlin Mission: The American Who Resisted Nazi Germany from Within.* New York: PublicAffairs, 2019.

Breitman, Richard, and Alan M. Kraut. *American Refugee Policy and European Jewry, 1933–1945.* Bloomington: Indiana University Press, 1987.

Breitman, Richard, and Allan J. Lichtman. *FDR and the Jews.* Boston: Harvard University Press, 2013.

Breitman, Richard, et al. *U.S. Intelligence and the Nazis.* Cambridge: Cambridge University Press, 2005.

"The Brits Who Fought for Hitler." Season 1, episode 2 of the TV series *Revealed.* Directed by James Cutler and Nigel Levy. Released in the United Kingdom on October 16, 2002. 47 minutes. London: A Real Life Media Production for Five (c) Channel 5 Broadcasting Ltd., 2002.

Brogiato, Heinz Peter. "Bartz, Fritz." In *Germany and the Americas: Culture, Politics, and History. A Multidisciplinary Encyclopedia,* edited by Adam Thomas, 119–20. Santa Barbara, CA: ABC Clio, 2005.

Brooks, Chay. "The Apostle of Internationalism: Stephen Duggan and the Geopolitics of International Education." *Political Geography* 49 (November 2015): 64–73.

Browder, George C. *Hitler's Enforcers: The Gestapo and the SS Security Service in the Nazi Revolution.* Oxford: Oxford University Press, 1997.

Brown, Jack Harold Upton. *Footsteps in Science.* Lanham, MD: University Press of America, 1993.

Browning, Christopher. *The Final Solution and the German Foreign Office: A Study of Referat D III of Abteilung Deutschland, 1940–43.* New York: Holmes & Meier, 1978.

Bryden, John. *Fighting to Lose: How the German Secret Intelligence Service Helped the Allies Win the Second World War.* Toronto: Dundurn Press, 2014.

Buckow, Anjana. "Allensbach Institute." In *Europe since 1945: An Encyclopedia,* edited by Bernard A. Cook, 32. London: Taylor & Francis, 2001.

Büdinger Forschungen zur Sozialgeschichte. Boppard am Rhein: Harald Boldt Verlag, 1982.

"Canaris, Wilhelm." *Jewish Virtual Library.* Accessed May 22, 2023. https://www.jewishvirtual library.org/wilhelm-canaris.

Caplan, Jane. *Government without Administration: State and Civil Service in Weimar and Nazi Germany.* Oxford: Clarendon Press, 1988.

Carlson, John Roy [Avedis Boghos Derounian]. *Under Cover: My Four Years in the Nazi Underworld of America—the Amazing Revelation of How Axis Agents and Our Enemies Within Are Now Plotting to Destroy the United States.* New York: E. P. Dutton, 1943.

Center for Antisemitism Research. "Antisemitic Attitudes in America: Topline Findings." Anti-Defamation League. January 12, 2023. https://www.adl.org/resources/report/anti semitic-attitudes-america-topline-findings.

Center for Cryptologic History, National Security Agency. "Cryptologic Aspects of German Intelligence Activities in South America during World War II." 2011. Accessed October 5, 2022. https://www.nsa.gov/portals/75/documents/about/cryptologic-heritage/historical -figures-publications/publications/wwii/cryptologic_aspects_of_gi.pdf.

Chicago Theological Seminary. *President's Newsletter.* Special ser., 13, no. 2, September 1979.

Clifford, Geraldine, T. Bentley Edwards, and Theodore Reller. "Frederic Lilge, Berkeley, 1911–1984, Professor Emeritus." Calisphere: Regents of the University of California, 2011. *Online Archive of California.* Accessed October 22, 2024. https://oac.cdlib.org/view?docId =hb4d5nb2om;NAAN=13030&doc.view=frames&chunk.id=div00098&toc.depth=1&toc .id=&brand=oac4.

Connelly, John, and Michael Grüttner. *Universities under Dictatorship.* University Park: Pennsylvania State University Press, 2005.

Conze, Eckart, Norbert Frei, Peter Hayes, and Moshe Zimmermann. *Das Amt und die Vergangenheit: Deutsche Diplomaten im Dritten Reich und in der Bundesrepublik.* Munich: Karl Blessing Verlag, 2010.

Conze, Werner, Erich Kosthorst, and Elfriede Nebgen. *Jakob Kaiser: Der Widerstandskämpfer.* 2nd ed. Stuttgart: Kohlhammer, 1970.

Cooper, Artemis. *Patrick Leigh Fermor: An Adventure.* New York: New York Review Books, 2013.

"Coor, Gertrude Marianne Achenbach." In *Dictionary of Art Historians.* Accessed May 25, 2019. http://www.arthistorians.info/coorg.

Cox, Caroline. "Dance in Nazi Germany." *Washington College Review* 25, W2. Accessed October 13, 2024. https://washcollreview.com/2018/07/16/dance-in-nazi-germany/.

Craig, John. *Peculiar Liaisons in War, Espionage, and Terrorism in the Twentieth Century.* New York: Algora Publishing, 2007.

Dahrendorf, Ralf. *Society and Democracy in Germany.* Garden City, NY: Doubleday and Co., 1967.

Daum, Andreas W. "Refugees from Nazi Germany as Historians: Origins and Migrations, Interests and Identities." In *The Second Generation: Émigrés from Nazi Germany as Historians,* edited by Andreas W. Daum, Hartmut Lehmann, and James J. Sheehan, 1–32. New York: Berghahn Books, 2016.

Deutscher Akademischer Austauschdienst. *Der Deutsche Akademische Austauschdienst 1925 bis 1975: Beiträge zum 50 jährigen Bestehen.* Bonn: Deutscher Akademischer Austauschdienst, 1976.

Deutscher Akademischer Austauschdienst / German Academic Exchange Service. "Geschichte–DAAD." Accessed February 5, 2021. https://www.daad.de/de/der-daad/wer-wir-sind /geschichte/.

Deutsche Forschungsgemeinschaft. "History of the DFG, Presidents of the DFG, Prof. Ger-

Bibliography   283

hard Hess." Modified August 26, 2024. https://www.dfg.de/de/ueber-uns/ueber-die-dfg/geschichte/praesidenten/hess.

"Dietlinde von Kuenssenberg Jehle Raisig, Obituary." Legacy.com. Accessed October 12, 2024. https://www.legacy.com/us/obituaries/buffalonews/name/dietlinde-raisig-obituary?id=4719308.

Ditscheid, Angelika. "German Resistance" [Father Laurentius Siemer]. Deutsche Welle, October 21, 2006. Accessed October 17, 2024. https://www.dw.com/en/memory-of-spiritual-leader-in-german-resistance-lives-on/a-2206790.

Doering-Manteuffel, Anselm. "Der deutsche Weg nach Westen." In *Leitbilder Der Zeitgeschichte: Wie Nationen Ihre Vergangenheit Denken*, edited by Martin Sabrow, 23–39. Leipzig: AVA Akademische Verlagsanstalt, 2011.

Doerries, Reinhard. "Transatlantic Intelligence in Krieg und Frieden." In *Deutschland und die USA in der Internationalen Geschichte des 20. Jahrhunderts: Festschrift für Detlev Junker*, edited by Manfred Berg and Philipp Gassert. Stuttgart: Steiner, 2004.

Dolibois, John. *Pattern of Circles: An Ambassador's Story*. Kent, OH: Kent State University Press, 2000.

Donovan, William, and Edgar Mowrer. *Fifth Column Lessons for America*. Washington, DC: American Council on Public Affairs, 1940.

Döscher, Hans-Jürgen. *Das Auswärtige Amt im Dritten Reich: Diplomatie im Schatten der "Endlösung."* Munich: Siedler, 1987.

"Dr. Fritz Tiller Memorial." *Assembly*, March 1983. United States Military Academy. Association of Graduates, West Point Alumni Association.

Duquenne, Robert. "In Memoriam: Anna Seidel (1939–1991)." *Japanese Journal of Religious Studies* 19, no. 1 (1992): 107.

"Egloff von Tippelskirch (1913–1946)." Dickinson College Archives and Special Collections, 2005. Accessed November 4, 2024. https://archives.dickinson.edu/people/egloff-von-tippelskirch-1913-1946.

Ehrenreich, Eric. *The Nazi Ancestral Proof: Genealogy, Racial Science, and the Final Solution.* Bloomington: Indiana University Press, 2007.

Eley, Geoff. "Hitler's Silent Majority? Conformity and Resistance under the Third Reich (Part One)." *Michigan Quarterly Review* 42, no. 2 (Spring 2003): 389–425.

———. "Hitler's Silent Majority? Conformity and Resistance under the Third Reich (Part Two)." *Michigan Quarterly Review* 42, no. 3 (Summer 2003): 550–583.

Episkopos, Mark. "The Importance of Fritz Ermarth." *National Interest*, January 23, 2022. Accessed August 26, 2023. https://nationalinterest.org/feature/importance-fritz-ermarth-199854.

Ericksen, Robert P. *Complicity in the Holocaust: Churches and Universities in Nazi Germany.* Cambridge: Cambridge University Press, 2012.

Evans, Richard. *The Third Reich in Power*. Reprint ed. New York: Penguin Books, 2006.

"Faculty Member of Alma College Disappears." *Ohio State Lantern*, January 31, 1945.

Farago, Ladislas. *The Game of the Foxes: The Untold Story of German Espionage in the United States*. Philadelphia: David McKay Publications, 1972.

Federal Bureau of Investigation. "Duquesne Spy Ring." *FBI History: Famous Cases and Criminals*. Accessed August 26, 2024. https://www.fbi.gov/history/famous-cases/duquesne-spy-ring.

Federal Bureau of Investigation. "History: Ludwig Spy Ring." Accessed March 18, 2023. https://www.fbi.gov/history/famous-cases/ludwig-spy-ring.

———. "Nazi Saboteurs and George Dasch." FBI History: Famous Cases and Criminals. Accessed May 11, 2024. https://www.fbi.gov/history/famous-cases/nazi-saboteurs-and-george-dasch.

Bibliography

Fest, Joachim C. *Plotting Hitler's Death: The Story of the German Resistance*. New York: H. Holt and Co., 1996.

Fleck, Christian. *Etablierung in der Fremde: Vertriebene Wissenschaftler in den USA nach 1933*. Frankfurt am Main: Campus Verlag, 2015.

Fox, Stephen. *America's Invisible Gulag: A Biography of German American Internment & Exclusion in World War II: Memory and History*. New York: Peter Lang, 2000.

Frederick, Rudolph. *The American College and University: A History*. Athens: University of Georgia Press, 1991.

Freeman, Clive, and Gwynne Roberts. *Der kälteste Krieg: Professor Frucht und das Kampfstoff-Geheimnis*. Berlin: Ullstein, 1982.

Friedman, Saul S. *No Haven for the Oppressed: United States Policy toward Jewish Refugees, 1938–1945*. Detroit: Wayne State University Press, 1973.

"Fritsch, Georg Freiherr von." In *Munzinger Online/Personen: Internationales Biographisches Archiv*. Accessed June 15, 2018. http://www.munzinger.de/document/00000008224.

"Fritsch, Werner von." In Alan Axelrod and Jack A. Kingston, *Encyclopedia of World War II*. New York: Facts on File, 2007, 367–68.

Frye, Alton. *Nazi Germany and the American Hemisphere, 1933–1941*. New Haven: Yale University Press, 1967.

Fuhrmeister, Christian. "Vom Führerbau zum Central Collection." In *Bergung von Kulturgut im Nationalsozialismus Mythen—Hintergründe—Auswirkungen*, edited by Pia Schölnberger and Sabine Loitfellner. Cologne: Böhlau, 2015.

Fülbier, Rolf Uwe. "Digging Deeper: German Academics and Universities under Nazi Tyranny—A Comment." *Accounting History* 26, no. 3 (2021): 375–85.

Füssl, Karl-Heinz. *Deutsch-amerikanischer Kulturaustausch im 20. Jahrhundert: Bildung–Wissenschaft—Politik*. Frankfurt am Main: Campus Verlag, 2004.

Gallagher, Charles. *The Nazis of Copley Square*. Cambridge, MA: Harvard University Press, 2017.

Gassert, Philipp. *Amerika im Dritten Reich: Ideologie, Propaganda und Volksmeinung 1933–1945*. Wiesbaden: Franz Steiner Verlag, 1997.

Gellately, Robert. *Backing Hitler: Consent and Coercion in Nazi Germany*. Oxford: Oxford University Press, 2001.

———. *The Gestapo and German Society: Enforcing Racial Policy, 1933–1945*. Oxford: Clarendon Press, 1992.

Gensichen, Hans-Werner. "My Pilgrimage in Mission." *International Bulletin of Missionary Research* 13, no. 4 (October 1989): 167–69.

"Georg Ferdinand Duckwitz." *Yad Vashem*. Accessed May 22, 2023. https://www.yadvashem.org/righteous/stories/duckwitz.html.

Gienow-Hecht, Jessica. "The Anomaly of the Cold War: Cultural Diplomacy and Civil Society since 1850." In *The United States and Public Diplomacy: New Directions in Cultural and International History*, edited by Kenneth Alan Osgood and Brian Craig Etheridge, 27–56. Leiden: Brill, 2010.

"Giftwolken—dort wäre die Hölle los: Der Spionagefall Frucht." *Der Spiegel*. Part 3 of a five-part series, June 26, 1978, 134–45; No. 27, July 3, 1978; no. 34, August 20, 1978; no. 39, September 23, 1978.

Giles, Geoffrey. "German Students and Higher Education Policy in the Second World War." *Central European History* 17, no. 4 (1984): 330–54.

———. "The Rise of the National Socialist Students Association and the Failure of Political Education in the Third Reich." In *The Shaping of the Nazi State*, edited by Peter D. Stachura, 160–85. London: Routledge, 2014.

Bibliography 285

———. *Students and National Socialism in Germany*. Princeton, NJ: Princeton University Press, 1985.

Gillingham, John. *Industry and Politics in the Third Reich: Ruhr Coal, Hitler and Europe*. 1985. London: Routledge, 2014.

Glatt, Benjamin. "The German Officer Who Saved 13 Jewish 'Spies' from the Nazis." *Jerusalem Post*, October 27, 2016. Accessed May 22, 2023. https://www.jpost.com/christian-news/saving-13-jewish-spies-470888.

Goldberger, Ludwig Max. *Das Land der unbegrenzten Möglichkeiten: Beobachtungen über das Wirtschaftsleben der Vereinigten Staaten von Amerika*. Berlin: F. Fontane & Company, 1903.

Goldschmidt, Nils. "Der Freiburger universitäre Widerstand und die studentische Widerstandsgruppe KAKADU." In *Universitäten und Studenten im Dritten Reich: Bejahung, Anpassung, Widerstand. XIX. Königswinterer Tagung vom 17.–19. Februar 2006*, edited by Joachim Scholtyseck and Christoph Studt, 143–58. Berlin: LIT Verlag, 2008.

Greenberg, Udi. *The Weimar Century: German Émigrés and the Ideological Foundations of the Cold War*. Princeton, NJ : Princeton University Press, 2014.

Grenville, Anthony, Jewish Museum, London, and the Association of Jewish Refugees in Great Britain. *Continental Britons: Jewish Refugees from Nazi Europe*. London: Association of Jewish Refugees, 2002.

Groothuis, Rainer Maria. *Im Dienste einer Überstaatlichen Macht: Die deutschen Dominikaner unter der NS-Diktatur*. Münster: Regensberg, 2002.

Gross, Daniel A. "The U.S. Government Turned Away Thousands of Jewish Refugees, Fearing That They Were Nazi Spies." *Smithsonian Magazine*, November 18, 2015. Accessed March 17, 2024. https://www.smithsonianmag.com/history/us-government-turned-away-thousands-jewish-refugees-fearing-they-were-nazi-spies-180957324/.

Gross, Stephen G. *Export Empire: German Soft Power in Southeastern Europe, 1890–1945*. Cambridge: Cambridge University Press, 2017.

Grunenberg, Nina. "Immer schön die Türen schließen: Dreißig junge Amerikaner leben in Krefeld in deutschen Familien." *Die Zeit*, April 8, 1967. Accessed January 9, 2022. https://www.zeit.de/1967/31/immer-schoen-die-tueren-schliessen.

Grüttner, Michael. "Die 'Säuberung' der Universitäten: Entlassungen und Relegationen aus rassistischen und politischen Gründen." In *Universitäten und Studenten im Dritten Reich: Bejahung, Anpassung, Widerstand. XIX. Königswinterer Tagung vom 17.–19. Februar 2006*, edited by Joachim Scholtyseck and Christoph Studt, 23–39. Berlin: LIT Verlag, 2008.

———. "Nationalsozialistische Wissenschaftler: Ein Kollektivporträt." In *Gebrochene Wissenschaftskulturen Universität und Politik im 20. Jahrhundert*, edited by Michael Grüttner, Rüdiger Hachtmann, Konrad H. Jarausch, Jürgen John, and Matthias Middell, 149–66. Göttingen: Vandenhoeck & Ruprecht, 2010.

———. *Studenten im Dritten Reich*. Paderborn: Ferdinand Schöningh, 1995.

Haase, Christian. *Pragmatic Peacemakers: Institutes of International Affairs and the Liberalization of West Germany, 1945–73*. Augsburg: Wissner-Verlag, 2007.

Halpern, Stephen Mark. "The Institute of International Education: A History." PhD diss., Columbia University, 1969.

"Hans Gatzke, 71, Dies: Taught History at Yale." *New York Times*, October 17, 1987.

Hansen, Jörg, and Gerald Vogt. *"Blut und Geist": Bach, Mendelssohn, und ihre Musik im Dritten Reich*. Eisenach: Bachhaus Eisenach, 2009.

Harrington, Austin. *German Cosmopolitan Social Thought and the Idea of the West: Voices from Weimar*. Cambridge: Cambridge University Press, 2016.

Hart, Bradley W. *Hitler's American Friends: The Third Reich's Supporters in the United States*. New York: Thomas Dunne Books, 2018.

Haugh, Michael. "Intercultural (im)politeness and the Micro-Macro Issue." In *Pragmatics across Languages and Culture*, edited by Anna Trosborg, 139–66. Berlin: Walter de Gruyter, 2010.

Hausmann, Frank-Rutger. *Anglistik und Amerikanistik im "Dritten Reich."* Frankfurt am Main: Klostermann, 2003.

———. "English and Romance Studies in Germany's Third Reich." In *Nazi Germany and the Humanities: How German Academics Embraced Nazism*, edited by Anson Rabinbach and Wolfgang Bialas, 341–64. London: Oneworld Publications, 2014.

Haynes, John Earl, Harvey Klehr, and Alexander Vassiliev. *Spies: The Rise and Fall of the KGB in America*. New Haven, CT: Yale University Press, 2009.

Heftrig, Ruth, Olaf Peters, and Barbara Maria Schellewald. *Kunstgeschichte im "Dritten Reich": Theorien, Methoden*. Berlin: Akademie, 2008.

Heideking, Jügen, and Christof Mauch, eds. *USA und deutscher Widerstand: Analysen und Operationen des amerikanischen Geheimdienstes im Zweiten Weltkrieg*. Tübingen: A. Franke Verlag, 1993.

Heimböckel, Dieter. "Zivilisation auf dem Treibriemen: Die USA im Urteil der deutschen Literatur um und nach 1900." In *Mythos USA "Amerikanisierung" in Deutschland seit 1900*, edited by Frank Becker and Elke Reinhardt-Becker, 49–69. Frankfurt am Main: Campus Verlag, 2006.

Heine, Jörg. "Geschichte einer Sprengstofffabrik." *Hirschagen*. Accessed May 11, 2024. https://hirschhagen.de/geschichte/.

Hellmann, Friedrich W. *Spuren in die Zukunft: Der Deutsche Akademische Austauschdienst 1925–2000*. Vol. 3, *Mit dem DAAD in die Welt: Ausländer und Deutsche erzählen von ihren Erlebnissen—ein Lesebuch*. Bonn: Deutsche Akademische Austauschdienst, 2000.

Hepler, Allison L. "'And We Want Steel Toes Like the Men': Gender and Occupational Health during World War II." *Bulletin of the History of Medicine* 72, no. 4 (1998): 689–713.

Herman, Stewart W., Jr. *It's Your Souls We Want*. New York: Harper, 1943.

Heschel, Abraham Joshua. *Moral Grandeur and Spiritual Audacity: Essays*. New York: Macmillan, 1997.

Hill, Leonidas E. "The National-Conservatives and Opposition to the Third Reich before the Second World War." In *Germans against Nazism: Nonconformity, Opposition and Resistance in the Third Reich: Essays in Honour of Peter Hoffmann*, edited by Francis R. Nicosia and Lawrence D. Stokes, 221–52. Rev. ed. New York: Berghahn Books, 2015.

Hockenos, Matthew D. *A Church Divided: German Protestants Confront the Nazi Past*. Bloomington: Indiana University Press, 2004.

Hoerlin, Bettina. *Steps of Courage: My Parents' Journey from Nazi Germany to America*. 2nd ed. Bloomington, IN: AuthorHouse, 2012.

Hoffmann, Peter. *Beyond Valkyrie: German Resistance to Hitler. Documents*. Montreal: McGill-Queen's University Press, 2011.

———. *History of the German Resistance, 1933–1945*. Montreal: McGill-Queens University Press, 1996.

———. *Widerstand-Staatsstreich-Attentat: Der Kampf der Opposition gegen Hitler*. Munich: R. Piper & Co., 1969.

Honan, William. "U.S. Professor's Criticism of German Scholar's Work Stirs Controversy." *New York Times*, August 27, 1997.

Hürter, Johannes, and Michael Mayer, eds. *Das Auswärtige Amt in der NS-Diktatur*. Berlin: Walter de Gruyter, 2014.

IMDb.com. "Pohlenz, Peter, aka Frank U. Peter Pohlenz." Accessed July 26, 2018. http://www.imdb.com/name/nm0688372/.

Impekoven, Holger. *Die Alexander von Humboldt-Stiftung und das Ausländerstudium in*

Deutschland, 1925–1945: Von der "geräuschlosen Propaganda" zur Ausbildung der "geistigen Wehr" des "Neuen Europa." Göttingen: V&R Unipress, 2013.

Jacobsen, Hans-Adolf. *Nationalsozialistische Außenpolitik, 1933–1938.* Frankfurt am Main: Metzner, 1968.

——. "Zur Rolle der Diplomatie im Dritten Reich." In *Das diplomatische Korps, 1871–1945,* edited by Klaus Schwabe, 171–200. Boppard am Rhein: H. Boldt, 1985.

Jacobsen, Hans-Adolf, and Arthur L. Smith. *The Nazi Party and the German Foreign Office.* New York: Routledge, 2007.

Jacqué, Sebastian Ignatius. "Constructing America: A Constructivist Contemplation of the Relationship between the Franco-German Americanization-Debate and National Identity, 1918–1933." PhD diss., Erasmus University, 2017.

Jarausch, Konrad H. *After Hitler: Recivilizing Germans, 1945–1995.* Oxford: Oxford University Press, 2008.

——. *Deutsche Studenten, 1800–1970.* Frankfurt am Main: Suhrkamp, 1984.

Jeffreys-Jones, Rhodri. *The Nazi Spy Ring in America: Hitler's Agents, the FBI, and the Case That Stirred the Nation.* Washington, DC: Georgetown University Press, 2020.

"Jessen, Jens." *Gedenkstätte Deutscher Widerstand.* Accessed October 20, 2024. https://www.gdw-berlin.de/en/recess/biographies/index_of_persons/biographie/view-bio/jens-jessen/?no_cache=1.

Jewish Virtual Library. "Great Britain & the Holocaust: The British Free Corps." Accessed August 18, 2018. http://www.jewishvirtuallibrary.org/the-british-free-corps.

Jonas, Manfred. *The United States and Germany: A Diplomatic History.* Ithaca: Cornell University Press, 1984.

Junker, Detlef. "The Continuity of Ambivalence: German Views of America, 1933–1945." In *Transatlantic Images and Perceptions: Germany and America since 1776,* edited by David E. Barclay and Elisabeth Glaser-Schmidt, 243–64. Cambridge: Cambridge University Press, 1997.

——. *Kampf um die Weltmacht: Die USA und das Dritte Reich 1933–1945.* Düsseldorf: Schwann-Bagel, 1988.

——, ed. *The United States and Germany in the Era of the Cold War, 1945–1990.* Vol. 1, *1945–1968: A Handbook.* New York: Cambridge University Press, 2004.

Kahn, David. *Hitler's Spies: German Military Intelligence in World War II.* New York: Collier Books, 1985.

Kappelt, Olaf. *Braunbuch DDR: Nazis in der DDR.* Berlin: Reichmann, 1981.

Keefe, IV, Mark A. "U.S. Army Ordnance vs. NRA: The Battle over the M1 Garand." *American Rifleman,* June 4, 2020. Accessed June 10, 2023. https://www.americanrifleman.org/content/u-s-army-ordnance-vs-nra-the-battle-over-the-m1-garand/.

Keiper, Gerhard. "Rantzau, Josias von." In *Biographisches Handbuch des Deutschen Auswärtigen Dienstes, 1871–1945,* edited by Maria Keipert, Peter Grupp, Gerhard Keiper, and Martin Kröger, 570. Paderborn: F. Schöningh, 2014.

Kellermann, Henry J. *Cultural Relations as an Instrument of U.S. Foreign Policy: The Educational Exchange Program between the United States and Germany, 1945–1954.* Washington, DC: U.S. Government Printing Office, 1978.

Kempner, R. M. W. "Vernetzung des Herrn von Twardowski am 11. August 1947." Institut für Zeitgeschichte. Accessed October 22, 2024. https://www.ifz-muenchen.de/archiv/zs/zs-0786.pdf.

Kennedy, Sean. "André Siegfried and the Complexities of French Anti-Americanism." *French Politics, Culture & Society* 27, no. 2 (Summer 2009): 1–22.

Kenny, Anthony. *The History of the Rhodes Trust, 1902–1999.* New York: Oxford University Press, 2001.

Kershaw, Ian. *Hitler, the Germans, and the Final Solution*. New Haven, CT: Yale University Press, 2008.

———. *The Nazi Dictatorship: Problems and Perspectives of Interpretation*. London: Bloomsbury, 2015.

Kersten, Andrew E. *Labor's Home Front: The American Federation of Labor during World War II*. New York: New York University Press, 2006.

"Kesseler, Ina." Obituary. *New York Times*, February 22, 2000.

Kesting, Robert. "The Black Experience during the Holocaust." In *The Holocaust and History: The Known, the Unknown, the Disputed, and the Reexamined*, edited by Michael Berenbaum and Abraham J. Peck. Bloomington: Indiana University Press, 2002.

Kimmich, Christoph M. *German Foreign Policy, 1918–1945: A Guide to Current Research and Resources*. Lanham, MD: Scarecrow Press, 2013.

Klein, Melanie. "Ursula Lamb, UA Historian, Dies at 82." *Arizona Daily Wildcat* (Tucson), August 21, 1996. Accessed October 12, 2024. https://wc.arizona.edu/papers/90/1/16_1_m .html.

Kleine, Georg H. "Interview of Werner von Rosenstiel: Dr. Werner H. von Rosenstiel Oral History Interview by Dr. Georg Kleine, August 15, 1996." University of Cincinnati, 1996.

Kłodzinski, Stanisław, and Zdzisław Jan Ryn. "Suicide in the Nazi Concentration Camps." *Medical Review: Auschwitz*, August 10, 2017. Originally published as "Z problematyki samobójstw w hitlerowskich obozach koncentracyjnych." *Przegląd Lekarski–Oświęcim* (1976): 25–46. Accessed August 28, 2024. https://www.mp.pl/auschwitz/journal/english /170046,suicide-in-the-nazi-concentration-camps.

Kohut, Thomas August. *A German Generation: An Experiential History of the Twentieth Century*. New Haven, CT: Yale University Press, 2012.

Kramer, Nicole. "'München ruft!'—Studentenaustausch im Dritten Reich am Beispiel der Akademischen Auslandsstelle München." In *Die Universität München im Dritten Reich Aufsätze*, edited by Elisabeth Kraus, 123–81. Munich: Herbert Utz, 2006.

Kramer, Paul A. "International Students and U.S. Global Power in the Long 20th Century." *Asia-Pacific Journal* 8, no. 3 (2010). Accessed August 26, 2024. https://apjjf.org/paul-a -kramer/3289/article.

———. "Is the World Our Campus? International Students and U.S. Global Power in the Long Twentieth Century." *Diplomatic History* 33, no. 5 (November 2009): 775–806.

Kroll, Frank-Lothar. "'. . . Gott schütze unser liebes Deutsches Volk!' Heinrich Lützeler im Dritten Reich." In *Universitäten und Studenten im Dritten Reich: Bejahung, Anpassung, Widerstand. XIX. Königswinterer Tagung vom 17.–19. Februar 2006*, edited by Joachim Scholtyseck and Christoph Studt, 75–104. Berlin: LIT Verlag, 2008.

Kulke, Ulla. "Ein undiplomatischer Diplomat und die Freiheitsliebe." *Welt*, April 9, 2007. Accessed July 1, 2020. https://www.welt.de/politik/article800571/Ein-undiplomatischer -Diplomat-und-die-Freiheitsliebe.html.

Kuropka, Joachim, and Bernhard Austing. *"Um den Karren Wieder aus dem Dreck zu Holen . . .": 50 Jahre Christlich Demokratische Union im Landkreis Vechta*. Vechta: Vechtaer Druckerei und Verlag, 1995.

"Kurt Gerstein." *Holocaust Encyclopedia*. United States Holocaust Memorial Museum, Washington, DC. Accessed May 22, 2023. https://encyclopedia.ushmm.org/content/en/article /kurt-gerstein.

Laitenberger, Volkhard. *Akademischer Austausch und auswärtige Kulturpolitik: Der Deutsche Akademische Austauschdienst (DAAD), 1923–1945*. Göttingen: Musterschmidt, 1976.

Langbein, Hermann. *People in Auschwitz*. Chapel Hill: University of North Carolina Press, 2005.

Lansen, Oscar E. "Dissension in the Face of the Holocaust: The 1941 American Debate over Antisemitism." *Holocaust and Genocide Studies* 24, no. 1 (Spring 2010): 85–116.

———. "Victims of Circumstance: Jewish Enemy Nationals in the Dutch West Indies, 1938–1947." *Holocaust and Genocide Studies* 13, no. 3 (Winter 1999): 127–48.

Larson, Erik. *In the Garden of Beasts: Love, Terror, and an American Family in Hitler's Berlin.* New York: Broadway Books, 2011.

Lauterbach, Iris. "Central Art Collecting Point (1945–1949)." In *Historisches Lexikon Bayerns.* Published October 4, 2016. Accessed July 26, 2018. https://www.historisches-lexikon -bayerns.de/Lexikon/Central_Art_Collecting_Point_(1945-1949).

Lauwers-Rechs, Magda. "The Influence of Nazism and World War II on German Studies in the United States." PhD diss., Ohio State University, 1985.

Leber, Annedore, ed. *Conscience in Revolt: Sixty-Four Stories of Resistance in Germany.* Elstree, UK: Vallentine, Mitchell & Co., 1957.

Lee, Calvin B. T. *The Campus Scene, 1900–1970: Changing Styles in Undergraduate Life.* New York: David McKay Co., 1970.

Leff, Laurel. "Combating Prejudice and Protectionism in American Medicine: The Physicians Committee's Fight for Refugees from Nazism, 1941–1945." *Holocaust and Genocide Studies* 28, no. 2 (Fall 2014): 181–239.

———. *Well Worth Saving: American Universities' Life-and-Death Decisions on Refugees from Nazi Europe.* New Haven, CT: Yale University Press, 2019.

Lehmann, Hartmut, and James Sheehan, eds. *An Interrupted Past: German-Speaking Refugee Historians in the United States after 1933.* Washington, DC: German Historical Institute, 1991.

Lerg, Winifred B. "Amerikanische Rundfunkmacher im Dienste des Dritten Reichs." *Studienkreis Rundfunk und Geschichte: Mitteilungen* 19, no. 4 (October 1993): 211–14.

Levine, David O. *The American College and the Culture of Aspiration, 1915–1940.* Ithaca: Cornell University Press, 1986.

Levine, Emily J. "Baltimore Teaches, Göttingen Learns: Cooperation, Competition, and the Research University." *American Historical Review* (June 2016): 780–823.

Lewis, Ralph. "Books That Germans Are Reading about America." *Library Quarterly* 29, no. 4 (October 1959): 246–50.

Lichtblau, Eric. *The Nazis Next Door: How America Became a Safe Haven for Hitler's Men.* Boston: Houghton Mifflin Harcourt, 2014.

Lifton, Robert Jay. *Nazi Doctors: Medical Killing and the Psychology of Genocide.* New York: Basic Books, 1986.

Lucas, Christopher J. *American Higher Education: A History.* 2nd ed. New York: Palgrave Macmillan, 2016.

Lusane, Clarence. *The Historical Experiences of European Blacks, Africans and African Americans during the Nazi Era.* London: Routledge, 2004.

MacDonnell, Francis. *Insidious Foes: The Axis Fifth Column and the American Home Front.* New York: Oxford University Press, 1995.

MacDonogh, Giles. *A Good German Adam von Trott Zu Solz.* London: Quartet Books, 1994.

Maddow, Rachel. *Prequel: An American Fight against Fascism.* New York: Random House, 2023.

Maguire, Peter. *Law and War: International Law and American History.* New York: Columbia University Press, 2010.

Manvell, Roger, and Heinrich Fraenkel. *The Men Who Tried to Kill Hitler.* New York: Skyhorse Publishing, 2008.

Martin, Benjamin G. *The Nazi-Fascist New Order for European Culture.* Cambridge, MA: Harvard University Press, 2016.

Matthews, James K. "My Pilgrimage in Mission." *International Bulletin of Missionary Research* 23, no. 1 (January 1999): 18.

Mauch, Christof. *The Shadow War against Hitler: The Covert Operations of America's Wartime Secret Intelligence Service.* Translated from the German by Jeremiah M. Riemer. New York: Columbia University Press, 2003.

"Max Dessoir." *Journal of Aesthetics and Art Criticism* 5, no. 3 (March 1947): 241.

McKean, David. *Watching Darkness Fall: FDR, His Ambassadors, and the Rise of Adolf Hitler.* New York: St. Martin's Press, 2021.

McMurry, Ruth Emily, and Muna Lee. *The Cultural Approach.* Chapel Hill: University of North Carolina Press, 1947.

Medoff, Rafael. " 'Retribution Is Not Enough': The 1943 Campaign by Jewish Students to Raise American Public Awareness of Nazi Genocide." *Holocaust and Genocide Studies* 11, no. 2 (Fall 1997): 171–89.

"Memorandum, Re: Ludwig Case." National Law Enforcement Memorial Fund Oral Histories, George H. Franklin addendum. Accessed March 18, 2023. http://www.nleomf.org/assests /pdfs/nlem/oral-histories/FBI_Franklin_addendum.pdf.

Merritt, Richard L. *Democracy Imposed: U.S. Occupation Policy and the German Public, 1945– 1949.* New Haven, CT: Yale University Press, 1995.

Mertens, Lothar. "Einige Anmerkungen zur NS-Wissenschafts- und Forschungspolitik." In *Wissenschaften und Wissenschaftspolitik: Bestandsaufnahmen zu Formationen, Brüchen und Kontinuitäten im Deutschland des 20. Jahrhunderts,* edited by Rüdiger vom Bruch and Brigitte Kaderas, 171–90. Stuttgart: Franz Steiner Verlag, 2002.

Metternich, Tatiana, and Mazal Holocaust Collection. *Purgatory of Fools: A Memoir of the Aristocrats' War in Nazi Germany.* New York: Quadrangle / New York Times Book Co., 1976.

Miller, Joan Irene. "Spies in America: German Espionage in the United States, 1935–1945." MA thesis, Portland State University, 1984.

Mogulof, Milly. *Foiled, Hitler's Jewish Olympian: The Helene Mayer Story.* Oakland, CA: RDR Books, 2002.

Moore, Michaela Hoenicke. *Know Your Enemy: The American Debate on Nazism, 1933–1945.* Cambridge: Cambridge University Press, 2010.

"More Deadly Than War." *Popular Mechanics,* March 1944, 66–71, 148.

Mowry, David P. "Cryptologic Aspects of German Intelligence Activities in South America during World War II." Center for Cryptologic History, National Security Agency. Series 4: Word War II. Vol. 11. 2011. Accessed June 17, 2023. https://www.nsa.gov/portals/75/docu ments/about/cryptologic-heritage/historical-figures-publications/publications/wwii /cryptologic_aspects_of_gi.pdf.

Mullen, Bill, and Chris Vials. *The U.S. Antifascism Reader.* London: Verso, 2020.

Murphy, David Thomas. "Hitler's Geostrategist?: The Myth of Karl Haushofer and the 'Institut für Geopolitik.' " *Historian* 76, no. 1 (2014): 1–25.

Nagel, Anne Christine. *Hitlers Bildungsreformer: Das Reichsministerium für Wissenschaft, Erziehung und Volksbildung, 1934–1945.* Frankfurt am Main: Fischer Taschenbuch-Verlag, 2012.

Nagorski, Andrew. *Hitlerland: American Eyewitnesses to the Nazi Rise to Power.* New York: Simon & Schuster, 2013.

Naval History and Heritage Command. "German Espionage and Sabotage." September 20, 2017. Accessed October 26, 2024. https://www.history.navy.mil/research/library/online -reading-room/title-list-alphabetically/g/german-espionage-and-sabotage.html.

"Nazi Looting Organisations: The So-Called Kunstschutz in the Art Looting Investigation

Red Flag Names." . . . *Open Art Data* . . . , July 18, 2020. Accessed October 12, 2024. https://www.openartdata.org/2020/07/nazi-looting-kunstschutz.html.

Neumann, Martina. *Theodor Tantzen: Ein widerspenstiger Liberaler gegen den Nationalsozialismus*. Hannover: Hahn, 1988.

Noakes, Jeremy. *Government, Party, and People in Nazi Germany*. Exeter: University of Exeter, 1980.

Nolan, Mary. *America's Century in Europe: Reflections on Americanization, Anti-Americanism and the Transatlantic Partnership*. Göttingen: Wallstein Verlag, 2023.

———. "Anti-Americanism and Americanization in Germany." *Politics & Society* 33, no. 1 (March 2005): 88–122.

———. *The Transatlantic Century: Europe and America, 1890–2010*. Cambridge: Cambridge University Press, 2012.

———. *Visions of Modernity: America Business and the Modernization of Germany*. Oxford: Oxford University Press, 1994.

Norwood, Stephen H. *The Third Reich in the Ivory Tower: Complicity and Conflict on American Campuses*. Cambridge: Cambridge University Press, 2011.

Oakes, Elizabeth H. *Encyclopedia of World Scientists*. New York: Facts on File, 2007.

Olson, Lynne. *Those Angry Days: Roosevelt, Lindbergh, and America's Fight over World War II, 1939–1941*. New York: Random House, 2013.

"On Capitol Hill." *Washington Post*, February 12, 1939.

O'Shaughnessy, Nicholas J. *Selling Hitler: Propaganda and the Nazi Brand*. London: Hurst, 2013.

Paterson, Lawrence. *Hitler's Brandenburgers: The Third Reich's Elite Special Forces*. Barnesley, S. Yorkshire: Greenhill Books; Annapolis, MD: Naval Institute Press, 2018.

Paulus, Stefan. *Vorbild USA? Amerikanisierung von Universität und Wissenschaft in Westdeutschland, 1945–1976*. Oldenburg: De Gruyter, 2010.

Pedersen, Paul. *The Five Stages of Culture Shock: Critical Incidents around the World*. Boston: Greenwood Press, 1995.

Pentlin, Susan L. "German Teachers' Reaction to the Third Reich, 1933–1939." In *Teaching German in America: Prolegomena to a History*, edited by David P. Benseler, Walter F. W. Lohnes, and Valters Nollendorfs, 228–52. Madison: University of Wisconsin Press, 1988.

Perels, Friedrich Justus. *Die Rolle der Juristen im Widerstand Gegen Hitler: Festschrift für Friedrich Justus Perels*. Edited by Stiftung Adam von Trott. Baden-Baden: Nomos, 2017.

Petersen, Peter B. "Occupational Safety in Time of Haste: Lessons Learned from American Workers on the Home Front during World War II." *Journal of Managerial Issues* 6, no. 4 (Winter 1994): 408–27.

Petropoulos, Johnathan. *Art as Politics in the Third Reich*. Chapel Hill: University of North Carolina Press, 1996.

———. *Artists under Hitler: Collaboration and Survival in Nazi Germany*. New Haven, CT: Yale University Press, 2014.

Phelps, Reginald. "Thomas Mann, LL.D., Harvard, and the Third Reich." *Harvard Magazine*, July–August 1986, 65–68.

Pilgert, Henry P. *The Exchange of Persons Program in Western Germany*. [Bad Godesberg]: Office of the U.S. High Commissioner for Germany, Historical Division, Office of the Executive Secretary, 1951.

Piller, Elisabeth. *Selling Weimar: German Public Diplomacy and the United States, 1918–1933*. Stuttgart: Franz Steiner Verlag, 2021.

Pine, Lisa. *Education in Nazi Germany*. London: Berg Publishers, 2010.

———. *Life and Times in Nazi Germany*. London: Bloomsbury, 2016.

"Portrait Ehemalige Geschäftsführer und Generalsekretäre." Deutscher Akademischer

Austauschdienst. Accessed October 12, 2024. https://www.daad.de/de/der-daad/wer
-wir-sind/organisation/ehemalige/.

Puckett, Dan J. "Reporting on the Holocaust: The View from Jim Crow Alabama." *Holocaust and Genocide Studies* 25, no. 2 (August 2011): 219–51.

Rabinbach, Anson, and Wolfgang Bialas, eds. *Nazi Germany and the Humanities*. London: Oneworld, 2014.

"Rantzau, Josias von." In *Biographisches Handbuch des deutschen Auswärtigen Dienstes 1871–1945*. Vol. 3, *L–R*, edited by Maria Giepert, 570. Paderborn: F. Schöningh, 2008.

Rasmussen, Chris. "'This Thing has Ceased to be a Joke'": The Veterans of Future Wars and the Meanings of Political Satire in the 1930s." *Journal of American History* 103, no. 1 (June 1, 2016): 84–106.

Rees, Peter. "Nathan Roscoe Pound and the Nazis." *Boston College Law Review* 60, no. 5 (2019): 1314–46.

Regis, Margret. *When Our Mothers Went to War: An Illustrated History of Women in World War II*. Seattle: NavPublishing, 2008.

"Reich Mourns Blast Dead." *New York Times*, June 19, 1935, 6.

Remy, Steven P. *The Heidelberg Myth: The Nazification and DeNazification of a German University*. Cambridge: Cambridge University Press, 2002.

Reuther, Thomas. *Die Ambivalente Normalisierung: Deutschlanddiskurs und Deutschlandbilder in den USA, 1941–1955*. Stuttgart: Franz Steiner Verlag, 2000.

Reynolds, Justin. *Against the World: International Protestantism and the Ecumenical Movement between Secularization and Politics, 1900–1952*. New York: Columbia University, 2016.

Ribuffo, Leo P. *The Old Christian Right: The Protestant Far Right from the Great Depression to the Cold War*. Philadelphia: Temple University Press, 1983.

Riebling, Mark. *Church of Spies: The Pope's Secret War against Hitler*. New York: Basic Books, 2015.

Riess, Curt, and Alan Sutton. *Total Espionage: Germany's Information and Disinformation Apparatus, 1932–40*. Stroud, UK: Fonthill Media, Reprint, 2016.

Ringer, Fritz K. *The Decline of the German Mandarins: The German Academic Community, 1890–1933*. Cambridge, MA: Harvard University Press, 1969.

Ritter, Nikolaus Adolf Fritz, Katharine R. Wallace, and Mary Barbier, eds. *Cover Name: Dr. Rantzau*. Lexington: University Press of Kentucky, 2019.

Rodgers, Marion Elizabeth. *Mencken: The American Iconoclast*. Oxford: Oxford University Press, 2005.

Ronald, Susan. *Hitler's Aristocrats: The Secret Power Players in Britain and America Who Supported the Nazis, 1923–1941*. New York: St. Martin's Press, 2023.

Ropp, Paul, and Douglas Little. "In Memoriam: Theodore H. von Laue, 1916–2000)." *Perspectives on History*, December 1, 2000. Accessed August 28, 2024. https://www.historians.org/perspectives-article/theodore-h-von-laue-1916-2000-december-2000/.

Rosenbaum, Robert A. *Waking to Danger: Americans and Nazi Germany, 1933–1941*. Santa Barbara, CA: Praeger, 2010.

Rosenzweig, Laura B. *Hollywood's Spies: The Undercover Surveillance of Nazis in Los Angeles*. New York: New York University Press, 2017.

Ross, Stephen. *Hitler in Los Angeles: How Jews Foiled Nazi Plots against Hollywood and America*. New York: Bloomsbury, 2019.

Rothfels, Hans. *The German Opposition to Hitler: An Appraisal*. Rev. ed. Translated by Lawrence Wilson. Chicago: H. Regnery, 1962.

Rouse, Hunter. "Arthur Thomas Ippen, 1907–1974." *Memorial Tributes*. Vol. 1. Washington, DC: National Academies Press, 1979.

Rout, Leslie B., Jr., and John F. Bratzel. *The Shadow War German Espionage and United States*

Counterespionage in Latin America during World War II. Frederick, MD: University Publications of America, 1986.

Rowold, Katharina. *The Educated Woman: Minds, Bodies, and Women's Higher Education in Britain, Germany, and Spain, 1865–1914.* New York: Routledge, 2010.

Rubin. Barry, and Judith Colp Rubin. *Hating America: A History.* New York: Oxford University Press, 2004.

"Rupp, Hans." *Munzinger.* Personen: Internationales Biographisches Archiv, no. 42, October 9, 1989. Accessed August 29, 2018. http://www.munzinger.de/document/00000007815.

Russell, John. "Prof. H. W. Janson Is Dead at 68; Wrote Best-Selling 'History of Art.'" *New York Times,* October 3, 1982.

"Ruth Hubbard Honored by Federal Republic of Germany." *News Bulletin of the Institute of International Education* 33–34 (1957): 313–314.

Ryerson, Jade. "Hazards on the Home Front: Workplace Accidents and Injuries during World War II." Disability and the World War II Home Front 5. National Park Service. Accessed May 11, 2024. https://www.nps.gov/articles/000/hazards-on-the-home-front-workplace-accidents-and-injuries-during-world-war-ii.htm.

Sahm, Ulrich. *Rudolf von Scheliha 1897–1942: Ein deutscher Diplomat gegen Hitler.* Munich: Beck, 1990.

Sams, Katharine. "Adam von Trott zu Solz: Early Life and Political Initiatives in the Summer of 1939." Master's thesis, McGill University, 1990.

Scherf, Rebecca. *Evangelische Kirche und Konzentrationslager (1933 bis 1945).* Göttingen: Vandenhoeck & Ruprecht, 2018.

Scheuer, Franziska. Review of the conference *German Military Art Protection in Italy (1943–1945). H-Soz-Kult,* January 10, 2011. Accessed January 9, 2022. https://www.hsozkult.de/conferencereport/id/tagungsberichte-3490.

Schneppen, Heinz. "Die Ämter und ihre Vergangenheit im 'Dritten Reich': 'Horte des Widerstands' oder 'verbrecherische Organisationen'? Das Auswärtige Amt." In *Die Ämter und ihre Vergangenheit im "Dritten Reich": "Horte des Widerstands" oder "verbrecherische Organisationen"?,* edited by Manuel Becker and Christoph Studt, 87–99. Augsburg: Wissner, 2013.

———. "Vom Jagdtrieb historischer Ermittler: Der Bericht der 'Unabhängigen Historikerkommission' zur Vergangenheit des Auswärtigen Amtes. *Zeitschrift für Geschichtswissenschaft* 7/8 (2011): 593–620.

Scholtyseck, Joachim. *Robert Bosch und der Liberale Widerstand gegen Hitler, 1933 bis 1945.* Munich: C.H. Beck, 1999.

———, and Christoph Studt, eds. Introduction to *Universitäten und Studenten im Dritten Reich: Bejahung, Anpassung, Widerstand. XIX. Königswinterer Tagung vom 17.–19. Februar 2006.* Berlin: LIT, 2008.

Schulte, Jan Erik, and Michael Wala, eds. *Widerstand und Auswärtiges Amt: Diplomaten gegen Hitler.* Munich: Siedler, 2013.

Schwabe, Klaus, and Büdinger Vorträge. *Das Diplomatische Korps 1871–1945: Büdinger Forschungen Zur Sozialgeschichte 1982.* Boppard am Rhein: H. Boldt, 1985.

Searle, A. "Letters of Robert Briffault." *British Library Journal* 3, no. 2 (Autumn 1977): 169–76.

Seckendorf, Martin. "Reichskommissariat Ostland." *Arbeit und Leben: Hochtaunus.* Accessed August 23, 2018. http://www.arbeit-und-leben-hochtaunus.de/Baltikum.Reichskommissariat_Ostland.pdf.

"Seger, Gerhart." *Gedenkstätte Deutscher Widerstand.* Accessed October 29, 2019. https://www.gdw-berlin.de/vertiefung/biografien/personenverzeichnis/biografie/view-bio/gerhart-seger/?no_cache=1.

Seidman, Michael. *Transatlantic Antifascisms: From the Spanish Civil War to the End of World War II*. Cambridge: Cambridge University Press, 2018.

Shain, Yossi. "The War of Governments against Their Opposition in Exile." *Government and Opposition* 24, no. 3 (1989): 341–56.

Sharlet, Jeff. *The Family: The Secret Fundamentalism at the Heart of American Power*. New York: Harper Collins, 2008.

Shea, Christopher. "Nazi Apologist or Noted Scholar? A Journal Reignites a Debate." *Chronicle of Higher Education*, August 8, 1997, A13.

Shrivastava, Anindya. "The Survival of the Mandarin Tradition in German Universities." PhD diss., Oxford Brookes University, 2004.

Siebe, Daniela. *"Germania docet": Ausländische Studenten, auswärtige Kulturpolitik und deutsche Universitäten, 1870 bis 1933*. Gießen: Husum Matthiesen, 2009.

Sims, Amy R. "Intellectuals in Crisis: Historians under Hitler." *Virginia Quarterly Review* 54, no. 2 (Spring 1978): 246–62.

———. "The Unsettling History of German Historians in the Third Reich." In *Flight of Fantasy: New Perspectives on Inner Emigration in German Literature, 1933–1945*, edited by Neil H. Donahue and Doris Kirchner, 277–91. New York: Berghahn Books, 2003.

Sirois, Herbert. *Zwischen Illusion und Krieg: Deutschland und die USA, 1933–1941*. Paderborn: Schöningh, 2000.

Smith, Woodruff D. *Politics and the Sciences of Culture in Germany, 1840–1920*. Oxford: Oxford University Press, 1991.

Snyder, Timothy. *Bloodlands: Europe between Hitler and Stalin*. London: Bodley Head, 2010.

Solomon, Harvey. *Such Splendid Prisons: Diplomatic Detainment in America during World War II*. Lincoln: University of Nebraska Press, 2020.

Spencer, Kyle York. "Modern Dance." *New York Magazine*, February 24, 2003.

Steinacher, Hans. *Hans Steinacher: Bundesleiter des VDA 1933–1937. Erinnerungen und Dokumente*. Boppard am Rhein: Harold Boldt, 1970.

Stob, Henry. *Summoning Up Remembrance*. Grand Rapids, MI: Eerdmans, 1995.

Strobel, Robert. "Der Wehrbeauftragte." *Zeit*, April 24, 1958.

Strote, Noah Benezra. "Emigration and the Foundation of West Germany, 1933–1963." PhD diss., University of California, Berkeley, 2011.

Strunz, Gisela. *American Studies oder Amerikanistik?: Die deutsche Amerikawissenchaft und die Hoffnung auf Erneuerung der Hochschulen und der politischen Kultur nach 1945*. Berlin: Springer, 2013.

Syga, Judith. "Philanthropic American Foundations and German Social Sciences in the Inter-War Period." PhD diss., École des Hautes Études en Sciences Sociales and the University of Bielefeld, 2010.

SWR (Südwestrundfunk). "Wiederaufbau des Rundfunks in den Besatzungszonen: Die Jahre 1941–1950." Accessed June 7, 2023. https://www.swr.de/unternehmen/organisation/artikel-ereignisse-der-jahre-1941-1950-100.html.

Szkudlarek, Betina. "Reentry—A Review of the Literature." *International Journal of Intercultural Relations* 34, no. 1 (2010): 1–21.

Taschka, Sylvia. *Diplomat ohne Eigenschaften? Die Karriere des Hans Heinrich Dieckhoff (1884–1952)*. Stuttgart: Franz Steiner Verlag, 2006.

Tate, Tim. *Hitler's Secret Army: A Hidden History of Spies, Saboteurs, and Traitors*. New York: Pegasus Books, 2019.

Thelin, John R. *A History of American Higher Education*. 3rd ed. Baltimore: Johns Hopkins University Press, 2019.

Theoharis, Athan G., Tony G. Poveda, Susan Rosenfeld, and Richard G. Powers. *The FBI: A Comprehensive Reference Guide*. Boston: Greenwood Press, 1999.

Bibliography 295

Thomsett, Michael C. *The German Opposition to Hitler: The Resistance, the Underground, and Assassination Plots, 1938–1945.* Updated ed. Horley, UK: Crux Publishing, 2017.

Tisch, Chris. "Soldier in Hitler's Army Fled to the U.S., Served as Translator in Nuremberg Trials." *St. Petersburg Times,* July 13, 2008.

Torodash, Martin. "Ursula Lamb (1914–1996)." *Hispanic American Historical Review* 77, no. 2 (May 1997): 281–82.

Trent, James F. "The Free University of Berlin: A German Experiment in Higher Education, 1948–1961." In *American Policy and the Reconstruction of West Germany, 1945–1955,* edited by Jeffry M. Diefendorf, Axel Frohn, and Hermann-Josef Rupieper, 237–56. Cambridge: Cambridge University Press, 1993.

Tuchel, Johannes. *Der Vergessene Widerstand: Zu Realgeschichte und Wahrnehmung des Kampfes Gegen die NS-Diktatur.* Göttingen: Wallstein, 2005.

United States. Congress. Senate. *Demobilization of Armed Forces: Hearings before the Committee on Military Affairs.United States Senate,* 79th Cong. First and Second Sessions on S. 1355, pt. 3. January 16–18, 1946.

United States. Department of Defense. "Explosive Accident Summary: World War II." DoD Explosives Safety Board, August 1992.

United States Holocaust Memorial Museum. "What Did Refugees Need to Obtain a U.S. Visa in the 1930s?" Accessed December 24, 2019. https://exhibitions.ushmm.org/americans-and-the-holocaust/what-did-refugees-need-to-obtain-a-us-visa-in-the-1930s.

United States Military Academy. Association of Graduates, West Point Alumni Association, Inc. "Dr. Fritz Tiller Memorial." *Assembly* 41, no. 3 (March 1983): 23.

University of Aberdeen. "Steps of Courage: Exploring Resistance in Hitler's Germany." Aberdeen in America, 2019. Accessed May 29, 2023. https://www.abdn.ac.uk/stories/steps-of-courage/.

Usdin, Steven T. *Bureau of Spies: The Secret Connections between Espionage and Journalism in Washington.* Amherst, NY: Prometheus Books, 2018.

Van Paassen, Pierre, and James Waterman Wise, eds. *Nazism: An Assault on Civilization.* New York: H. Smith and R.Haas, 1934.

Van Roon, Ger. *German Resistance to Hitler: Count von Moltke and the Kreisau Circle.* Translated by Peter Ludlow. London: Van Nostrand Reinhold Co. [1971].

Vasey, Christopher. *Nazi Intelligence Operations in Non-occupied Territories: Espionage Efforts in the United States, Britain, South America and Southern Africa.* Jefferson, NC: McFarland & Company, 2016.

Vogt, Susanne. " 'Herzlich willkommen, meine lieben jungen Freunde': Der Lebensweg von Heinz Haber." *Marchivum,* June 22, 2020. Accessed January 6, 2021. https://www.marchivum.de/de/blog/nachlasswelten-10.

Vom Bruch, Rüdiger, and Brigitte Kaderas, eds. *Wissenschaften und Wissenschaftspolitik: Bestandsaufnahmen zu Formationen, Brüchen und Kontinuitäten im Deutschland des 20. Jahrhunderts.* Stuttgart: Franz Steiner Verlag, 2002.

Von Braun, Christina. *Stille Post: Eine andere Familiengeschichte.* Berlin: Propyläen Verlag, 2007.

Von Eckardt, Wolfgang. "Reviving German Propaganda." *New Leader,* May 17, 1954, 13–14.

Von Hassell, Agostino, Sigrid MacRae, with Simone Ameskamp. *Alliance of Enemies: The Untold Story of the Secret American and German Collaboration to End World War II.* New York: Thomas Dunne Books, 2006.

"Von Kessel, Albrecht." *Gedenkstätte Deutscher Widerstand.* Accessed October 21, 2024. https://www.gdw-berlin.de/en/recess/biographies/index_of_persons/biographie/view-bio/albrecht-von-kessel/?no_cache=1.

Von Klemperer, Klemens. *German Resistance against Hitler: The Search for Allies Abroad, 1938–1945.* Oxford: Clarendon, 1994

———. "Hans Rothfels, 1891–1976." *Central European History* 9, no. 4 (December 1976): 381–83.

Wagner, Patrick. "Forschungsförderung auf der Basis eines nationalistischen Konsenses: Die Deutsche Forschungsgemeinschaft am Ende der Weimarer Republik und im Nationalsozialismus." In *Gebrochene Wissenschaftskulturen Universität und Politik im 20. Jahrhundert*, edited by Michael Grüttner, Rüdiger Hachtmann, Konrad H. Jarausch, Jürgen John, and Matthias Middell, 183–92. Göttingen: Vandenhoeck & Ruprecht, 2010.

Wala, Michael. " 'Gegen eine Vereinzelung Deutschlands': Deutsche Kulturpolitik und akademischer Austausch mit den Vereinigten Staaten von Amerika in der Zwischenkriegszeit." In *Deutschland und die USA in der internationalen Geschichte des 20. Jahrhunderts*, edited by Manfred Berg and Philipp Gassert, 303–15. Stuttgart: Franz Steiner Verlag, 2004.

Walker, Frank. *Traitors: How Australia and Its Allies Betrayed Our ANZACs and Let Nazi and Japanese War Criminals Go Free*. Sydney: Hachette Australia, 2017.

Wall, Wendy L. *Inventing the "American Way": The Politics of Consensus from the New Deal to the Civil Rights Movement*. Oxford: Oxford University Press, 2008.

Waller, Douglas. *Wild Bill Donovan: The Spymaster Who Created the OSS and Modern American Espionage*. New York: Free Press, 2011.

Watson, Francis J. *The Nazi Spy Pastor: Carl Krepper and the War in America*. Santa Barbara, CA: Praeger, 2014.

Weale, Adrian. *Army of Evil: A History of the SS*. New York: New American Library / Caliber, 2010.

Weber, Thomas. *Hitler's First War: Adolf Hitler the Men of the List Regiment and the First World War*. Oxford: Oxford University Press, 2010.

Weihsmann, Helmut. *Bauen unterm Hakenkreuz: Architektur des Untergangs*. Vienna: Promedia, 1998.

Weinberg, Gerhard L. "Hitler's Image of the United States." *American Historical Review* 69, no. 4 (July 1964): 1006–21.

Weinke, Annette. "Das 'neue' Auswärtige Amt und der Widerstand." In *Die Ämter und ihre Vergangenheit im "Dritten Reich": "Horte des Widerstands" oder "verbrecherische Organisationen"?*, edited by Manuel Becker and Christoph Studt, 73–86. Augsburg: Weissner, 2013.

Weinreich, Max. *Hitler's Professors: The Part of Scholarship in Germany's Crimes against the Jewish People*. New Haven, CT: Yale University Press, 1946.

Weinstein, Allen, and Alexander Vassiliev. *The Haunted Wood: Soviet Espionage in America—the Stalin Era*. New York: Modern Library, 2000.

Weis, Andrea. " 'On Behalf of My Comrades': Transnational Private Memories of German Prisoners of War in U.S. Captivity." PhD diss., University of Kansas, 2008.

Weiss, Sheila Faith. *The Nazi Symbiosis: Human Genetics and Politics in the Third Reich*. Chicago: Chicago University Press, 2010.

Welsh, Addison E. "Long Term Effects of Reverse Culture Shock in Study Abroad." PhD diss., University of the Pacific, 2015.

Welzer, Harald. "The Collateral Damage of Enlightenment: How Grandchildren Understand the History of National Socialist Crimes and Their Grandfathers' Past Knowledge." In *Victims and Perpetrators: 1933–1945. (Re)Presenting the Past in Post-Unification Culture*, edited by Laurel Cohen-Pfister and Dagmar Wienroeder-Skinner, 285–95. Berlin: Walter de Gruyter, 2006.

Werner, Marion A. "I Was Proud of America." *Saturday Evening Post*, November 16, 1946.

"Werner von Rosenstiel Obituary." *Tampa Bay Times*, July 10, 2008.

Wesemann, Hans. *The Brown Network: The Activities of the Nazis in Foreign Countries*. New York: Knight Publication, 1936.

Whiting, Charles. *Hitler's Secret War: The Nazi Espionage Campaign against the Allies*. London: Leo Cooper, 2000.

Wiesen, S. Jonathan. *Creating the Nazi Marketplace: Commerce and Consumption in the Third Reich*. Cambridge: Cambridge University Press, 2011.

Wighton, Charles, Erwin von Lahousen, and Günter Peis. *Hitler's Spies and Saboteurs: Based on the German Secret Service War Diary of General Lahousen*. New York: Holt, 1958.

"Wilhelm Canaris." *Jewish Virtual Library*. Accessed May 22, 2023. https://www.jewishvirtuallibrary.org/wilhelm-canaris.

Williams, Michael. *To Pass on a Good Earth: The Life and Work of Carl O. Sauer*. Charlottesville: University of Virginia Press, 2014.

Windlof, Paul. *Expansion and Structural Change: Higher Education in Germany, the United States, and Japan, 1870–1990*. London: Routledge, 2018.

Windsor, Tara. "Rekindling Contact: Anglo-German Academic Exchange after the First World War." In *Anglo-German Scholarly Networks in the Long Nineteenth Century*, edited by Heather Ellis and Ulrike Kirchberger, 212–31. Leiden: Brill Publishers, 2014.

Winston, Rachel. "The 1926 Lake Denmark Explosion: An Extraordinary Mishap That Changed Military Safety Standards." *New Jersey Studies* 7, no. 1 (Winter 2021): 345–60. Accessed August 24, 2024. doi.org/10.14713/njs.v7i1.230.

Wirmer: "Josef Wirmer." Kartellverbandes katholischer deutscher Studentenvereine Westphalia-Berlin. Accessed October 20, 2024. http://www.kstvguestphaliaberlin.de/wirmer.htm.

———. "Josef Wirmer." Pfad der Erinnerung. Accessed October 18, 2024. https://pfad-der-erinnerung.berlin/en/josef-wirmer-2/.

Wistrich, Robert S. *Who's Who in Nazi Germany*. London: Routledge, 1995.

Witkop, Bernhard. "Remembering Heinrich Wieland (1877–1957): Portrait of an Organic Chemist and Founder of Modern Biochemistry." *Medicinal Research Reviews* 12, no. 3 (1992): 195–274.

Wonschik, Helmut, ed. *Briefe aus Bautzen II: Maria und Adolf-Henning Frucht*. Berlin: Morgenbuch, 1992.

Yeide, Nancy H., Konstantin Akinsha, and Amy L. Walsh. *The AAM Guide to Provenance Research*. Washington, DC: American Association of Museums, 2001.

Zacharias, Ellis M. *Secret Mission: The Story of an Intelligence Officer*. New York: G.P. Putnam's Sons, 1946.

Zacharias, Klaus. "Johannes Schlüter." In Altertumsverein Paderborn and Verein für Geschichte Paderborn: Westfälische Biographien. Modified August 20, 2012. Accessed October 12, 2024. https://www.pacelli-edition.de/kurzbiografie.html?idno=14038.

Zacharasiewicz, Waldemar. *Images of Germany in American Literature*. Iowa City: University of Iowa Press, 2007.

"Zeitgenossinnen Inhalt.indd—Stadt Krefeld." Accessed October 15, 2024. https://www.yumpu.com/de/document/view/9939092/zeitgenossinnen-inhaltindd-krefeld.

Zeman, Z. A. B. *Nazi Propaganda*. New York: Oxford University Press, 1964.

INDEX

Abwehr and espionage and covert operations, 158–68

Achenbach, Gertrude (exchange student): photograph of, 84–85; postwar US academic career, 187–88; pre-exchange anti-Nazism claims, 134–35; rejection of espionage demands, 39

African Americans and exchange students, 90, 112–14

Akademische Auslandsstelle. *See* University Foreign Affairs Offices

America First Committee, 3

American academics opposed to Nazism: 10, 33, 38, 78, 90–102, 110, 151–55, 163, 172; and cancellation of German exchange programs, 5, 70

American college students. *See* college students (American)

American Nazi sympathizers, 2–4, 6, 9, 10, 137, 150, 182, 216n65, 235n48; and covert activities against the US, 2–6, 9–10, 150, 169, 176–77, 182; lack of influence of, 2, 5–6, 23, 78, 93, 126, 150, 173–74, 198

Americans' perception of German exchange students: general interest in, 24, 86, 91–93; negative perceptions of, 23, 38, 99–102, 120; positive perceptions of, 78, 93, 103–4, 109, 198. *See also under* college students (American)

Americans' perceptions of Nazi Germany, 78, 88, 90, 97–98, 101, 149–50, 166, 197–99, 203

antisemitism (in the US), 4–5, 90, 93–94, 98, 173, 203

asylum and immigration (US), 4; bureaucratic obstacles in, 129, 139, 201; exchange students' personal accounts of, 109, 130, 136–40, 143–44, 179; rules and regulations governing, 127–29, 138, 201

Bavaria Project, 11

Bergsträsser, Arnold (German educator): postwar career, 184; prewar career, 27, 53, 184. *See also* West Germany, Americanization of

Bildungsbürgertum, 17, 23, 116, 122 193, 200, 205; and attitudes toward Nazism, 12; and German exchange student families, 19, 54, 90, 125 195

Blanke, Gustav (exchange student), 106, 113, 157, 175; Americanization of, 109–10, 112; as Americanizer of West Germany, 180, 186; attempts to secure refuge in US, 14, 109, 139–40. *See also* exchange students: Americanization of

Boas, Franz (German American educator), 151

Bonhoeffer, Dietrich (resistance figure). *See* resistance groups

"brain drain" and German-American exchange program, 175, 187–88 191–92, 205

"brown scare" thesis, 9, 170; and John Roy Carlson (author), 9–10, 170; and John Spivak (author), 9

Burmeister, Wilhelm (DAAD official): as DAAD managing director, 30, 33, 38, 52, 62–65, 68, 70–76, 101, 110; and Holocaust, 178–79; and postwar life, 184

careers of German exchange students: in postwar West Germany, 184–87; in the Third Reich, 21, 24, 76, 132, 137–38, 146, 164, 176, 178, 200; in the US, 156, 172, 182, 186–89; with US occupation authorities, 176–77, 181–83, 204

Carl Schurz Vereinigung, 30, 45, 218n27; Emil de Haas, secretary general of, 30, 143–44, 215n39, 237n101. *See also* Sonthoff, Herbert

Catholics (German): involvement in anti-Nazi circles, 11, 21, 43, 56, 58, 145; involvement in

300 Index

Catholics (German) (*cont.*)
  German-American exchange, 30, 42, 58, 80–81, 133, 135, 241n78; and Margildis Schlüter (exchange student), 30, 58, 80–81, 135
choice-supportive bias, 200
Chroust, Anton-Hermann (exchange student), 137; clashes with German diplomatic corps, 134, 137; as exchange student leader, 71–74, 79, 108, 134; Harvard education years, 137–39, 154; photograph of, 72; postwar academic career in US, 134, 188, 191; Roscoe Pound's (American educator) defense of, 137, 235n48; self-exoneration attempts, 134–39, 180; wartime internment, vii, 134, 179
cognitive dissonance, 122, 146, 201
cognitive inertia, 200
college students (American): and campus life, 24, 79, 86, 103–05, 120, 155, 198, 232n248; negative perceptions of exchange students / Nazism, 97–105, 120, 126, 191; positive perceptions of exchange students / Nazism, 93–94, 103–4, 191; and social hierarchy, 103–4, 198; and sports, 106; uninterest in foreign affairs, 95, 198–99
college students (German), attitudes toward Nazism, 17–18, 20, 65, 195–96
Committee on Un-American Activities / Dickstein and Dies Committees, 34, 151, 216n65
Confessing Protestant Church: and exchange students, 56–58, 133, 135
Coughlin, Charles (American Nazi sympathizer), 3–5

DAAD (Deutscher Akademischer Austauschdienst): continuity across German eras, 22, 75, 183, 190–91, 205, 213n146; dismissal of Jewish students and employees, 22, 28–29, 56; Ingrid Dybwad (DAAD official), 28–29, 49; early history of, 13, 20, 22–23, 26–27, 32, 51, 71, 87, 149; Kurt Goepel (DAAD official), 29; Gerhard Gräfe (DAAD official), 29–30, 95; Adolf Morsbach; and Nazi radicalization, 23, 28, 31–32, 78, 195, 197–98; and New York City branch office, 34–35, 38; non-Nazi influences in, 23, 27, 29, 34, 40, 68, 76; postwar rebirth of, 189, 213n146; relations with IIE, 32, 33–34, 38, 49, 65–66, 72–73, 120, 190; Eva Schröder (exchange student) incident, 86, 95, 101 Georg von Fritsch (DAAD official), 29, 34, 183; World War II history of, 189. *See also*

Burmeister, Wilhelm; exchange students: application and selection of; exchange students: training of: Rettig, Georg; Schutzstaffel (SS); Von Gienanth, Ulrich
Das Amt und die Vergangenheit, 12–13
diplomatic corps (German). *See* German diplomatic corps
Duggan, Lawrence (IIE official): death of, 189; as IIE director, 33, 189; as Soviet espionage agent, 189
Duggan, Stephen (IIE official), 26, 33–34, 38, 40, 66, 95, 106, 122–23, 142, 148, 189, 197; and exchange student covert activities, 70, 89–90, 99, 151, 164; and foundation of IIE, 27; and German exchange disruptions, 33, 39, 56, 70, 89, 91, 99, 120, 122, 164; photograph of, 80–81; and Wilsonian internationalism, 10. *See also* Institute of International Education (IIE)
Duquesne ring, 160–61, 163–64, 166–67, 241n73

Education Ministry: and DAAD, 30, 32, 35, 37, 44–45, 52–53, 67
Einstein, Albert, 57, 238n16; and fear of exchange students, 152
Ermarth, Fritz (exchange student), 235n55; and Karl Haushofer (German educator), 157; as pro-American student, 157, 181; suicide of, 181
espionage and covert operations (German), 143, 149; and the Abwehr, 158–68; Duquesne ring, 160–61, 163–64, 166–67, 241n73; dysfunction of, 6, 9, 25, 37–40, 158–60, 165–66, 173, 195, 203; and German diplomats in US, 15, 39–40, 156, 159; Griebl ring, 160; Lonkowski ring, 160; Nicolaus ring, 164–65; Operation Elster, 7; Operation Ludwig, 7; Rumrich ring, 160, 167; SS-SD, 155, 157; Von Hausberger–Bergmann debacle, 167–68. *See also* exchange students, espionage; Haushofer, Karl; Nazi Party Foreign Organization
espionage training, 149, 203
exchange student leaders, 35, 71–74. *See also* Chroust, Anton-Hermann; Von Gienanth, Ulrich
exchange students: Americanization of, 21, 24, 32, 68, 75, 78, 92, 109–12, 122–25, 128, 139–48, 154, 191–92, 199–201; application and selection of, 20, 23, 32, 42–48, 50–52, 54, 56, 59–61, 67, 75, 127, 130, 190; and campus life, 24, 103–6, 125, 199; and collegiate sports, 103, 104–6, 140, 142, 199;

courier duties, 150–51, 157, 159, 162, 164, 166; espionage and covert operations of, 148, 156–61, 164–66, 169–70, 173, 202–3; Florida vacations of, 1, 73, 79, 107–10; and Jewish Americans, 10, 98–100, 106, 111–12, 120, 151; monitoring refugees and "liberal" exchange students, 152–55, 173; negative perceptions of Americans, 115–16, 118–20, 129, 190, 200; non-/anti-Nazi proclivities of, 11, 21, 23–24, 57, 76, 92, 109–12, 114, 130, 133–35, 140–43, 236n72; and organizations making use of student operatives, 152–59, 164, 203; overt propaganda of, 24, 27, 48, 62–63, 69–70, 75, 79, 86–87, 89–91, 104, 120, 150, 153; photograph of annual student assembly, 69; positive perceptions of Americans, 24, 78, 103, 107–9, 114, 120–26, 130, 143, 190, 199; pro-Nazi proclivities of, 45, 61, 89–90, 92, 115, 130; recruitment of, 152, 158–59, 163–64, 195; repatriation of, 14, 21, 24, 59, 65, 68, 106, 123, 125, 128, 133–34, 137, 140, 142, 155, 187, 200–202; reverse culture shock, 128, 141–42, 191, 202; and romantic relationships or marriages with Americans, 105, 112–13, 128, 138–39, 142, 235n55; and school loyalty 105–7, 142; and social life of, 103–7, 199; and "Swing Youth," 194, 247–248n1; training of, 23, 27, 32, 61–62, 64–65, 68–71, 75, 197; and travel around US and Mexico, 107–8, 115, 118–19; wartime internment of, vii, 48, 131, 133–34, 170, 179. *See also* careers of German exchange students; espionage and covert operations (German); refugees; *and names of individual exchange students*

exile, opposition through, 12, 129, 201–2

FBI (Federal Bureau of Investigation), 5–6, 14, 58, 123, 130, 136, 138–39, 143, 145, 155, 157, 159–61, 163, 165–67, 169, 170, 172–74, 178, 189, 202–3

Fehling, August (German official): postwar career, 183, 190; prewar career, 52–53. *See also* West Germany, Americanization of

Foreign Ministry (Third Reich), 185; Cultural Affairs Department (Kulturabteilung), 15, 178; Nazi suspicion of, 13, 37; non-/anti-Nazi proclivities of some officials, 12–13, 40, 53, 195; and role in German student exchanges, 32, 34–35, 37, 40, 44, 51–52, 73, 76, 137; Fritz von Twardowski, 15–16, 52–53

Foreign Ministry (West Germany), 185

Franco-German soft power rivalry in the US, 66

Freiburg circle. *See* resistance groups

Friedrich, Carl Joachim (German American educator), 153, 182–83; and Americanization of West Germany, 153, 183; and German-American exchanges, 182

Frucht, Adolf Henning (exchange student): involvement in resistance circles, 21, 145–46, 187; postwar career, 187

Gatzke, Hans (exchange student): investigation by Gestapo, 155; photograph of, 82–83; postwar US academic career, 141, 188; pro-Americanism of, 141, 155; and refugee status, 141; and reverse culture shock, 128, 141. *See also* exchange students: Americanization of

Geist, Raymond (American official): as American consul in Berlin, 133, 140, 143; and consulate staff, 65, 143–44. *See also* Sonthoff, Herbert

Gensichen, Hans-Werner (exchange student), 58, 152

Gensichen, Johannes (anti-Nazi minister), anti-Nazi activities of, 58

German academics: with Jewish ancestry, 44, 53, 59, 183–84; and possible non-/anti-Nazi proclivities of, 18–19, 40, 43–44, 47, 76, 135, 196

German Americans and covert activities against US, 4, 6, 148, 150, 154, 157, 161, 165, 169, 173, 203, 241n73

German diplomatic corps in US, 5, 10, 13, 33–34, 66, 134; and espionage, 13, 15, 39–40, 158, 166; and non-/anti-Nazi proclivities of, 13; Josias Rantzau (German official), 15; and relations with Nazi organizations, 13, 40, 73–74; Fritz von Twardowski (German official), 15–16. *See also* Gyssling, Georg; Scholz, Herbert; Thomsen, Hans

German Student Union (Deutsche Studentenschaft, or DSt), 19, 28, 45–47, 57, 67–68, 71, 74, 95; incompetence of, 20, 76; and Kiel controversy, 19, 47–48; and Lausanne controversy, 67–68; and role in exchange student selection, 32, 45, 51–52, 63, 76, 152

German-American exchange program. *See* DAAD; exchange students; Institute of International Education (IIE)

German-American exchange program, decline of, 38–40, 70, 91, 97, 203

Gestapo: activities in US, 15, 35, 74, 158, 170; and exchange student candidates, 48, 52, 58, 76, 136, 147, 196; and returned exchange students, 21, 142, 145, 155; and suspect non-/anti-Nazi officials, 15–16, 57–58, 145

Goebbels, Josef, 35; attempts to gain control of DAAD, 34–35. *See also* Propaganda Ministry

Goerdeler circle. *See* resistance groups

Gothelf, Ina (exchange student): as college student, 132, 166; concerns about Nazism, 133–34; decision to remain in US, 133–34; as German covert agent, 166; internment of, 131, 133, 179; and Jewish ancestry, 130–32; photograph of, 132; postwar life in US, 185; pro-Nazism of, 133, 166

Gothelf, Irene (exchange student): as college student, 166; concerns about Nazism, 133; decision to return to Germany, 133; as German covert agent, 133, 153, 166; internment of, 48, 131, 133, 179; and Jewish ancestry, 130; photograph of, 131; pro-Nazism of, 127, 133

Griebl ring. *See* espionage and covert operations (German): Griebl ring

Gyssling, Georg (German official): as German consul in Los Angeles, 6–7, 13–15, 159; and Hollywood film industry, 14, 170; and Los Angeles Jewish Community Committee, 14–15; as US informant, 13–14

Hanfstaengl, Erika (exchange student): attempt to remain in US, 137–38; family background of, 55, 137–38; involvement in Nazi stolen art program, 138, 181–82; photograph of, 82–83; work for US occupation authorities, 182

Haushofer, Karl (German official), 156–57: and amateur espionage, 156–57; and Fritz Ermarth, 157; as Nazi geographer, 156

Heimatrundbrief deutscher Austauschstudenten in den U.S.A., 110, 205–6

Hitler in Los Angeles, 2–5

Hitler's American Friends, 3–5, 8

Hollywood's Spies, 2, 4

Holocaust, 16, 21; and Bruno Weber (exchange student), 178; and Kurt Weege (exchange student), 84–85, 178, 218n21. *See also* Burmeister, Wilhelm

Hoover, J. Edgar, 5–6, 14, 160, 167, 170, 173, 203. *See also* FBI (Federal Bureau of Investigation)

Hörhager, Herbert (exchange student), 60, 105–6, 110

Hubbard, Ruth (IIE official): as manager of German-American exchanges, 48–49, 61, 95, 101, 104, 153, 166; photograph of, 80–81, 124; postwar career of, 190, 247n97; relationships with exchange students, 56–57, 86, 106–7, 110, 122–25, 131, 138–42, 144, 157; relationship with DAAD, 30, 33–34, 38–39, 73

Institute of International Education (IIE), 26, 48–49, 54, 61, 66, 79, 94, 104–5, 130, 189, 198, 247n97; foundation of, 10, 27; funding of, 27, 40; and German student propaganda, 89–94, 97; photographs of IIE officials, 80–84; postwar history of, 40, 189–90; and problems with German students, 40, 72, 109, 122, 139, 155, 160, 164; and refugee status sought by students, 139, 141; relations with DAAD, 32, 33–34, 38, 49, 65–66, 72–73, 120, 190; relations with US government, 39–40, 189–90; responses to anti-German sentiments, 5, 38. *See also* Duggan, Lawrence; Duggan, Stephen; Hubbard, Ruth

interventionism, 3, 153, 173–74, 183, 203

isolationism, 64, 95, 147, 149, 168, 173, 199

Janson, Horst (exchange student): as college student, 112, 134, 138–39, 153–54; and exchange student selection process, 52, 59; life during World War II, 179; photograph of, 84–85; postwar US academic career of, 188

Jewish Germans: 188; academics relocating to US, 33, 44, 151, 152, 153, 183–84; antisemitism in Nazi Germany, 4, 28–29, 44, 88–89, 194; antisemitism in US, 4; attitudes toward, among exchange students, 64, 88–89, 99–100, 111–13, 151, 152–53; exchange students' associations with, 42, 59–60, 130–35, 139, 219n50; among professoriate in Germany, 53–54; refugees, 143, 208n18

Kreisau circle. *See* resistance groups

Kristallnacht, 4, 38, 134

Lankowski ring. *See* espionage and covert operations (German): Lankowski ring

Lautsch, Marianne (exchange student): photograph of, 82–82; postwar life in West Germany, 185; and reverse culture shock, 90, 124, 128, 141

Lilge, Frederic (exchange student): as college student, 56; photograph of, 80–81; as postwar American educator, 1, 19, 188; wartime anti-Germanism of, 179–80

Los Angeles Jewish Community Committee, 4; and anti-Nazi investigations, 5, 14–15, 151. *See also* Gyssling, Georg

Lüdtke, Gerhard Wolfgang (exchange student), 43, 55, 140

Ludwig ring, 7

Mann, Erika (German American author): anti-Nazi speaking tour, 163; interaction with German exchange students, 105, 111

Mayer, Helene (exchange student): as college student, 56; and Jewish ancestry, 56; participation in 1936 Olympics, 188; post-Olympics life, 189; residency in US, 56

Mexico: exchange student visits to, 107, 166, 230n153; and German espionage, 158, 162–66. *See also* von dem Hagen, Annaliese; Weber, Karl Max

Morsbach, Adolf (DAAD managing director): imprisonment of, 31; and management of Nazi-era DAAD, 28–31, 51–52, 68, 72; and management of Weimar-era DAAD, 27; photograph of, 28

munitions plant disasters in war, 8, 209n50

National Socialist German Students' League (NSDStB), 15, 19–20, 32, 35, 45, 67; and exchange student espionage, 32; ineffectiveness of, 15, 19; role in selecting exchange students, 32, 45, 47, 136, 195

Nazi organization infighting, 27; Kiel scandal example, 47–48; Lausanne example, 67–68

Nazi Party Foreign Organization (NSDAP/ Auslands-Organisation, or NSDAP/AO), 13, 28, 44, 71, 73–74, 159; and amateur espionage, 9, 150, 155–56, 158, 195

Nazis of Copley Square, 2, 6–7, 10

Noelle, Elisabeth (exchange student), 43–44, 48, 135–36, 230n172; antisemitism of, 88, 112; journalism career during the Reich, 49, 176–77; meeting with Adolf Hitler, 48, 137, 219n45; photograph of, 49; postwar career as demographer, 49, 186–87; propaganda work in US, 38, 87

Nolan, Mary, 21

Non-/anti-Nazi German officials, examples, 11, 76; Emil Dovifat (German professor), 43–44, 135, 241n78; Emil de Haas (German official), 30, 142–44; Ulrich von Hassell (German diplomat), 15, 21, 146, 197. *See also* Fehling, August; Goepel, Kurt; Gyssling, Georg; Rantzau, Josias; Thomsen, Hans; Wiedemann, Fritz

Olympics of 1936, 133, 188–89

Operation Elster, 7

Operation Hummingbird, 32, 35, 58

Operation Ludwig, 7

Pohlenz, Ulrich (exchange student): as college student, 123, 136, 139; and Gestapo attention, 139; and identity fluidity, 145, 237n106; and Jewish brother-in-law, 60, 113, 134, 139; and marriage, 139; photograph of, 171; and post-exchange life in US, 145, 170, 172, 179–80, 243–44n128, 243n121–22

POWs (prisoners of war): former German exchange students as, 177, 180, 204; Hans Werner Roepke (exchange student), 177

Prequel: An American Fight against Fascism, 6, 8, 10

Propaganda Ministry, 166; and DAAD, 19, 28, 34–35; and exchange student employees, 19, 35, 42, 74, 76, 176–77, 182, 187. *See also* Goebbels, Josef

refugees, 12–13, 21, 53, 58, 65, 98, 110, 129–30, 153

refugees and exchange students, 22–23, 32, 40, 63, 72, 87, 111, 128–32, 134, 137–39, 147, 152, 155

"remigrants." *See* West Germany, Americanization of

resistance groups, 11, 20, 146, 185, 204, 211n100; and Dietrich Bonhoeffer (German anti-Nazi minister), 57, 135; Freiburg circle, 17, 53; Goerdeler circle, 15, 53, 135, 146, 220n74; Kreisau circle, 15, 146; Siemer-Wirmer circle, 21, 145. *See also* Frucht, Adolf Henning; Sonthoff, Herbert; Von Braun, Sigismund

Rettig, Georg (DAAD administrator): as amateur espionage coordinator, 32, 39, 154, 158, 163–64; and American exchange student recruitment, 37–38; as DAAD manager, 32–34, 37–39, 50–52, 62, 65, 71, 75–76, 86, 109–10; as head of DAAD New York City branch, 34, 38–39; and intimidation of exchange students, 34, 57, 154, 162, 164;

Rettig, Georg (DAAD administrator) (*cont.*)
as manager of German-American exchanges, 32–34, 37–39, 50–52, 62, 65, 71, 75–76, 86; pre-DAAD managerial career, 31–32; relations with IIE, 33
reverse culture shock, 24, 141–42; of Marianne Lautsch (exchange student), 90, 124, 141. *See also* Gatzke, Hans
Richter, Hans (exchange student): post-exchange career in US, 180, 188, 221n102; as pro-American, 57–58
Richter, Julius (German academic): and Dietrich Bonhoeffer (German anti-Nazi minister), 17, 57; as father of Hans Richter, 17, 57; Gestapo investigation of, 17; involvement in German-American exchange, 57; professor at University of Berlin, 17; role in anti-Nazi activity, 17
Roepke, Hans Werner (exchange student): and communication with Middlebury College alumni, 176–77; as Waffen-SS recruiter, 176–77, 244n9
Roosevelt, Franklin, 39, 55, 105; and interventionism, 3, 169–70, 173, 203; and revelation of impending Japanese attack, 14
Rothfels, Hans (German American educator), 16; and exchange student selection, 53–54, 217n14; involvement in German-American exchange, 53; as postwar Americanizer, 183–84, 246n55; as refugee in US, 53, 183. *See also* West Germany, Americanization of
Rumrich ring, 160, 167
Rundbrief deutscher Austauschstudenten in den U.S.A., 79, 86, 105–06, 113–16, 121

Schäfer, Ursula (exchange student), 44, 109, 116–18, 130, 134, 136, 153–54, 188, 231n203, 235n55, 239n27, 247n82
Scheibe, Fritz Hubertus (exchange student), 114–15, 121, 130, 190
Scholz, Herbert (German official): as amateur covert director, 7, 9, 150, 153, 209n39; and exchange students, 153, 155; as German consul in Boston, 137, 146; as SS official, 150
Schutzstaffel (SS), 35, 51, 58, 71, 136, 150, 177–78; infiltration of DAAD, 12, 20, 26, 31–32, 34, 76, 161, 195, 202; influence over German-American exchange program, 12, 20, 23, 32, 45, 52, 62; in the US, 6, 9, 12, 20–21, 37

Schutzstaffel-Sicherheitsdienst (SS-SD), 3, 35, 62, 74, 137, 147, 158, 184. *See also* espionage and covert operations (German); exchange students, espionage and covert operations of; Von Gienanth, Ulrich
Siemer-Wirmer circle, 21, 145
Sonthoff, Herbert (exchange student): Catholicism and SS membership, 58, 135–36; as college student, 119; early life, 56, 58; efforts to return to US, 119, 143–44; life during World War II, 138–39, 144–45, 154–55, 171–72, 179–80; and Operation Hummingbird, 58; photograph of, 59, 82–83; postwar career, 144–45, 188; pre-exchange life, 43, 135; repatriation period, 135–36, 142–43, 162; and Siemer-Wirmer resistance group, 21, 145; and Walter von Hausberger (German saboteur), 168
spying. *See* espionage and covert operations (German)

Thomsen, Hans (German official): as German chargé d'affaires in Washington, 39–40, 166–67; as US informant, 13–14
Trojandt, Gerda (exchange student applicant): pro-French scandal and, 46–47

University Foreign Affairs Offices (Akademische Auslandsstelle, or AKA), 28, 31–32, 43–44, 46–47, 65, 114, 138
US Army and exchange students, 139, 179, 204, 241n73

von Braun, Sigismund (exchange student): anti-Nazi activity, 15, 21, 146; postwar career, 146, 182, 185; and Ulrich von Hassell (German diplomat), 15, 21, 146
von dem Hagen, Annaliese (exchange student), 44, 48, 64, 86, 92, 162, 218n18; amateur espionage activities, 146, 154–55, 162–64; difficulties with Georg Rettig (DAAD official), 162; life in US, 86, 92; photograph of, 162
von Fritsch, Georg (DAAD official), 29, 34, 183
von Gienanth, Ulrich (German official): and American antisemitic movement, 6; background, 35; as covert operations director, 32, 40, 77–79, 137–39, 150–51, 153–58, 161, 170; and DAAD, 31–32, 37; and espionage training of, 155; and exchange student espionage, 79, 153–58, 161;

as exchange student leader, 35, 37, 74, 79, 109, 156, 158, 224n190, 240n59; and individual exchange students, 137, 139, 153–54, 161; as Nazi/SS official, 31, 35–37, 74, 77, 155, 158, 216n73–74; photograph of, 36, 84–85; post-1939 career, 167, 184–85; pre-exchange career, 31, 35

von Lilienfeld, Georg (exchange student): as college student, 103–4, 119; photograph of, 82–83; work in Reich Foreign Ministry, 146, 176–78, 182; work in West German Foreign Ministry, 185–86. *See also* exchange students: positive perceptions of Americans

von Rosenstiel, Werner (exchange student): Americanization of, 104–5, 110–11; as college student, 47, 105, 111, 134, 154; photograph of, 83–84; post-exchange life in Germany, 142; postwar career in US, 188; questions regarding return to US, 134, 139, 145; as a target of exchange student "monitoring," 142, 154; wartime military service in US, 179

von Tippelskirch, Kurt (German official): and Anton-Hermann Chroust, 73; as German consul in Boston, 137; non-Nazi proclivities, claims of, 134, 211n91

Weber, Bruno (exchange student): and Auschwitz, 178; photograph of, 84–85

Weber, Karl Max (exchange student): and amateur espionage in US, 164–65; and expulsion from Mexico, 165. *See also* espionage and covert operations (German): Duquesne; Mexico: German espionage

Weimar-era student exchanges. *See* DAAD: early history of

West Germany, Americanization of, 190; role of exchange officials in, 21–22, 25, 175, 182–85, 190–92, 247n97; role of exchange students in, 21–22, 175, 180, 185–86, 190–91; role of remigrants in, 25, 204. *See also* Bergsträsser, Arnold; Blanke, Gustav; Friedrich, Carl; Rothfels, Hans

Wickert, Erwin (exchange student): as anti-American author, 116–18, 129; as college student, 88, 110, 129; photograph of, 84–85, 117; work in Reich Foreign Ministry, 178; work in West German Foreign Ministry, 186

Wiedemann, Fritz (German official): anti-Hitlerism of, 14; as German consul in San Francisco, 14; and German exchange students, 14, 130; as US informant, 14

World War II: 174, 180–82; and American attitudes toward Germans, 94; German espionage in, 159; internment of exchange students, 131, 134; for repatriated exchange students, 175–78, 203–4; and sabotage in US, 8, 209n50; and US asylum for exchange students, 139–40